COMPARATIVE CONSTITUTIONAL DESIGN

This volume brings together essays by many of the leading scholars of comparative constitutional design from myriad disciplinary perspectives, including law, philosophy, political science, and economics. The authors collectively assess what we know – and do not know – about the design process as well as particular institutional choices concerning executive power, constitutional amendment processes, and many other issues. Bringing together positive and normative analysis, it provides the state of the art in a field of growing theoretical and practical importance.

Tom Ginsburg is the Leo Spitz Professor of Law and Political Science at the University of Chicago. He is the coauthor of *The Endurance of National Constitutions* (2009, with Zachary Elkins and James Melton), which won the best book award from the Comparative Democratization Section of the American Political Science Association. His other books include *Rule by Law: The Politics of Courts in Authoritarian Regimes* (2008, with Tamir Moustafa) and *Judicial Review in New Democracies* (2003), which won the American Political Science Association's C. Herman Pritchett Award for best book on law and courts.

Comparative Constitutional Design

TOM GINSBURG
University of Chicago, School of Law

CAMBRIDGE
UNIVERSITY PRESS

CAMBRIDGE UNIVERSITY PRESS
Cambridge, New York, Melbourne, Madrid, Cape Town,
Singapore, São Paulo, Delhi, Mexico City

Cambridge University Press
32 Avenue of the Americas, New York, NY 10013-2473, USA

www.cambridge.org
Information on this title: www.cambridge.org/9781107020566

First published 2012
Reprinted 2013

A catalog record for this publication is available from the British Library.

Library of Congress Cataloging in Publication Data

Comparative constitutional design / Tom Ginsburg.
p. cm.
Includes bibliographical references and index.
ISBN 978-1-107-02056-6 (hardback)
1. Constitutional law. I. Ginsburg, Tom.
K3165.C576 2012
342–dc23 2011048126

ISBN 978-1-107-02056-6 Hardback

Contents

Figures

Tables

Contributors

Susan Alberts recently received her PhD from the Department of Political Science, Georgetown University.

Tamar Asadurian is an Analyst at the U.S. International Trade Commission in Washington, DC, and holds a PhD from the Department of Politics, New York University.

Justin Blount is PhD candidate, Department of Political Science, University of Illinois.

Anjali Thomas Bohlken is Assistant Professor of Political Science, University of British Columbia.

Robert D. Cooter is Herman Selvin Professor of Law, Berkeley Law School.

Rosalind Dixon is Assistant Professor, University of Chicago Law School.

Zachary Elkins is Associate Professor of Government, University of Texas at Austin.

Jon Elster is Robert K. Merton Professor of Social Sciences, Columbia University.

John Ferejohn is Samuel Tilden Professor of Law, New York University Law School.

Tom Ginsburg is Leo Spitz Professor of International Law, University of Chicago Law School.

Ran Hirschl is Canada Research Chair in Constitutionalism, Democracy, and Development, University of Toronto Faculty of Law, Canada.

Richard Holden is Professor of Economics, Australian School of Business, University of New South Wales, Australia.

James Melton is Post-Doctoral Fellow, IMT Institute for Advanced Studies, Italy.

Martha C. Nussbaum is Ernst Freund Distinguished Service Professor of Law and Ethics, University of Chicago.

Pasquale Pasquino is Global Distinguished Professor, New York University.

Randall Peerenboom is Professor of Law, La Trobe University, Australia.

Eric A. Posner is Kirkland & Ellis Professor of Law, University of Chicago.

Adam Przeworski is Carroll and Milton Petrie Professor of European Studies and Professor of Politics and Economics, New York University.

Neil S. Siegel is Professor of Law and Political Science, Duke University School of Law.

Adrian Vermeule is John H. Watson Professor of Law, Harvard Law School.

Chris Warshaw is PhD candidate, Department of Political Science.

Barry R. Weingast is Senior Fellow, Hoover Institution, and Ward C. Krebs Family Professor, Department of Political Science, Stanford University.

Acknowledgments

Thanks to Dean Michael Schill and the Russell Baker Scholars Fund at the University of Chicago Law School for support for this project. Chantelle Hougland and Angela Kim provided research assistance. Cooter and Siegel acknowledge the editors of the *Stanford Law Review*, who published related material in Volume 63 (2010). Thanks also to the editors of the *William and Mary Law Review*, who published material from Chapter 13 in Volume 52 (2011), and the *Annual Review of Law and Social Science*, who published material from Chapter 2 in Volume 5.

1

Introduction

Tom Ginsburg

In contemporary practice, constitutional systems usually originate with bold acts of purposive institutional design, embodied in a founding document for the polity. These designs involve borrowing, learning, and accommodation, but they also involve moments of creative innovation and experimentation. Gathering together disparate elements from the real or mythical national past and the varied experience of other polities, constitution makers produce a document to structure government and express fundamental values. Viewed in this light, constitutional design is nothing if not audacious. Founders attempt to regulate future human conduct on the basis of speculative predictions of how institutions, sometimes untried, will actually function, and in the midst of heated political conflicts that render compromise inevitable.

This audacious practice has given rise to a long history of scholarly efforts seeking to analyze the successes and failures of constitutions, and this volume falls within that tradition. The focus is on constitutional design, and the volume brings together many leading students of constitutions. The contributions are a mix of positive analysis of the constraints and conditions of constitution making, along with normative analysis of particular design elements.

At the outset, it must be acknowledged that the term "constitutional design" is contested, and appropriately so. Design implies a technocratic, architectural paradigm that does not easily fit the messy realities of social institutions, especially not the messy process of constitution making. Even after decades of scholarship on political institutions, our knowledge of the interaction of particular practices with environmental factors is quite limited, and predictions of how institutions will operate are, at best, probabilistic guesses. Indeed, Horowitz (2002) argues that constitutional process, not design, is the better metaphor to understand how constitution making works. Hirschl (2009) explores other design sciences for potential analogies and generally finds the field of constitutional design wanting on a number of dimensions. In particular, unlike in other fields, constitutional designers may not be motivated by technocratic desire to get the results right, but may be self-interested. And even with the best of intentions, most constitutional designs fail on the throes of unanticipated consequences, unforeseen external events, and new information revealed by counterparties (Elkins et al. 2009).

Even if constitution making is more art than science, however, it would be too rash to give up on the possibility of comparative knowledge. No two situations are quite the same, but there are recurring problems faced by constitutional designers, and therefore there is the possibility of learning from prior experience. Constitution making is always, and always has been, comparatively informed; it involves a balance between borrowed models and local tailoring, between conventional choices and creative innovation. As long as there is constitution making, there will be *attempts* at constitutional design, and it thus behooves us to keep the term around, so long as we have the requisite humility with regard to our ambitions and maintain a healthy suspicion of mechanistic recommendations.

ANTECEDENTS

The field of comparative constitutional studies can be traced back at least to Aristotle's systematic evaluation, in the *Politics*, of the constitutions of the Greek city-states. Aristotle's views, like those of his counterparts in ancient China, India, and elsewhere, were couched in normative and universalist terms, notwithstanding the discovery of variation in the analysis. Aristotle emphasized the mixed constitution, rejecting ideal types, as best suited for the ideal polity.

Modernity brought with it a new set of analysts, including Machiavelli, Montesquieu, and John Stuart Mill, who undertook comparative analysis to inform normative design. In the seventeenth century, state-builders in the Netherlands undertook extensive study of ancient and contemporary models to resolve constitutional problems of the nascent Dutch republic, finding particular inspiration in the proto-federalism of the biblical Israelites (Boralevi 2002). In the eighteenth century, besides Montesquieu's foundational exploration, lesser-known figures such as Gottfried Achenwall and Johann Heinrich Gottlieb von Justi undertook surveys of political forms (González Marcos 2003: 313). Comparative constitutional study thus has a long and distinguished lineage.

Constitutional design in its contemporary sense is associated with the rise and spread of the written constitutional form, conventionally understood to have emerged in full flower in the late eighteenth century in the United States, France, and Poland. These nation-states drew on earlier efforts in Corsica (Carrington 1973) and the American colonies. Conceiving the constitution as a written document led to a discrete emphasis on constitution making as an act of purposive institutional design. The integrated constitutional text also transformed the idea of the constitution from a kind of applied political theory toward a more technical, even legal enterprise. The Enlightenment thinkers of the French, Polish, and American projects saw written constitutions as devices to channel self-interest into larger public ends. Theirs was a modernist project, but it was also a comparative one, for which wide study was a desirable, even necessary, feature. Drafters thus engaged in extensive examination and debate about the appropriateness of particular models. Modern constitutions were from the beginning informed by comparative inquiry, toward rationalist ends of optimal design.

The next wave of constitution making came in Latin America, in which liberal models were channeled through the 1812 Spanish Constitution of Cadiz. This in turn influenced the 1821 Constitution of Gran Colombia, the 1830 and 1832 Constitutions of New Granada, the 1830 Constitution of Venezuela, the 1823 and 1828 Constitutions of Peru, the Argentine Constitution of 1826, the Uruguayan Constitution of 1830, and the Chilean Constitution of 1828. In each instance, new nationalists sought to borrow the best from other models while tailoring them to local conditions and introducing new innovations. Some of these innovations, such as Bolivar's idea of a tricameral legislature, have faded away; others, such as the single-term executive who could run again after a term out of power, were very influential for a long time (as documented in Chapter 13 of this volume).

Elsewhere in the nineteenth century, new state-builders, initially in Western Europe but also in Japan, sought to adopt the new technology of the written constitution, and in doing so needed to engage in practical comparisons about which institutions were optimal. As a result, constitutional compilations became more popular, focusing on both European and Latin American countries (Marcos 2003: 314–16). The method involved a mix of normative and positive analysis, and in turn informed drafting exercises in new states and old (Takii 2006).

Early scholarship on constitutions and constitutional design tended to be case-driven and responsive to new constitutional events. Scholarly interest tended to come after waves of constitutional changes, such as those triggered by the end of World War I and the associated dissolution of empires. Much of this work was purely descriptive in character (Davidson 1925; Pollock 1923), or provided only minimal analysis (Albert et al. 1894; Moses 1893). The description focused on institutions, particularly executive-legislative relations, but also on regionalism (Dedek 1921; Quigley 1924) and rights (Bentwich 1924; Clark 1921).

Two developments in the late twentieth century – one academic and one in the world – coalesced to provide a fruitful environment for the explosive recent growth of comparative constitutional studies. The academic development was the revival of various institutionalisms in the social sciences (March and Olsen 1989; Powell and Dimaggio 1991). Sociologists and some political scientists began to (re)emphasize that individual agents were embedded in broader institutional structures, and that these structures helped determine outcomes. From another angle, economists moving away from neoclassical models began to understand that rules were important (Buchanan and Tullock 1961; North 1991). Institutions were defined as the rules of the game that structured behavior. Constitutions, as the social devices that structure the creation of rules, were the ultimate institutions worthy of analysis. Hence there was a turn in economics to understanding constitutional structures. With some exceptions, the literature in constitutional political economy focused more on theory than on empirics, but it did provide a set of working assumptions and hypotheses for analyzing constitutions.

The late twentieth century also saw epochal changes in the real world that made it hard for academics to ignore constitutions. The third wave of democracy beginning in the mid-1970s brought new attention to constitutions as instruments of democratization, and the emergence of new states following the end of the Cold War prompted a new round of efforts to theorize and analyze institutional design (Elster et al., 1998; Holmes 1995; Sunstein 2001). In particular, constitutional design became a central focus for ethnically diverse states in the hope that proper institutions could ameliorate conflict (Choudhry 2008; Ghai 2001; Horowitz 1991). There was a revival of interest in federalism and other design techniques (LeRoy et al. 2006), and a number of intelligent comprehensive surveys (Lutz 2006; Murphy 2007; Schneier 2006).

THE STATE OF KNOWLEDGE

Today, there is much demand for wisdom and knowledge, largely driven by real-world constitutional designers. In any given year, five to ten countries are engaged in major acts of constitutional design or redesign. Most of the participants in these exercises are not repeat players, and they are not experts in comparative government or law. Instead, their aspiration is to find enduring solutions to political conflict or to incorporate technical adjustments in the constitution to improve governance and performance. Drafters are rarely on their own in trying to navigate these shoals; they are frequently accompanied by a large number of international organizations and assistance providers eager to help. This institutional environment naturally favors the search for "best practices," and so it is worth inquiring what we as scholars can say about the state of the field.

The answer is that there is less consensus on the major issues of institutional design than might be hoped. To take one high-profile example, two decades of furious debate over the relative merits of presidentialism and parliamentarism have not produced definitive results as to which design is superior. Cheibub's (2007) state-of-the-art analysis shows that, notwithstanding simple associations between presidentialism and regime failure, the causal connections are more ambiguous. In identifying selection effects that led to the simple association, he suggests that the constitutional design choices are only intervening variables on the ultimate outcomes of interest. The unobservable deep structures of societies, rather than consciously designed institutions, may, in the end, be what are determining outcomes.

When one moves down from the grand choices toward more mundane ones, however, we do have a bit more knowledge about what works and what does not. Electoral systems, for example, have been the subject of extensive study, as have mechanisms of judicial appointments. Still, there are relatively few "best practices" in constitutional design, and much copying occurs without a strong social-science basis for asserting that it is based on actual learning.

To some degree these tensions reflect the difficulty of using positive social science for normative ends. Constitutional design is more art than science, and there are always myriad factors that can interfere with the best-laid plans. What this volume seeks to do is to bring together our best students of constitutional design from myriad disciplinary perspectives, including law, philosophy, political science, and economics, to see what we know about the design process in general as well as about particular constitutional institutions. It is intended as a stock-taking exercise, blending normative and positive perspectives.

OVERVIEW OF THE VOLUME

This volume is divided into three sections. The first section focuses on design processes. Jon Elster, who has for more than two decades been the leading analyst of constitutional design processes, begins by revisiting his classic tripartite framework of reason, passion, and interest as forces motivating constitution making. In Chapter 2, he revises his earlier view that reason, rather than passion or interest, should be the dominant mode in constitutional design. He nevertheless focuses on how to enhance public-spirited motivation through design processes, arguing for the need to "clear and strengthen" the channels of constitution making. His forward-looking analysis starts by identifying six intermediate variables likely to produce a good constitution. Elster states that an optimal constituent process ought to be guided by reason, which includes beliefs about the means as well as the ends. He assigns new weight to the role of passion, self-interest, and cognitive biases in collective decision making and states that each has varying effects on the constituent process. By studying and manipulating these variables, he argues, one may be able to eliminate distorting influences and enhance motivation and information, producing a better product.

Justin Blount, Zachary Elkins, and Tom Ginsburg then review the empirical evidence on design processes, revisiting some of Elster's classic conjectures with new data drawn from the Comparative Constitutions Project (CCP). Consistent with the earlier analysis, they find that there has been more theoretical speculation than empirical testing in this area. Elster's work had argued that institutional self-dealing was a major concern, and hence that legislatures ought to be disfavored as constitutional drafters; other writers and international organizations have argued that public participation ought to be enhanced in constitutional design processes. Blount and colleagues provide evidence that some of the assumptions of institutional self-dealing do not play out in constitutional design, whereas others do; they also find little direct support for the participation hypothesis. They conclude optimistically, suggesting that new data sources will facilitate a positive research program in this area. Together Chapters 2 and 3 point toward developing more precise variables in the study of constitution making, in terms of both interests and process and the need to connect these with outcomes.

The second section of this volume concerns constraints and conditions on design processes. In their contribution, Susan Alberts, Chris Warshaw, and Barry R. Weingast draw on a well-known literature arguing that successful democratic transitions are a product of the balance of power between opposing groups, but introduce into the argument the importance of constitutional design choices that lower the costs of upholding the democratic bargain. Using Chile as a central case study, they emphasize the role of countermajoritarian constitutional designs that allow the erstwhile authoritarians a role in the new democratic order, domesticating political conflict. Careful constitutional design, then, can facilitate democratization. The argument partially echoes Hirschl's (2004) notion of hegemonic preservation, but has a different normative spin: Whereas Hirschl had been critical of the constitutional entrenchment of neoliberal principles in the polities he examined, Alberts and colleagues point out that constitutionalization can facilitate credible commitments to dictators, and hence induce them to step down. The chapter emphasizes one of the central constraints on design processes: power. The assumption is that, given a particular balance of power between rising democrats and falling authoritarians, a carefully crafted solution can broker the transition that might otherwise not occur. They show in their model, however, that such outcomes are not predetermined.

Adam Przeworski, Tamar Asadurian, and Anjali Thomas Bohlken examine precisely such a set of historically contingent negotiations between new parliamentary elites and established monarchies. Even in monarchic constitutional schemes, the power of the purse led to some de facto power for the legislature, and it was the interaction of this legislature with the monarch that led to, alternatively, formalization of monarchical power, a republican revolution, or the emergence of parliamentary monarchy. In tracing these alternative paths, they make an important general point about the conditions under which things get written down in formal texts. The authors identify a structural incongruence between written texts and actual practices in the nineteenth-century parliamentary monarchies. Those constitutions that provided for parliamentary responsibility were violated, whereas parliamentary responsibility flourished even without formal provision in many other countries. The idea is that when everyone observes the equilibrium balance of powers, there is no need to write it down. Once monarchic rule was formalized, however, it tended to be undermined. The generalizable implication is that some of the factors that lead to written constitutional norms perversely lead to their violation.

The gap between text and practice is picked up in a case study of constitutions in a dynamic authoritarian regime – Randall Peerenboom's analysis of China's Living Constitution. Peerenboom reviews the uses of the formal constitution in the country and the functional need to constrain Communist Party activity while guaranteeing the Party a leading role in China's development. This design goal was difficult to achieve, given the country's history of using constitutions for political rhetoric rather than empowerment of institutional constraints on the government. Even though the Chinese constitution is not judicially enforceable, it has nevertheless served to structure competition among different institutions and has also become a basis for popular discourse by claimants seeking to advance a variety of goals. In his review of various likely trajectories for constitutionalism in China, Peerenboom echoes Przeworski and colleagues' analysis of monarchs and the perverse results of formalization. The story also hints, however, at the possibility for a more formal process of constitutional design in China's future.

In his contribution, Ran Hirschl discusses the reasons why constitutional law and constitutional courts are so appealing to secularist and other antireligious social forces. He argues that among the key secularist appeals of constitutionalism is a logic of co-optation: By explicitly incorporating religion into the formal constitutional design, secular forces can gain influence over religious governance. In addition, the structure and logic of constitutionalism, in which the constitution is highest law, make it an attractive enterprise to those who wish to contain religiosity and assert state authority over religion. And because the jurisprudence of constitutional courts generally reflects a less radical view of religious identity, constitutional law and courts have become the natural companions of the groups that are against the spread of principles of theocratic governance.

Together these four chapters offer a typology of constitutional design situations amid some, but not all, kinds of drafting circumstances. Alberts and colleagues focus on democratization and the ability of constitutional design to accommodate erstwhile authoritarians; Hirschl's focus is on a related problem, namely how establishment secularists can tame the rising forces of religion. In each case, the question is how to bring together the past and the potential future into some kind of accommodation. Przeworski and colleagues' account of negotiation between monarchs and parliaments also reflects the need for accommodation between established and rising political forces, with the additional twist that formalization produces perverse consequences. And Peerenboom's case study examines a very different type of constitution, a stable authoritarian regime in which constitutional discourse begins to make the design relevant to real politics, despite the intentions of the founders to keep the document symbolic. We can summarize the section as reminding us that constitutional design reflects political constraints and opportunities of the drafting circumstances, and that there is slippage between the goals of designers and actual political practice.

The third section of the book addresses particular issues in institutional design. Rosalind Dixon and Richard Holden focus on amendment rules, the very central institutions for formal constitutional change. They examine an under-analyzed feature of amendment rules, namely that the difficulty of amendment is determined not only by the threshold required in any voting body (majority, two-thirds, three-quarters, etc.), but also by the size of the body. As the denominator goes up, the practical difficulty of marshalling any particular threshold increases. After showing this theoretically, they go on to develop an empirical test using data from American states. They find a statistically significant negative relationship between the size of legislative voting bodies and the rate of constitutional amendment in various states. They then explore possible institutional corrections. There are clear implications for constitutional design, extending even beyond the context of constitutional amendment to any voting rule for a multimember institution.

Robert D. Cooter and Neil Siegel combine traditional methods of constitutional interpretation with economic analysis to produce a positive and normative account of the federal powers possessed by the U.S. Congress. Although developed in the context of the United States, their theory of "collective action federalism" has natural implications for other multijurisdictional settings. The basic idea is that the national government is best situated to solve problems of collective action for substates. Such problems include interstate externalities and impediments to interstate markets. The technical characteristics of these problems impede the ability of substates to solve them on their own. Cooter and Siegel argue that in the United States, courts ought (and, to a large extent, do) to interpret the founders' division of labor between national and state governments, articulated in Article I, Section 8 of the U.S. Constitution, in accordance with this structural approach.

Martha Nussbaum's contribution tackles modes of accommodation in systems of religious pluralism, using the example of personal laws in India to orient the discussion. The British colonialists, like many others, sought to give a good deal of autonomy to local communities in matters of religion, which typically encompass what we would call family law. Going further than simply accommodating the local communities, the British undertook efforts to codify religious custom, which had the perverse effect of freezing illiberal practices. In turn, the early leaders of independent India were reluctant to challenge powerful religious communities and left intact the personal laws for selected religious groups, despite their frequent conflict with constitutional guarantees of equality and dignity. Rooting her argument in the comparative constitutional history of religious establishment, Nussbaum demonstrates the flaws in the current Indian scheme, while elaborating the difficult constitutional politics of moving toward a more just order. It is a cautionary tale for constitutional designers who may be tempted to accommodate illiberal religious practices; however, her story is also one that suggests a role for sensitive and careful constitutional adjudication in resolving conflicts.

Constitutional adjudication is the theme of the contribution from John Ferejohn and Pasquale Pasquino. The large literature on comparative constitutional review tends to focus on the German, French, and American models as ideal types. Ferejohn and Pasquino undertake the important corrective of emphasizing the Italian model, in which cases come to the court through referral from lower courts. This design is also found now in the European Union and in many Latin American countries. The Italian design has certain advantages over the others. Because it does not allow direct access from citizens through a constitutional complaint, it has not been subjected to tremendous backlogs as has the German court. At the same time, there is no need for political sponsorship to raise a claim, as is found in the French system of 1958–2008. The system also minimizes institutional conflicts between the ordinary and constitutional judiciary that have plagued other systems. In short, this is a call to consider a fresh but proven option in designing constitutional adjudication.

Eric A. Posner and Adrian Vermeule focus on executive power in Chapter 12, which they call "Tyrannophobia" – the fear of dictatorship that has been a longstanding theme of American political discourse. Fear of monarchy was pervasive among the founding fathers, yet they chose a constitutional design – a popularly elected president – which was amenable to the great expansion of executive power. Tyrannophobia, one might think, is itself a constraint that has helped limit executive aggrandizement, but Posner and Vermeule find no evidence for this proposition. Instead, they find that tyrannophobia in the United States is an irrational political attitude that has interfered – and continues to interfere – with needed institutional reform.

This section concludes with Zachary Elkins, Tom Ginsburg, and James Melton's contribution on executive term limits, one of the devices used to minimize the possibility of tyranny. The chapter traces the origins of term limits and demonstrates that they are widespread within presidential systems. It also evaluates their consequences: Term limits are not associated with constitutional crisis and tend to be observed in democratic systems. The normative conclusion is that term limits are a vital and effective arrow in the quiver of constitutional design.

Together, the chapters in this section call into question many conventional assumptions about core institutions. Designing amendment rules involves more than picking the level of supermajoritarian entrenchment. Federalism is a device not only for political accommodation, but also for effective economic regulation. Accommodating religious communities is a typical strategy of constitutional design, but it risks unanticipated consequences. Constitutional court models are not restricted to the French and German archetypes. Executive power need not be irrationally feared, and institutions such as term limits can serve as effective constraints on presidents. Each of these propositions implicates an active literature in institutional design and moves it forward with unconventional argument or empirical evidence.

CONCLUSION

"Constitutions," noted the political theorist Hanna Pitkin, "are made, not found" (1987: 168). While constitutions no doubt require continuous reenactment through ongoing practices, they also involve self-conscious institutional choices that can become quite sticky once adopted. The chapters in this volume illustrate the importance of institutional choice, and thus reiterate the high stakes in constitutional design. Good designs can facilitate democracy and tame religious radicals; they can encourage executive turnover and promote responsive adjustment to new circumstances through constitutional amendments. Bad designs, on the other hand, can exacerbate intercommunal conflict and perpetuate unjust outcomes for women; they can block transitions to superior institutions; and they can clog channels of citizen redress through the courts.

It will be helpful to close with a final note on the place of this volume in the literature. This is the first volume in a new series of books published by Cambridge University Press on *Comparative Constitutional Law and Policy*. The contributors to this volume share a sense that our work is only beginning to scratch the surface of possibilities for the field. We do not, and cannot, produce acontextual or mechanistic statements about the universal effect of social institutions. We can, however, aspire to the more modest goal of raising issues for consideration by designers and students of design, and offer normative suggestions informed by comparative experience. It is hoped that future volumes will advance knowledge in this spirit.

REFERENCES

Albert, Charles, S. M. Lindsay, and Leo S. Rowe. 1894. Supplement: Constitution of the Kingdom of Italy. *Annals of the American Academy of Political and Social Science* 5:1–44.

Bentwich, Norman. 1924. The Constitution of Egypt. *Journal of Comparative Legislation and International Law* 6 (1):41–49.

Blaustein, Albert P., and Jay A. Sigler, eds. 1988. *Constitutions That Made History*. New York: Paragon House Publishers.

Boralevi, Lea Campos. 2002. Classical Foundational Myths of European Republicanism: The Jewish Commonwealth, in Martin van Gelderen and Quentin Skinner (eds.),

Republicanism: A Shared European Heritage, New York: Cambridge University Press, pp. 247–61.

Buchanan, James and Gordon Tullock. 1961. *The Calculus of Consent*. Ann Arbor: University of Michigan Press.

Carrington, Dorothy. 1973. The Corsican Constitution of Pasquale Paoli (1755–1769). *The English Historical Review* 88 (348):481–503.

Chapman, Charles E. 1925. The Cuban Constitution and Congress. *California Law Review* 14 (1):22–35.

Cheibub, Jose. 2007. *Presidentialism, Parliamentarism and Democracy*. New York: Cambridge University Press.

Choudhry, Sujit. 2008. Constitutional Design for Divided Societies: Integration or Accommodation? Oxford: Oxford University Press.

Clark, R. T. 1921. The Constitution of Estonia. *Journal of Comparative Legislation and International Law* 3 (4):245–50.

Davidson, Nigel G. 1925. The Constitution of Iraq. *Journal of Comparative Legislation and International Law* 7 (1):41–52.

Dedek, Vladimir. 1921. The Constitution of Czecho-Slovakia. *Journal of Comparative Legislation and International Law* 3 (1):115–22.

Elkins, Zachary, Tom Ginsburg, and James Melton. 2009. *The Endurance of National Constitutions*. New York: Cambridge University Press.

Elster, Jon. 1998. *Institutional Design in Post-Communist Societies: Rebuilding the Ship at Sea*. New York: Cambridge University Press.

Ghai, Yash (ed). 2001. *Autonomy and Ethnicity: Negotiating Competing Claims in Multiethnic States*. New York: Cambridge University Press.

González Marcos, Miguel. 2003. Comparative Law at the Service of Democracy: A Reading of Arosemena's Constitutional Studies of the Latin American Governments. *Boston University Law Review* 21:259–324.

Hirschl, Ran. 2004. *Towards Juristocracy*. Cambridge, MA: Harvard University Press.

2009. The Design Sciences and Constitutional "Success." *Texas Law Review* 87: 1339–74.

Holmes, Stephen. 1995. *Passions and Constraint: On the Theory of Liberal Democracy*. Chicago: University of Chicago Press.

Horowitz, Donald. 1991. *A Democratic South Africa? Constitutional Engineering in a Divided Society*. Berkeley: University of California Press.

2002. Constitutional Design: Proposals Versus Processes, in Andrew Reynolds (ed.), *The Architecture of Democracy: Constitutional Design, Conflict Management, and Democracy*. Oxford: Oxford University Press, pp. 15–36.

Kammen, Michael. 1986. *A Machine That Would Go of Itself: The Constitution in American Culture*. New York: Alfred A. Knopf.

Le Roy, Katy and Cheryl Saunders (eds). 2006. *Legislative, Executive and Judicial Governance in Federal Countries*. Montreal: McGill University Press.

Lutz, Donald S. 2006. *Principles of Constitutional Design*. New York: Cambridge University Press.

March, James G. and Johan P. Olsen. 1989. *Rediscovering Institutions*. New York: Free Press.

Marcos, Miguel González. 2003. Comparative Law at the Service of Democracy: A Reading of Arosemena's Constitutional Studies of the Latin American Governments. *Boston University Law Review* 21: 259–324.

Moses, Bernard. 1893. Supplement: Constitution of the Republic of Colombia. *Annals of the American Academy of Political and Social Science* 3:1–70.
Murphy, Walter F. 2007. *Constitutional Democracy: Creating and Maintaining a Just Political Order*. Baltimore: Johns Hopkins University Press.
North, Douglass. 1991. *Institutions, Institutional Change and Economic Performance*. New York : Cambridge University Press.
Pitkin, Hanna Fenichel. 1987. The Idea of a Constitution. *Journal of Legal Education* 37: 167–69.
Pollock, James K. Jr. 1923. The Constitution of Latvia. *The American Political Science Review* 17 (3):446–48.
Powell, Walter and Paul Dimaggio. 1991. *The New Institutionalism in Organizational Analysis*. Chicago : University of Chicago Press.
Quigley, Harold Scott. 1924. The Constitution of China. *The American Political Science Review* 18 (2):346–50.
Reeves, Jesse S. 1933. The New Spanish Constitution and International Obligations. *Michigan Law Review* 31 (3):386–89.
Schneier, Edward. 2006. *Crafting Constitutional Democracies*. New York: Rowman and Littlefield.
Sunstein, Cass. 2001. *What Constitutions Do*. New York: Oxford University Press.
Takii, Kazuhiro. 2007. *The Meiji Constitution: The Japanese Experience of the West and the Shaping of the Modern State*. Tokyo: International House of Japan.
Vermeule, Adrian. 2007. *Mechanisms of Democracy*. New York: Oxford University Press.

PART I

Design Processes

2

Clearing and Strengthening the Channels of Constitution Making

Jon Elster

INTRODUCTION

A main task of the courts, said John Hart Ely (1980), is that of clearing the channels of political change. In this chapter, I consider the task of clearing the channels of constitution making. In addition, I discuss the more constructive task of strengthening these channels. I do not assume that the tasks will be undertaken by any particular agent, such as the convener of the assembly or the assembly itself. Rather I consider in the abstract how an omnipotent designer of a constituent assembly ought to structure the selection of delegates, the organization of the assembly, and the mode of ratification (if any). The advice of Bentham (1788/2002) to Louis XVI at the eve of the convocation of the Estates-General offers an example of this kind of exercise. In practice, of course, constituent assemblies believe themselves to be omnipotent once they come into being; otherwise they would be a *pouvoir constitué* rather than a *pouvoir constituant*.

As background, let me first state how the argument I present differs from some of my earlier discussions of constitution making (Elster 1995a, 2000). Drawing on the French moralists, I distinguished among three generic motivations that can animate framers: interest, reason, and passion. The implication was that an optimal constituent process ought to be guided by reason – an impartial concern for the common good in the long term – and eliminate as far as possible the influence of passion and interest. I do not exactly repudiate this idea, but I have come to see that things are more complicated. First, the idea of reason should be expanded to include informed beliefs about means as well as impartial ends (Elster 2008). Second, the role of passion does not need to be exclusively negative (Rudenfeld 2001). Third, the appeal to self-interest is not necessarily ruled out on normative grounds, if one allows other parties to appeal to *their* self-interest (Mansbridge et al. 2010). Lastly, the designer has to overcome the tacit traditional assumption that biases in collective decision making spring mainly from passion, and to acknowledge the importance of cognitive or "cold" biases (Eskridge and Ferejohn 2002).

In this perspective, the negative task – clearing the channels – consists in eliminating the impact of bias, interest, and passion, as far as possible and as far as desirable. One may (1a) prevent the selection of interested, passionate, or biased individuals or organize the process so that it will (1b) weaken or (1c) be less vulnerable to these attitudes. As for limits to possibility, random idiosyncratic effects can never be completely eliminated. A domineering individual may exercise an undue influence on the outcome, and a spoiler may ruin the whole process. Some systematic biases may also be hard to eradicate. As for limits to desirability, I just asserted that passion and interest may have a positive or at least a nonnegative role. In addition, the cost and especially the opportunity cost of distortion-removing machinery might also be prohibitive. Constituent tasks are often *urgent*.

The positive task – strengthening the channels – consists in enhancing the motivations of the framers and improving the information available to them. One may (2a) select impartial and well-informed individuals or organize the process so that it will (2b) foster or (2c) be responsive to these qualities. We may observe that (2a) is not merely the opposite of (1a), given that the *strength* of the concern for the public good is an important independent factor. A framer might be not only dispassionate and disinterested, but also uninterested in his task. We may also note that in selecting for information, one should aim at creating an informed group of individuals, not a group of informed individuals (see discussion later in the chapter).

I have listed six *intermediate variables*, (1a) through (2c). To affect them in desired ways, a designer could, in principle, use any number of *institutional variables*:

- the mode of election or selection of delegates
- the qualifications (age, gender, income, literacy, etc.) of electors
- the qualifications of delegates
- the number of delegates
- the seating of the delegates in the assembly
- secrecy or publicity of debates and votes during and after the tenure of the assembly
- allocation of time to speakers
- allowing or forbidding deputies to read from written speeches
- the task of the assembly (constituent only or constituent and legislative)
- the location of the assembly
- the (minimal or maximal) duration of the assembly
- the (minimal or maximal) length of the constitutional text
- the procedures of ratification of the constitution
- the date of promulgation of the constitution.

Not all of these have been used in designing actual assemblies. Some of them would not (indeed should not) be used today. I nevertheless discuss some of the latter, such as elector and delegate qualifications, when they have been proposed or could be proposed for the purpose of affecting the intermediate variables.

It would now seem natural to ask how the intermediate variables affect the *outcome variable* – the constitution. Reasoning backward, one would first try to determine the intermediate variables likely to produce a good constitution and then the institutional variables likely to produce the desired intermediate variables. This is not how I proceed, however. Rather, my reasoning will be forward-looking – from favorable conditions to the presumption of a good outcome, or as good as one can expect.

Consider the three forms of procedural justice discussed by Rawls (1971, §14). Clearly, we cannot understand the task of constitution making as involving *perfect procedural justice*, exemplified by Harington's two girls ("I divide, you choose"). Even if we had independently defined criteria for what constitutes a good constitution, no procedure could track that outcome perfectly. Given that we do not, in fact, have any such criteria, the idea of *imperfect procedural justice*, exemplified by jury verdicts, will not do either.

It might seem more plausible to characterize good constitution making in terms of *pure procedural justice*, exemplified by Rawls's own theory, in which "there is a correct or fair procedure such that the outcome is likewise correct or fair, whatever it is, provided that the procedure has been properly followed." Even this requirement is too strong, however. As virtually all processes of collective decision making, constitution making is subject to *incorrigible distortions* and to *indeterminate trade-offs*. In a deliberating group, the susceptibility of participants to vanity and *amour-propre* may be reduced but not eliminated. *Being right* will always, for some, loom larger than *getting it right*. Also, when an institutional variable has two opposite effects on an intermediate variable, one negative and one positive, the designer may not know how to strike the right balance. The relation between the size of an assembly and its epistemic quality illustrates this case, as we shall see. Indeterminacy can also obtain when a given institutional variable, such as publicity of the debates and votes, has the desirable effect of reducing the role of interest and the (sometimes) undesirable effect of enhancing the role of passion.

The best one can hope for, then, may be a variety of good collective decision making that Rawls does not mention – *impure procedural justice*. When distortions that can be reduced by institutional means have been reduced, and trade-offs have been made on an intuitive basis, the designer cannot do any better than let the chips fall where they may.

In pursuing some of these ideas, I shall proceed as follows. In the second section, I consider whether public-spirited motivations can be enhanced by mechanisms

(2a), (2b), or (2c). In the third section, I ask the same question with regard to rational belief formation. In the fourth section, I address the issue of reducing the impact of interest by mechanisms (1a), (1b), or (1c). In the fifth section, I ask the same question with regard to passions. In the sixth section, I briefly consider cognitive bias in the same perspective. The seventh section offers summary concluding comments. Although the most important historical examples will be the eighteenth-century constituent assemblies in Philadelphia and Versailles (later Paris), I also draw on a number of other constituent episodes.

ENHANCING IMPARTIALITY

The quality of impartiality or public-spiritedness – the concern for the common good in the long run – is more crucial in constituent assemblies than in ordinary legislatures. In the latter, partisan majority decisions can be reversed by a later majority; moreover, the expectation of an alternation in power may cause partisan majorities to pull their punches. In a constituent assembly, a small partisan majority may be able to impose its preferences not only on the current minority, but also on a posterity in which it may itself be in a minority. This future tyranny of the minority is made possible by the fact that the majority required to amend a constitution is typically a qualified one, whereas the document itself is always adopted by a simple majority. At the Federal Convention, for instance, Gouverneur Morris tried to lock in the future when he warned that if you "[g]ive the votes to people who have no property, [...] they will sell them to the rich who will be able to buy them. We should not confine our attention to the present moment. The time is not distant when this Country will abound with mechanics & manufacturers who will receive their bread from their employers" (Farrand 1966, II, p. 160).

As the stability of the constitution over time is a large part of its *raison d'être*, it would be pointless to make the decisions of the constituent assembly as easily reversible as those of a legislature. To counteract the risk of a lock-in by the present on the future, we may look to solutions along the lines of (2a), (2b), and (2c). To enhance the likelihood that public-spirited delegates will be selected, one might require qualifications in the electors or in the delegates themselves. However, there are few if any objective characteristics that are demonstrably correlated with public-spiritedness. Education and age are conducive to a better understanding of means-ends relations but are neutral with regard to the quality of the ends themselves. Income and property mainly induce a stake in the status quo. There is no evidence for the claim, frequently made in the nineteenth century, that the possession of land induces a permanent interest in the well-being of the community. Equally implausibly, one might require that framers have large families to give them a personal inducement to consider long-term consequences.

If direct selection for impartiality is unfeasible, the indirect method of *cross-voting* might seem more promising (Elster 2006). In the elections to the Estates-General of 1789, the large majority of electoral districts chose delegates from the three orders separately, the clergy, the nobility and the third estate each choosing its own deputies. In a handful of districts, notably the Dauphiné, the three orders jointly chose the deputies for each estate, each elector casting three votes. (An even more extreme version was used in the elections in Brittany to the Estates-General in 1576 and 1614: Deputies for the clergy were chosen by the nobility and the third estate, those for the nobility by the clergy and the third estate, and those for the third estate by the clergy and the nobility [Picot 1888, vol. V, p. 271–72].) The hope was that the method would favor the election of moderate deputies motivated at least in part by the general interest rather than of extremists motivated only by the interests of their particular orders (Tocqueville 2004a, pp. 531, 541). In general, however, the procedure is fragile because it can also create an incentive for the members of one group to vote for the most insignificant members of the other estates – *raiding* rather than *hedging* (Cho and Kang 2008). A similar concern was voiced by Madison at the Federal Convention (Farrand 1966, II, p. 114).

It is tempting, then, to look for ways in which the process itself might foster or be responsive to impartial motivations. In an admittedly unrealistic proposal, one might delay the promulgation of the constitution for some years, to create a veil of ignorance behind which framers would have to "put themselves in the place of all," given that nobody would know exactly how the document would affect them personally. More realistically, publicity of debates and votes would induce, if not impartial motivations, at least verbal and nonverbal behavior consistent with such motivations ("the civilizing effect of hypocrisy"). Publicity does not rule out self-serving uses of impartial arguments (Elster 1995b, 1999, ch. V), but it can to some extent limit opportunism.

Yet even though hypocrisy can mimic impartiality, it does not provide the strength of motivation required for a sustained participation. If their absence goes unnoticed or unsanctioned, deputies may take time off for their private affairs rather than showing up for work in committees or plenary debates. (Note the difference between this impact of private interest and that discussed in the fourth section of this chapter.) Beginning with the *Constituante* of 1789, French assemblies have addressed this issue by publishing the names of those not responding to roll calls (Pierre 1893, p. 479–80), in the hope that blame and shame might counteract private interest.

We can take the proportion of deputies' time devoted to the constituent task as a proxy for strength of motivation. To increase that proportion, one may try to ensure not only that they show up in the assembly, but also that when there, they devote all their time to the task. (During the conclave for electing a new pope, cardinals are not allowed to devote themselves to any other task.) It follows that constituent assemblies ought not to serve as legislative assemblies as well. Among the reasons why a separation of constituent power and legislative power is desirable one can, in fact, cite the sheer scarcity of time and the need to work in a sustained manner. The intense focus of the Federal Convention stands in stark contrast to the constituent efforts of the Assemblée Constituante, which were constantly interrupted by legislative and, increasingly, executive tasks.

Needless to say, strength of motivation – like competence (see discussion later in the chapter) – is to be valued only if deputies are impartial or can be induced to behave as if they were. If the worst are full of passionate conviction, they will neither be impartial nor ashamed to show their partiality, which, in their eyes, is righteousness itself. As explained earlier, cross-voting was intended to prevent election of such extremists.

ENHANCING RATIONAL BELIEF FORMATION

The efficient promotion of impartial ends requires rational beliefs about ends-means causality. Impartiality and rationality interact multiplicatively rather than additively. The capacity for rational belief formation makes no independent contribution to the goodness of decisions; it can help constitution wreckers as well as constitution makers, extremists as well as moderates, to realize their goals more effectively.

Beliefs are based on the possession and processing of information. At the individual level, *competence* or expertise is a multiplicative function of acquired information and innate ability to process it. In principle, one might select competent delegates by requiring that they (or their electors) possess a certain level of literacy or education. Yet what matters for present purposes is collective rather than individual competence. The idea of "collective wisdom" in its various manifestation is highly complex (Landemore and Elster, forthcoming). Here I want to emphasize three aspects: how diversity at the group level might trump competence at the individual level; how larger assemblies might be better at processing information; and how small assemblies might be better at acquiring information.

Page (2007) shows that under certain conditions, "diversity trumps ability" with regard to problem solving. As far as I understand, it is impossible to verify whether these conditions are satisfied for actual assemblies. Yet it makes good intuitive sense to think that if members of an assembly represent a cross-section of the population, they might outperform a less representative group of more competent individuals both with respect to identifying the most important problems (where the shoe pinches) and with respect to solving them (how to make good shoes).

There are two main ways of achieving representativeness. In classical Athens, the lawgivers or *nomothetai* were chosen by lot from the citizens or, more accurately, from the citizens who presented themselves on the day of the meeting.

(The element of self-selection may have reduced representativeness.) In modern constituent assemblies, universal suffrage combined with some kind of proportional representation will, in general, yield a representative assembly. In communities where elections to ordinary legislatures have imposed economic qualifications on the voters, these have sometimes been lifted in the election to constituent assemblies. Thus in the elections to the 1780 constituent legislature in Massachusetts, the assembly "enfranchised all free adult male town inhabitants for the duration of the constitution-making process" (Kruman 1997, pp. 30–31; see also Hoar 1917, pp. 203–07). Proportional voting, too, is often seen as especially appropriate for constituent assemblies. In 1990, Vaclav Havel imposed this system in the first free elections, to allow a place for his former communist enemies in the constituent assembly. He paid a high price, however, for his impartiality. The communists, notably the deputies from Slovakia, ended up as constitution wreckers rather than constitution makers (Elster 1995c).

The Condorcet jury theorem asserts, in nontechnical terms, that if each member of a jury or an assembly has a better than random chance of "getting it right" and if they form their opinions independently of each other, the chance that the majority will "get it right" increases with the number of members, converging to 100 percent as the number increases indefinitely. The relevance of this theorem for actual assemblies, and the feasibility of verifying that the two conditions obtain, are more than dubious. For present purposes, the important question is whether there is any intuitive reason to think that sheer numbers will enhance epistemic accuracy. Would the addition of identical twins with identical life histories to the assembly improve its capacity to get it right? As far as I can see, there is no reason to think it would.

In fact, as Bentham first showed, adding the twins might make things worse. We know that Bentham was aware of Condorcet's 1785 Essay, since there is an ironic reference to it in a work from 1808 (Bentham 1808/1843). I do not know whether he was already familiar with it when he wrote his two essays for the Estates-General, but internal evidence suggests that he was. In his first essay, he admits that "It is certain that with a larger number [of delegates] there is also a larger probability of a good rather than a bad decision" (Bentham 1788/2002, p. 35). Yet, he goes on to say, experience from the British parliament suggests that "the greater the number of voters the less the weight and the value of each vote, the less its price in the eyes of the voter, and the less of an incentive he has in assuring that it conforms to the true end and even in casting it at all." In the second essay, he first states the argument for a large assembly: "With the number of members increases the chances of wisdom (*sagesse*). So many members, so many sources of enlightenment" and then objects that "the reduction that this same cause brings in the strength of the motivation to exercise one's enlightenment offsets this advantage" (Bentham 1788/2002, p. 122).

Well before Grossman and Stiglitz (1980), Bentham here puts his finger on the problem of informational free-riding. The motivation to acquire information to form rational beliefs about how to realize the public good will be diluted when the size of the assembly increases. Now, given that information itself is a public good, this claim might seem incoherent. The question is deeper, however, since in a group of public-spirited deputies, each has a reason to seek out information if and only if others do not. Barring implausible mixed strategies, there is no stable point between the underproduction of information, leading to bad decisions, and the overproduction of information, leading to costly redundancy. As Vermeule (2007, p. 228–31) argues, however, the assembly can overcome this collective action problem by setting up a separate information-gathering structure staffed by officials who are paid to determine the facts.

The same solution will also take care of the less esoteric but practically more important problem that delegates will usually *not* be exclusively concerned with the public interest. When allocating their time between conducting their private affairs and informing themselves about public matters, the amount they invest in assuring that their vote "conforms to the true end" will, for the reasons Bentham stated, decrease with the number of fellow deputies. These considerations may perhaps explain the otherwise puzzling decision by the Belgian parliament in 1875 that no proposition of law could be signed *by more* than six members (Pierre 1893, p. 724).

REDUCING THE IMPACT OF INTEREST

In this section, I consider only how the interest of the deputies might have an impact on the substance of their *decisions*, leaving behind the impact, discussed earlier, on their *participation*. I distinguish between personal interest and group interest. The normative status of these interests in the constitution-making process differs widely. Whereas personal interests are intrinsically undesirable influences on the decisions, group interests may or may not be inappropriate.

In modern constituent assemblies, the personal interests of the framers are a minor factor, because group interests, especially party interests, are overwhelmingly important. Although the recent transitions in Eastern Europe offer a few examples of constitutional provisions clauses owing their origin to vested interests of individual framers (Elster 1993, p. 191), personal interest usually has little purchase on the decisions. In the two great eighteenth-century assemblies, however, many individual framers had a great deal to gain or to lose under the respective constitutions. No effort whatsoever was made to prevent the election of individuals with strong interests. In America, the burning issue of the assumption of federal and state debts by the new government might have triggered a decision to exclude large holders of such debts from the Convention. This anachronistic thought did not, of course, occur to anyone. Self-selection is another matter. Thus Gouverneur Morris claimed that he had deliberately refrained from acquiring such holdings so "that he might urge with more propriety the compliance with public faith" (Farrand 1966, II, p. 329).

An assembly can reduce the impact of personal interest by *exposing* its decisions to publicity or by *insulating* them from that motive. Concerning the first, we may cite Bentham (1791/1999, p. 37): "Is it objected against the régime of publicity that it is a system of *distrust*? This is true, and every good political institution is founded upon that base." In the canonical modern formulation, "Sunlight is the best disinfectant." The Abbé Sieyes lost much of his prestige in the French Constituante when he objected (with perfectly valid arguments!) to the abolition of the tithe. At the Federal Convention, "four men – Gerry, King, Sherman, and Ellsworth – were obviously working ardently for the interests represented by their own investments" (McDonald 1992, p. 106). If the debates on the assumption of the debts had taken place before an audience, they might have spoken more prudently. Oliver Ellsworth, who owned federal debts only, argued that the new government ought to assume these debts and no others. In the presence of an audience, the civilizing force of hypocrisy might at least have induced him to extend the assumption to state debts, thus satisfying the "imperfection constraint" on self-serving arguments (Elster 1999, chapter V). (Sherman and King, both of whom held state debts only, argued for the assumption of all debts.)

In addition, an assembly can try to *insulate* its decisions from personal interest. When designing a future institution, framers can include features that ensure that they will not benefit from it personally. In the two eighteenth-century assemblies, framers as different as Benjamin Franklin and Robespierre made proposals to this effect. When the question of paying a salary to the future Senators came up, Franklin asserted that he "wished the Convention to stand fair with the people. There were in it a number of young men who would probably be of the Senate. If lucrative appointments should be recommended we might be chargeable with having carved out places for ourselves" (Farrand 1966, I, p. 329). His motion that Senators should not receive a salary failed by a five-to-six vote. By contrast, Robespierre's motion on May 16, 1791 that members of the constituent assembly should be ineligible to the first ordinary legislature was adopted unanimously. Although some of the deputies may have been "drunk with disinterestedness," in the words of the biographer of one of them (Lebègue 1910, p. 261), many were probably afraid of being *perceived* as insufficiently disinterested (Elster 2009a, chapter 10).

Consider now group interests, beginning with party interests. In many cases, these have an undesirable impact on the outcome. A large party may be able to impose a majoritarian electoral system because it favors large parties, just as a coalition of small parties may be able to impose a proportional system. The Spanish constituent assembly of 1931 illustrates the first possibility. The second is illustrated by several postcommunist constitutions. A party with a popular presidential candidate may be able to impose a strong presidency and popular election of the president, unless its opponents in the assembly manage to impose a weak presidency and election of the president by the legislature. The constituent episode in France in 1958 illustrates the first possibility, that of Poland in 1921 the second. Although undesirable, such effects may be inevitable. To avoid them, framers would have to be selected on a non-partisan basis, as were the Athenian *nomothetai*. In the contemporary world, this idea is unthinkable.

Group interest can also take other forms. At the Federal Convention, the interests of the *states* operated in a number of ways to shape the outcome, notably by the threat of the small states to leave the Convention unless they achieved an equal representation in the Senate and the threat of the slave states to leave unless slavery was protected. These influences were predictably obnoxious, the first distorting American politics to the present day and the second creating massive and durable injustices. In general, however, to the extent that the interests of states in federal systems reflect the interests of their populations, they are not necessarily disreputable. When the interests of Catholics and Protestants or of Francophones and Anglophones diverge, there is no well-defined public interest that can trump interest-based bargaining and voting. When interests of farmers and manufacturers diverge, there may be a public interest, but no reliable procedure to determine it.

One may nevertheless try to create conditions of *fair bargaining* or, alternatively, *reduce the scope for bargaining*. The first aim could be met by imposing a time limit on the constitutional process, so as to prevent some participants from getting their way by virtue of their superior "inside options" (ability to hold out). Similarly, the threat of filibustering can be reduced by limiting the time allocated to a given speaker (or speakers from a given party) on a given issue. Secrecy of the *debates* may also be seen as a means to the same end, since it prevents the bargainers from using the public as an amplifier on their demands. Also, secrecy of the *votes* can reduce the scope for bargaining by blocking the credible promises that are a precondition for logrolling.

In any case, even with public votes, the one-off nature of constituent assemblies will tend to weaken the incentive to keep promises. At the Federal Convention, the compromise in which the large states agreed to equal representation for all states in the Senate in exchange for denying the Senate the right to initiate *and amend* money bills was undone later when the right to amendment crept in. In the West German assembly of 1948, "the Minister President of Bavaria persuaded the SPD to vote for [the institution of] a Bundesrat in exchange for a momentary advantage and concessions which were subsequently all but abandoned" (Merkl 1963, p. 69). During the debates over the Spanish constitution in 1978, the Union of the Democratic Center was accused "of breaking a painstakingly negotiated set of compromises" (Bonime-Blanc 1987, p. 56). In a legislature, such reneging would be severely punished. In constituent assemblies, the shadow of the future is less effective. It is an open question whether members of a constituent assembly are aware of the fact that it may be hard to sustain logrolling promises by the fear of punishment. It is also an open question whether a reduced capacity for logrolling is desirable or not (see Riker and Brahms 1973 ; Stratmann 1997; Mueller 2003, pp. 104–12).

REDUCING THE IMPACT OF PASSION

Let me first enumerate some of the cognitive and motivational mechanisms by which emotions can distort decision-making processes (see also Elster 2009b). First, they may induce temporary preference changes that differ from the permanent and stable attitudes of the agents. Second, they may prevent the agents from realizing that these changes are indeed temporary. Third, they may induce insufficient investment in information-gathering. Fourth, they can induce wishful thinking or counterwishful thinking: "Each man believes easily what he fears or what he hopes." Finally, sheer *amour-propre* can make an agent stick to his beliefs, in the face of contrary evidence, simply because they are *his* beliefs. Here I limit myself to mechanisms that can to some extent be neutralized by institutional design.

The passions of framers can be exogenous or endogenous. On the one hand, they come to their task with preexisting emotions of fear, resentment, envy, contempt, and the like. On the other hand, the process itself may generate strong emotions. I consider these in turn.

When, as is often the case, constitutions are adopted under the threat of violent uprisings or as part of turbulent regime transitions, strong exogenous passions are inevitably present. Shays' Rebellion had strongly impressed many of the framers in Philadelphia. Writing to William Smith on November 13, 1787, Jefferson asserted that "Our Convention has been too much impressed by the insurrection of Massachusetts: and in the spur of the moment they are setting up a kite [hawk] to keep the hen-yard in order." He is clearly implying that the framers were acting under the impulse of visceral fear and not merely out of prudential fear. Although some scholars minimize the importance of the rebellion for the proceedings of the Convention (Feer 1966; Ackerman and Katyal 1995), I tend to believe that Jefferson knew what he was talking about. At Versailles, the abolition of feudalism on August 4, 1789 certainly owed something to the visceral fear of the *constituants* that their castles might be burned and their families slaughtered (see, for instance, Ferrières 1932, p. 109 ff.). The committee drafting the constitution of the Second French Republic moderated its initially radical proposals after the invasion of the

Assembly by the Parisian crowds on May 16, 1848. The constitution of the Fifth French Republic was adopted when the parliamentarians of the Fourth Republic granted full powers to de Gaulle under the pressure of events in Algeria. In his own inimitable words, "In 1958 I had a problem of conscience. I could just let things take their course: the paratroopers in Paris, the parliamentarians in the Seine, the general strike, the government of the Americans: it was written on the wall. Finally a moment would have come when everybody would have come looking for de Gaulle, but at what price? Thus I decided to intervene in time to prevent the drama" (Peyrefitte 1995, p. 262).

These exogenous emotions cannot be fully neutralized by institutional means, but procedural design may prevent them from escalating. When debates and votes take place behind closed doors or in a location far from major urban agglomerations, passions may more easily be contained. The framers in Philadelphia were completely insulated from the rest of the country. The choice of Weimar as the birthplace for the 1919 German constitution was dictated by the need to be away from the fighting in Berlin. During the 2007–2008 constituent process in Ecuador, framers were sequestered in a small village. They could leave it, but visitors needed a special permit, which was hard to get, to pass the police roadblocks (Adam Przeworski, personal communication).

Even if it were possible to neutralize the emotions of framers, it might not be desirable. Hegel claimed that "Nothing great in the world has been accomplished without passion." Tocqueville (2004b, p. 228) wrote that "a man facing danger rarely remains as he was: he will either rise well above his habitual level or sink well below it." The Federal Convention, in his opinion, illustrated the first case. According to Bentham (1788/2002, p. 31), "the time of great crises is also the time of great virtues; virtue is a good that, like any other, is multiplied by demand." One of the most impressive of the *constituants* of 1789, the Comte de Clermont-Tonnerre, said that "Anarchy is a frightening yet necessary passage, and the only moment one can establish a new order of things. It is not in calm times that one can take uniform measures" (AP, 9, p. 461). To overcome interest, reason may need to form an alliance with passion. If the *constituants* had deliberated behind closed doors, they might not have been able to make a clean break with the past. Needless to say, however, this effect of publicity is too unpredictable to be used as a basis for institutional design.

Endogenous emotions arise in the interaction among framers and in the interplay between framers and audience. Although the exogenous emotion of fear was a central force behind the decrees of August 4, the endogenous emotions of malice and resentment that arose as framers sacrificed one another's privileges (Elster 2007) also mattered. Thus after the bishop of Chartres had proposed the abolition of exclusive hunting rights, the Duc du Châtelet said to his neighbors, "Ah! he takes our hunting, I'll take his tithe," and proposed that the tithe be abolished with compensation (Droz 1860, II, p. 308). As this exchange shows, the passions were grounded in the strong material interests of the framers. The idea of selecting framers with no personal interest in the outcome would, of course, have been as unthinkable as in the American case.

An important endogenous emotion is *vanity* induced by speaking before an audience. In Madison's classic defense of the secrecy at the Convention, "had the members committed themselves publicly at first, they would have afterwards supposed consistency required them to maintain their ground, whereas by secret discussion no man felt himself obliged to retain his opinions any longer than he was satisfied of their propriety and truth, and was open to the force of argument. ... No constitution would ever have been adopted by the convention had the debates been public" (Farrand 1966, III, p. 479). Framers did indeed change their mind in the course of the debates at the Convention. By contrast, I have not come across any publicly expressed changes of opinion at the French *Constituante*. As the records of this assembly amount to some twenty-odd thousand double-column pages in small print, there may, of course, be examples that I missed.

To reduce the role of vanity in assemblies while also ensuring publicity of the debates, Bentham (1791/1999, p. 64) proposed to exclude women from the galleries. "It has been found that their presence gave a particular turn to the deliberations – that self-love played too conspicuous a part – that personalities were more lively – and that too much was sacrificed to vanity and wit." For some time after 1778, this practice was, in fact, observed by the British parliament (*ibid.*, note 1). I do not know whether the reason for excluding women was that adduced by Bentham. When the French Convention in 1795 decided to exclude women from the galleries, it was because they had been among the most active among the invaders of the parliamentary arena (Pierre 1893, p. 826).

As most speeches at the *Constituante* were written, speakers did not really talk to one another and try to refute one another's arguments. Rather, they were speaking to the audience and to the readers of the numerous newspapers that would report their speeches the next day. If they had wanted to overcome this problem and create a genuine debate, they might have adopted the British practice of banning prepared speeches. Only Mirabeau, however, proposed this radical step (Pierre 1893, p. 899). In addition to the fact that written speeches paralyze debate, it is worthwhile citing the objection to written speeches made (in a written speech!) by the President of the French Assemblée Nationale in 1862: "If [a written speech] is long and diffuse, it chills the debate and is pronounced before empty benches. If it is bitter and violent, it causes a deep irritation, because nothing produces a more painful impression than calculated bitterness and violence that does not have the excuse of improvisation" (Pierre 1893, p. 900).

REDUCING COGNITIVE BIAS

I understand bias as a cognitive or "cold" mechanism that shapes beliefs in normatively inappropriate ways. There is little doubt that these operate in collective decision making, either at the level of individual participants or through their interaction. It is widely argued, for instance, that jurors are deeply shaped by hindsight bias and anchoring bias when awarding compensatory and punitive damages. If subject either to the "sunk cost fallacy" or to the "planning fallacy," members of an assembly may form unrealistically optimistic beliefs about the economic viability of projects. In addition to these individually based distortions, bias may arise through interaction. The "recency effect" and the "first-impression effect," for instance, can distort decisions by lending excessive weight to the arguments made by the last and the first speakers in the debate. (The "availability bias" corresponds to the first of these.) Conjecturally, these effects may also arise in voting.

Our knowledge about such biases comes mainly from the studies of juries and other small groups. Little is known about the importance of bias in assemblies in general and constituent assemblies more specifically. Nor, to my knowledge, is much written on how to reduce or prevent assembly bias by institutional design (see Eskridge and Ferejohn 2002 for some skeptical comments). Even though the remedies of bicameralism, executive veto, and judicial review may reduce some bias in legislatures, they are not available for constituent assemblies. In any case, bias reduction (debiasing) is in general less effective than bias prevention (Wilson, Centerbar, and Brekke 2002).

The political thinker who has devoted the most thought to these matters is, no doubt, Bentham, notably in *Political Tactics*. Thus if the recency effect and the first-impression effect arise in voting, one could prevent them by votes being public but simultaneous (Bentham 1791/1999, p. 106ff.). To prevent memory-induced biases, Bentham (*ibid.*, p. 45) recommended the construction of "a very simple mechanical apparatus for exhibiting to the eyes of the assembly the motion on which they are deliberating." When deputies tend to seat themselves with others of the same political persuasion, they should speak from a central tribune rather than from their seats, to relieve "the individual from the association of ideas which would connect him with a given party" (*ibid.*, p. 54). Alternatively, one could follow the practice of the French Convention and have the deputies seated randomly (Pierre 1893, p. 829).

CONCLUSION

The procedural approach to good collective decision making has been studied and applied in several settings, notably jury decisions, academic hiring decisions, and decisions by central banks, committees, or constitutional courts. By manipulating the mode of appointment to these bodies, their voting rules, the secrecy or publicity of their debates and votes, and many other variables, one hopes to eliminate distorting influences of the kind I have mentioned and to enhance the motivation and information of their members.

These are all small-group decisions. The extension of this approach to political assemblies – including constituent ones – is in its infancy, and may perhaps remain there forever. Although we can draw on a vast amount of historical knowledge, it is mostly anecdotal. It can help us identify possible causal mechanisms that may be at work, without enabling us to assess their net effects and to make positive recommendations. The study of the successes and failures of past constituent assemblies can nevertheless be useful if it makes conveners and members of future assemblies pause and reflect before they make potentially important design decisions.

REFERENCES

Ackerman, Bruce and Neil Katyal (1995), "Our unconventional founding," *University of Chicago Law Review* 62, 475–573.

AP = *Archives Parlementaires*, Serie I: 1787–1799, Paris 1875–1888.

Bentham, Jeremy (1788/2002), "Lettre d'un Anglois" and "Considération d'un Anglois," in Bentham, *Rights, Representation and Reform*, Oxford: Oxford University Press, pp. 3–146.

(1791/1999), *Political Tactics*, Oxford: Oxford University Press.

(1808/1843), "Scotch reform," in J. Bowring (ed.), *The Works of Jeremy Bentham*, vol. 5, Edinburgh: William Tait, pp. 1–54.

Bonime-Blanc, A. (1987), *Spain's Transition to Democracy*, Boulder: Westview Press.

Cho, S. and Kang, I. (2008), "Open primaries and crossover voting," Working Paper, Yale University.

Droz, J. (1860), *Histoire du règne de Louis XVI*, Paris: Renouard.

Elster, Jon (1993), "Rebuilding the boat in the open sea: Constitution-making in Eastern Europe," *Public Administration* 71, 169–217.

(1995a), "Forces and mechanisms in the constitution-making process," *Duke Law Journal* 45, 364–96.

(1995b), "Strategic uses of argument," in K. Arrow et al. (eds.), *Barriers to the Negotiated Resolution of Conflict*, New York: Norton, pp. 236–57.

(1995c), "Transition, constitution-making and transition in Czechoslovakia," *Archives Européennes de Sociologie* 36, 105–34.

(1999), *Alchemies of the Mind*, Cambridge: Cambridge University Press

(2000), "Arguing and bargaining in two constituent assemblies," *University of Pennsylvania Journal of Constitutional Law* 2, 345–421.

(2006), "Altruistic behavior and altruistic motivations," in S.-C. Kolm and J. M. Ythier (eds.), *Handbook on the Economics of Giving, Reciprocity, and Altruism*, Amsterdam: Elsevier, vol. 1, pp. 183–206.

(2007), "The night of August 4 1789," *Revue Européenne de Sciences Sociales* 45, 71–94.

(2008), *Reason and Rationality*, Princeton: Princeton University Press

(2009a), *Le désintéressement*, Paris: Seuil.

(2009b), "Emotions," in P. Hedstrom and P. Bearman (eds.), *The Oxford Handbook of Analytical Sociology*, Oxford: Oxford University Press.
(forthcoming), "The optimal design of a constituent assembly," in H. Landemore and J. Elster (eds.), *Collective Wisdom*, New York: Cambridge University Press.
Ely, John Hart (1980), *Democracy and Distrust*, Cambridge, MA: Harvard University Press.
Eskridge, William and John Ferejohn (2002), "Structuring lawmaking to reduce cognitive bias: A critical view," *Cornell Law Review* 87, 616–47.
Farrand, M. (1966), *Records of the Federal Convention*, New Haven: Yale University Press.
Feer, R. (1966), "Shays' rebellion and the Constitution: A study in causation," *New England Quarterly* 42, 388–410.
Ferrières, Marquis de (1932), *Correspondance inédite*, Paris: Armand Colin
Grossman, S. and Stiglitz, J. (1980), "On the impossibility of informationally efficient markets," *American Economic Review* 70, 393–408.
Hoar, R. S. (1917), *Constitutional Conventions*. Boston: Little, Brown.
Kruman, M. (1997), *Between Authority and Liberty: State Constitution Making in Revolutionary America*, Chapel Hill: University of North Carolina Press.
Landemore, H. and Elster, J. (eds.) (forthcoming), *Collective Wisdom*, New York: Cambridge University Press.
Lebègue, E. (1910), *Thouret*, Paris: Felix Alcan
Mansbridge, Jane et al. (2010), "The place of self-interest and the role of power in deliberative democracy," *Journal of Political Philosophy* 18, 64–100.
McDonald, F. (1992), *We the People: The Economic Origins of the Constitution*, New Brunswick: Transaction Books.
Merkl, P. (1963), *The Origin of the West German Republic*, Oxford: Oxford University Press.
Mueller, Denis (2003), *Public Choice III*, Cambridge: Cambridge University Press.
Page, S. (2007), *The Difference*, Princeton: Princeton University Press.
Peyrefitte, A. (1995), *C'était de Gaulle*, vol. 1, Paris: Fayard.
Picot, G. (1888), *Histoire des Etats-Généraux*, Paris: Hachette.
Pierre, E. (1893), *Traité de droit politique, électoral et parlementaire*, Paris : Librairies-Imprimeries Réunies.
Rawls, John (1971), *A Theory of Justice*, Cambridge, MA: Harvard University Press.
Riker, W. and Brahms, S. (1973), "The paradox of vote trading," *American Political Science Review* 62, 1235–47.
Rudenfeld, Jed (2001), *Freedom and Time*, New Haven: Yale University Press.
Stratmann. T. (1997), "Logrolling," in D. Mueller (ed.), *Perspectives on Public Choice*, Cambridge: Cambridge University Press.
Tocqueville, Alexis de (2004a), *Oeuvres* (éd. de la Pléiade), vol. III, Paris: Gallimard.
(2004b), *Democracy in America*, New York: Library of America.
Vermeule, Adrian (2007), *Mechanisms of Democracy*, Oxford: Oxford University Press.
Wilson, T., Centerbar, D., and Brekke, N. (2002), "Mental contamination and the debiasing problem," in T. Gilovich, D. Griffin, and D. Kahneman (eds.), *Heuristics and Biases*, Cambridge: Cambridge University Press, pp. 185–200.

3

Does the Process of Constitution-Making Matter?

Justin Blount, Zachary Elkins, and Tom Ginsburg

INTRODUCTION

Constitution making is as ubiquitous as it is mysterious. In any given year, by our estimate, some four or five constitutions will be replaced, ten to fifteen will be amended, and another twenty or so proposals for revision will be under consideration (Elkins, Ginsburg, and Melton 2009). These revisions represent potentially far-reaching changes to fundamental political rules. Yet our knowledge of constitutional (re)design processes and their consequences is cloudy at best. More than a decade after Elster (1995, 1997) lamented the dearth of theory on constitutional design (and, we would add, systematic empirical evidence), the field retains a frontier quality – exciting but unchartered – notwithstanding Elster's own valuable contributions. Many of us likely suspect that the conditions and rules under which founders write, deliberate, and ratify will be consequential. We just cannot say with any authority how they matter, or to what extent.

At the same time, there is genuine reason for optimism about the prospects of improved knowledge. If the field is thin with respect to rigorous comparative research, it is becoming thicker and richer in case studies that can conceivably motivate researchers and shape theory. Founding moments are generally historical, if mythical, affairs, and historians have documented classic cases (e.g., Golay 1958; Moore and Robinson 2004; Rakove 1997) in some depth. More recent cases have also been the subject of detailed accounts (e.g., Bannon 2007; Brandt n.d.; Congleton 2003; Ghai, Lattimer, and Said 2003; Goldwin and Kaufman 1988; Haysom 2004; Hyden and Venter 2001; Keogh and McCarthy 2007; Moehler 2006; Rubin 2004; Selassie 2003; for an extensive bibliography of sources relating to post-1975 cases of constitutional design, see Widner 2005b.)[1] These accounts offer a rich source of inspiration for a literature whose needs are clear: conceptualization and measurement of the

[1] For a truly mythical take on both the process of constitutional design and political transition, see Murphy's (2007) account of a fictional constitutional convention in which the delegates intelligently

process, rigorous theorizing about the effects of different aspects of the process, and the testing of these theories with suitable empirical designs. More extensive comparative empirical work looms on the horizon, and we can expect steady growth, if not a boom, in research on the topic (see Carey 2007; Moehler 2007; Samuels 2006; Widner 2005a, 2007a).

Our goals in this chapter are largely cartographic. We seek to chart the frontiers of our collective knowledge of constitutional drafting and adoption processes. Our particular focus is on the links between process and outcomes. We begin with a historical review of the literature and a description of different modes of constitutional design processes, including both the typical actors involved and the activities in which they are engaged. We then explore some of the micro-foundational assumptions that undergird theory regarding the consequences of different processes; in particular, we address the motivations of participating actors. The bulk of the essay is devoted to identifying hypotheses (or, more accurately, thoughtful conjecture) that appear in the literature on the relationship between these processes and various outcomes of interest. We describe existing evidence bearing on these hypotheses and suggest promising approaches to testing these claims further. Occasionally we draw on new cross-national data that we have at our disposal (Elkins, Ginsburg and Melton 2007) to sketch some baseline associations. These analyses are not at all meant to be conclusive, but rather to serve as a point of departure for further research.

LITERATURE ON CASES

Constitutional compilations in the modern era have existed since at least 1783 when the French ministry of foreign affairs, at the request of Benjamin Franklin, authorized the publication of an anthology of U.S. state constitutions (Blaustein and Sigler 1988). Early scholarly literature (~1890–1945) on constitutions and constitutional design was largely case-driven and responsive to new constitutional events. Not surprisingly, the end of World War I and the wave of new national constitutions that emerged in the breakup of empires spawned quite a bit of scholarly interest. These efforts were largely descriptive, in some cases going through new constitutional texts section by section (Davidson 1925; Pollock 1923) and in others simply providing a brief introduction to the constitutional text (Albert et al. 1894; Moses 1893). These early analyses are generally not concerned with process, but instead focus on describing institutions such as executive-legislative relations and regionalism (Dedek 1921; Quigley 1924). The issues of human rights (or, in the parlance of

engage scholars, experts, and each other in discussions of both general principles and specific rules relating to the foundation of a democratic, constitutional state.

the time, the rights of man) and democratic theory are also raised in discussions of particular constitutional texts (Bentwich 1924; Clark 1921; Morse 1919).

There are exceptions to this general characteristic of atheoretical, institutional description, of course. Kantorowicz's (1927) examination of the Weimar constitution is motivated by ascertaining the political goals of the designers and how well they met them by comparing the new republican constitution with the old imperial one. He also contrasts the operation of the constitution with its de jure provisions. Chapman (1925) attempts a similar undertaking in endeavoring to explain the disjunction between Cuba's constitution and political reality (a culture of corruption, particularly in the Congress), ultimately concluding that the solution may be beyond the scope of any constitution.

Other works are more centrally focused on issues related to constitutional design processes such as legitimacy and the exercise of constituent power. Arangio-Ruiz (1895), for example, explicitly addresses the evolution of constituent power in Italy from 1848 onward. Even though plans were made for an elected Constituent Assembly to establish a permanent constitution for Italy, they were never realized, and so the constituent function was never clearly assigned. This constitutional silence allowed parliament progressively to assume a constituent function. Perhaps motivated by institutional self-interest, Italian deputies and senators resisted calls for a constituent assembly. Likewise, they resisted the notion of a constituent power residing in the people, who were deemed incapable of exercising it. Arangio-Ruiz approvingly notes the objections of the parliamentarians that, given Italy's recent despotic past and lingering conservatism in the state bureaucracy and police services, locating constituent powers in the people would be a grave mistake.

Another historical work that speaks to contemporary themes is Currier's (1893) analysis of the circumstances surrounding the French constitution of 1875. As in the Italian case, Constituent Assembly elections scheduled for October 1870 were cancelled. The National Assembly elected the following February concluded peace with Germany and asserted implicit authorization to proceed with the drafting and adoption of a new constitution. Although the political and legal circumstances were muddied, the National Assembly was elected by universal suffrage and could justifiably claim to be a constituent body representing the "will of the nation and the sovereignty of the people" (Currier 1893: 132). As Saleilles (1895) notes, however, such an action was out of line with previous French constitutional history. In an argument that anticipates Elster (2006), Saleilles maintains that the constituent, or sovereign, power cannot simultaneously lay in a constituted power such as a parliament.

Whereas single-country case studies have been and will continue to be an invaluable source of knowledge about specific episodes of constitutional design, recent decades have seen the emergence of volumes attempting to situate constitutional design process in a cross-national, comparative framework. Goldwin and Kaufman

(1988) is an invaluable example of this approach, involving a series of papers by contributors, who are, with but one exception, all former constitution writers themselves. The case studies provide insights into different aspects of the process in order to facilitate a better understanding of choices faced and decisions made as they worked to craft a new constitution for their respective countries. In a companion volume, Goldwin, Kaufman, and Schambra (1989) replicate their previous task but with a specific focus on the issue of ethnic, linguistic, racial, and religious diversity. Banting and Simeon (1985) highlight the political, rather than the legal or institutional, conflicts associated with constitutional change in select industrial countries.

More recently, both Reynolds (2002) and Hyden and Venter (2001) have contributed edited volumes that address various aspects of constitutional design. Reynolds combines single-country case studies with thematic ruminations on institutional design to explore the extent to which constitutions can reduce civil conflict and promote democratic governance. As noted later, the conflict resolution literature has provided a good deal of the recent work on constitutional design, taking an instrumental approach.

Hyden and Venter's analysis of constitution making in four African countries is among the most theoretical and explicitly comparative studies in this vein. They construct a common theoretical framework and evaluate constitutional design processes as to the representativeness of the process, the mechanisms used to create the document and aggregate interests, and finally, the extent of popular participation in the process. In a similar manner, Samuels's (2006) twelve-country study commissioned by the International Institute for Democracy and Electoral Assistance (IDEA) evaluated constitutional design processes on the dimensions of inclusiveness, representativeness, and popular participation, in part to determine to what extent a democratic design process can help generate democratic outcomes.

CONSTITUTIONAL DESIGN: MODES, ACTORS, AND CONSTRAINTS

Any particular instance of constitutional design must deal with certain basic questions of organization and process. These include designating *who* is to be involved; *when* that involvement takes place; and *how* the actors are to proceed in terms of formulating, discussing, and approving a text. There are conceivably as many variants on the process as there are constitutions, but several common patterns emerge.

Constitution making occurs in discernible stages, some of which resemble an ordinary legislative process familiar to many drafters in consolidated democracies. Jennifer Widner (2007b) has provided a very useful schematic of design processes that should guide researchers and practitioners. Widner identifies the phases of constitution making as including drafting, consultation, deliberation, adoption, and ratification. Banting and Simeon (1985) begin even earlier, focusing on the stage of mobilization of interests (and counterinterests) prior to the preparation of a text. They call this the "idea-generating stage" at which large parameters are laid out and the process itself may be determined.

These different stages interact with the possible actors who might fill the roles to create a matrix of options for designers. Afghanistan's constitution of 2004, for example, was drafted in relative secrecy by a commission with foreign advice and then sent to the president's office before deliberation and adoption at an inclusive constituent assembly, the Loya Jirga (Huq 2009). In this model – which appears to be relatively common – each stage is potentially consequential, although it is likely that inertial forces and the power of agenda setting will apportion disproportionate influence to those actors involved at earlier stages. Still, it is quite possible that early-stage actors will anticipate the preferences and needs of later-stage actors, thus mitigating any sequence effects. Elster (1995: 373–75) develops the vivid distinction between "upstream" and "downstream" constraints in the process: Upstream constraints are imposed by the powers setting up the constitution-drafting body, whereas downstream constraints result from the anticipation of preferences of those involved in later stages. Ratification by public referendum, for example, is a downstream constraint that can hamstring leaders in an earlier stage, who recognize that their document must ultimately obtain public approval.

As this discussion of constraints implies, a critical variable in constitution making has to do with which actors are included in the process. Institutional scholars are used to thinking of actors as "veto players" (Tsebelis 2002), and the constitutional design realm is no different. As Widner (2007b) describes, actors involved in constitution making can include expert commissions, legislative bodies or committees, the executive, the judiciary, national conferences, elite round tables, transitional legislatures, specially elected constituent assemblies, interest groups and nongovernmental organizations, foreign advisors, and the public itself. Public involvement, discussed later in the chapter, has become the subject of particular attention in recent years, and is urged by scholars, governments, and international organizations (Banks 2008; Commonwealth Human Rights Initiative 1999; Elkins, Ginsburg and Blount, 2008; Samuels 2006). But not all constitutions involve the public, and some are drafted by a handful of leaders behind closed doors.

To sketch some patterns of actor involvement, we have gathered data on the process of adoption for 460 of the 899 national constitutions promulgated in the period between 1789 and 2005. (In a larger project – the Comparative Constitutions Project – we are engaged in the collection of data on the *content* of all 899 constitutions). The information on process reveals a pattern of constrained variation in the choice of actors. The principal actors include constituent assemblies, executives, ordinary legislatures, and the public through ratification referenda. At least one of these actors is formally included in 95 percent of the design processes in the sample.[2] As Table 3.1 reveals, however, there is some variation in how various design processes utilize the actors. Slightly less than one-half of processes utilize a single actor.

This accounting does not reveal anything about the depth or quality of involvement. Executives, for example, were involved in some manner in 51 percent of processes we analyzed. In some cases, however, executive involvement may have been merely formal, such as acting as the last official to sign the constitution, whereas in other cases, it may have been more substantial.[3] For some analyses, it is useful to identify the institution, or actor, with the *most* influential role in the shaping of the document (Elster 2006). We engage in this sort of categorization when we turn to some preliminary analysis questions of "self-dealing" (see discussion later in the chapter).

Certainly, a central dimension on which constitution-making processes differ is the degree of public participation. Because the constitution is the highest level of lawmaking and provides the ultimate rule of recognition for lawmaking processes (Hart 1961; Kelsen 1945), it requires the greatest possible level of legitimation in democratic theory. In an ideal world, one would desire universal consent over the rules of society, a standard that is obviously impractical (Buchanan and Tullock 1962). Our sense is that actual constitutional design processes employ scattered and usually rather anemic forms of popular participation and oversight to substitute for actual consent. Higher levels of participation are presumed to function like supermajority rules, restricting the adoption of undesirable institutions and protecting prospective minorities in the democratic processes that are established. Participation thus legitimates and constrains, substituting process for consent to make effective government possible.

2 The twenty-two cases that do not fit this categorization are generally either former UK colonies whose independence constitutions were negotiated at elite-level constitutional conferences and passed as Parliamentary Acts in London with the Queen's formal consent or represent cases of adoption/ratification by subnational legislatures or federal units such as Bosnia-Herzegovina in 1995 and Germany in 1871. The United States is classified as a constituent-assembly-centered process.

3 We adopted special coding rules vis-à-vis the executive role in constitutional design processes for two subtypes of authoritarian regimes. Adoption by a political party in a civilian dictatorship was judged equivalent to the role of an executive in the design process. Two texts were classified by this rule. By Article 73, the Mozambique constitution of 1975 was "Approved by acclamation by the Central Committee of the Mozambique Liberation Front on 20 June 1975." The second case was the Burma Socialist Programme Party-created Myanmar constitution of 1974 that was eventually approved at referendum. In both cases, the party or party organs are interpreted as executive in nature, leading to classifications of executive and referendum-executive design processes. Military regimes (which make up 92 out of 291 cases for which regime type is available) are an additional special case of executive action. The modal design process choice for such regimes is the referendum-executive model with thirty-six constitutions coming into force in this manner. Overall, forty-seven of the ninety-two constitutions adopted and promulgated by military regimes held ratification referenda. In contrast, there are only ten instances of executive-only design processes. In eleven cases, ratification referenda were held by military regimes with no additional information provided about other actors. On the assumption that the leadership is clearly a gatekeeper of the referenda process in such regimes, these processes were categorized as involving executive action.

TABLE 3.1. *Actors and processes (N = 460)*

	Number	Frequency (%)
Constituent Assembly	53	12
Constituent Legislating Assembly	15	3
Constituent Legislature	89	19
Executive	40	9
Referendum	6	1
Constituent Assembly + Executive	42	9
Constituent Assembly + Legislature	0	0
Constituent Assembly + Referendum	13	3
Constituent Legislating Assembly + Executive	9	2
Constituent Legislating Assembly + Referendum	2	<1
Constituent Legislature + Executive	78	17
Constituent Legislature + Referendum	9	1
Referendum + Executive	57	12
Constituent Assembly + Executive + Legislature	4	<1
Constituent Assembly + Executive + Referendum	3	<1
Constituent Assembly + Legislature + Referendum	1	<1
Constituent Legislature + Executive + Referendum	16	4
Constituent Assembly + Executive + Legislature + Referendum	1	<1
Other	22	5

Note: Coding rules are described in an online appendix at http://www.comparativeconstitutionsproject.org

The modal form of participation in constitutional design is the power to approve the charter, usually by referendum on the final document as a whole. Figures 3.1 and 3.2 present historical data on the processes of promulgating constitutions, and on public promulgation in particular. Figure 3.1 plots the percent of constitutions in force, by year, whose text requires public ratification. The plot suggests a significant trend, accelerating in the early twentieth century, toward public ratification. We emphasize that the denominator here includes only those constitutions that specify the promulgation procedure in the text itself. As Figure 3.2 attests, although a majority of modern constitutional texts provide information on promulgation, most nineteenth-century texts were silent on the topic. We thus treat the findings in Figure 3.1 with some caution, although it seems unlikely to us that the shift in norms regarding the appearance of promulgation procedures in the text biases the results significantly. Indeed, our review of extratextual case information for a smaller sample suggests that the trend implied by the cases plotted in Figure 3.1 is fairly representative of the trend within the full universe of cases. Thus, it seems likely that public ratification has been on the rise since the turn of the twentieth century.

Approval by referendum may be an increasingly popular mode of public involvement, but it is clearly a limited one in that it involves only an up-or-down vote over

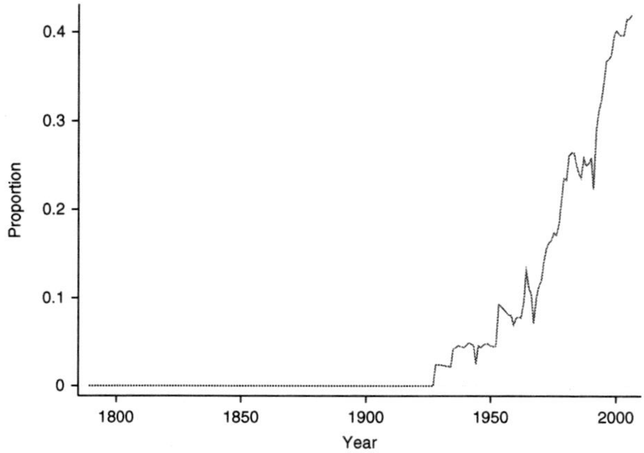

FIGURE 3.1. Proportion of constitutions in force that provide for public ratification
Note: Universe: National constitutions that specify promulgation procedures.

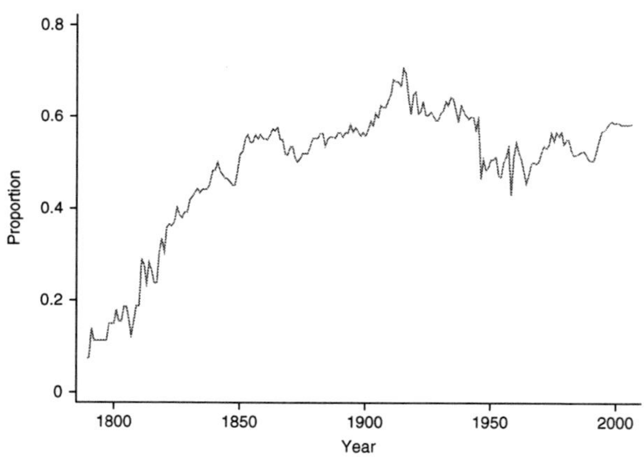

FIGURE 3.2. Proportion of constitutions in force that specify some promulgation procedure.

a package of provisions.[4] Since at least World War II, however, participation in constitutional design has become more direct and has penetrated deeper (or at least earlier) in the process. One common approach is to involve the public in selecting those who will draft or deliberate over aspects of the charter (Widner 2005a: 7–8). This sort of voice is possible whether the representative group is a constituent assembly elected expressly for the purpose or a regular legislature that takes on the project

4 Interestingly, the 1978 Ecuadorian referendum held by the military government provided for a choice of constitutions. A "yes" vote indicated support for the newly drafted text whereas a "no" vote indicated support for the previously abrogated 1945 constitution.

in addition to other duties. Some constitutional processes have experimented with more bottom-up methods of direct democracy, such as the citizen initiative, in which ideas can bubble up from civil society. We cannot say much yet about the effect of such methods, although anecdotal accounts, such as the report that citizens submitted 64,000 proposals to the Brazilian 1987–1988 assembly (Benomar 2004), suggest the magnitude of the challenges involved in absorbing public suggestions.

Still another mode of participation involves direct consultation with the public or representative groups at various stages, which might occur before, during, or after the drafting of the initial text (Ghai 2004; Ghai and Galli 2006; Samuels 2006; Selassie 2003; Widner 2007a;). The drafting phase would seem to be especially crucial, because we can expect a fair degree of inertia in the later stages of the process. But the phase is also likely to be the least participatory, given the challenges of writing-by-committee, much less "writing-by-nation." Indeed, in some well-known cases, the public is excluded from the drafting process and not consulted at all.

Of course, actors and their accompanying constraints may come from outside, as well as inside, a state's borders. An extreme case is that of the "Occupation Constitution" (Elkins, Ginsburg, and Melton 2008; see also Feldman 2005), a document drafted when a country is under the control of a foreign military power. Such constitutions are usually presumed to have less involvement on the part of local actors, and hence to be less legitimate. Burnell (2008) believes that international involvement creates disincentives to enforce the constitution locally, as actors will strategically acquiesce to conditions they have no intention of fulfilling simply to remove external oversight. He cites Zimbabwe and the Lancaster House Agreement of 1979 as a prime example of this kind of behavior.

The voluminous literature on policy diffusion reminds us that policy reform is a highly interdependent process. Constitution making – often undertaken during moments of crisis when states are at their most amenable to foreign models and "suggestions" – may be especially interdependent and "networked" (Elkins 2009). Certainly, scholars have long noted a high degree of similarity across documents, and nearly anyone privy to the details of a case of constitution making can recount an episode of international borrowing. John Meyer and other sociologists working within the "world society" perspective point to constitutional isomorphism as case in point in their compelling globalization narratives (Go 2003; Meyer et al. 1987). The persistence of presidentialism in Latin America, the use of French and Westminster models of government in former colonies, and the recent use of national conferences in Francophone Africa (Clark 1994) are all examples of diffusion, which occur on a subglobal level.

Given the persistent centrality of the U.S. constitution to the American legal academy, there has been a fair amount of interest in documenting the influence of the U.S. constitution over the years (e.g., Billias 1990), but other constitutional models have also had some impact (Elkins 2003). In public law, much of this research has found its way into a series of compilations of work on "constitutional borrowing," which cover a decidedly heterogeneous set of transnational issues involving both constitutional design and interpretation (see, e.g., Choudhry 2006; special issues on the subject in the *International Journal of Constitutional Law* (2003: 177–324) and *Texas Law Review* (2004: 1653–737).

Of course, international constraints on constitution making can range in their intensity and degree of "coordination," ranging from borrowing to imposition. External influence need not be as blatant as in Occupation Constitutions. Constitutional drafting that occurs concurrently with peace negotiations often attracts international advisers and interests, be they donors, creditors, interested states, or the United Nations. Samuels and Wyeth (2006) briefly discuss the sometimes unintended but nonetheless negative consequences of such "benign" intervention. Also, some models exhibit pull-through proximity: The prospect of future membership in the European Union, for example, led some Eastern European countries to make modifications to their draft constitutions at the behest of the Council of Europe (Elster 1997: 129). Many accounts of foreign borrowing point to the decisive role of influential consultants (e.g., Davis 2003), and several scholars have sought to profile these consultants and describe their behavior (Perry 1992; Reynolds n.d.).

There are other potentially consequential aspects of process apart from the identity of the actors involved. Some constraints reflect the circumstances that lead to constitution making in the first place. The conventional wisdom is that constitution making is coincidental with a cataclysmic event of some kind, such as war, coup, economic crisis, or revolution (Elster 1995; Russell 1993). In fact, the evidence suggests that, although crises do frequently precede constitutional reform, the degree of non-crisis constitution making is probably underestimated (Elkins, Ginsburg, and Melton 2008).[5] Sweden's 1972 reform of its 163-year-old constitution is a prominent example of crisis-free reform (Congleton 2003). The various socialist constitutions, such as those in the Soviet Union (1936, 1977) and China (1982), seem to follow the installation of new leaders, a practice that was often justified by the Marxist view of evolution in stages (see Go 2003). These different patterns, reflecting various degrees of crisis or continuity, will affect the process, creating either an atmosphere of urgency or of deliberation.

The process can also vary in terms of time involved. At one extreme, the secretive process that led to Myanmar's 2008 constitution took seventeen years.[6] At the other

[5] Approximately half of new constitutions in our sample are promulgated within three years of a military conflict, economic or domestic crisis, regime change, territorial change, or coup (Elkins, Ginsburg, and Melton 2009).

[6] One of the ironies of the Burmese constitution is that the military government insisted that the referendum on the document continue as scheduled during one of worst natural disasters in the country's history; this after years of delay in the drafting!

extreme, a small group of American bureaucrats working for the occupation authorities drafted the basic form of Japan's 1946 constitution in a little more than a week, and the entire process, including elections, legislative deliberation, and approval by the emperor, took a mere eight months (Moore and Robinson 2004). Which of these cases is closer to the mean? Japan, it seems, by a long shot. We randomly sampled 150 of the 806 cases of constitution making (new and replacement constitutions) since 1789, and were able to identify the start and end dates for the processes in 148 of those cases.[7] On average, constitution making took 1.32 years in those 148 cases, with a standard deviation of 1.84. The median process length of the surveyed cases was 0.83 years.

Anecdotally, those constitution-making processes involving either a very short or very long amount of time seem to occur in non-democracies. Speedy processes do not allow sufficient time for mobilization of the public and civil society, whereas extended processes are unlikely to hold public attention for the duration. The record for shortest process, formally at least, may belong to the Romanian constitution of 1938, which instituted a brief period of royal dictatorship. A new cabinet taking power on February 12 of that year announced its intention to appoint a commission to draft a new constitution. A new text was published February 21, a referendum conducted using oral voting under a state of siege was held on February 24, with promulgation by the king occurring three days later. This was an expeditious process, to say the least.

Another dimension on which processes differ is the size of the deliberative body. Bannon (2007) argues that the Kenyan constitutional design process was too bloated, with more than 600 delegates and two bodies producing drafts. Textual coherence and internal consistency appear to have been casualties of the process. Even Yash Ghai, the former chairperson of the Review Commission, noted that Uganda and South Africa managed the process with 300 delegates. To mitigate this problem in the future, Bannon recommends a smaller deliberative body with a greater focus on public consultation at the expense of extensive representation of all interests.

Recent studies have also begun to examine the institutional structure of constituent bodies. Generalizing models from the area of legislative studies, Proksch (2007) and Tsebelis and Proksch (2007) find evidence in the European Union constitutional convention of both agenda-setting power on the part of convention's Praesidium and

[7] Starting dates were identified in one of six ways, in decreasing order of priority: official announcement of intention to draft a new constitution, including statements as to the identity of the drafting or adopting body; date of elections to the drafting and/or adopting body, if relevant; date of first meeting of the drafting and/or adopting body; date of formation of drafting subcommittees in either constituent assemblies or legislatures; for Commonwealth countries, the opening day of the first constitutional conference prior to independence; date of successful coup d'etat. Ending dates reflect the day of promulgation or, if unavailable, the date of final approval.

subcommittees. One implication of this is that representative, inclusive constituent bodies may not be a sufficient condition for representative, inclusive texts if the possibility exists for biased committees. In effect, the level of analysis most commonly applied to design processes may be misleading. Continued systematic examination of the inner workings of constituent bodies and application of social science analytic methods to their proceedings hold the promise of leading to a better understanding of how particular provisions make their way into a text, and how participation is channeled.

In sum, processes of constitutional design and adoption vary widely along many dimensions. There is much speculation, but relatively little evidence, about the impact of these processes on different outcomes. The remainder of this essay considers the range of hypotheses regarding this impact and reviews the available evidence.

CONNECTING PROCESS AND OUTCOME: MICRO-FOUNDATIONAL ASSUMPTIONS

Assumptions about the motives of those participating in the process, be they elites or citizens, turn out to be central to hypotheses about the relation between process and constitutional outcomes. Nearly all the normative and positive work on constitutions proceeds from the assumption that constitutional politics are fundamentally different in character from ordinary politics. This is a central assumption of constitutional political economy (Buchanan and Tullock 1962), but also of much other thinking about constitutions and constitutionalism (Ackerman 1993). The basic idea is that legal or political entrenchment distinguishes choice *about* rules from choice *within* rules. Because constitutional designers operate without certain knowledge of their prospective position in postconstitutional governance, they are presumed to pay greater attention to the public rather than the private interest. Furthermore, it is argued, constitutions are typically adopted during moments of crisis, and so likely to produce more attention to the general welfare and less likely to be dominated by special interests.

Assumptions about motive also inform normative work on constitutional design processes. If one believes designers will act in their own self-interest, one might want to ensure maximum participation in the process to counter this tendency. On the other hand, if one believes that designers can take the public interest into account, one might design a process with more limited public involvement so as to facilitate elite deliberation.

Elster (1995) postulates three types of motivations that necessarily are balanced in the constitutional design process: reason, passions, and interests. Reason represents disinterested principles; passions refers to emotional factors such as religious or ethnic animosities or sudden, impulsive desires; and interests may refer to those motives identified with the welfare of drafters, or broader groups or institutions of which they are a part. Elster believes that balance is necessary: A constitution that is too crudely identified with self-interest may fail to be adopted, as might one that is perfect in theory but fails to meet key needs of certain players (see also Ghai 2006). Elster (1997:130) concludes that direct self-interest of the framers is of less importance than the interests of their constituents, but also (Elster 1996) finds that institutional interests dominated in Eastern European constitution making.

In a recent article, Brown (2008) modifies some of Elster's claims. Noting that even in the best of worlds, there is a certain amount of unpredictability in the process, Brown (2008) argues for the notion of "passionate rationality." In his conception, actors seek to pursue ends efficiently but do not always recognize what these ends are, much less how to pursue them. As a result, miscalculation and unintended consequences may loom large in constitutional design (Smith and Remington 2001). Elster (2006) provides several examples of miscalculation and its consequences: the decision by Louis XVI to allow parish priests rather than bishops to represent the clergy in the Estates General; the adoption of proportional voting by the Weimar Assembly in 1919, despite the fact that it was against the interests of the Socialist government to do so; and Vaclav Havel's insistence on proportional voting that allowed communists into the Constituent Assembly where they became "constitution wreckers rather than … constitution makers" (Elster 2006: 189). Scheppele (2008) echoes this point in cautioning that the crucial variables for constitutional success are beyond the ability of designers to control, and so "constitutional luck" plays an important role in the ultimate success or failure of constitutional arrangements.

Assumptions regarding the motives of actors undergird expectations about how process affects outcomes. In large part, these assumptions lead scholars to focus on the negotiators and drafters, with the idea that the identity of the constitution's authors will go far to explain its content. Constitutions, of course, may not simply be the sum of the interests of those involved; it is likely, for example, that decision rules and other conditions will also prove consequential. Nonetheless, strong theory and predictions regarding the "who" of the constitutional process is a good place to start.

HYPOTHESES AND EVIDENCE LINKING PROCESSES TO OUTCOMES

In this section, we identify a set of hypotheses regarding process and outcome and summarize the available evidence. Our focus, in particular, is on expectations regarding the interests and influence of institutional loyalists, international actors, and the public – all of whom are thought to play an increasingly consequential role in constitutional design.

Institutional Self-Dealing

It is common to think of constitutions as the product of various competing interest groups organized along economic goals, ethnic claims, or political ideology.[8] It also seems plausible that drafters who occupy or seek to occupy government positions may act in the interest of their respective institutions. Once we consider this possibility, the institutional identity of actors in the design process becomes paramount. One theme in the literature is suspicion of legislators as constitution makers. As we described earlier, the legislative model of constitutional design involves electing a legislature to accomplish both ordinary and constitutional rule making, so that choices about constitutional design are bundled with the concerns of ordinary law. One problem with this bundling concerns interest aggregation: the voter's constitutional preferences may be traded off against other concerns in choosing a representative. It may be that the qualities that make a legislator attractive to a voter (e.g., attention to local interests) are not what that voter would look for in a founding father or mother. More centrally, however, there is a reasonable suspicion that legislators will aggrandize their own institution in designing a governance structure. As summarized by Elster (1998:117): "To reduce the scope for institutional interest, constitutions ought to be written by specially convened assemblies and not by bodies that also serve as ordinary legislatures. Nor should legislators be given a central place in ratification."

The skepticism regarding institutional self-interest is certainly not limited to sitting legislatures. The critiques of legislative-centered processes would presumably be even more scathing for constitutions drafted in executive-centered processes, given the distrust of heavy-handed executive rule in democratic governance. Indeed, it is hard to imagine that a constitution such as that recently produced in Myanmar, ruled by a military junta that handpicked the drafters and the deliberative body, would undercut executive power. In another example, the Armed Forces Ruling Council in Nigeria, which reserved for itself a decisive editing role at the end of the constitutional process, rejected as tautological a provision drafted by the Constituent Assembly that would have made coup participants punishable by law (Ehindero 1991). A general expectation of institutional self-dealing means that we ought to expect that executive-centered processes will lead to stronger executives in the resulting constitution.

The evidence of institutional self-dealing is largely anecdotal (Elster 1996; Chesterman 2005: 952; Ghai 2005; Ghai and Galli 2006; Samuels 2006). Drawing on

[8] Following Beard's (1913) classic argument, for example, McGuire and Ohsfeldt (1986, 1989a, 1989b) use statistical analysis to evaluate the voting behavior of the delegates to the U.S. constitutional convention and subsequent state ratification processes, and find some support for public choice hypotheses of economic self-interest among participants.

our own cross-national data on the content of constitutions, we provide here some preliminary findings on these questions intended only to provoke further inquiry, and certainly not to settle the questions. Recall our sample of 460 constitutions for which we had gathered information on the identity of actors involved in each of the processes. We can categorize these processes, following Elster (2006) as either executive-centered, constituent assembly, constituent legislating assemblies, constituent legislatures, or a residual category for other cases. The labels can be confusing, but the intuitions are straightforward. The principal contrast is between "constituent assemblies," which are elected especially to design a constitution and then disband, and "constituent legislatures," which are legislatures that take on the added task of constitution making. The "constituent legislating assembly" refers to an intermediate category of cases in which assemblies elected specially for constitutional design transform themselves into a sitting legislature. Executive-centered processes include those adopted solely by an executive or by an executive and approved through referendum. We were able to categorize 411 of our 460 cases without difficulty according to these four categories, leaving 49 in the "other" category. Given that representatives in the "constituent legislating assembly" category likely aspire to a career in the legislature, we combine this category with that of the "constituent legislature" into a category of processes that we call "legislature centered."

We next drew on our own data from the Comparative Constitutions Project to create an index of legislative power, based on a parallel set of items from Fish and Kroenig's (2009) Parliamentary Powers Index. Fish and Kroenig aggregate thirty-two dimensions of legislative power, equally weighted, into an index representing the level of legislative power in a constitutional system. Their measure, which relies on expert coding, is a de facto measure of legislative power, whereas our parallel measure is a de jure measure based on the formal provisions of the text. We employ a set of variables from the CCP that map onto Fish and Kroenig's items, and score cases a 1 for each provision present in the constitution. We then calculate the mean of these twenty-one binary variables, resulting in an index that ranges between 0 and 1, with 1 representing the maximum amount of legislative power. If the hypothesis of institutional self-interest has merit, we would expect that legislative-centered processes would feature stronger legislatures than would constituent-assembly-centered process, whereas executive-centered processes would feature weaker legislatures than either. Table 3.2 provides the mean value of our de jure measure of parliamentary power as provided in the constitutions produced by processes in each of the three process categories. Table 3.3 provides additional detail.

Interestingly, we find no bivariate support for the hypothesis that legislatures produce constitutions with more parliamentary power than do constituent assemblies: The mean value for the parliamentary power index for cases of constituent assembly is actually *higher* than that of those centered in the legislature, although

TABLE 3.2. *Constitutional design processes and average de jure parliamentary power*

	Number	Mean level of de jure parliamentary power
Constituent Assembly-Centered	103	.38
Constituent Legislating Assembly-Centered	26	.41
Constituent Legislature-Centered	178	.37
Executive-Centered	84	.30
Other	20	.20

TABLE 3.3. *Proportion of constitutional texts containing de jure parliamentary power provisions, by design process*

De jure parliamentary power provisions	Constituent assembly-centered (N=103)	Legislature-centered[1] (N=204)	Pr(T=t)
Parliamentary Power Index	.38	.37	0.31
The legislature alone, without the involvement of any other agencies, can impeach the president or replace the prime minister.	.55	.54	0.88
Ministers may serve simultaneously as members of the legislature.	.25	.33	0.17
The legislature has powers of summons over executive branch officials, and hearings with executive branch officials testifying before the legislature or its committees are regularly held.	.79	.65	0.02
The legislature can conduct independent investigations of the chief executive and the agencies of the executive.	.32	.30	0.70
The legislature has effective powers of oversight over the agencies of coercion (the military, organs of law enforcement, intelligence services, and the secret police).	.08	.10	0.56
The legislature appoints the prime minister.	.27	.26	0.89
The legislature's approval is required to confirm the appointment of individual ministers; or the legislature itself appoints ministers.	.04	.06	0.37
The country lacks a presidency entirely; or there is a presidency, but the president is elected by the legislature.	.29	.43	0.02

De jure parliamentary power provisions	Constituent assembly-centered (N=103)	Legislature-centered[1] (N=204)	Pr(T=t)
The legislature is immune from dissolution by the executive.	.59	.41	0.00
Any executive initiative on legislation requires ratification or approval by the legislature before it takes effect; that is, the executive lacks decree power.	.20	.29	0.09
Laws passed by the legislature are veto-proof or essentially veto-proof; that is, the executive lacks veto power, or has veto power but the veto can be overridden by a simple majority in the legislature.	.31	.43	0.05
The legislature's laws are supreme and not subject to judicial review.	.38	.32	0.30
The legislature has the right to initiate bills in all policy jurisdictions; the executive lacks gatekeeping authority.	.68	.71	0.57
Members of the legislature are immune from arrest and/or criminal prosecution.	.07	.09	0.54
All members of the legislature are elected; the executive lacks the power to appoint any members of the legislature.	.88	.82	0.17
The legislature alone, without the involvement of any other agencies, can change the constitution.	.39	.37	0.79
The legislature's approval is necessary for the declaration of war.	.70	.61	0.12
The legislature's approval is necessary to ratify treaties with foreign countries.	.86	.76	0.03
The legislature reviews and has the right to reject appointments to the judiciary; or the legislature itself appoints members of the judiciary.	.08	.03	0.10
The chairman of the central bank is appointed by the legislature.	0	.03	0.06
Legislators are eligible for reelection without any restriction.	.23	.11	0.01

[1]Legislature-centered category includes constituent legislatures and constituent legislating assemblies.

differences of means tests do not meet standard levels of significance. Executive-centered processes, on the other hand, yield significantly less power for legislatures than do processes in the other two categories.[9] Elster's conjecture about institutional self-interest, it seems, is evident only relative to executive-centered processes.

This finding that constituent assemblies are more likely to empower the legislature than are the legislatures themselves is striking. Of course, the finding could still reflect institutional self-dealing in that members of a constituent assembly foresee themselves inhabiting the legislature at some point in the future, even if that career path is not guaranteed. The finding could also reflect the possibility that members of a constituent body – sitting and reflecting as a representative body – are philosophically and politically inclined toward representative government, as opposed to a more hierarchical form that they would identify with executive power. Finally, the bivariate association could be the product of any number of confounds or statistical artifacts. One obvious confound is time. Our sample includes cases dating to the early nineteenth century. To the extent that constitutional processes and legislative power both covary with time, we may be capturing a simultaneous, but unrelated, pair of trends. However, if we de-trend the data (by running a simple regression with year as a covariate), the results remain: Constituent assembly products are indistinguishable from legislative-centered texts with respect to legislative power, but both texts provide significantly more legislative power than do texts written in executive-centered processes.[10]

Still, this analysis is plagued by another methodological concern that affects nearly all empirical work on process and outcome: endogeneity. In this case, a state's predisposition toward strong legislatures might influence both their formal constitutional text *and* the process they use to produce the text. This sort of endogeneity, however, should produce a bias toward a positive association between legislative power in the text and legislature-centered processes. Given the direction of this bias, and our finding of no difference between constituent assembly and legislature processes, we have rather strong exculpatory evidence that legislatures are not guilty of self-dealing. Nonetheless, our results here represent simply an initial baseline finding: Deeper exploration of this relationship is certainly warranted.

International Actors

The role of international actors in constitution making is varied and so too are the empirical expectations. One basic expectation is that outside actors will export

[9] A t-test indicates that the difference in means is significant at the .0001 level.

[10] We regressed the legislative power index on year and dummy variables for legislature-centered processes and constituent assembly processes, with executive processes as the residual category.

constitutional provisions from their home country. This presumption seems most likely in situations in which the sovereignty of the host country is compromised, such as the case of occupation. The assumption is that constitutions drafted under the watchful eye of an occupying power will involve the more or less forcible transfer of institutions from the occupier to the occupied. Even if not motivated by self-interest on the part of the occupying power, one might expect a certain amount of institutional propagation to take place, if only through the occupier's institutional habits or even deferential mimicry on the part of the occupied. Through a number of complementary mechanisms, therefore, we should expect that such constitutions bear some similarity to the occupying powers. It may be, however, that the coercive relationship between occupier and occupied plays out in more subtle ways with respect to constitutional design. Failing outright adoption of the occupier's institutions, we may suspect at the very least that the occupier's presence would disrupt the host country's normal search process for relevant constitutional models (Elkins, Ginsburg, and Melton 2008). Of course, military occupations represent an extreme case, and international actors may be influential even in less coercive situations. States are enmeshed in any number of international networks that render the experiences and constitutions of certain countries more relevant than others.

It also seems possible that occupation and other sorts of international processes will have strong effects on the fit and functionality of constitutional provisions. Elkins (2003, 2009) has sought to uncover these sorts of social welfare effects with respect to constitutional diffusion. At the extremes, we see two plausible, but divergent, effects. External participation may lead drafters to adopt suboptimal or inappropriate provisions designed for the needs of others. Alternatively, outsiders may lead drafters to adopt provisions superior to those that drafters have the resources or knowledge to engineer for themselves. It seems likely that these effects will vary according to the kind and extent of external participation and the conditions under which it occurs.

The evidence for these sorts of international hypotheses is growing steadily as a result of a noticeable increase in scholarly interest in transnational mechanisms of institutional reform. With respect to the hypotheses regarding military occupation – specifically those with respect to endurance and imposition – we can report findings from Elkins, Ginsburg, and Melton (2008), who survey forty-two instances of constitutions adopted under occupation or shortly thereafter and develop an index of similarity to compare constitutional dyads. They find that on average, occupation constitutions are moderately more similar to those of the principal occupying nation. With regard to two prominent constitutions drafted under American occupations, for example, they find some similarity between the U.S. constitution and that of Japan in 1946, but find very little with respect to the Iraqi constitution of 2005. Although they find that occupation constitutions are less enduring than other constitutions, this result does not hold in a multivariate specification (Elkins, Ginsburg, and Melton 2009).

Public Participation and Oversight

Elster (1997: 125) generalizes that constitutions produced in more democratic processes will tend to be more democratic. Given the recent trend toward participation in constitutional design, it is worth inquiring how constitutions produced through participatory processes may be systematically different from other constitutions. A small literature nested in the larger trove of work on political participation more generally has generated a host of hypotheses.

First, participatory constitutional design processes may undermine textual coherence (Voigt 2003). As Horowitz (2002) notes, even under the best of circumstances, constitutional "design" – a term he reserves for a cohesive process – is quite rare, with some process of incremental construction more the norm. Constitution making frequently consists of a combination of institutional borrowing, wholesale grafting, logrolling, and improvisation. As new, and more, actors become involved in the process, bargaining and negotiation becomes both more extensive as well as intensive. In addition, the populace may be subject to cascades that exacerbate the element of "passion" in constitutional design (Elster 1995). The constitution that emerges from this process will almost certainly be an ad-hoc creation, rife with internal inconsistencies and institutional mismatches. The loss of design consistency may be offset by resultant gains in legitimacy (Horowitz 2002), but it may also render the constitutional scheme unworkable. Additionally, simply increasing the number of actors is no guarantee of a more equitable outcome. The composition of a deliberative body is as important to the ultimate outcome as the number of members; extreme outcomes can emerge from a collective decision-making process (Sunstein 2001).

A related point is that participation may also lead to more specific and detailed constitutional documents (Elkins, Ginsburg, and Melton 2008; Voigt 2007). Analogizing to the contracts literature, more diverse parties are likely to want to specify their bargain in greater detail because of distrust of counterparties and concerns about strategic nondisclosure of preferences during the bargaining process. Thailand's 1997 document, for example, was designed to limit political institutions by setting up a large number of watchdogs, all elaborated in excruciating detail in the constitution. Similarly, if the public perceives opportunities for participation to be episodic, there may also be a tendency to seek to constitutionalize various institutions that would ordinarily be left to nonconstitutional politics. An example here is Brazil, whose 1988 process was a model of public participation involving citizen proposals on content. The resulting document is one of the world's longest, at more than 40,000 words.

We know of no empirical study that has systematically analyzed constitutions for coherence or related concepts. That constitutions contain a complex array of institutions certainly poses a challenge to research design. Undoubtedly, one can find examples of poor drafting, internal contradictions, or errors, but no one has been able to tie these directly to participation. Cross-national approaches might focus on issues of constitutional length and scope, either of which might be construed as indicators of specificity or even incoherence. Even then, it seems likely that these sorts of questions will ultimately be best suited to case-oriented research.

A different line of critique emphasizes the difficulty of reaching agreement. More actors will, *ceteris paribus*, increase the transaction costs of negotiation, particularly when participants have veto powers over the adoption of new rules (Tsebelis 2002). A more open process can also make bargaining and the granting of concessions more difficult (Arato 1995; Elster 1995; Sunstein 2001). This is in part because the drafters will feel the need to signal positions to their constituents outside the process, potentially leading to more extreme positions. The drafters may also be interested in using the bargaining process to grandstand, decreasing the possibility of agreement. Open processes of negotiation will tend to hinder tough choices and compromise. This suggests that participatory processes are less likely to produce a constitution, although arguably the documents that do emerge will be more legitimate.

The claim that participatory design processes generate constitutions with higher levels of legitimacy and popular support has been subject to only limited study. We can find case studies that seem to support both the more optimistic and more pessimistic hypotheses. South Africa is rightly celebrated as a case in which participation was extensive, and the resulting document scores well on measures of rights, endurance, and enforcement. On the other hand, Eritrea, Ethiopia, and Thailand utilized broadly participatory processes that had little to no effect on the subsequent political system (Ghai and Galli 2006; Selassie 2003). Thailand's 1997 process included a provision disallowing constitutional drafters from running for post-constitutional office for a period – a suggestion approved by the theoretical literature (Voigt 2003: 217) – but this did not prevent electoral corruption from reviving. In fact, Thailand's participatory process appears not to have built a reservoir of support for the constitution, which died in a coup in 2006 without much ado (Kuhonta 2008). On the other hand, the constitutional orders in Germany, Japan, and Eastern Europe appear healthy despite the fact that these documents were either imposed by foreign powers or were the result of elite-level round table negotiations (Elster, Offe, and Preuss 1998; Ghai and Galli 2006; Moore and Robinson 2004).

In perhaps the most extensive study of the question to date, Moehler (2006) provides evidence from the highly participatory Ugandan process, and found that citizens who were active in the process were no more likely to support the constitution than other citizens.[11] She found that individual-level support for the constitution was influenced more by their support for the National Resistance Movement (NRM) regime and elite opinion than even the respondent's own participation in the design process. This is a nuanced result, suggesting legitimacy is conditional on factors other than process, particularly the mediating factor of elite opinion as well as other aspects of the context (see also Bannon 2007). Moehler (2007) also found that participation in constitution making had downstream effects on the process, fostering attachment to democratic principles and closer monitoring of government action downstream.

As Moehler's studies exemplify, much of the recent emphasis on constitutional design process has emanated from the conflict resolution literature (Hart 2001, 2003; Samuels 2005; Widner 2005a, 2005b, 2007a, 2008). These authors link the successful resolution of (primarily) internal conflict to episodes of constitutional design. The most comprehensive student of the question, Widner, finds a correlation between the representativeness of the main deliberative body and the level of violence five years after ratification. With popularly elected representatives, violence decreased in approximately 42 percent of cases and remained roughly the same in 35 percent of cases. Among executive-appointed bodies, the respective figures were 24 percent and 36 percent.

One of the strongest theoretical claims about popular participation concerns its implications for constitutionalism – that is, a constitution's ability to constrain government. If citizens are to effectively police the actions of government, it must be sufficiently clear what constitutes a violation of the limits of governmental power so that citizens can mobilize to prevent it. Constitutions help resolve this coordination problem by generating common knowledge about the scope of acceptable government behavior and by providing a focal point for citizens to organize enforcement efforts (Carey 2000; Przeworski 1991; Weingast 1997). To the extent that popular participation in a constitutional design process serves to construct focal points, it will facilitate the coordination needed to deter potential constitutional violations by government. In the most optimistic scenario, the presence of a focal point in the written text, when coupled with the more robust civil society that emerged as part of a participatory design process, will ensure that the constitution will be enforced and not serve as a mere parchment barrier (Carey 2000).

It follows logically that constitutional endurance, an important criterion of constitutional success (Voigt 2003), will be closely related to enforcement. Public involvement should enhance endurance by making enforcement more likely. Elkins, Ginsburg, and Melton (2009), in a book-length study of constitutional endurance at the national level, find that public involvement in constitutional adoption, as captured in the existence of a referendum or popularly elected constitutional assembly,

[11] Comparatively speaking, however, the Ugandan constitution enjoys higher levels of support than the constitutions of seven other sub-Saharan countries (Moehler 2006).

was positively correlated with constitutional lifespan, at least for democracies. For example, South Africa's celebrated 1996 document has already lasted longer than the historical mean for constitutions on the African continent. Even though the world's oldest constitution (that of the United States) was not adopted by referendum, there was a relatively high level of involvement in its approval if not its drafting. The Japanese case, it should be noted, is anomalous in this regard (Elkins, Ginsburg, and Melton 2008; Moore and Robinson 2004).

We might also speculate on further implications of participation for constitutional design. One influential view of constitutions conceives of them as a social contract among the citizenry, designed to limit demands by the state. In this view, one would expect that more participatory processes work like supermajority rules. As the veto power of minorities increases, one might expect the adoption of more minoritarian institutions, such as judicial review (Ginsburg 2003), bicameralism, and, assuming that relevant cleavages are geographically concentrated, federalism. Supermajoritarian processes might produce supermajoritarian rules and institutional configurations, to the extent that a rule-making body will produce others in its likeness. One can also expect that the use of referenda to approve the constitution may be mimicked with direct democracy institutions in the constitution itself.

Voigt (2003) develops a set of hypotheses relating inclusive participation to substantive outcomes. He suggests that inclusive processes will lead drafters to create more independent bodies, delegating powers away from the legislature. This is a corollary, of sorts, to the prediction that the legislative model will concentrate powers in the legislature (Chesterman 2005: 952; Elster 1995). Voigt also believes that participatory documents will be more stable, in that there will be fewer demands for renegotiation down the road, and more legitimate.

We might also expect that as the power of the citizenry in design processes increases, the number and extent of constitutional rights will increase as well. The American case, in which the Bill of Rights was inserted only after public discussion and debate, makes the point quite dramatically (Arato 1995: 225). The Anti-Federalists wanted to include a bill of rights in the original bargain, and were able to gain agreement on this during the ratification process as a condition of approval (Rakove 1997). Participation, then, begat a more extensive set of limitations on federal power. In more recent examples, we might expect that participation would be associated with "positive" socioeconomic rights, as the constitution becomes an instrument of redistribution.

These hypotheses regarding content would seem most amenable to analysis. What evidence there is seems to support the prevailing wisdom. IDEA's survey of twelve constitutional design processes suggests that more participatory processes result in more progressive rights provisions and a higher quality of democracy (Samuels 2006). Their general finding is that "more representative and inclusive constitution building processes resulted in constitutions favoring free and fair elections, greater political equality, more social justice provisions, human rights protections and stronger accountability mechanisms" (Samuels 2006: 668). This finding deserves further testing on a broad set of cases. Ghai (2001) has also shown that rights provisions emerging from deliberation and negotiation have more of an indigenous character and are more fervently defended and respected. Rights provisions imposed by outsiders such as former colonial masters or handed down by elites are frequently not understood or appreciated. Thus, leaders have little compunction about derogating from them.

We are able to offer some cross-national data relevant to this question, again as an effort to start the conversation rather than end it. We divide all constitution-making processes into two categories, based on whether or not they utilize a public referendum to approve the document. If Samuels's finding is to be generalized, it would suggest that those processes involving a public referendum would be more likely to have various rights provisions than those processes without a referendum. This is because ratification by referendum forms a downstream constraint shaping the drafting process. The IDEA results also suggest that constitutions in which the public had an approval role would be more likely to involve the public in various decisions thereafter. For example, we might expect that constitutions approved by referendum would be more likely to use direct democracy devices such as the referendum in ordinary governance. We might also expect that the scope of elections would be broader.

We have gathered some descriptive data on these issues as part of the Comparative Constitutions Project. The descriptive data in Tables 3.4 and 3.5 provide partial support to the conjecture about public participation. Processes involving a referendum produce constitutions that are more likely to have virtually every category of right. The anomalous exception is health care: Whereas referendum constitutions are more likely to provide for a right to health care, they are less likely to state that health care is to be provided free of charge. However, given the referendum trend shown in Figure 3.1 and the likelihood that the extent of rights provisions also covary with time, de-trending the data is necessary. A simple-count model of the number of rights provisions in a text with the year of adoption and use of a referendum as the sole covariates yields a statistically significant, negative coefficient for the effect of referenda on rights. The most likely explanation for this startling finding is the frequent pairing of referenda with executive-centered design processes. An additional test using year, executive-only, executive-referendum and non-executive-referenda processes as covariates reveals a positive effect ($p = .057$) on rights for referenda when not paired with executives that approaches standard levels of statistical significance. Our sense from these preliminary analyses is that referenda may indeed serve as a downstream constraint, particularly for nonauthoritarian drafting processes.

TABLE 3.4. *Proportion of constitutions containing direct democracy provisions, by use of referendum*

Constitutional provision	Referendum (N=100)	No referendum (N=326)	Pr(T=t)
Popularly elected head of state (hos)	.64	.36[1]	0.00
Popularly elected head of government (hog)	.03[2]	.01[3]	0.20
Popularly elected deputy executive	.18[4]	.31[5]	0.08
Popularly elected lower (or only) legislative chamber	.96	.78	0.00
Popularly elected subnational legislature	.61[6]	.42[7]	0.05
Popularly elected municipal officials	.54[8]	.51[9]	0.62
Dismissal of head of state	.71	.66[1]	0.39
Public proposal of hos dismissal	.01	.02	0.46
Public approval of hos dismissal	.04	.01	0.07
Dismissal of head of government	.92[2]	.89[3]	0.60
Public proposal of hog dismissal	0	0	.0
Public approval of hog dismissal	.01	0	0.07
Dismissal of legislator(s)	.49	.58[1]	0.11
Public role in dismissal of legislator(s)	.06	.06	0.86
Dismissal of judges	.49	.70	0.00
Public role in dismissal of judge(s)	.01	.04	0.17
Universal suffrage	.75	.40	0.00
Voting by secret ballot	.84	.56	0.00
Right to form political parties			
Sovereignty of people	.74	.41	0.00
Reference to democracy	.32[10]	.32[11]	0.98
Referendum	.91	.34	0.00
Initiative	.15	.12	0.43
Public challenge to constitutionality of legislation	.17	.13	0.34
Public initiation of legislation	.09	.06	0.38
Public proposal of amendments	.13	.08	0.13
Public approval of amendments	.66	.13	0.00
Public last body to ratify/approve amendments	.54	.09	0.00

[1]N=324; [2]N=71; [3]N=149; [4]N=44; [5]N=175; [6]N=36; [7]N=113; [8]N=59; [9]N=233; [10]N=93; [11]N=299.

Referendum constitutions also appear more likely to provide for universal suffrage, a secret ballot, a referendum process in ordinary governance, and a public role in approving constitutional amendments. We do not, however, find statistically significant differences between public referendum processes and non-referendum processes in electing or recalling various public officials, although in most cases the direction of the difference is consistent with the predictions.

Still, it seems prudent to reserve judgment about any causal inferences with respect to these results. As with the legislative-constituent assembly analysis, because

TABLE 3.5. *Proportion of constitutions containing selected rights provisions, by use of referendum*

Constitutional provision	Referendum (N=100)	No referendum (N=326)	Pr(T=t)
Rule of law	.35	.21	0.00
Equality, equal rights, and/or nondiscrimination	1	.87	0.00
No rights restrictions on certain groups	.94	.84	0.01
Freedom of religion	.91	.80	0.01
Separation of church and state	.27	.16	0.02
Socioeconomic rights mentioned	.30	.12	0.00
Equal payment for work	.47	.30	0.00
Right to join trade union	.76	.48	0.00
Right to strike	.59	.24	0.00
Right to rest and leisure	.35	.29	0.27
Right to adequate standard of living	.19	.18	0.84
Right to transfer property freely	.12	.15	0.49
Right to transfer property freely after death	.08	.07	0.83
Inheritance rights	.26	.20	0.17
Intellectual property mentioned	.21	.38	0.00
Right to conduct/establish business	.34	.28	0.24
Consumer rights/consumer protection mentioned	.10	.08	0.59
Financial support of particular groups	.64	.42	0.00
Right to own property	.89	.66	0.00
Occupational freedom	.38	.44	0.28
Safe and/healthy working conditions	.27	.22	0.28
Limits on child employment	.16	.19	0.46
Shelter and/or housing	.23	.16	0.12
Right to marry	.38	.26	0.03
Right to found a family	.30	.18	0.01
Matrimonial equality	.22	.22	0.99
Rights of children guaranteed	.53	.30	0.00
Right to health care	.46	.29	0.00
Free health care	.26[1]	.48[2]	0.01
Life	.56	.52	0.50
Prohibition on slavery	.33	.43	0.09
Prohibition on torture	.61	.46	0.01
Cruel, inhuman or degrading treatment	.61	.46	0.01
Privacy	.72	.62	0.08
Movement	.79	.70	0.09
Opinion, thought and/or conscience	.89	.72	0.00
Expression or speech	.91	.85	0.11
Petition	.41	.62	0.00
Prohibition on censorship	.26	.38	0.03
Press	.63	.49	0.02

Constitutional provision	Referendum (N=100)	No referendum (N=326)	Pr(T=t)
Assembly	.89	.79	0.03
Association	.91	.78	0.00
Conscientious objection to military service	.10	.10	0.88
Bear arms	.01	.03	0.21
Jury trials	.14	.20	0.16
Citizen involvement in indictment process	0	.02	0.17
Regulation of collection of evidence	.51	.57	0.31
Habeas corpus	.71	.57	0.01
Pretrial release	.15	.24	0.06
Nulla poena sine lege	.68	.58	0.07
Right of appeal	.32	.23	0.06
Explicit mention of due process	.14	.06	0.00
Right to examine evidence or confront witnesses	.11	.18	0.08
Ex post facto	.84	.64	0.00
Fair trial	.33	.22	0.02
Speedy trial	.21	.19	0.71
Public trial	.54	.50	0.45
Presumption of innocence	.69	.36	0.00
Trial language	.17	.23	0.20
Double jeopardy	.25	.31	0.23
Right to silence and/or protection from self-incrimination	.25	.43	0.00
Right to counsel	.55	.45	0.08
Right to counsel, state expense	.38[3]	.24[4]	0.06
Compulsory education	.63[5]	.58[6]	0.42
Free education	.62	.57	0.38
Academic freedom	.26	.28	0.67
Access to higher education	.25	.14	0.00

[1]N=46; [2]N=93; [3]N=56; [4]N=148; [5]N=92; [6]N=271.

processes are themselves selected at some upstream point in constitution making, it is likely that the association between public involvement on the one hand and rights and democracy on the other reflects the common impact of an unobserved variable. For example, a set of elites might conclude a private agreement to democratize in which constitution making is part of the process. The elites might then seek to ensure that the process of adoption is more open and democratic, in which case both the process and result reflect a level of antecedent agreement. This problem of endogeneity is endemic in efforts to tie process to outcomes, and hence there is an important role for the careful work of case study literature to try to untangle the causal relationships.

The complement to public participation is public oversight, or the visibility of the design process. There is reason to think that transparency will have decisive effects on the manifestations of self-interest. Constitution making typically, albeit not always, involves discrete moments that occur with great public fanfare. This greater visibility may reduce rent seeking and self-interest, as interest groups seek to exploit the relative anonymity of ordinary politics (Mueller 2000). Appeals to public reason, rather than private interest, are presumed to be prevalent during constitutional drafting. On the other hand, publicity may lead to grandstanding, as political leaders seek to mobilize their own supporters (Brown 2008). Along these lines, Stasavage (2007) provides a game-theoretic justification for limiting transparency, arguing that rather than generate consensus, open deliberation has the potential to lead to mass polarization.

Analyzing the French and American experiences, Elster (2000) finds that secrecy and transparency matter, and that publicity explains some of the failures of the French constitutional assemblies around 1789. Secrecy, in his view, is amenable to hard bargaining, whereas publicity facilitates arguing. As a solution to this tension between transparency and secrecy, Elster (2006) employs an hourglass metaphor to describe the optimal role of the public in the process with participation via public hearings at the upstream stage and some form of ratification possible at the downstream stage. The actual writing and deliberation (the neck of the hourglass) should be shielded from the public eye to avoid the pitfalls described earlier. Banting and Simeon (1985) cite the Spanish constitution of 1978 as mostly achieving this ideal with the small private working groups that hammered out the final draft being bookended by public scrutiny. The precise need for each form of negotiation may depend on particular contextual circumstances.

The visibility of constitutional design also might affect the ability of certain kinds of interests to organize, particularly those groups focused on the general interest. Public-interest groups that face collective action problems in ordinary politics may be more likely to organize for the relatively infrequent iterations of constitutional politics (Boudreaux and Pritchard 1993; but see Sutter 1995: 129). If the profile of the participating interest groups veers toward the public good in this way, constitutional politics might indeed achieve the normative ambition of greater focus on the common good. On the other hand, there is the offsetting consideration of stakes. Private interest groups may invest more energy in playing for rules at the constitutional level precisely because of the presumptively higher stakes in the selection of rules, thus discounting the increased participation of public interest groups.

CONCLUSION

This chapter has explored the theoretical and empirical relationships between the process of constitutional design and constitutional outcomes. On the theoretical side, we found a broad consensus in the literature about the importance of public involvement as well as an apparent trend in practice. Yet many of the assumptions of proponents of participation remain untested, and the precise relationships between participation and desirable outcomes of interest remain underspecified.

In general, scholars have been far better at generating hypotheses relating process to outcomes than testing them. Individual case studies have provided some insights, but large-n work has been hindered by a lack of data and a need for conceptual refinement. Our own analysis utilizing data from Widner and the CCP suggests an association between processes that involve the public in the adoption of the constitution and the presence of rights and certain democratic institutions in the resulting document. This is consistent with the case study literature, although we are cautious about drawing conclusions about causality. On the other hand, we find little support for the claims about institutional self-interest on the part of legislatures that control constitutional design.

Constitutional design processes are loaded with expectations about endurance, efficacy, the resolution of conflicts, and political reconstruction (Arjomand 2007). In the real world, however, most constitutions fail (Scheppele 2008). A key normative question is whether aspects of process can be manipulated to reduce the probability of failures, but this question requires much more positive work on the complex relationships among process, content, and outcomes.

LITERATURE CITED

Ackerman, Bruce. 1993. *We the People*. Cambridge, MA: Harvard University Press.

Albert, C., Lindsay, SM., and Rowe, LS. 1894. Supplement: Constitution of the Kingdom of Italy. *Annals of the American Academy of Political and Social Science* 5:1–44.

Arangio-Ruiz, Gaetano. 1895. The Amendments to the Italian Constitution. *Annals of the American Academy of Political and Social Science* 6:31–57.

Arato, Andrew. 1995. Forms of Constitution Making and Theories of Democracy. *Cardozo Law Review* 17:191–231.

Arjomand, Said, ed. 2007. Constitutionalism and Political Reconstruction. Leiden: E.J. Brill.

Banks, Angela. 2008. Expanding Participation in Constitution Making: Challenges and Opportunities. *William and Mary Law Review* 49(4):1043–69.

Bannon, AL. 2007. Designing a Constitution-Drafting Process: Lessons from Kenya. *Yale Law Journal* 116(8):1824–72.

Banting, KG., and Simeon, R. eds. 1985. *Redesigning the State: The Politics of Constitutional Change*. Toronto: University of Toronto Press.

Barber, Benjamin. 1984. *Strong Democracy: Participatory Politics for a New Age*. Berkeley: University of California Press.

Beard, Charles 1913. *An Economic Interpretation of the Constitution*. New York: Macmillan.

Benomar, Jenna. 2004. Constitution-Making after Conflict: Lessons for Iraq. *Journal of Democracy* 15(2):81–109.

Bentwich, N. 1924. The Constitution of Egypt. *Journal of Comparative Legislation and International Law* 6(1):41–49.
Biggs, F. 2001. Public Participation in Constitution Making. In *Constitution-Making and Democratization in Africa*, ed. G. Hyden and D. Venter. Pretoria: Africa Institute of South Africa.
Billias, George Athan, ed. 1990. *American Constitutionalism Abroad*. New York: Greenwood.
Blaustein, Albert P., and Sigler, JA., eds. 1988. *Constitutions That Made History*. New York: Paragon House Publishers.
Boudreaux, D, and Pritchard, AC. 1993. Rewriting the Constitution: An Economic Analysis of the Constitutional Amendment Process. *Fordham Law Review* 62(1):111–62.
Brandt, Michelle n.d. UN Assistance to Constitution-Making Processes: The Cases of East Timor, Cambodia and Afghanistan. UNDP/BCPR.
Brown, Nathan. 2008. Reason, Interest, Rationality, and Passion in Constitution Drafting. *PS: Political Science and Politics* 6(4):675–89.
Buchanan, James, and Tullock, Gordon. 1962. *The Calculus of Consent*. Ann Arbor: University of Michigan Press.
Burnell, P. 2008. The Relationship of Accountable Governance and Constitutional Implementation, with Reference to Africa. *Journal of Politics and Law* 1(3):10–24.
Carey, John M. 2000. Parchment, Equilibria, and Institutions. *Comparative Political Studies* 33:735–61.
2007. *Does It Matter How a Constitution Is Created?* Presented at Exporting democracy: What democracies can and cannot do, April 21, University of Texas, Austin, TX.
Chapman, CE. 1925. The Cuban Constitution and Congress. *California Law Review* 14(1):22–35.
Chesterman, Simon. 2004. *You the People: The United Nations, Transitional Administration and State Building*. New York: Cambridge University Press.
2005. Imposed Constitutions, Imposed Constitutionalism, and Ownership. *Connecticut Law Review* 37: 947–54.
Choudhry, Sujit. 2006. *The Migration of Constitutional Ideas*. New York: Cambridge University Press.
Clark, JF. 1994. The National Conference as an Instrument of Democratization in Francophone Africa. *Journal of Third World Studies* 11:304–35.
Clark, RT. 1921. The Constitution of Estonia. *Journal of Comparative Legislation and International Law* 3 (4):245–50.
Commonwealth Human Rights Initiative. 1999. *Promoting a Culture of Constitutionalism and Democracy in Africa*. Recommendations to the Commonwealth Heads of Government. Available at http://www.humanrightsinitiative.org/publications/const/constitutionalism_booklet_1999.pdf
Congleton, Roger. 2003. *Improving Democracy through Constitutional Reform: Some Swedish Lessons*. Boston: Kluwer Academic Press
Converse, PE. 1961. The Nature of Belief Systems in the Mass Publics. In *Ideology and Discontent*, ed. David Apter. New York: Free Press.
Currier, CFA. 1893. Supplement: Constitutional and Organic Laws of France. *Annals of the American Academy of Political and Social Science* 3:1–77.
Dahl, Robert. 2001. *How Democratic Is the American Constitution?* New Haven, CT: Yale University Press.
Davidson, NG. 1925. The Constitution of Iraq. *Journal of Comparative Legislation and International Law* 7(1):41–52.

Davis, Dennis M. 2003. Constitutional Borrowing: The South Africa Experience. *International Journal of Constitutional Law* 1(2):181–95.
Dedek, V. 1921. The Constitution of Czecho-Slovakia. *Journal of Comparative Legislation and International Law* 3(1):115–22.
Diamond, Larry. 2006. *Squandered Victory*. New York: Times Books.
Ehindero, SG. 1991. *The Constitutional Development of Nigeria 1849–1989*. Nigeria: Ehindero (Nigeria) Ltd.
Elkins, Zachary. 2003. *Designed by Diffusion: International Networks and the Spread of Democracy*. PhD Dissertation, University of California, Berkeley.
2009. Constitutional networks. In *Networked Politics: Agency, Power, and Governance*, ed. M. Kahler. Ithaca, NY: Cornell University Press.
Elkins, Zachary, Tom, Ginsburg, and James Melton. 2007. The Comparative Constitutions Project. Available at http://netfiles.uiuc.edu/zelkins/constitutions
Elkins, Zachary, Tom, Ginsburg, and Justin Blount. 2008. Citizen as Founder: Participation in Constitutional Design. *Temple Law Review* 81(2):361–82.
Elkins, Zachary, Tom, Ginsburg, and James Melton. 2009. *The Endurance of National Constitutions*. New York: Cambridge University Press.
2008. Baghdad, Tokyo, Kabul...? Constitution-Making in Occupied States. *William and Mary Law Review* 49:1139–78.
Elster, Jon. 1995. Forces and Mechanisms in the Constitution-Making Process. *Duke Law Journal* 45:364–96.
1996. The Role of Institutional Interest in East European Constitution-Making – Explaining Legislative Dominance. *East European Constitutional Review* 5(6):63–65.
1997. Ways of Constitution-Making. In *Democracy's Victory and Crisis*, ed. A. Hadenius 123–42. Cambridge: Cambridge University Press.
2000. Arguing and Bargaining in Two Constituent Assemblies. *University of Pennsylvania Journal of Constitutional Law* 2:345–421.
2006. Legislatures as Constituent Assemblies. In *The Least Examined Branch: The Role of Legislatures in the Constitutional State*, ed. R. W. Bauman and T. Kahana. Cambridge: Cambridge University Press.
Elster, Jon, Claus, Offe, and Ulrich Preuss. 1998. *Institutional Design in Post-Communist Societies: Rebuilding the Ship at Sea*. Cambridge and New York: Cambridge University Press.
Feldman, Noah. 2005. Imposed Constitutionalism. *Connecticut Law Review* 37:857–90.
Fish, M. Steven, and Kroenig, M. 2009. *The Handbook of National Legislatures: A Global Survey*. New York: Cambridge University Press.
Frey, Bruno. 1979. Economic Policy by Constitutional Contract. *Kyklos* 32(1–2):307–19.
Ghai, Yash. 2001. *Human Rights and Social Development: Toward Democratization and Social Justice*. New York: United Nations Research Institute for Social Development.
2004. The Constitution Reform Process: Comparative Perspectives. Presented at Toward Inclusive and Participatory Constitution Making, August 3–5 at Kathmandu.
2005. A Journey around Constitutions: Reflecting on Contemporary Constitutions. *South Africa Law Journal* 122:804–31.
Ghai, Yash, and Galli G. 2006. Constitution Building Processes and Democratization. In *Democracy, Conflict, and Human Security: Further Readings*. Stockholm: IDEA.
Ghai, Yash, Lattimer, M, and Said, Y. 2003. *Building Democracy in Iraq*. London: Minority Rights Group International.
Ginsburg, Tom. 2002. Ways of Criticizing Public Choice: Empiricism and the Use of Theory in Legal Scholarship. *University of Illinois Law Review* 2002:1139–66.

2003. *Judicial Review in New Democracies: Constitutional Courts in Asian Cases*. NewYork: Cambridge University Press.
Go, Julian. 2003. A Globalizing Constitutionalism. *International Sociology* 18:71–95.
Golay, JF. 1958. *The Founding of the Federal Republic of Germany*. Chicago: University of Chicago Press.
Goldwin, RA, and Kaufman, A., eds. 1988. *Constitution Makers on Constitution Making: The Experience of Eight Nations*. Washington, DC: American Enterprise Institute for Public Policy Research.
Goldwin, RA, Kaufman, A, and Schambra, WA., eds. 1989. *Forging Unity Out of Diversity: The Approaches of Eight Nations*. Washington, DC: AEI Press.
Habermas, Jurgen. 1996. *Between Facts and Norms*. Cambridge, MA: MIT Press.
Hart, HLA. 1961. *The Concept of Law*. Oxford: Oxford University Press.
Hart, Vivien. 2001. Constitution-Making and the Transformation of Conflict. *Peace & Change* 26(2):153–76.
2003. *Democratic Constitution Making* (107). Washington, DC: United States Institute of Peace.
Haysom, Nicholas. 2004. Lessons from the South African Transition. Paper read at Toward Inclusive and Participatory Constitution Making, August 3–5, 2004 at Kathmandu, Nepal.
Henkin, Louis, and Rosenthal, Albert J. 1990. *Constitutionalism and Rights: The Influence of the United States Constitution Abroad*. New York: Columbia University Press.
Horowitz, Donald L. 2002. Constitutional Design: Proposals versus Processes. In *The Architecture of Democracy*, ed. A. Reynolds. Oxford: Oxford University Press.
2008. Conciliatory Institutions and Constitutional Processes in Post-Conflict States. *William and Mary Law Review* 49(4):1213–48.
Howard, AED. 1993. *Constitution-Making in Eastern Europe*. Baltimore: Johns Hopkins University Press.
Huntington, Samuel. 1968. *Political Order in Changing Societies*. New Haven, CT: Yale University Press.
Huq, Aziz. 2009. The Story of Hamid Karzai: The Paradoxes of State-Building and Human Rights. In *Human Rights Advocacy Stories*, ed. D. Hurwitz, M. Satterthwaite, and D. Ford. Eagan, MN: West Publishing.
Hyden, G, and Venter, D., eds. 2001. *Constitution-Making and Democratisation in Africa*. Pretoria: Africa Institute of South Africa.
Kantorowicz, H. 1927. The New German Constitution in Theory and Practice. *Economica* 19:37–62.
Kelsen, Hans. 1945 (1961). *General Theory of Law and State*, tr. A. Wedberg. New York: Russell and Russell.
Keogh, D, and McCarthy, AJ. 2007. *The Making of the Irish Constitution*. Mercier Press.
Kuhonta, EM. 2008. The Paradox of Thailand's 1997 "People's Constitution": Be Careful What You Wish For. *Asian Survey* 48(3):373–392
Lemont, ED., ed. 2006. *American Indian Constitutional Reform and the Rebuilding of Native Nations*. Austin: University of Texas Press.
Levinson, Sanford. 2006. *Our Undemocratic Constitution*. New York: Oxford University Press.
Lipset, Seyomour Martin. 1959. Some Social Requisites of Democracy: Economic Development and Political Legitimacy. *American Political Science Review* 53(1):69–105.
1963. *Political Man: The Social Bases of Politics*. Garden City, NY: Doubleday.
Lupia, Arthur, and McCubbins Mathew. 1998. *The Democratic Dilemma: Can Citizens Learn What They Need to Know?* New York: Cambridge University Press.

Mansbridge, Jane. *Does Participation Make Better Citizens?* February 11–12, 1995. Available from http://www.cpn.org/crm/contemporary/participation.html (accessed November 7, 2007).
McGuire, R, and Ohsfeldt R. 1986. An Economic Model of Voting Behavior: The Ratification of the United States Constitution. *Journal of Economic History* 46(1):79–111.
McGuire, R, and Ohsfeldt R. 1989a. Self-Interest, Agency Theory, and Political Voting Behavior: The Ratification of the United States Constitution. *American Economic Review* 79(1):219–34.
McGuire, R, and Ohsfeldt R. 1989b. Public Choice Analysis and the Ratification of the Constitution, in *The Federalist Papers and the New Institutionalism*, ed. B. Grofman and D. Wittman. New York: Agathon, 175–204.
Meyer, JW, Boli, J, Thomas, G, and Ramirez, FO. 1987. *Institutional Structure: Constituting State, Society and the Individual*. Newbury Park, CA: Sage.
Moehler, Devra. 2006. Public Participation and Support for the Constitution in Uganda. *Journal of Modern African Studies* 44(2):275–308.
2007. *Distrusting Democrats: Outcomes of Participatory Constitution-Making*. Ann Arbor: University of Michigan Press.
Moore, RA, and Robinson DL. 2004. *Partners for Democracy: Crafting the New Japanese State under MacArthur*. New York: Oxford University Press
Morse, HB. 1919. The New Constitution of China. *Journal of Comparative Legislation and International Law* 1(3):183–95.
Moses, Bernard. 1893. Supplement: Constitution of the Republic of Colombia. *Annals of the American Academy of Political and Social Science* 3:1–70.
Mueller, Denis. 2000. *Constitutional Democracy*. New York: Oxford University Press
Murphy, Walter F. 2007. *Constitutional Democracy: Creating and Maintaining a Just Political Order*, in *The Johns Hopkins Series in Constitutional Thought*, ed. S. Levinson and JK. Tulis. Baltimore: The Johns Hopkins University Press.
Pateman, C. 1970. *Participation and Democratic Theory*. Cambridge: Cambridge University Press.
Perry, Barbara. 1992. Constitutional Johnny Appleseeds: American Consultants and the Drafting of Foreign Constitutions. *Albany Law Review* 55:767–92.
Pollock, JK., **Jr.** 1923. The Constitution of Latvia. *The American Political Science Review* 17(3):446–48.
Proksch, SO. 2007. Ideology and the Politics of Constitution Making: The Institutional Organization of the European Convention. Paper read at 10th Biennial Conference of the European Union Studies Association, May 17–19, Montreal, Canada.
Przeworski, Adam. 1991. *Democracy and the Market*. New York: Cambridge University Press.
Quigley, HS. 1924. The Constitution of China. *The American Political Science Review* 18(2):346–50.
Rakove Jack. 1997. *Original Meanings: Politics and Ideas in the Making of the Constitution*. New York: Vintage.
Rawls, John. 1971. *A Theory of Justice*. Cambridge: Harvard University Press.
Reeves, JS. 1933. The New Spanish Constitution and International Obligations. *Michigan Law Review* 31(3):386–89.
Reynolds, Andrew, ed. 2002. *The Architecture of Democracy*. New York: Oxford University Press.
2005. First Do No Harm: Seeing Constitutional Design through the Eyes of Medicine. *Journal of Democracy* 16(1):54–68.
n.d. Academics as Democratic Designers: The Moonlighting of Political Scientists as Constitutional Engineers around the Globe. Unpublished manuscript.

Rubin, Barney R. 2004. Crafting a Constitution for Afghanistan. *Journal of Democracy* 15(3):5–19.
Russell, Peter. 1993. *Constitutional Odyssey: Can Canadians Become a Sovereign People?* Toronto: University of Toronto Press.
Saleilles, R. 1895. The Development of the Present Constitution of France. *Annals of the American Academy of Political and Social Science* 6:1–78.
Samuels, Kirsti. 2005. Post-Conflict Peace-Building and Constitution-Making. *Chicago Journal of International Law* 6(2):663–82.
2006. *Constitution Building Processes and Democratization: A Discussion of Twelve Case Studies*. Stockholm: IDEA.
Samuels, Kirsti, and Wyeth, VH. 2006. *State-Building and Constitutional Design after Conflict*. New York: International Peace Academy.
Sartori, Giovanni. 1997. *Comparative Constitutional Engineering*. New York: New York University Press.
Scheppele, Kim Lane. 2008. A Constitution between Past and Future. *William and Mary Law Review* 49(4):1377–1407.
Schwartzberg, Melissa. 2007. *Democracy and Legal Change*. New York: Cambridge University Press
Selassie, Berekat Habte. 2003. *The Making of the Eritrean Constitution: The Dialectic of Process and Substance*. Trenton, NJ: Red Sea Press.
Smith, S. and Remington, T. 2001. *The Politics of Institutional Choice: The Formation of the Russian State Duma*. Princeton, NJ: Princeton University Press.
Starr, JR. 1936. The New Constitution of the Soviet Union. *The American Political Science Review* 30(6):1143–52.
Stasavage, David. 2007. Polarization and Publicity: Rethinking the Benefits of Deliberative Democracy. *Journal of Politics* 69(1):59–72.
Sunstein, Cass. 2001. *Designing Democracy*. Oxford: Oxford University Press.
Sutter, D. 1995. Constitutional Politics within the Interest-Group Model. *Constitutional Political Economy* 6(2):127–37.
2003. Durable Constitutional Rules and Rent Seeking. *Public Finance Review* 31(4):413–28.
Tsebelis, George. 2002. *Veto Players: How Political Institutions Work*. Princeton, NJ: Princeton University Press.
Tsebelis, George, and Proksch, SO. 2007. The Art of Political Manipulation in the European Convention. *Journal of Common Market Studies* 45(1):157–86.
Tullock, Gordon. 2000. Some Further Thoughts on Voting. *Public Choice* 104:181–82.
Voigt, Stefan. 2003.The Consequences of Popular Participation in Constitutional Choice – Toward a Comparative Analysis. In *Deliberation and Decision*, eds. Anne van Aaken et al. Aldershot: Ashgate Publishing.
2007. Constitutional Garrulity. Unpublished manuscript.
Weingast, Barry R. 1997. The Political Foundations of Democracy and the Rule of Law. *American Political Science Review* 91(2):245–63.
Widner, Jennifer. 2005a. *Constitution Writing and Conflict Resolution*. Helsinki: United Nations University – World Institute for Development Economics Research.
2005b. Constitution Writing & Conflict Resolution: Data & Summaries. First posted August 2005 and accessed at http://www.princeton.edu/~pcwcr/index.html on December 17, 2008.

2007a. The Effects of Constitution Writing Procedures on Choice of Terms & Patterns of Violence: Some Data, Some Observations, and Many Reasons for Modesty. Paper read at Stanford Workshop in Comparative Politics, January 22, Palo Alto, CA.

2007b. Proceedings, Workshop on Constitution Building Processes. Princeton University, May 17–20, Bobst Center for Peace and Justice, Princeton University in conjunction with Interpeace and International IDEA.

2008. Constitution Writing in Post-Conflict Settings: An Overview. *William and Mary Law Review* 49(4):1513–41.

PART II

How Do We Get to Constitutional Design? Constraints and Conditions

4

Democratization and Countermajoritarian Institutions

Power and Constitutional Design in Self-Enforcing Democracy

Susan Alberts, Chris Warshaw, and Barry R. Weingast

"So that one cannot abuse power, power must check power."
Montesquieu, *Spirit of the Laws* (1989[1748])

INTRODUCTION

Most democratic constitutions fail to endure. The estimated half-life of a democratic constitution adopted between 1789 and 2005 is just sixteen years (Elkins, Ginsburg, and Melton 2008: 135). The purpose of this chapter is to explore some of the conditions that support constitutional and democratic survival. For democracy to survive, it must be self-enforcing in the sense that all parties with the power to disrupt democracy – such as an incumbent who may refuse to honor an electoral defeat or another group that might use force to take power – choose not to do so, instead honoring the rules (Mittal and Weingast, 2010).

Building on this perspective, we provide a new model of a self-enforcing constitution to address a series of questions: Why do some authoritarian regimes democratize whereas others remain stable? Why do some countries sustain stable democracy whereas others fail?[1] How does constitutional design contribute to the emergence of self-enforcing democracy? With respect to the last question, we observe that many successful cases of democratization involved specific types of countermajoritarian features that constrain the power of elected majorities; for example, malapportionment may benefit the old, authoritarian elite, an upper chamber may represent geographic units, or other forms of veto power over majorities. These questions identify core problems of democratization.

[1] Since the beginning of the "third wave" of democracy in 1974, the record of democratic success is mixed. On the one hand, most of the sixty-three countries that experienced a democratic transition during this period have, so far, remained democracies (Diamond 2008: 54–55). Others, however, have either returned to new forms of authoritarian rule (Russia) or limped along with unconsolidated and crisis-prone democratic regimes (Ecuador, Bolivia).

Our approach to answering these questions joins two literatures. The first involves models of democratization based on citizens' threats to elites' economic interests, such as Acemoglu and Robinson (2006) and Boix (2003). These works argue that authoritarians choose democracy when forced to by opposition groups, specifically when the authoritarians find that the costs of sharing power are lower than attempting to sustain their regime in the face of potentially violent opposition. The second literature is a small group of scholars who model issues in self-enforcing democracy, such as Alberts (2008), Inman and Rubinfeld (2008), Mittal and Weingast (2010), and Weingast (1997). Combining these two literatures, we show that successful democratic transitions are a product of the balance of power between opposing groups and constitutional design choices that lower the costs of upholding the democratic bargain.

We begin with an authoritarian in power and an opposition seeking democratization. When the latter is insufficiently strong – that is, incapable of imposing sufficiently large costs on the authoritarian regime – the authoritarian regime is stable. Democratization arises when the opposition can threaten the authoritarian with sufficient costs that it prefers democratization over attempting to retain authoritarian power (Acemoglu and Robinson 2006; Boix 2003).

This insight is important for understanding democratization. Nonetheless, it provides an incomplete understanding of democratization. Although revolt, disorder, disruptions, and violence by the opposition impose costs on the authoritarian regime, so too does democracy. Democratization typically imposes large costs on the authoritarian regime and their constituents; for example, democracy may result in reprisals or expropriation, or it may open the door to previously suppressed sources of conflict (ideological, ethnic, religious, economic, and so forth). We argue that the struggle to democratize is, therefore, not simply about redistribution from the elite protected by the authoritarian regime to the masses who support democratization. Rather, it often entails a broader range of conflict. Moreover, a critical element missing from the Acemoglu and Robinson's and Boix's frameworks is the extent to which constitutional design can facilitate the peaceful resolution of conflicts and promote a transition to self-enforcing democracy.[2] Also missing from this literature is the attention to what sustains democracy over time given that political leaders have the power to subvert it.

Democratization processes frequently involve constitutional negotiations that reduce the stakes of democracy by protecting the interests of the incumbents (Mittal and Weingast 2010). When democratizing, authoritarian regimes often seek constitutional arrangements that contain countermajoritarian features designed to

[2] Acemoglu and Robinson (2006: 207–11) have a short section on this issue, but it is not the central concern of their book.

constrain majorities ex post. These features lower the costs of democratization for the authoritarian regime and its supporters and provide incentives to refrain from reversing democracy. Many successful cases of democratizations are characterized by institutional features crafted to constrain majorities, including the early United States under the new Constitution; Great Britain in the early reforms; Germany's initial steps toward democracy in 1871; and many twentieth-century cases of democratization, including Spain, Chile, South Africa, and Uruguay. To succeed, constitutional provisions must be self-enforcing in the sense that the players have incentives to abide by them.

One of the main lessons of our approach, indicated in the Montesquieu headnote, is that successful democratization and subsequent constitutional stability require incentives for both pro-authoritarian and prodemocratic groups to adhere to the constitutional bargain once the new constitution is in place. The initial transition to democracy may occur when the threat of social unrest is such that the costs of repression outweigh the costs of adopting democratic institutions. Sustaining democracy thereafter involves the reciprocal ability to impose costs on the other group for deviating from the constitutional bargain.

This chapter proceeds as follows. The second section discusses a range of democratizations with countermajoritarian features. The third section presents our model of self-enforcing democratization. The fourth section studies the implications of the model for the questions raised earlier. In the fifth section, we provide an in-depth examination of Chile. The sixth section raises some potential extensions. Our conclusions follow.

COUNTERMAJORITARIAN CONSTITUTIONS AND SUCCESSFUL DEMOCRATIZATION

The democratization literature is replete with examples of "third wave" political transitions or historical cases of democratic development whose success is attributed to a high degree of accommodation among elite actors (Lijphart 1977; O'Donnell and Schmitter 1986; Linz 1990; Valenzuela 1990; Huntington 1991; Higley and Gunther 1992). Such accommodation is linked to the creation of institutional frameworks capable of processing conflict peacefully, thereby promoting stable democracy. An important characteristic behind many of these success stories is the presence of countermajoritarian constitutional features aimed at protecting the fundamental interests of groups key to democratization, particularly those with the ability to overthrow democracy.

Countermajoritarian constitutional provisions come in many varieties, but all share the common characteristic of protecting the rights and interests of minorities from infringement by a majority. Many of the standard rights entrenched in

FORM

SCOPE	*Structural*	*Procedural*
Diffuse	-constitutional court with judicial review	-super-majority to pass certain types of laws -protections for basic rights -limits on government power
Targeted	-advisory council with veto power -appointed legislative body -legislative body with territorial representation -federalism	-power sharing - electoral malaportionment -restrictions on legal prosecution of former officials -protected status for certain groups

FIGURE 4.1. Countermajoritarian provisions typology.

democratic constitutions are meant to guard against the abuse of power by majorities, and thus can be considered countermajoritarian elements. Other countermajoritarian provisions, however, are more narrowly conceived and often respond to unique, contextual circumstances. Given the variety of countermajoritarian provisions and their role in a number of successful transitions to democracy, it is useful to distinguish among them.

Countermajoritarian provisions can be classified along two dimensions: the form they take (whether they create structures or procedures) and their scope (whether they protect diffuse interests or the interests of a targeted group within the population) (see Figure 4.1).

A constitutional court with judicial review illustrates a countermajoritarian structure providing diffuse protection. The court's power to reverse majority decisions infringing constitutional rights, for example, is a potent means of protecting a wide range of minority interests.

Examples of countermajoritarian structures that provide targeted protections include legislative bodies with territorial representation; advisory councils with veto power over elected officials' decisions; appointed legislative members or bodies; and federalism. Territorial representation in the legislature protects the interests of citizens in sparsely populated areas by giving their vote equal weight with densely populated areas. Appointed councils and legislative bodies dilute the power of elected officials and limit their impact on policy making. Federal systems can devolve critical policies to regional (and more homogeneous) levels of government, protecting against overly onerous redistribution or expropriation and privileging local concerns.

Countermajoritarian procedures providing diffuse protections include guarantees of basic civil and political rights; limits on government power; and the requirement of a supermajority to pass certain types of laws (including, but not limited to, constitutional amendments). Targeted countermajoritarian procedures, on the other hand, include electoral rules that overrepresent certain groups; power sharing; special protections for certain groups or organizations; and restrictions on the legal prosecution of former regime officials for human rights abuses or other violations (as in Uruguay, Chile, South Africa, and former communist regimes in Eastern Europe.)

Countermajoritarian provisions vary in their long-term effect on democracy once the immediate transition period ends. In this regard, these provisions can be conceptualized as ranging along a continuum from moderate, "democracy-enhancing" to extreme, "democracy-eroding" effects. At the democracy-enhancing end of the continuum are constitutional provisions necessary for baseline democratic functioning, such as guarantees of fundamental civil and political rights. Moderate examples of institutional engineering can also be situated toward this end of the continuum (such as electoral rules that moderately overrepresent rural as opposed to urban voters, or a bicameral legislature in which one house gives equal representation to geographical units of the state whereas in the other house, representation is based on population).

At the opposite end are more extreme democracy-eroding features that severely limit popular sovereignty and potentially undermine democratic legitimacy. The presence of extreme countermajoritarian provisions may place a regime in the territory of "democracy with adjectives," signifying a type of diminished democracy (Collier and Levitsky 1997).[3] Extreme countermajoritarian provisions include those that exclude certain groups from suffrage rights or fielding candidates for office, award some seats in the legislature by appointment rather than free elections, or prohibit elected officials from policy making in specified areas, such as military affairs.

Numerous cases demonstrate the various ways in which countermajoritarian constitutional features contributed to democratic survival. After a cycle of civil wars, Uruguay's 1919 Constitution established power sharing between the country's two major parties by means of a nine-person collegial executive. This and other power-sharing arrangements (through electoral rules and administrative posts) contributed

3 "Democracy with adjectives" refers to the various labels for diminished types of a democratic regime, such as "tutelary" or "protected" democracy, where the elected government lacks full power to govern; "limited" democracy, in which some segments of the population are denied suffrage; or "illiberal" democracy, where civil liberties are curtailed.

to Uruguay's record as one of the most long-lived and successful democracies in Latin America. Colombia, although long troubled by violence, is another enduring Latin American democracy whose longevity is due in part to the adoption of countermajoritarian constitutional provisions. The "National Front" power-sharing pact lasted from 1958 to 1974. This agreement (incorporated into the Constitution by means of a 1957 plebiscite) stipulated that the country's two major parties would alternate in the presidency; it also divided all elected and administrative positions evenly between them. In the Chilean transition, the 1980 Constitution (discussed in the fourth section) included countermajoritarian elements such as electoral rules designed to overrepresent supporters of the Pinochet regime, appointed senators, and reserved policy domains. These provisions limited the elected government's authority and protected the interests of pro-authoritarian groups by restricting policy making on the part of elected officials. In the antebellum United States, federalism combined with the balance rule (equal representation of free and slave states) and the three-fifths clause (allowing additional representatives for Southerners by counting slaves as equal to three-fifths of a white person) to protect the interests of slaveholders (Weingast 1998).

In other regions and contexts, successful democratic transitions in Portugal, Spain, Poland, and South Africa were characterized by constitutions and pacts that restricted the ability of majorities to implement their preferred policies. From 1976 until it was amended in 1982, Portugal's constitution gave the Council of the Revolution (predominated by the military) the power to pass their own laws and to judge the constitutionality of all laws passed by the legislature. Spain's constitution of 1978 guaranteed the special status of the Catholic Church, established a quasi-federal system, and included an electoral system with a rural bias favoring groups that supported the previous authoritarian regime. In the 1989 elections to the Polish legislature (the *Sejm)*, only 35 percent of the seats were freely contested; the communist military government appointed the remaining seats. Finally, South Africa's 1996 constitution provided for proportional power sharing in the Cabinet for any party winning at least twenty seats in the legislature and a federal system that devolved important taxation and spending issues to regions (reducing redistributive costs for the white population). The South African constitution also requires a two-thirds majority in both houses of the legislature to amend the constitution (Inman and Rubinfeld 2008).

Depending on the nature of the countermajoritarian rule, the composition of the protected minority or the effect of the provision (or both) may change over time. The critical point is that these types of provisions contribute to successful democratization based on the logic that, to succeed, all parties to the pact to democratize must believe themselves better off under the newly established institutional agreements. Without this condition, they are not likely to agree to democratization or, having agreed to it, are likely to subvert it (Mittal and Weingast 2010). Where this condition is fulfilled, however, opposing groups are more likely to uphold the formal rules of democracy and process a broad range of conflicting interests within democratic institutions, including the modification of targeted countermajoritarian provisions that initially facilitated the transition to democracy but subsequently proved harmful to democratic stability. This perspective allows us to see that even extreme democracy-eroding countermajoritarian provisions may allow evolution toward constitutional stability if, as in the case of Chile, such provisions are eventually modified peacefully, within the framework of the formal constitutional rules.

These observations fit within the larger democratization literature's emphasis on the importance of pacts to democratic transitions. Constitutions are pacts establishing the formal rules of the game of democratic politics and governance. As with other pacts, they must be self-enforcing to endure (Mittal and Weingast 2010). The new institutional framework created by the constitution is, in large part, responsible for providing credible protections to opposing groups. Countermajoritarian provisions are an essential building block of credible protection.

We now turn to a model of these agreements to see how and under what circumstances they work.

THE MODEL

We develop our full model of self-enforcing democracy in two steps, beginning with a simple model and then adding complexity. The first parallels an aspect of the approaches in Acemoglu and Robinson (2001, 2006) and Boix (2003), two of the leading models of democratization. In our second model, we relax two of the key assumptions used by Acemoglu, Robinson, and Boix and incorporate several new elements. Before beginning, we raise an important feature of democracy central to Acemoglu and Robinson's approach, namely that democracy potentially provides a commitment device on the part of the elite to redistribute over time. We abstract from this point, instead focusing on two other features of democracy: the role of constitutional design and the potential for leaders to subvert democracy.

We consider a political environment with two players: G1 represents an incumbent authoritarian and its supporters who initially hold power, and G2 is the principal opposition group. In general, we think of the opposition group, G2, as being larger in size than the authoritarian faction and therefore constituting a majority of the population. The two sides can also be conceptualized as warring factions from different regions or two opposing groups seeking different policies on a left-right spectrum.

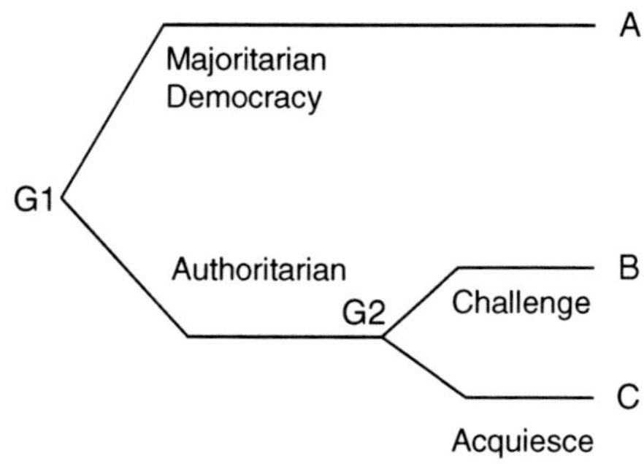

FIGURE 4.2A. Model 1.

Model 1

Our approach relies on an extensive form game with perfect information and begins with G1 holding power (Figure 4.1). The sequence of interaction is as follows. At the outset of the game, G1 has two choices. First, G1 can adopt a majoritarian system where the median voter in the electorate determines policy outcomes. Second, G1 may decide not to democratize, attempting to maintain the authoritarian regime. G2 must then decide whether to challenge or acquiesce. The potential types of challenges include a range of tactics that imposes costs on G1, such as a revolution, secession, riots, a general strike, and other forms of disruption and disorder. We assume that challenges impose costs on both sides and lead to a move by nature that determines which player wins the challenge. For ease of exposition, we suppress the move by nature, representing it through an expected value on the allocation of distributive payoffs after the challenge. The group that wins the challenge sets policy to its ideal point. We let p be the probability that G2 wins the challenge.

Payoffs

We assume that ideological policy exists on a standard one-dimensional policy space, X, equal to the real line. Each group possesses an ideal point over the ideological policy space, $X_i \in X$. We also assume that the ideal point of G_1 is to the right of the median voter, which, in turn, is to the right of G2: $X_2 < X_m < X_1$. Additionally, we assume that challenges are costly. Challenging creates turbulence in the economy and destroys economic wealth for both groups (Acemoglu and Robinson 2006: 120–21). We denote the reduction in group i's payoffs due to a challenge as C_i.

Taken together, we assume quadratic preferences over these two dimensions of utility, (x, C_i), where x is a policy resulting from political choice. Thus, each group's utility is decreasing in the distance between the policy and its ideal point and as the costs due to challenges rise.

We model each group's payoffs at the three terminal nodes of the game. For simplicity, these terminal nodes can be labeled as T = {A, B, C}. The reduced form representation of each group's utility at terminal node *t* can be represented as: $u_i(T)$.

Analysis

Given that this is a game of perfect information, the appropriate equilibrium concept to solve the game is subgame perfection. To analyze the equilibria of the game, we use backward induction. Thus, we analyze each player's strategies beginning with the terminal nodes of the game and then work backward toward the beginning of the game. This equilibrium of this game depends on the relative payoffs associated with various parameters.

First, we analyze the authoritarian subgame where G1's initial choice is to continue the authoritarian regime. G2 must then decide whether to challenge the authoritarian regime or acquiesce. G2 will challenge *if* it receives a greater payoff from challenging than acquiescing, $u_2(B) > u_2(C)$. Thus, when G2 chooses to acquiesce, authoritarian rule continues. In contrast, if G2 prefers to launch a challenge, the outcome is node B. Because G1 can set policy at its ideal point at node C, G1 receives a higher payoff at this node than any other terminal node in the game.

Looking at the first node of the game, G1 must decide between majoritarian democracy and continuing authoritarian rule. Suppose p, the probability that G1 wins the challenge, and C_i are such that G1's preferences rank the outcomes as C, A, B; that is, G1 prefers authoritarian rule first, majoritarian democracy second, and fighting third. If G2 prefers not to challenge in the authoritarian subgame, G1 will choose to maintain the authoritarian regime. If G2 prefers to challenge, then G1 will choose majoritarian democracy.

This game captures one of the main theses of Acemoglu and Robinson (2006) and Boix's (2003): Democratization occurs when the opposition is sufficiently strong so that the incumbent regime prefers to democratize rather than face the challenge. The model shows that G1 will not democratize when G2 lacks the ability to threaten a challenge (that is, it prefers C to B) in the authoritarian subgame. If G2 credibly threatens a challenge so that G1 is worse off attempting to maintain the authoritarian regime, G1 will democratize.

Model 2

Model 1 makes two critical assumptions. First, it assumes that the only strategy choices available to authoritarian regimes facing an opposition strong enough to challenge it is to establish a majoritarian democracy or to remain steadfast in the authoritarian regime and face a challenge. In many cases, however, authoritarian regimes have a third option of establishing a democracy with countermajoritarian provisions that protect the authoritarian's interests by preventing policy outcomes under democratization from moving completely to the median voter's ideal point. In these cases, democratization occurs, but with constitutional restrictions that force those in power to deviate from majoritarian/median policy outcomes; for example, in the direction of the authoritarian's interests. The discussion of countermajoritarian provisions in the previous section suggests both the range and applicability of these constitutional features.

Second, model 1 assumes that G2 has no strategic choice after the establishment of the majoritarian democracy; instead, G2 automatically implements the will of the median voter.[4] In some cases, however, G2 is likely to have both the incentive and the ability to subvert majoritarian democracy to move policy toward its ideal point away from the median.[5] Similarly, in a countermajoritarian democracy, G2 may also have incentives either to renege on the constitution and establish a majoritarian democracy or to subvert the constitution entirely by moving policy outcomes to its own ideal point.

In our second model, we relax both of these assumptions. The sequence of play for this game is shown in Figure 4.2. As in model 1, the game begins with G1 holding power. G1 has an initial choice among three options. It can decide to continue the authoritarian regime or it can adopt a majoritarian system as in model 1. However, G1 now has an additional option: It can opt for democracy with countermajoritarian constitutional provisions.

If G1 attempts to maintain an authoritarian regime, then, as in model 1, G2 decides whether to challenge or acquiesce. If G1 chooses to initiate majoritarian democracy, G2 takes power and must next decide whether to honor the institutions or to subvert. In either case, G1 then must decide whether to challenge or acquiesce.

Finally, if G1 chooses to negotiate a countermajoritarian constitution, G2 takes power and must decide whether to honor the constitution, renege on the constitutional bargain and institute majoritarian rule, or subvert the constitution to increase its own power (as in the majoritarian subgame). After observing G2's choice, G1

4 For instance, Acemoglu and Robinson (2006: 94, 98) assume that "the policy that wins in a direct democracy must be the ideal point of the median voter." This assumption is made in many of the previous models of democratization in the comparative political economy literature.

5 Spain in 1936, prior to the outbreak of the Civil War, provides an example. Here, the left-wing Popular Front government threatened to enact more advanced social polices than would be supported by the median voter (Carr and Fusi 1981: 3) Similarly, in Venezuela, the victory of Acción Democrática's presidential candidate in the 1948 elections was followed a short nine months later by a military coup that rescinded numerous reforms that had alienated domestic business groups, the Catholic Church, and other more conservative elements (Coppedge 1994: 324).

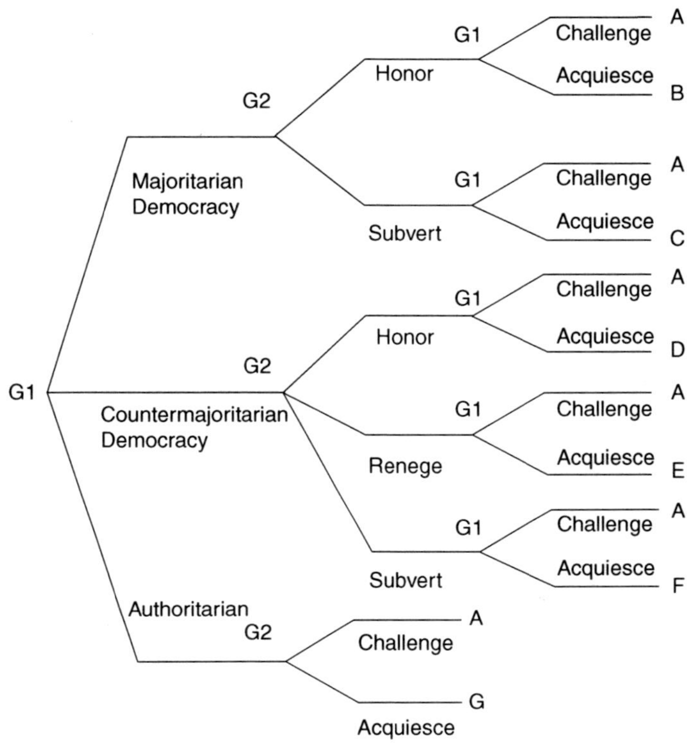

FIGURE 4.2B. Model 2.

then decides whether to challenge or acquiesce. As with model 1, we assume that challenges impose costs on both sides and lead to a move by nature that determines whether the form of de jure institutions changes.[6]

Payoffs

The outcomes of the countermajoritarian subgame are determined in part by the institutional constraints established by the constitution. If G2 honors the constitution, it must set a policy subject to constitutional constraints, resulting in X_{cj}. If G2 reneges on the constitution by instituting majoritarian democracy and G1 does not challenge, then G2 sets a policy outcome at the preferred outcome of the median voter, X_m. If G2 subverts the constitution and G1 does not challenge, G2 sets policy at its own ideal point, X_r. Alternatively, if G1 challenges G2's choice in

6 In the figure, we suppress the move by nature, representing it through an expected value on the allocation of distributive payoffs after the challenge that affects each side's expected utility. In what follows, we explicitly analyze the probabilities.

the countermajoritarian subgame, the group that wins is determined by a move by nature, which we represent through an expected payoff for each group.

We make four assumptions about the model:

- (A1) The probability that G1 (G2) wins a challenge is p (1–p) regardless of who initiates the challenge.[7] [NOTE TO READER: The next draft will generalize this, allowing three different probabilities of success for G1, depending on the subgame.]
- (A2) A challenge results in one of two outcomes, depending on who wins. If G1 wins, it imposes its ideal X_1. If G2 wins, it imposes its ideal X_2.
- (A3) The costs of challenging, C_i, are constant across the different subgames.
- (A4) Finally, we assume that the idea points are ordered as follows:

$$X_2 < X_m < X_{cj} < X_1. \qquad \text{(Ineq 1)}$$

In general, we will assume that X_m is closer to X_2 than X_1, and X_{cj} is closer to X_1 than X_2, but in some cases, we will explicitly relax this assumption.

These assumptions have several implications. First, when G1 challenges in either the majoritarian or the countermajoritarian subgames, the outcome is the same, labeled A at each terminal node where a challenge occurs. The same outcome (A) occurs when G2 challenges in the authoritarian subgame. The terminal nodes can therefore be labeled as T = {A, B, C, D, E, F, G}. Second, when G1 chooses to acquiesce in the majoritarian subgame, $B = X_m$ and $C = X_2$. Third, when G1 chooses to acquiesce in the countermajoritarian subgame: $D = X_{cj}$, $E = X_m$, and $F = X_2$. Fourth, in the authoritarian subgame, $G = X_1$.

The preceding assumptions afford many payoff configurations, depending on the various parameters and the location of the four outcomes. Figure 4.3 provides a spatial configuration of the preferences consistent with these assumptions. In the figure, raising (lowering) C_i moves A down (up). Similarly, raising (lowering) p moves A to the right (left).

Analysis

In this subsection, we consider several sets of preferences, each resulting in a different equilibrium outcome.

7 This is clearly a simplifying assumption, and it holds in many cases. In the Chilean and Spanish cases, for example, the army (supporting G1) remained independent of the new government in the earlier transition. The assumption also held for the American Civil War where what mattered was not which side held the national government, but the relative resources of the two regions.

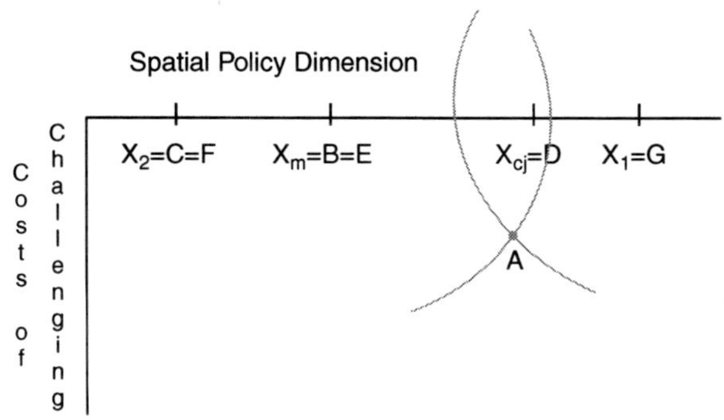

FIGURE 4.3. Spatial preference map, countermajoritarian equilibrium (outcome D).

Equilibrium countermajoritarian democratization. We begin with the preference configuration of Figure 4.3 (recall that X_i is Gi's ideal point). For now, assume that X_{cj} is exogenously given. In the majoritarian subgame: If G2 honors, then G1 will challenge if C_1 is not too large; challenging yields outcome A: $pX_1 + (1-p)X_2 - C_1$, whereas acquiescing yields outcome B, X_m. If G2 subverts, and G1 challenges, the outcome is A, whereas acquiescing yields outcome C = X_2. Given the preference configuration of Figure 4.3, G1 prefers A to both X_m and X_1, so regardless of G2's choice, it will challenge. In the countermajoritarian subgame: If G2 honors, then G1 will acquiesce; challenging yields A: $pX_1 + (1\text{-}p)X_2 - C_1$, whereas acquiescing yields outcome D = X_{cj}, which by preference configuration in Figure 4.3 it prefers to A. If G2 chooses to renege, we duplicate the first calculation in the majoritarian subgame (G1 chooses challenge); and if G2 chooses to subvert, we duplicate the second calculation in the majoritarian subgame (G1 chooses challenge). Given the preferences in Figure 4.3, G2 will choose to honor ($u_2(D) > u_2(A)$); and G1 will honor ($u_1(D) > u_1(A)$). In the authoritarian subgame, G2 will challenge when C_2 is not too large; challenging yields A: $pX_1 + (1-p)X_2 - C_2$, whereas acquiescing yields G, X_1. Thus, when p and C_2 are not too large so that $u_2(A) > u_2(G)$, G2 will challenge. Given these choices in the subgames, G1 will choose countermajoritarian democratization at the first node.

To summarize the logic that supports the countermajoritarian constitutional equilibrium: inequality (1) specifies the relationship among the outcomes; p and C_1 are such that G1 prefers A to X_m, and D to A; and p and C_2 are such that G2 prefers outcome A to G and D to E and A.

Authoritarian equilibrium. In comparison with Figure 4.3, if C_2 is large (or if p is large), then G2 prefers to acquiesce in the authoritarian subgame. In this case, G1 chooses to maintain its authoritarian regime, and this is an equilibrium. This behavior results in outcome G, the best possible for G1.

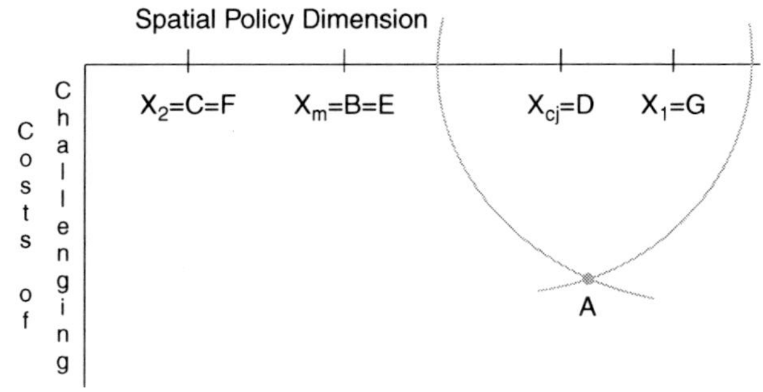

FIGURE 4.4. Spatial preference map, authoritarian equilibrium (outcome G).

Figure 4.4 illustrates a spatial configuration that supports this case. In comparison with Figure 4.3, A is much lower, reflecting larger costs of challenging, C_i, so that X_1 = G is inside G2's indifferent curve through A. The outcomes of the other two subgames necessarily produce lower utility for G1.

A majoritarian equilibrium. Consider again the preference configuration in Figure 4.3. Suppose that X_m moves close to X_{cj} (specifically, X_m moves inside G1's indifference curve through A) and all other points remain the same. The new outcome relationships generate preferences that produce an equilibrium in the majority subgame whereby if G2 honors, G1 will acquiesce. The same logic means that if G2 reneges in the countermajoritarian subgame, G1 will acquiesce. Moreover, because in this subgame G2 prefers renege/acquiesce to both honor/acquiesce and subvert/challenge, it will renege on the countermajoritarian institutions and impose majoritarian democracy. In this case, at the first node, G1 is indifferent between choosing the majoritarian and the countermajoritarian subgame (and prefers both those outcomes to the outcome of the authoritarian subgame, A). This case arises in the presence of inequality (1); when p and C_1 are such that G1 prefers X_m to A; and p and C_2 are such that G2 prefers A to G.

This special case, requiring that X_m is close to X_{cj}, produces a counterintuitive result. It arises when the majority of the population's policy orientation is closer to G1 than to G2. Oddly, despite this situation, the authoritarian cannot assure itself of a countermajoritarian constitution. From the authoritarian faction's point of view, it is not worth fighting to maintain countermajoritarian institutions when the majoritarian policy outcome is close to the outcome that results from countermajoritarian institutions.

This special case is one of the few circumstances where we expect a democratic transition to result in majoritarian political institutions. However, we suspect that X_m will rarely be this near X_{cj} unless G1 is very weak (i.e., C_1 is very high and p is

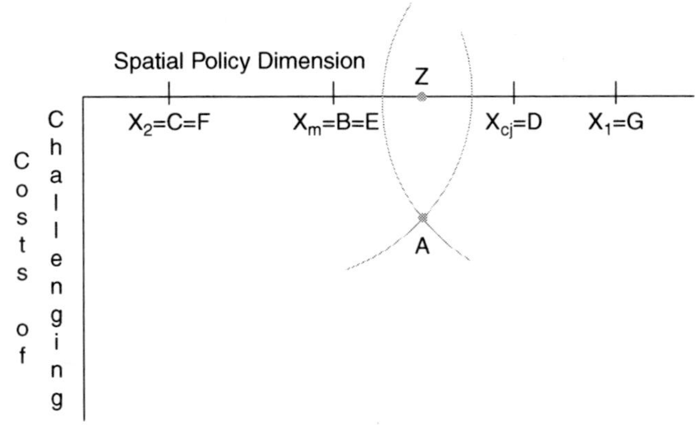

FIGURE 4.5. Spatial preference map, an equilibrium with mutual defection.

low). The main implication is that democratizations will rarely result in majoritarian political institutions.[8]

Comparing the countermajoritarian equilibrium in Figure 4.3 to this majoritarian equilibrium, we find that majoritarian democracy emerges where it is not very costly to G1; but when it is costly, G1 engineers a credible countermajoritarian constitution. In both of these cases, the amount of policy movement from X_1 – the policy under the authoritarian regime – is not very dramatic.

An equilibrium with fighting. Suppose that p is considerably lower than we assumed in Figure 4.3. This results in the spatial configuration of preferences in Figure 4.5, which places the outcome of challenges by G1 (e.g., A) and challenges by G2 (outcome A) up and to the left in comparison with those in Figure 4.3.

Suppose as well that institutions are difficult to mold so that the only possible outcomes on the policy space are X_2, X_m, X_{cj}, and X_1. Then, in the majoritarian subgame, G2 is indifferent between honoring and subverting because G1 challenges in both, yielding the same outcome. In the countermajoritarian subgame, G2 also chooses to subvert (it prefers A over D) and G1 will challenge (it prefers A over F = X_2). In the authoritarian subgame, G2 will challenge. In short, challenging is the outcome of every subgame, so G1 is indifferent among them. In this setting, violence occurs in equilibrium. The reason is the mix of the non-malleability of institutions in combination with the threat point: None of the four possible outcomes Pareto-dominates the challenge outcome. In every subgame where a player can challenge, they prefer challenging to acquiescing. In principle, a policy such as Z would make both parties

8 For example, this situation may occur with a moderate-to-conservative society that nonetheless rejects the repression under authoritarian rule. As a possible illustration, Uruguay restored democracy in 1984 by simply restoring the prior constitution with no added countermajoritarian features.

better off than fighting. However, the lack of institutions to sustain Z means that Z is not an option.[9] Instead, both parties prefer to challenge than accept another outcome.

An equilibrium with X_{cj} endogenous. Consider again the preference configuration of Figure 4.3. Suppose that X_{cj} is endogenous and that institutions are sufficiently rich to allow them to be constructed to support any point in the policy space. In terms of the game, this means that, at the first node of the countermajoritarian subgame, when G2 chooses to honor, it also chooses the location of X_{cj}.

In this setting, G2 will set X_{cj} so that G1 just prefers X_{cj} to A (that is, G2 will set X_{cj} where G1's indifference curve through A crosses the horizontal line in Figure 4.3). To see this, recall the countermajoritarian equilibrium. As before, G2 will challenge in the authoritarian subgame, yielding A. The placement of X_{cj} yields maximum benefits along the policy line to G2 subject to G1 preferring X_{cj} to A. If G2 reneges or subverts in the countermajoritarian subgame, G1 will challenge, yielding A. If G2 honors, then G1 will acquiesce. By construction of X_{cj}, G1 prefers X_{cj} (honor) instead of A (reneging or subverting), and so too does G2. The equilibrium choices in the majoritarian and authoritarian subgames are as before, so G1 prefers the outcome of countermajoritarian democratization to that of either majoritarian democratization or attempting to maintain the authoritarian regime. Self-enforcing countermajoritarian democracy occurs in this equilibrium, but with the institutions more favorable to G2 than G1 when X_{cj} was exogenous (or when G1 sets X_{cj}).

This model affords interesting comparative statistics depending on the relative power of the two groups. The less favorable is the threat point to G1 (that is, the lower is p or the higher is C_1), the further toward X_1 is X_{cj}.

IMPLICATIONS

An important implication of the approach is that democratization is more likely to occur when the countermajoritarian option is available to an authoritarian than when majoritarian democracy alone is available. In comparison with model 1, the additional option of constitutional restrictions afforded by the countermajoritarian subgame in model 2 means that G2 does not have to be capable of imposing as high a cost on G1 in order to induce G1 to abandon the authoritarian regime and establish a democracy.

To see this, in model 1 when G2 prefers B to A, then G1 will choose majoritarian democratization whenever $Xm \geq pX_1 + (1\text{-}p)X_2$. In model 2, G1 will choose countermajoritarian democratization whenever $Xcj \geq p'X_1 + (1-p')X_2 - C_1$. Because

[9] This argument parallels Fearon's (1995) classic argument about why wars occur.

G1 prefers X_{cj} to X_m, $p' < p$: the minimum strength of G2 necessary to force the authoritarian to democratize is lower. Moreover, the bigger the utility difference between X_{cj} and X_m, the lower is the minimum p' necessary for G1 to choose democratization. Put simply, the countermajoritarian features make democratization less costly for G1 than in a purely majoritarian system. Of course, countermajoritarian democracy may also impose onerous restrictions on majorities.

The model reveals important insights into the circumstances that sustain democracy. In a two-group setting with an authoritarian incumbent (G1) and a principal opposition group (G2), both sides have the opportunity to defect from the bargain. The model shows that the transition to a self-enforcing democracy arise with the reciprocal ability of both groups to punish each other for defecting. Self-enforcing democracy, therefore, requires that both sides have incentives not to defect. In terms of model 2, G2 must be strong enough to challenge G1 if it attempts to maintain the authoritarian regime. Further, G1 must be strong enough in the democratic regime to prevent G2 from reneging on the countermajoritarian constitutional features.

This result adds to the literature on democratic transitions: Paralleling Acemoglu and Robinson (2006) and Boix (2003), the model shows that an authoritarian regime is stable when the opposition group G2 is insufficiently strong to challenge it. Equally importantly, however – and missing from those accounts – the maintenance of self-enforcing democracy in model 2 requires that the authoritarian group in power, G1, be sufficiently strong after the transition to ensure that G2 has incentives to honor the constitutional bargain once it gains power. If this latter condition fails, G2 may well prefer to attempt to maintain the authoritarian regime and fight G1, resulting in disorder or civil war. Thus, our model demonstrates institutional and contextual foundations of self-enforcing democratization and consequent long-term democratic survival. In the (countermajoritarian) democratization equilibrium, both sides have the ability to punish the other for defection, and therefore maintain democracy. This analysis suggests that if one side is too strong, democracy is not stable.

The institutional aspects of our approach contrast with the models in Boix (2003) and Acemoglu and Robinson (2006). Precisely because majoritarian democracy can be median-driven, or through subversion can result in policy outcomes beyond the median, authoritarians are likely to resist this form of democracy. They are more likely to initiate a democratic transition and subsequently refrain from overthrowing democracy when a third option is pursued: democracy with constitutional constraints that mitigate the effects of unconstrained, median-driven majority rule.[10]

[10] Indeed, the availability of the constitutional democracy with countermajoritarian features means that G1 is unlikely to voluntarily establish a majoritarian democracy (subject to the qualification above – when X_m is close to X_{cj}).

These ideas yield an important prediction. Although we observed that majoritarian democratization was possible in model 2, we also suggested that the circumstances producing it were not very likely. This implies that when authoritarians democratize, they are more likely to achieve stable democracy when it is countermajoritarian than when it is not.

This insight with respect to countermajoritarian democracy helps explain another frequent feature of most democratizations emphasized in the substantive literature but missing from existing models: pacts. A pact is an agreement that defines the rules governing the exercise of power and provides guarantees for the vital interests of those entering into the pact (O'Donnell and Schmitter 1986: 37). Pacts often occur when neither competing group can unilaterally impose its preferred solution on the other. Although they acknowledge that pacts are not always viable, O'Donnell and Schmitter (1986: 38–39) argue that pacts strongly enhance the probability of establishing a viable democracy.[11]

In contrast, pacts play no role in the Acemoglu and Robinson's and Boix's approach. The authoritarian has nothing over which to negotiate. In our approach, pacts emerge naturally at the moment of constitutional bargaining that creates the constitution, typically with countermajoritarian features, and the credible commitments to maintain those features. Our model helps explain why some pacts pave the way for self-enforcing democratization whereas others fail: Those that succeed not only include countermajoritarian features protecting one or both parties to the pact, but they also involve the reciprocal ability to punish the other if the other defects. In terms of the model, pacts construct the appropriate location for X_{cj}. Self-enforcing pacts are those consistent with the countermajoritarian equilibrium (when X_{cj} is exogenous) or with the endogenous countermajoritarian equilibrium. In both cases, both G1 and G2 must be better off at X_{cj} than at the threat point of mutual defection.

The results of model 2 also parallel an insight from Mittal and Weingast (2010): Successful transitions to stable democracy reduce the stakes of power. The model shows that democratization is more likely in the face of limits on the power of majorities. When the stakes are too high (majority movement to the median or beyond the median toward G2's ideal) so that policy movements are too costly for the authoritarian, the latter is more likely to fight to remain authoritarian, possibly leading to civil war and other forms of disorder.

Another aspect of the Acemoglu and Robinson's and Boix's approaches is that a central feature of democracy concerns redistribution from the rich to the poor, as

11 Spain, Portugal, Venezuela, Colombia, and (to a lesser extent) Brazil all experienced pacted democratic transitions that, according to O'Donnell and Schmitter, seemed to presage viable democracy. In contrast, with the exception of Costa Rica, O'Donnell and Schmitter (1986: 45) did not view as promising the prospects for democratic consolidation among the unpacted democratic transitions that occurred in Peru, Ecuador, Argentina, Bolivia, and the Dominican Republic.

represented by the median. Viewing the policy space in our models as representing the degree of redistribution, the main lesson is that some redistribution takes place, but the countermajoritarian features of the constitution are designed to place limits on the extent of that redistribution. The creation of democracy with countermajoritarian features helps explain why so many of the early democratizations in Western Europe and the Anglo-American countries of the nineteenth and early twentieth centuries involved relatively little redistribution, at least for several generations.

The model implies that successful democracy, beyond simply holding elections, requires attention to constitutional design, specifically the inclusion of countermajoritarian features that protect one or more parties to the constitutional pact creating democracy. Without such protections, those in power are less likely to accept democracy in the first place. Without credible commitments to honor such features, self-enforcing democracy is a less likely outcome. As we have noted, a large proportion of successful democratizations have these features.

Finally, the model also provides an answer as to why we observe such different outcomes of attempts at democratization across different countries. Different parameter values lead to different equilibria: Some countries will remain authoritarian (e.g., when G2 is weak), whereas others successfully create democracy that lasts more than a generation. In yet other cases, democratization may occur followed by some form of democratic failure (such as subversion or coups); for example, when G1 is not sufficiently strong after the transition, or when G2 loses strength so that G1 challenges.

APPLYING THE APPROACH: CHILE, 1973–PRESENT

Chile's transition to democracy in 1989 illustrates the model's predictions. Our point in developing this case is not to prove our model using a single example, but instead to show how countermajoritarian institutions work in practice. Specifically, we argue that self-enforcing democracy with countermajoritarian features is established when:

- A democratic opposition (G2) poses a credible challenge to an authoritarian regime (G1), leading to the initiation of a democratic transition with countermajoritarian constitutional provisions.
- G1 is sufficiently strong to present a credible challenge to G2 if it reneges on the constitutional bargain.
- G1 receives a higher payoff from upholding the constitutional bargain as opposed to challenging and attempting to bring back authoritarian rule.
- G2 receives a higher payoff from upholding the constitutional bargain as opposed to attempting to establish majoritarian democracy or subverting the government to establish its own policy preferences.

The 1973 military coup deposed Chile's socialist President Salvador Allende Gossens, beginning seventeen years of authoritarian rule under a military junta led by General Augusto Pinochet. An important element behind the consolidation of the military's hold on power in the years after the coup was the judgment on the part of economic elites and other sectors that the Allende period represented "a definitive threat to their existence" (Garreton in O'Donnell, Schmitter, and Whitehead 1986: 100). The remainder of the 1970s witnessed severe repression, economic transformation toward a free-market model, and a largely silent civil society. At the same time, a commission appointed by the junta elaborated a new constitution as a means of securing the regime's legitimation and institutional foundations. This text was approved in a 1980 referendum and took effect in March 1981.[12]

The constitution of 1980 formed the cornerstone of the military regime's foundational project, which centered on revitalizing the economy, preventing the resurgence of Marxist ideology, and restructuring Chilean politics by creating a so-called protected democracy with a guiding role for the military (Barros 2002). The constitution contained transitory articles extending military rule until 1989 as well as permanent articles that would go into effect after a plebiscite scheduled for 1988. The purpose of the 1988 plebiscite was to approve the military's candidate for president, which would presumably be Pinochet. If the military's candidate won, he would hold power for another eight years. If he lost, however, open elections would be held in 1989 for president and for a bicameral legislature.[13]

The constitution's permanent articles included extreme countermajoritarian provisions commonly referred to as "authoritarian enclaves" because they removed areas of authority and decision making from elected officials. These included nine designated senators (out of a total of twenty-six), a National Security Council dominated by the military and endowed with broad powers, restrictions on the president's power to appoint and remove the heads of the military services, and the exclusion from politics of individuals, parties, or movements deemed hostile to democracy (Valenzuela 1994: 205–08). Amending the constitution required a large supermajority and passage by two consecutive legislatures. These features placed Chile's constitution (until 2005) at the far extreme "democracy-eroding" end of our continuum.[14]

[12] Lack of unanimity within the junta and among regime supporters on the desirability of indefinitely prolonging military rule as opposed to establishing a constitutional basis for the regime and a timetable for the reintroduction of some democratic elements ultimately led to the adoption of the Constitution. An increase in international pressure in the latter half of the 1970s and a more critical stance on the part of the Catholic Church and pro-regime communications media also contributed to Pinochet's decision to finalize the constitution. (Garreton 1986).

[13] See Barros (2002) for the events surrounding this period and dynamics within the junta. See Magaloni (2008) and Cox (2009) on the rationale for holding elections in authoritarian regimes.

[14] The authoritarian enclaves were removed by the legislature in 2005. The electoral system designed by the military regime remains unreformed but is not technically an authoritarian enclave, nor can it be classified as undemocratic.

The plan to hold a plebiscite, which appeared to be a safe bet for Pinochet in 1980, turned out to be instrumental to the unraveling of the authoritarian regime and Chile's return to democracy. As 1988 approached, the democratic opposition seized the opportunity afforded by the plebiscite to challenge the regime. Previously divided parties of the center and left formed a coalition, registered voters, and carried out a highly effective "Campaign for the No."[15] Pinochet, who thought himself invulnerable, lost the plebiscite 54 percent to 43 percent.

The regime's defeat initiated the strategic interactions described in the authoritarian and countermajoritarian subgames (Figure 4.2). The result of the vote demonstrated the strength of popular opposition to the authoritarian regime and paved the way for democratic elections in 1989. Consistent with the model, G2's strength in the authoritarian subgame led G1 to initiate a democratic transition in which extreme countermajoritarian provisions lowered the stakes for the regime and its constituents.[16] As shown in Figure 4.5, the countermajoritarian policy outcomes are endogenous to the Chilean case.

Further evidence of G1's perception of G2's strength can be adduced from the negotiations carried out between the center-left democratic opposition, the regime, and its allies on the right during 1989, resulting in the adoption of fifty-four constitutional reforms. The reforms maintained the extreme countermajoritarian character of the constitution but eliminated some provisions and softened others. For example, the total number of elected Senators was increased from twenty-six to thirty-eight, diluting the impact of the nine unelected Senators; the supermajority for amending the constitution and organic constitutional laws was slightly reduced; the requirement that constitutional amendments be passed by two consecutive legislatures was dropped; and the provision (aimed at the communists) of banning political participation of antidemocratic groups was removed. The autonomy of the armed forces was maintained, as were mechanisms for military oversight of Chile's political institutions and the continuation of Pinochet as head of the army until 1998. Moreover, organic laws issued by the junta created an electoral system that overrepresented right-wing parties, established a guaranteed source and minimum level of funding for the military, and provided for military involvement in naming members of the Constitutional Court, regulatory, and semiautonomous agencies. Finally,

[15] Other factors contributed to the authoritarian defeat. For example, during the 1980s, the regime's bases of support began to fragment owing in part to an economic crisis and the effects of the Latin American debt crisis, which hit Chile particularly hard.

[16] Although Pinochet wanted to ignore the plebiscite results and hold on to power, other members of the junta refused to go along (Londregan 2000: 80). They (and others in the military) were interested in a "soft landing" and a return to military rather than political concerns (Valenzuela 1994: 212) The Constitution's provisions provided assurances of the continuation of their institutional project for the country.

the constitution also protected right-wing interests by establishing an independent central bank and enshrining the inviolability of private property – a principal source of conflict in the period prior to 1973 (Scully 1996: 106–07; Valenzuela 1994: 214–15). These institutions provided the framework in which subsequent elected governments operated.

As the model suggests, mutual awareness of each sides' reciprocal ability to inflict punishment helped foster the transition, the 1989 negotiations and elections, and the opposition's acceptance of an extreme countermajoritarian constitutional framework. The military regime (G1), cognizant of the fact that they lacked the support of a majority of the population, moderated its strategy, engaged in negotiations to secure the survival and legitimation of their basic constitutional design, and held elections. As Siavelis notes, "the military and its allies were concerned that if they did not negotiate and appeared inflexible, the opposition might succeed in building a popular movement to do away with Pinochet's entire institutional framework" (Siavelis 2008: 193). The democratic opposition (G2), acutely aware of both the military's strength and the fact that more than 40 percent of the voters in 1988 supported continued military rule, pursued a moderate strategy in which it accepted a return to civilian rule under an extreme countermajoritarian constitution.

Mutual Restraint: Governance under the 1980 Constitution

Patricio Aylwin, the Christian Democratic candidate of the center-left coalition *Concertación por la Democracia*, won the 1989 presidential elections and took office in March 1990.[17] The *Concertación* won a majority in the legislature's lower house, the Chamber of Deputies, and a plurality in the Senate. The effects of the regime's electoral law (which overrepresents second-place winners, which during this period were parties on the right) combined with the nine designated senators to mean that the government lacked enough votes to pass legislation on its own. The right consistently held a veto over policy making.

The model helps interpret these events. The authoritarian regime valued the countermajoritarian constitutional provisions, restricting the behavior of an elected democratic government, and so chose this route for democratization rather than majoritarian democracy that could have proved disastrous to their interests. Further, according to the countermajoritarian subgame in model 2, G1's strength and credible threats to punish defections from the constitutional bargain raised the payoffs to G2 for working within constitutional constraints.

[17] The *Concertación por la Democracia* is a coalition of center-left and left-wing parties, which won all presidential elections from 1990 through 2005. Chile's other main political grouping, a center-right coalition, was called *Alianza por la Democracia* until changing its name in mid-2009 *to Coalición por el Cambio.* The *Coalición*'s presidential candidate, Sebastián Piñera, won the presidency in 2009.

This picture accurately describes the situation in Chile in the aftermath of the return to civilian rule. The Chilean military at the time of the transition and for some time afterward was considered to be a significant threat to democracy (Linz and Stepan 1996: 205). Even before President Aylwin took office, the military made it clear that any violation of the constitution would provoke military intervention. In June 1989, army generals issued a warning that they would resort to the "legitimate use of force" against anyone attempting to ignore the constitution. Several months later, sending a clear signal with respect to the future government's handling of military involvement in human rights violations during the dictatorship, Pinochet declared that the military would not allow any of their members to be vilified for their actions aimed at saving Chile (*Latin American Weekly Reports*, July 6, 1989 and Sept. 7, 1989). Furthermore, when the transition began, Pinochet's authoritarian project commanded a considerable degree of support among business elites, producer organizations, and parties of the right (the UDI and RN) (Siavelis 2008: 196). *Concertación* leaders understood that the support of business elites was critical to the success of the transition (Boylan 1996).

Given the credible military threat, democratic elites in Chile viewed reneging or subverting the constitution as undesirable. Indeed, despite the fact that it did not relish operating under the military-imposed constitution, the opposition (and subsequently the new government) "wanted to avoid giving Pinochet any excuse to renege on the constitutional deal that had been struck" (Siavelis 2008: 193).

Examining the Aylwin administration's actions in three areas provides evidence supporting the model's insights that a transition to self-enforcing democracy rests on the reciprocal ability of opposing groups to punish each other for defecting from the constitutional bargain and, furthermore, that countermajoritarian constitutional provisions sustain an equilibrium wherein opposing groups' best strategy is to honor the constitution, constraining majoritarian policy making. In three highly contentious areas – human rights violations by the military, economic policy, and constitutional reform – the Aylwin government (1990–1994) as well as subsequent *Concertación* administrations worked within institutional constraints and pursued moderate policies. The strength of the military and the Right generated strong incentives for each successive *Concertación* government to honor the constitutional bargain. In so doing, the government, of necessity, took into account the interests of the military and right-wing groups and incorporated them into policy making. In turn, as the model predicts, given the strategic choice of democratic governments to honor the constitution, the best strategy for the military and its allies on the right was to acquiesce.

Civil-military relations, and particularly the issue of past human rights violations by the military, arguably posed the most delicate challenge for the new democratic government. The composition of the courts and the countermajoritarian structure of the Senate,[18] in combination with occasional warning signals by the army, forced the Aylwin administration to move slowly on addressing past human rights violations. President Aylwin issued a public rebuke to Pinochet in 1990 for the military's explicit threats to the government,[19] but sensitive issues – such as the application of the military' self-granted 1978 amnesty, the transfer of human rights trials from military to civil courts, and a date at which such trials would end – continued to be debated through the succeeding *Concertación* administrations of Presidents Eduardo Frei and Ricardo Lagos.

The gradual, negotiated approach produced slow progress. The administration set a pragmatic course by adopting a policy of "justice within the possible" (*justicia possible*), such as clarification of the truth and material compensation to victim's families, but stopping short of trial and punishment of the perpetrators (Rabkin 1992).[20]

In this context, the Aylwin government's economic policy was similarly moderate, steering a course between the Scylla of right-wing revolt and the Charybdis of social unrest. "Growth with Equity" was the government's slogan.[21] In the early years of the transition, the likelihood of a backlash from conservative elites if the new government strayed too far from Pinochet's economic model was high. But ignoring the needs of the middle and lower sectors also posed grave risks (Boylan 1996; Siavelis 2008: 182). In particular, the Aylwin government was concerned with the possibility of popular demands for immediate benefits that would endanger sound economic policy, trigger inflation, and undermine democratic stability (Weyland 1997: 40). Reacting to these forces, the government pursued a strategy that balanced fiscal prudence and sound macroeconomic policies with targeted increases in social spending to address the growth in poverty and inequality that took place during the Pinochet years.[22]

The Aylwin administration's first piece of legislation was a major tax reform bill negotiated with business groups and the right-wing RN party. As Boylan notes, the government wanted more than it got, but the *Concertación*'s lack of votes in the

[18] During the Aylwin administration, the *Concertación* was two votes short of a simple majority and six votes short of the supermajority needed for constitutional amendments.

[19] In December 1990, the army garrisoned its troops, fueling speculation of a coup, as military leaders (including Pinochet's son) were the focus of judicial and congressional investigations. In 1993, unhappy over a court ruling that could make it easier to investigate human rights cases, army units dressed in battle fatigues, with armored transport vehicles and antitank missiles, surrounded public buildings in downtown Santiago.

[20] A round table dialogue on human rights abuses was initiated during the Frei administration with the participation of the Minister of Defense. During the Lagos administration (2000–2005), the armed forces finally accepted that human rights investigations should be handled in civilian rather than military courts (a bone of contention since 1990) (Siavelis 2008: 198–99).

[21] The slogan was so successful that it was still invoked in 2009 by President Michelle Bachelet (http://www.as-coa.org/article.php?id=1898).

[22] In 1987, 44.7% of Chileans lived in poverty and 16.8% were classified as indigent (Scully 1995: 101).

Senate made right-wing support necessary. The bill's moderate character reassured the right with respect to the government's economic approach. At the same time, the government used the increased revenue to finance new spending on social programs. Despite the expectations that the government would respond to popular demands for social justice, "the reform was tailored far more to the interests of an economically powerful and politically visible business class" (Boylan 1996). Cautious spending, sound management of the economy, and attention to the demands of Chile's business and landholding groups continued through successive center-left administrations.[23] Chile's growth rates since the return of democracy have been consistently high, inflation has been kept under control, poverty rates have declined, and in 2005, the country had the highest GDP per capita in South America.

Finally, President Aylwin and all subsequent *Concertación* presidents repeatedly tried to amend the constitution's authoritarian enclaves, but these attempts were always according to the constitutionally mandated procedures for amendment. As in other policy areas, the threat of punishment for defecting (for example, trying to impose constitutional changes) combined with the lack of votes to enact reforms to force *Concertación* governments to negotiate with parties on the right, for the most part unsuccessfully.[24]

No comprehensive reforms passed until 2005, during the administration of socialist President Lagos. These reforms eliminated all nonelected Senate seats, altered the composition of the National Security Council and made it a purely advisory body, and restored the president's powers to name, fire, and promote high-level military officials. Several changes from 1989 to 2005 facilitated the constitutional revision within the rules. Over time, both sides had moderated. Although the military and right-wing groups still had sufficient power to disrupt the government, they had redefined their interests. Over time, more and more segments of the right and the military came to support the median's position, especially as the median had come to accept the system and the results it produced. Moderation and growth set the stage for consensual removal of these provisions. The center-left government found it could retain power and produce growth through moderation. Although the constitutional changes eliminated the targeted protections provided by the authoritarian enclaves, the right had become less worried about the consequences.

A frequent question is how to explain Chile's "exceptionalism" in achieving a stable, consolidated democracy; maintaining a sound economy; and avoiding populist

[23] Scully (1995: 112–13) notes that the authoritarian enclaves within the Constitution reinforced consensus building and attention to the demands of groups outside the center-left coalition, such as business and landholding elites, as well as providing a legal and institutional framework to reinforce policies of economic liberalization.

[24] Under the Aylwin administration, a municipal reform bill was passed, allowing for direct elections at the local level.

pressures, particularly in the Latin American context. Common answers include social learning from the mistakes of the past, the narrowing of ideological differences, the strength of Chile's parties, the presence of other encompassing organizations capable of pursuing collective goods, and the influence of Chile's prior experience with democratic governance (Scully 1996; Weyland 1997; Siavelis 2006, 2008).

These approaches identify important contributing factors but overlook the central role played by the constitution's countermajoritarian features and the power relations that helped enforce them. We conclude our discussion of Chile's transition by pointing to a paradox: Although many scholars now recognize the importance of incentives for consensual governance generated by the constitution's extreme countermajoritarian features, the tendency is to take a negative view of such provisions because they inhibit full democracy (Scully 1995, 1996; Linz and Stepan 1996). To be sure, democracy in Chile could not be considered consolidated until the undemocratic provisions of the constitution were removed, as Linz and Stepan (1996: 215) observe. Yet, at the same time, these provisions helped ensure that Chile's democratic transition would lead to self-enforcing democracy while preventing a disastrous return to military government. Consistent with the model, countermajoritarian provisions allowed a democratic transition without threatening the right, which maintained the power to challenge the government by taking back control at any time. The countermajoritarian institutions led to a relatively quiescent military and a center-left government that moderated its policies and protected issues deemed critical by the right. At the same time, these policies produced growth and moved toward greater equity. In combination, moderation and growth provided the opportunity for removing the most onerous countermajoritarian provisions down the line. Although Chile's countermajoritarian provisions were at the extreme end of the continuum, the larger lesson is that institutionalized protections for the interests of all key groups (particularly those with the power to subvert democracy) and the reciprocal ability to punish defections from the constitutional bargain are critical for a transition to sustainable democracy.

CONCLUSIONS

In this chapter, we study two issues at the heart of democratic development: Why do some authoritarian regimes democratize, and why do some countries sustain stable democracy? We develop a new model of democratization and show that these questions are not independent but intimately related. Members of an authoritarian regime worry not only about the immediate consequences of democratization, but also about its long-term stability, specifically whether the majority that takes over after elections will honor the constitution or subvert it. Central to our model is the insight that the design of democratic institutions is critical for stable democracy.

This view contrasts with that in the recent literature emphasized by Acemoglu and Robinson (2006) and Boix (2003). These scholars highlight the role of redistribution as a major motive for democratization, backed up by a threat from the masses to use violence and disorder as a means of forcing a rich elite to democratize. Their approach ignores the problem of upholding the constitutional bargain and maintaining democracy after a transition, when the de facto power of citizens often wanes. Understanding the creation of stable democracy requires attention to how self-enforcing democracy comes about and to the mechanisms that undergird credible commitment to constitutional bargains.

Our work is nonetheless in the spirit of this literature. Both model 1 and model 2 incorporate features of the Acemoglu and Robinson's framework, in particular the notion that an authoritarian regime initiates democracy because of the threat from the majority opposition. We then add to this framework in two ways. First, we allow democracy to occur through constitutional design with countermajoritarian features that constrain the policy discretion of the majority and protect the authoritarian regime and its constituents ex post. Second, we explicitly model the question of democratic stability. Not only must the authoritarians choose to democratize rather than retain an authoritarian regime, but, once in power, the opposition must choose not to subvert the system.

We show that the relative power of each group matters; in particular, the reciprocal nature of threats is central in explaining the adoption of a countermajoritarian constitution, *and* it helps to sustain democracy after the transition. We suggest that stable democracy arises where the opposition poses a credible threat to the authoritarian regime, but that constitutional stability occurs when the constituents of the former regime have the ability to impose sufficient costs on the new, democratic leaders if they try to subvert the constitution. Another result concerns the relative strength of the opposition. In contrast to majoritarian democracy, countermajoritarian democracy imposes lower costs on the authoritarian regime. Authoritarians will, therefore, democratize with countermajoritarian features in the face of weaker threats than they would when the only option is majoritarian democracy. In our framework, sustainable democracy is more likely to occur when countermajoritarian institutions are adopted.

Finally, we suggest that democratization is not simply about redistribution. Whereas democracy is less likely to be stable where massive redistribution is a possibility, as exhibited by Chile in 1973 and Kenya in 2008, where democratization involves constitutions containing targeted countermajoritarian features, policy is likely to be more moderate. Rather than centering on conflict involving redistribution, in our framework, sustainable democracy hinges on the ability to adopt institutions that at once allow policy change in favor of the majority but also lower the costs of adhering to the constitutional pact.

Countermajoritarian provisions are common features of successful democratizations. By reducing the stakes of political decision making, these provisions lower the probability of disruptions, in particular the probability of a coup. In contrast, many majoritarian transitions fail because the stakes are too high, resulting in disruptions or violence rather than a self-enforcing democracy. When threatened, groups use extra-constitutional actions to protect themselves, destroying democracy (Mittal and Weingast 2010).

The Chilean case illustrates the model: The new constitutional arrangements adopted at the end of the authoritarian regime gave both sides incentives to honor the countermajoritarian constitution. In particular, the opposition demonstrated that it had enough strength to challenge (disrupt) the regime in the late 1980s when it forced the regime to negotiate and initiate a transfer to civilian rule. The transition, however, occurred with extreme countermajoritarian provisions that protected the interests of the former regime's constituents on the right. The left's willingness to honor the constitution allowed it to gain power, but the countermajoritarian provisions forced it to moderate its policies. Over the long run, however, the left in power slowly came to control some of the veto enclaves and, fifteen years later, altered the constitution to remove them. Importantly, the democratically elected governments chose to alter the constitution within the provisions allowing for amendment rather than to renege on the countermajoritarian provisions and toss them out. The Chilean case also suggests the important role of countermajoritarian provisions in allowing a phased transition to democracy over more than a decade in a way that is unlikely to have occurred had the opposition been able to force majoritarian democracy.

Another feature of the Chilean case illustrates the difference between our approach and that of Acemoglu, Robinson, and Boix: In the presence of the countermajoritarian constitution, the left's moderation limited redistributive policies. The left's economic policies under its platform of "growth with equity" led to continued economic growth along with significant reductions of poverty, making a large proportion of Chilean population better off. Whereas the Allende regime prior to the 1973 coup threatened massive redistribution away from the right, the new constitutional institutions favored moderate policies that complemented economic growth. In the long run, the leftist government's moderation helped maintain support among the population while not alienating the business elite, protecting their property and businesses and promoting growth, ultimately allowing the removal of the most egregious, democracy-eroding countermajoritarian constitutional features.

Other successful democratizations illustrate both these points: the countermajoritarian features of the constitution and restraints on redistribution. The American case involved a range of strong countermajoritarian constitutional features protecting slavery, including the three-fifths clause, federalism, and the informal constitutional norm of the balance rule (Weingast 1998). The latter, for example, granted Southerners a veto over national policy making, preventing any attempt by the national government to alter rights in slaves. As the party of majority rule and free soil, the rise of the new Republican Party threatened these countermajoritarian institutions, causing Southern secession. Neither the national nor state governments engineered significant redistribution during this era, which became important only during the 1930s, nearly 150 years after the Constitution.

Another canonical case in the recent democratization literature concerns the transition in nineteenth-century Great Britain. Democracy emerged through a series of steps – the various "Reform Acts" of 1832, 1867, and 1884 and the Redistribution of Seats Act of 1885. These laws, however, created neither majoritarian democracy nor significant redistribution. Instead, they created a countermajoritarian democracy that gave a major constituency of the previous oligarchic regime a veto over policy making through the budget process (only ministers can make spending proposals) and, to an extent, the House of Lords. These processes prevented any major redistributive act. Significant redistribution did not begin with the critical Second Reform Act of 1867, but rather only after the conclusion of World War I in the twentieth century, fifty years later.[25]

We conclude with several observations concerning the importance of countermajoritarian constitutions for sustainable democracy. First, we have emphasized that countermajoritarian features in many cases make democracy more likely – the lower stakes mean the authoritarian regime and their constituents will fight less and will turn to democracy earlier if they feel the countermajoritarian features will protect them ex post. Second, the reciprocal punishment mechanisms at the heart of our model are not the only way to protect democracy and countermajoritarian restrictions. As Fearon (1995), Mittal and Weingast (2010), and Weingast (1997) show, democracy also involves a coordination problem for the opposition and the citizenry more broadly. An alternative (and potentially complementary) means of protecting the constitution arises when constitutions create focal solutions to this coordination problem so that citizens react in concert against constitutional violations, regardless of their source (that is, violations by G1 or G2). Third, creating countermajoritarian features at the inception of democratization may at first involve inimical features, including the protection of drug lords, protection of slaveholders, privileges for the military, or protection of old, large landholders who hold most of a society's wealth. As the case of Chile suggests, however, when these features create a stable regime that protects the former authoritarians, they may also help pave the way toward self-enforcing

[25] Democratization in Great Britain did not concern redistribution of wealth, but rather granting the disenfranchised the same rights as the narrow, previously enfranchised elite: rights to the courts, to participate in markets, and to be free from arbitrary actions by the elite against them.

majoritarian or moderate countermajoritarian democracy in a way that moving all at once to majoritarian democracy would fail to accomplish. Many of the historic cases of democratization involved steps toward fuller democracy, as the British case suggests.

In toto, these observations suggest that democracy is not simply about redistribution; indeed, redistribution may be a secondary motivation. Instead, countermajoritarian provisions that limit redistribution and other policies adverse to the previous authoritarian regime and its supporters are often at the core of successful democratization.

ACKNOWLEDGMENTS

The authors thank Roger Myerson, Kenneth Shepsle, and Jed Stiglitz for helpful comments. Weingast gratefully acknowledges the John Templeton Foundation for partial support.

REFERENCES

Acemoglu, Daron and James Robinson. 2001. "A Theory of Political Transitions." *The American Economic Review* 91 (4): 938–63.

2006. *Economic Origins of Dictatorship and Democracy*. Cambridge: Cambridge University Press.

Alberts, Susan. 2008. "Why Play by the Rules? Constitutionalism and Democratic Institutionalization in Ecuador and Uruguay." *Democratization* 15 (5): 850–67.

2009. "How Constitutions Constrain." *Comparative Politics* 41 (2): 122–43.

Barros, Robert. 2002. *Constitutionalism and Dictatorship*. Cambridge: Cambridge University Press.

Boix, Carles. 2003. *Democracy and Redistribution*. Cambridge: Cambridge University Press.

Boylan, Delia M. 1996. "Taxation and Transition: The Politics of the 1990 Chilean Tax Reform." *Latin American Research Review* 1: 7–31.

Carr, Raymond and Juan Pablo Fusi. 1981. *Spain: Dictatorship to Democracy*, 2nd ed. London: George Allen and Unwin.

Collier, David and Steven Levitsky. 1997. "Democracy with Adjectives: Conceptual Innovation in Comparative Research." *World Politics* 49 (3): 430–51.

Coppedge, Michael. 1994. "Venezuela: Democratic Despite Presidentialism." In Juan J. Linz and Arturo Valenzuela, eds. *The Failure of Presidential Democracy in Latin America: The Case of Latin America*. Baltimore: The Johns Hopkins University Press.

Cox, Gary W. 2009. "Authoritarian Elections and Leadership Succession, 1975–2004." Paper prepared for delivery at the Annual Meetings of the American Political Science Association Meetings, Toronto, Canada, September 3–6.

Diamond, Larry. 2008. *The Spirit of Democracy*. New York: Harry Holt and Co.

Elkins, Zachary, Tom Ginsburg, and James Melton. 2008. *The Endurance of National Constitutions*. Cambridge: Cambridge University Press.

Fearon, James D. 1995. "Rationalist Explanations for War." *International Organization* 49 (Summer): 379–414.

Fogel, Robert William. 1989. *Without Consent or Contract: The Rise and Fall of American Slavery*. New York: W.W. Norton.
Garreton, Manuel Antonio. 1986. "The Political Evolution of the Chilean Military Regime and Problems in the Transition to Democracy." In Guillermo O'Donnell, Philippe C. Schmitter, and Laurence Whitehead, eds. *Transitions from Authoritarian Rule: Latin America*. Baltimore: The Johns Hopkins University Press.
Haber, Stephen, Armando Raxo, and Noel Maurer. 2003. *The Politics of Property rights: Political Instability, Credible commitments, and Economic growth in Mexico*. Cambridge: Cambridge University Press.
Higley John and Richard Gunther, eds. 1992. *Elites and Democratic Consolidation in Latin America and Southern Europe*. New York: Cambridge University Press.
Huntington, Samuel P. 1991. *The Third Wave: Democracy in the Late Twentieth Century*. Norman: The University of Oklahoma Press.
Inman, Robert P. and Daniel L. Rubinfeld. 2008. "Federal Institutions and the Democratic Transition: Learning from South Africa." NBER Working Paper No. 13733.
Latin American Weekly Reports, http://www.latinnews.com
Lijphart, Arend. 1977. *Democracy in Plural Societies: A Comparative Exploration*. New Haven, CT: Yale University Press.
Linz, Juan J. 1990. "Transitions to Democracy." *The Washington Quarterly* 13 (3): 143–62.
Linz, Juan J. and Alfred Stepan. 1996. *Problems of Democratic Transition and Consolidation*. Baltimore: The Johns Hopkins University Press.
Londregan, John. 2000. *Legislative Institutions and Ideology in Chile*. New York: Cambridge University Press.
Magaloni, Beatriz. 2008. "Credible Power Sharing and the Longevity of Authoritarian Rule." *Comparative Political Studies* 41 (April): 715–41.
Mittal, Sonia and Barry R. Weingast. 2010. "Self-Enforcing Democracy." Working Paper, Hoover Institution, Stanford University.
O'Donnell, Guillermo and Philippe C. Schmitter. 1986. *Transitions from Authoritarian Rule: Tentative Conclusions about Uncertain Democracies*. Baltimore: The Johns Hopkins University Press.
Rabkin, Rhoda. 1992. "The Aylwin Government and 'Tutelary' Democracy: A Concept in Search of a Case." *Journal of Interamerican Studies and World Affairs* 34 (4): 119–94.
Schlesinger, Arthur Meier, Sr. 1922. "The State Rights Fetish," in Arthur M. Schlesinger, Sr. ed. *New Viewpoints in American History*. New York: Macmillan.
Scully, Timothy. 1995. "Reconstituting Party Politics in Chile." In Scott Mainwaring and Timothy Scully, eds. *Building Democratic Institutions in Latin America*. Stanford, CA: Stanford University Press.
1996. "Chile: The Political Underpinnings of Economic Liberalization." In Jorge I. Dominguez and Abraham F. Lowenthal, eds. *Constructing Democratic Governance: South America in the 1990s*. Baltimore: The Johns Hopkins University Press.
Siavelis, Peter. 2008. "Chile: The End of the Unfinished Transition." In Jorge I. Dominguez and Michael Shifter, eds. *Constructing Democratic Governance in Latin America*. Baltimore: The Johns Hopkins University Press.
2006. "Accommodating Informal Institutions and Democracy in Chile." In Gretchen Helmke and Steven Levitsky, eds. *Informal Institutions and Democracy: Lessons from Latin America*. Baltimore: Johns Hopkins University Press.

Valenzuela, Arturo. 1990. "Chile: Origins, Consolidation and Breakdown of a Democratic System." In Larry Diamond, Juan Linz, and Seymour Martin Lipset, eds. *Politics in Developing Countries: Latin America*. Boulder, CO: Lynne Rienner.

1994. "Chile: Government and Politics." In Rex A. Hudson, ed. *Chile: A Country Study*. Washington, DC: Federal Research Division, Library of Congress.

Weingast, Barry R. 1997. "The Political Foundations of Democracy and the Rule of Law." *American Political Science Review* 91: 245–63.

1998. "Political Stability and Civil War: Institutions, Commitment, and American Democracy." In Robert Bates, Avner Greif, Margaret Levi, Jean-Laurent Rosenthal, and Barry R. Weingast, eds. *Analytic Narratives*. Princeton, NJ: Princeton University Press.

2004. "Constructing Self Enforcing Democracy in Spain." In Irwin L. Morris, Joe A. Oppenheimer, and Karol Edward Soltan, eds. *Politics: From Anarchy to Democracy*. Stanford, CA: Stanford University Press.

Weyland, Kurt. 1997. "Growth with Equity in Chile's New Democracy." *Latin American Research Review* 32 (1): 37–67.

5

The Origins of Parliamentary Responsibility

Adam Przeworski, Tamar Asadurian, and Anjali Thomas Bohlken

"Toute Constitution est un régicide."
l'abbé Rauzan, quoted in de Wasquerel and Yvert 2002: 61

INTRODUCTION

The topic of this chapter is the origins of government responsibility to parliaments, the shift of the power to appoint governments from the monarch to elected assemblies. Whereas one can adduce several reasons to study the history of parliamentary responsibility, the motivation here is most trivial, namely that it has not been done, or at least not done well.[1] As luck would have it, however, histories of constitutional monarchies turn out to be mischievously subversive: Countries in which the principle of parliamentary responsibility was written into constitutions did not practice it, whereas some practiced it long before it was constitutionalized. Thus questions abound: Why write a constitution that would not be observed? Why constitutionalize a status quo that is already an equilibrium without being written down? And the elephant in the room: What, if any, is the effect of constitutions on the actual political practices?

The text is organized as follows. Parliamentary responsibility is defined and constitutions of monarchies are described first. The structure of conflicts engendered by these constitutions is then analyzed and the feasible historical paths of constitutional monarchies are distinguished. Finally, the actual histories are summarized.

[1] There are surprisingly few comparative studies of the subject. In spite of its subtitle that promises to cover the period from 1789 to 1999, von Beyme's (2000) book devotes only one chapter to historical evolution, summarizing it in rather cursory tables. Lavaux (1998) is perhaps the most informative but he, as well as Van Caenegem (1995), focus on selected cases. Herb (2004) compares some Western European cases to the Middle Eastern monarchies. Some papers by economists (Congleton 2007; Huang 2008) offer promising titles but are too abstract to be useful here.

For lazy readers, sketches of histories of particular countries are relegated to the Appendix, but the devil is in the detail, so they should be consulted.

PARLIAMENTARY RESPONSIBILITY

The origins of parliamentary responsibility are a slippery topic for two reasons: the ambiguity between legal and political responsibility of governments, and the fact that the practice did not always correspond to the law. Already Hegel, in the essay on "The Reform Bill," observed that, in spite of the constitutional rights of the crown, formation of the ministry was the center of contestation in the monarchical systems (Lavaux 1998: 53). This contestation makes it difficult to date the rise of parliamentary government. In England, for example, it can be dated to the Glorious Revolution of 1688, the explicit recognition of the principle of parliamentary responsibility in a speech in the House of Lords in 1711 (Lavaux 1998: 188), the first collective resignation of the cabinet of Lord North in 1782, the formation of the first explicitly partisan government by Pitt in 1803, or the reinstatement of the Melbourne government after the election of 1834. Such ambiguities arise in several countries.

To define parliamentary responsibility – that is, collective political responsibility of governments to the parliament – it is necessary to distinguish it from other mechanisms of responsibility. In turn, to date its origins, one must be able to discern which of the episodes in which governments changed partisan colors were just contingent outcomes of interplay of forces and which constituted an application of principles, informal conventions, or legal norms. Clearly, the uncertainty is resolved if and when norms are enshrined in laws and the laws are complied with, but, as we shall see in what follows, several countries experienced periods in which parliamentary responsibility was practiced without being legalized whereas in some other countries it was constitutionalized but not practiced. Note that the practice of parliamentary responsibility is observable only if an opposition to the forces supported by the monarch becomes majoritarian in the parliament: If the opposition does not win, we cannot observe whether it would have been allowed to assume office had it won.

In all monarchical constitutions, the monarch was the chief executive. He or she was not responsible to the parliament or the courts. De Lolme's (2002: 59) argument – the "King himself cannot be arraigned before Judges; because, if there were any that could pass sentence upon him, it would be they, and not he, who must finally possess the executive power" – was standard. The monarch governed assisted by his ministers, councilors, or advisers, whom he could choose. But whereas the person of the King was inviolable, ministers were "responsible." The French Constitutions of 1814 and 1830 were prototypical: "The person of the King is inviolable and sacred. To the King belongs the executive power. His ministers are responsible" (Articles 13 and 14 in 1814; 12 and 13 in 1830).

What that meant is far from clear, and often it was not clear to the constitution writers themselves (Wasquerel and Yvert 2002). It is necessary to distinguish (1) the actions for which ministers were responsible, (2) the procedures according to which they could be held responsible, (3) the sanctions to which the ministers were subject, and (4) whether their responsibility was individual or collective. To anticipate, *parliamentary responsibility is a mechanism in which (1) the actions for which the government is responsible are not specified ex ante (the sanctioning body, which is the legislature, does not have to specify any reasons for invoking responsibility); (2) the procedure is some version of vote of no confidence (the requirement to remain in office is that the government cannot be formally rejected by a majority of the legislature); (3) the only sanction is that ministers must leave office (but may return); and (4) the responsibility is collective.* Thus defined, parliamentary responsibility may coexist with other mechanisms but is distinct from them. Importantly, the actions for which ministers are held responsible may be political whereas the procedure for exacting responsibility may still be legal, as in the 1815 model of Benjamin Constant.

As with many distinctions, these are easier to make than to apply. Typically, in the European monarchical constitutions:

1. Although the actions for which ministers could be held responsible may have been defined broadly and loosely, the ministers had to be accused of having committed (or omitted) previously specified acts. In England, according to De Lolme (2002: 59), ministers could be prosecuted for spending money in a manner contrary to the declared intention of the Parliament, "any abuse of power … or, in general, anything done contrary to the public weal." The Swedish Constitution of 1720 (article 14) also defined responsibility in terms so general that it comprised political acts. The Jordanian Constitution of 1952 (article 51) specifies that the government is responsible "in respect of the public policy of the State." In contrast, the French *Charte* of 1814 (article 56) specified that ministers "can be accused only for the fact of treason or corruption (concussion)." The Prussian Constitution of 1850 specified that "To be valid, all the acts of the King's government need to be signed by a minister, who in this way assumes responsibility for them," but this "responsibility" was to be defined by ordinary legislation, which never came (Schmitt 1993: 478). Thus the sanctionable actions may have been purely criminal (treason, corruption) or may have been also political ("anything done contrary to the public weal"). Responsibility, however, applied only to previously specified actions.
2. The procedure was everywhere one of "impeachment" or "censure" – that is, legal. Both the 1814 and the 1830 French constitutions gave the *Chambre des députés* the right to accuse ministers before the *Chambre des pairs*, which

would judge them. According to the Norwegian 1814 constitution, the lower house served as the accuser and a specially formed court adjudicated.

3. Almost everywhere, the sanctions were only political – that is, removal from office. The Norwegian Constitution of 1814 is unique, according to Elster (2007a), in that, "In theory, an accused politician could be sentenced to prison. That has never happened, but fines and removal from office have been imposed in several cases. The most frequent charge has been the government's neglect to provide parliament with the information it needs to enact laws."
4. The responsibility was individual. For example, in France in 1815, when an eminent prisoner condemned to death easily escaped from prison, the *Chambre* initiated an investigation against the Minister of Police, Decazes. The typical reference was to the "Ministry," which was a collection of individual ministers, not necessarily hierarchical or disciplined. In the German Constitution of 1871 (article 17), only the Chancellor was "responsible." In Sweden, two ministers of equal status were. In contrast, collective responsibility means that members of the government must publicly support its collective decisions and, in consequence, are jointly responsible for all decisions. The difference between individual and collective responsibility is illustrated by the contrast between Article 13 of the French Constitution of 1852, which says, "Each minister is responsible only for those acts of the government which concerns him; there is no solidarity among them," and Article 6 of the (republican) constitution of 1875, according to which, "The ministers are solidaristically responsible … for the general policy of the Government and individually for their personal acts."

To get an intuition of the ambiguities such systems generated, examine the Swedish Constitution of 1809. It stated that, "The King alone shall govern the realm," that the king can dismiss ministers, who are his advisers, and has a qualified right to dismiss the parliament. The parliament could not call the king to account for his conduct (Article 3). Yet all executive acts were to be countersigned by a minister and ministers were obliged to object against king's unconstitutional actions. The parliament could impeach a minister in case of "manifest violation of the fundamental laws or failure to refuse countersignature." Article 9 stated that, "Should at any time the unexpected event occur that the King's decision would be plainly contrary to the fundamental or general laws of the realm, it shall be the duty of the members of the Council of State to make a vigorous protest against such decision. Any member who does not separately enter his opinion in the minutes shall be held for the decision as if he had advised the King to make it." Article 38 specified that, "Should a Minister presenting a matter think that any order of the King is in conflict with the Constitution, he shall remonstrate against in the Council of State: if the King should still insist upon issuing the order it shall be the Minister's right and duty to refuse the countersignature thereto and, as a consequence, to resign from his office which he shall not resume until Parliament has examined and approved his conduct." Parliament controlled the Council of Ministers through its Constitution Committee, which examined the minutes of the Council of State (or King-in-Council). If the Committee discovered that there had been a manifest violation of the fundamental laws or failure to refuse countersignature, as indicated in Article 38, it was to instruct Parliament's Office of Justice to impeach the minister before the Court of Impeachment (Article 106). Where there was a less serious misdemeanor, such as "the failure of the Minister or even the whole Council of State to pay due regard to the welfare of the State," the Constitutional Committee was to bring the matter before parliament, which could request the King in writing to remove from the Council of State and from office the person or persons criticized (Article 107). The latter was known as the "political responsibility" in contrast to the "juridical responsibility" of Article 106.

KINGS AGAINST PARLIAMENTS

Constitutional monarchs were chief executives, not responsible to anyone in any manner, who governed with the advice and consent of their ministers. Parliaments could at most impeach or censure individual ministers for having committed previously specified acts. Yet there were many instances in which parliamentary majorities forced monarchs to dismiss or accept governments against their will. As Schmitt (1993: 475) observed, the difference between the practice of parliamentary responsibility in Belgium, as opposed to France or Prussia, "was not due to legal dispositions, but to its use in the public life of the nation. It is a practical rule which resides in the spirit of the constitution; the latter says nothing of it."

The power of the parliaments stemmed from their control over legislation, particularly budgets. Monarchs needed money to govern. Control over the budget by the parliament was a central feature of the "English constitution": The very existence of the Commons, De Lolme (2002: 54) argued in 1771, depended on its exercise of this prerogative. Moreover, "If any other person, besides the Representatives of the People, had a right to make an offer of the produce of labour of the people, the executive power would soon have forgot, that it only exists for the advantage of the public." Already in 1626, the Commons refused to approve the budget unless the unpopular Buckingham was dismissed by the King (von Beyme 2000: 23). So did the Belgian second chamber in 1841, the Swedish *Rikstag* in 1868, German *Reichstag* in 1887, 1892, and 1907, and many others.

Hence, parliaments had a powerful instrument to impose their wills on the monarchs. They could use it not only to control expenditures but to pressure the king to choose ministers to their liking. And because parliaments used or threatened to use this power, kings at times considered their wishes. Historians tell us that in Sweden, "after 1840, the King had to pay attention in choosing Ministers" (Verney 1957); in Belgium, "The principle was soon established that a cabinet had to have the support of a majority not only in the House of Representatives, the predominant chamber, but also in the Senate." (Lorwin 1966: 119); in Great Britain, "The executive, which used to be in the hands of the King and his secretaries, passed to the cabinet of ministers, who were politicians" (Van Caenegen 1995: 120). Yet when the Prussian parliament refused to approve the budget in 1862 and in 1866, the government continued to manage without the budget, presenting the situation as abnormal but not unconstitutional (Schmitt 1993: 478). The same happened in Denmark, where in 1877 and between 1885 and 1894, the Conservative leader, Elstrup, prorogued Parliament and on his own responsibility issued a provisional budget (Jespersen 2004: 67).

In turn, except in Norway, kings could dismiss parliaments. Incumbent governments managed elections and could use the apparatus and the resources of the state to secure a desired outcome, so monarchs often used this prerogative to bring the composition of the parliament closer to their wishes. Most of the time they succeeded: Elections were administered by the Ministry of Interior and validated by the newly elected legislature (Lehoucq 2003), so winning them was not very difficult. In several countries, control over the elections was so perfect that a regular alternation between parties was orchestrated from above. The favor of these arrangements is best captured by Garrido (1998: 218), writing about Spain: "The electorate did not elect Parliament, and it did not elect the government. The system worked from 'top to bottom': the King named his head of government, who convoked elections, which had, of necessity, to bestow a large majority on his party."

Hence seeds of conflict were built into this system: The king appointed the ministers but did not control the budget; parliaments held the purse but could not choose the ministers; the king could dissolve the parliament.

It is useful to analyze this structure of conflicts somewhat schematically. First, looking at the situation from the point of view of monarchs, it is obvious that ideally they would want to appoint whatever governments were to their liking and to have their budgets approved by parliaments. Having to tolerate governments chosen by parliaments against their will was not only unpleasant but was often seen as an affront against royal majesty. Nevertheless, facing a hostile government was preferable to not having a budget, particularly a budget for military expenditures. Finally, the worst possible outcome would have been for the monarch to be deposed or the monarchy abolished.

Now, as long as the pro-royalist forces won elections, the issue of parliamentary responsibility was not on the table. The issue appeared on the political agenda only when pro-royalist governments were not able to pass important legislation. Thus, for example, in France in 1827, "For the first time since 1814, the royal power found itself in face of majoritarian opposition. The question that was latent since the origins of the regime between royal and parliamentary preponderance is directly posed" (de Wasquerel and Yvert 2002: 396). The choices available to monarchs in such situations included: (1) dissolving the parliament and calling for a new election; (2) suppressing the parliament, either by dissolving it sine diem, or changing electoral rules by decree and holding a new election under the changed rules (as did Tsar Nicolai II in 1907 and King Hussain of Jordan in 1993), or taking power directly into their own hands; or (3) yielding to the parliament in choosing the government.

These actions were not without political consequences. Dissolutions bore the risk that the royalist force would do even worse in the subsequent election. Changing electoral rules by executive decree reduced this risk but generated a new one, namely that the repression would engender opposition by those charged with exercising it, and that the military might take power into their own hands, or that it would intensify popular opposition, bringing the population to the streets. Monarchs ran some risk of being deposed even when they won elections, but repression intensified this risk, as witnessed by the fate of Charles X, Prince Alexander of Bulgaria, King Gyanendra of Nepal, and several others who entered on this path. Hence, when choosing the course of action following an electoral defeat, monarchs had to look at political consequences beyond the immediate moment.

Assume now that monarchs did what they thought was best for them, whether dissolve, suppress, or yield. Histories of constitutional monarchies may have followed any of several diverse sequences of such actions, where in the end monarchs would either yield – that is, adopt the practice of parliamentary responsibility – or be overthrown. As varied as these sequences may have been, however, it is apparent that the feasible historical paths of constitutional monarchies fall into three patterns:

1. The principle of parliamentary responsibility is not tested because the monarch never loses elections or wins every election after a dissolution. Note that monarchs who always win elections can be still overthrown.
2. The monarch loses some elections, mixes dissolutions and suppressions when he loses, and is overthrown.
3. The monarch loses some elections, mixes dissolutions and suppressions, survives, and at one time yields.

Of these paths, only the last one leads to parliamentary monarchies. In the first path, the principle is never tested and, as seen in the later discussion, monarchy was abolished or stripped of executive power in all countries that followed this pattern. The second path leads to republican revolutions. Monarchs end up reigning but not governing only along the third path.

CONSTITUTIONS AND PRACTICES

Constitutional monarchies are systems in which the head of state bears a title of monarch and which have a constitution providing for an at least partially elected legislature with a power to approve the budget. Only those countries that were independent as constitutional monarchies are included in the following discussion, which explains the absence of Tunisia, which passed an abortive constitution in 1861.

The paths to parliamentary monarchy turned out to be narrow: Of the thirty-two countries that at one time established a constitutional monarchy, eighteen are now republics. It was traversed only in Belgium, Denmark, Japan (where the Emperor lost even the nominal executive power in 1947), Lesotho (where the monarch lost executive power in 1993), Netherlands, Norway, Sweden (where the monarch lost executive power in 1974), Thailand, and the United Kingdom. Monarchy was reestablished in Spain in 1978, but the monarch has no executive power. Jordan, Kuwait, Morocco, and Swaziland continue as monarchies in which the monarchs appoint and dismiss governments at their discretion.

Table 5.1 presents a summary of the histories of particular monarchies.

The constitutions (or other organic laws) of Serbia in 1869, Iran in 1907, Egypt in 1923, Iraq in 1925, Albania in 1928, Thailand in 1932, Jordan in 1952, Morocco in 1962 and 1996, Nepal in 1959 and 1980, and Lesotho in 1966 provided for the principle of parliamentary responsibility, with explicit procedures of nonconfidence. Periods in which oppositions to the monarch were allowed to govern occurred, however, only in Serbia between 1903 and 1918 and in Nepal between 1991 and 2008, albeit with a royal coup d'état in 2005. The history of Thailand is convoluted because of the active role of the military, which alternated with civilians in claiming royal support. In the remaining countries and periods, this constitutional norm was observed only if the parliamentary majority was royalist, which was always true in Albania as well as Iraq and most of the time in the rest of the countries listed. When the royalist parties did not enjoy sufficient support in the parliament, monarch dissolved parliaments and either won the subsequent elections or ruled without legislatures. In Iran, the parliament was dismissed whenever monarchs were displeased with their actions and monarchs assumed dictatorial powers in 1907, 1911–1914, 1949–1951, and 1961–1963. In Jordan, King Hussain allowed the National Socialist opposition to form a government in 1956, but sacked the government and declared martial law as soon as he was reassured of the support of the army one year later. The parliament was restored only in 1983 and political parties were legalized only in 1992, but the king changed the electoral laws before the multiparty elections of 1993, and pro-royalist forces won all subsequent elections. In Morocco, when the opposition UNFP won the election in 1965, King Hassan II suspended the parliament and served as his own prime minister

TABLE 5.1. *Summary of constitutions and practices*

Law/Practice	Yes	No	Not tested
Yes	Thailand 1932–	Iran 1907–1979	Albania 1928–1946
Yes	Nepal 1990–2008	Jordan 1952–	Iraq 1925–1958
Yes	Serbia 1903–1918	Morocco 1962–1970	
Yes		Morocco 1996–	
Yes		Nepal 1959–1962	
Yes		Egypt 1923–1952	
Yes		Serbia 1869–1903	
Yes		Lesotho 1966–1993	
No	Belgium 1847–1892	Austria 1867–1918	Bulgaria 1887–1918
No	Denmark 1901–1953	Brazil 1824–1891	France 1830–1848
No	Netherlands 1868–	Bulgaria 1878–1886	France 1852–1870
No	Norway 1884–	Bulgaria 1918–1947	Germany 1871–1918
No	Sweden 1917–1974	France 1815–1830	Japan 1887–1947
No	United Kingdom 1834–	Hungary 1867–1918	Portugal 1822–1910
No	Greece 1875–1910	Nepal 1962–1990	Spain
No	Italy 1861–1925	Ottoman 1876–1920	
No		Romania 1866–1947	
No		Russia 1906–1917	
No		Yugoslavia 1921–1945	
No		Kuwait 1962–	
No		Swaziland 1968–	

Notes: "Law" indicates whether the principle of parliamentary responsibility was present in a constitution, where the test of the principle is whether a constitution provides for a procedure of nonconfidence. "Practice" is classified as "No" unless there were periods in which governments not supported by monarchs were allowed to govern and the parliament served a full term. Cases in which constitutionalization followed practice are not listed. The unit of observation is the continuous constitutional status of parliamentary responsibility or a dynasty.

during two years. The opposition won the plurality election in 1998 and formed the government, but this event is generally considered to have been engineered by the king. In Nepal, the opposition Nepal Congress party won a majority in 1959 and formed the government, but in the following year the king suspended the parliament, appointed his own Cabinet, and ruled directly. Political parties were legalized in 1990, and governments were supported by shifting parliamentary majorities until 2005, when King Gyanendra took office in a royal coup d'état. Although power was restored to the parliament one year later, the monarchy was abolished in 2008. In Lesotho, the constitution was suspended as soon as an opposition party seemed to be winning the first election after independence in 1970. In the end, all the constitutions that provided for parliamentary responsibility were violated, in several countries repeatedly. Why write down rules that would not be obeyed?

In turn, the principle of parliamentary responsibility was absent from all European monarchical constitutions. The principle was perhaps for the first time tacitly recognized in the United Kingdom in 1834. With time, it was explicitly accepted and regularly practiced in several European countries: The best dates seem to be 1847 in Belgium (where the constitution dated to 1831), 1861 in Italy (1861), 1868 in the Netherlands (1815), 1875 in Greece (1844), 1884 in Norway (1814), 1901 in Denmark (1849, 1866), and 1917 in Sweden (1809). Hence, the practice developed without constitutional changes. Indeed, the principle of submitting governments to the will of parliamentary majorities was either constitutionalized only decades after it was well entrenched or continues until today without being constitutionalized: in Belgium in 1892 (see later in the chapter), Denmark in 1953, Norway either in 1928 or not until now (see later in the chapter), Sweden in 1974, and not until now in the Netherlands and the United Kingdom. Why write down as a formal rule something that has been practiced and would continue to be practiced without it? If constitutions only describe equilibria, why write down the rules that political actors follow anyway?

The dating of when parliamentary responsibility became a norm, convention, or principle that everyone expected to be obeyed is obviously problematic. Isolated instances in which monarchs consented to governments that were against their liking do not suffice to treat parliamentary responsibility as a principle regulating the existence of governments. After all, Charles X yielded in 1828 but two years later had to be reminded that, in the words of the French Chambre of 1830, "The permanent harmony of the political views of your Government with the wishes of your people is the indispensable condition for the conduct of public affairs. Sire, our loyalty, our devotion oblige us to tell you that this harmony does not exist" (cited in Bury 1962: 39). Kings Hussain of Jordan, Hassan of Morocco, Mahendra of Nepal, Fuad of Egypt, and several others at one time allowed the opposition to form the government only to clamp down soon after. Hence, sporadic instances in which monarchs yielded to parliamentary majorities do not necessarily indicate that they were ready to do so in the future. The problem is to distinguish periods in which the outcomes of conflicts were purely contingent on the relations of political forces from periods during which these outcomes were regulated by unwritten constitutional norms, or in Elster's (2007a) terms, "constitutional conventions." As he observes, such norms do not emerge through the sheer passage of time. Something more is needed. This "something" is that: (1) "Unwritten norms cannot have causal efficacy unless one believes that other relevant actors believe in them and will act on them"; (2) "For their existence, CC [constitutional conventions] require that individuals hold true beliefs (or at least do not hold false beliefs) about how others will react to a violation"; (3) "If violating a norm causes no reaction … it never existed in the first place" (Elster 2007a, various pages). The first two criteria add up to saying that constitutional conventions support equilibria: Everyone knows that everyone knows what others will do in and out of equilibrium. The third criterion, in turn, implies that if we were to observe an out-of-equilibrium action – that is, a violation of the convention – we should also observe a reaction. An example is provided by Denmark, where parliamentary responsibility was accepted as a principle in 1901 but was not codified until 1953, and where in 1920 Christian X decided on his own initiative to dismiss the government and appoint another without backing by the parliament, only to be defeated in the face of popular unrest (Jespersen 2004: 79). It may thus appear that this criterion provides an observational principle for determining whether a convention was in place. Yet it fails to do so because it does not imply its converse: An action to a unilateral imposition by a king need not constitute a reaction against violation of a norm. Charles X was overthrown in 1830 when he attempted to impose his will, but he may not have been; his successor dissolved the parliament four times, won the subsequent elections, and did not provoke a reaction. In the end, we have no way of knowing whether no convention was in place or it was in place but was violated. Hence, the dates used here are, of necessity, somewhat arbitrary: These seem to be the best dates, because many people thought at the time that a principle was at stake and because historians think, in retrospect, that it was. Moreover, except for Greece, all governments subsequent to these dates enjoyed parliamentary support regardless of the outcomes of elections.

In sum, except for short periods in Serbia and Nepal, when constitutions provided for parliamentary responsibility, it was not practiced, whereas in other countries, the practice took hold without having been constitutionalized. The power of constitutions thus appears paltry. What, then, is the role of constitutions in regulating political life? Neither Elster's (1984, but see 2007b) view of constitutions as commitments nor Hardin's (1989, also Kornhauser 1999) argument that constitutions pick one coordination equilibrium among several are supported by the experience of monarchical constitutions. At most, constitutions construct a game – grant institutional status to players and attribute to each a set of actions – within which different outcomes may ensue, depending on exogenous conditions, their hunger for power, and perhaps also luck. Certainly, the future of monarchies could not be predicted by reading their constitutions. What was inexorable was that the monarchs would lose power, but whether they would also lose the crown was not foretold.

Why did some monarchies succeed is losing power but preserving the crown while others lost both? In the end, l'abbé Rauzan was right: Once they constitutionalized their rule, monarchs could not keep power and survive. The monarchs who were too good at using the state apparatus to manage elections – and many were – saw their monarchies abolished. Those who clung to power when they happened to have lost also ended being overthrown. To keep the crown on their heads, they had to know when to give up. They did not like it. King Wilhelm of Netherlands abdicated rather than accept a parliamentary government, as did King Prajadhikop of Thailand, whereas Queen Victoria was insulted by having to accept it. So only a handful had the wisdom of embarking on the road to oblivion.

Conflicts over government responsibility were sharp, often violent, but in retrospect they appear strangely inconsequential. Parliamentary republics these days are indistinguishable from parliamentary monarchies: Whether the ceremonial head of state is elected by the parliament or inherits her mantle seems to have no practical consequences. Antimonarchical sentiments are at times fed by royal families intruding into the news, but juicy stories about the lives of the royals are just a folklore of parliamentary monarchies. The sharpest line distinguishing political regimes in the nineteenth century – monarchies versus republics – has been completely effaced.

Again ironically, the structure of conflicts that permeated constitutional monarchies is endemic in presidential systems: The president chooses the cabinet, the legislature controls the budget, the president needs the budget to govern, the legislature has preferences about the cabinet. Hence, the strategies and the conflicts that ensue are similar to those of monarchies. In Chile in 1881, for example, "a group of deputies attempted to cut off funds for the war effort, as a means of pressuring [President] Pinto to reshuffle his cabinet" (Collier and Sater 1996: 145). In 1890, the Congress rejected a budget proposal of President Balmaceda, who then announced that he would govern with previous year's budget, which was not enabled by the constitution. In response, the Senate threatened to impeach the president, for which it did not have constitutional authority either. A civil war ensued, in which about 3,000 people were killed, and Balmaceda was deposed. Simon Bolívar had it right when he remarked, "We elect monarchs whom we call presidents." True, presidents are elected, but it is not obvious that this fact changes the strategic situation. In turn, with minor exceptions, presidents do not have dissolution power, which means that if they are stuck with a hostile legislature, they have to wait until the next scheduled election. But, contrary to Linz (1994), this structure induces presidents to be more conciliatory than were monarchs, building government coalitions and making policy concessions (Cheibub, Przeworski, and Saiegh 2004). Perhaps this explains why no presidential system in history evolved into a parliamentary one.

APPENDIX: HISTORICAL PATHS

Principle Not Tested, Dynasty Deposed or Monarchy Abolished

Never Lost

In these cases, the principle was never tested because either anti-royalist forces never won an election or each time they had won the parliament was dissolved and pro-royalists won the ensuing elections.

Albania: The 1928 constitution replaced the republic established in 1925 with monarchy. According to this constitution, executive power was vested in the king, to be exercised through the government, which had to maintain the confidence of the parliament (Article 113: "A Cabinet which does not obtain a vote of confidence from Parliament is obliged to hand in its resignation to the King.") In practice, King Zog (who reigned from 1928 to 1939) changed his ministers at will, and because political competition was not permitted, "parliament was an assembly of handpicked individuals … entirely dependent upon the King" (Skendi 1957: 95). The pro-Zog parties won elections in 1928, 1932, and 1937. In 1935, the King made a conciliatory move and allowed the formation of a new "relatively liberal" government. However, when a vote of no confidence – probably inspired by King Zog – brought the new cabinet to an end, Zog gave the office back to the original holder, and elections in 1937 produced unanimous support for the government (Fischer 1984: 244–47). Monarchy was abolished in 1946.

France, 1830–1848: The 1830 Constitution did not provide for parliamentary responsibility. Several governments fell, however, when they lost an important – budget or foreign policy – vote in the *Chambre*. Still, they were always replaced by cabinets appointed by the King. At four moments (in 1831, 1834, 1837, and 1839), Louis Philippe resorted to dissolving the parliament, hoping to solidify his parliamentary support, but all elections that followed dissolutions resulted in reproducing the balance of forces – that is, a small margin in favor of the incumbent government. The monarchy was abolished in 1848, to be followed by a short-lived republic.

France, 1852–1870: The 1852 Constitution did not provide for parliamentary responsibility. The government won all elections during the Second Empire. Napoleon III introduced parliamentary responsibility on May 21, 1870, but too late to prevent his overthrow and with him of the monarchy.

Germany: The Constitution of 1871 recognized only the Reich Chancellor as a minister, giving him the responsibility for cosigning laws. The Reichstag was dissolved in 1887 when it refused to approve military appropriations. In the ensuing election, the government won. The same occurred in 1892 and in 1907. In a sequel to the 1907 election, Bülow created a parliamentary bloc and changed the cabinet to get its support. According to Carr (1969: 206), "[T]his was the first firm association between a government and the majority parties and, as such, a step on the road to parliamentary government. When the *bloc* threatened to fall apart in December 1907, Bülow summoned party leaders and threatened resignation unless they continued to support him; in other words, a chancellor made his continuation in office dependent, not on the emperor's pleasure, but on the willingness of majority parties to cooperate with him." In 1909, a finance bill was defeated and Bülow resigned. Quoting Carr (1969: 208) again, "the manner of his departure was important, for, unwittingly perhaps, he had established some kind of causal relationship between resignation and the defeat of a government bill." However, his successor was still appointed by the Emperor. The phrase "The Chancellor of the Reich requires the confidence of the Reichstag to exercise his functions" was first introduced as an amendment to the 1871 Constitution on October 18, 1918 and then incorporated (as article 54) into the Weimar Constitution, after the monarchy had been abolished.

Iraq: The original Iraqi constitution was drafted by the British in 1921, and the final version was adopted by an elected Constituent Assembly in 1925. According to Brown (2002: 43), it provided for parliamentary responsibility, with explicit procedures of nonconfidence. Yet no government, not even a single minister, was dismissed because of a parliamentary vote of nonconfidence. The military entered into politics in the late 1930s, but the constitution remained in force until 1958, when the monarchy was abolished.

Rotation

In several countries, during sometimes long periods, control over governments rotated between parties or factions either according to a preestablished agreement or as a consequence of monarchs seeking to maintain a balance between them. In such systems, the monarch appointed governments of parties different from the incumbents either just before a scheduled election or before dissolving the parliament. The new government would then administer the election and invariably win.

One can think differently about such systems. On the one hand, the monarch exercised total control over the choice of governments. On the other hand, the monarch felt obliged to change their partisan composition. If one thinks that the monarch was just accurately reading the mood of the political elite, he was anticipating the results that would have ensued in competitive elections, which may be seen as anticipatory parliamentary responsibility: Governments rotated and always enjoyed parliamentary support. Yet only governments that were palatable to the monarch participated in the rotation, so even if they bore different labels, they were all pro-royalist.

Note that not all cases of rotation are included in this section. If rotation was followed by suppression, they are included in the "Suppression" section (Austria, Romania).

Brazil: The 1824 Constitution (Article 101, paragraph VI) granted the emperor unlimited freedom to appoint and dismiss governments. The parliament was dissolved in

1842. A major reform occurred in 1847, when the Decree 523 created the position of the President of the Council of Ministers, to be appointed by the emperor but with the prerogative of forming the rest of the government. Historians do not agree whether the government was to be formally responsible to the parliament in addition to the emperor (da Silva Soares and Dalmiro n.d.; Mota Barbosa 2007). According to da Silva Soares, when a government did not enjoy the support of the majority of deputies, it was the role of the emperor to resolve the situation. He could – and at times did – change the prime minister but appoint another one from the same party or dissolve the parliament and call for a new election, which occurred in 1868, 1884, 1885, and 1889. Because parties in office always won elections, the emperor could maintain political balance by changing prime ministers before elections. Fausto (1999: 99) summarizes this period as follows:

> A parliamentary government was only to begin, and even at that in an unusual and restricted form in 1847. In that year, by decree, the position of president of the council of ministers was created. He would be appointed by the emperor. This political agent would appoint the ministry, which together formed the council of ministers or the cabinet. They controlled executive power. For the system to work, it was presumed that the cabinet would need the confidence of the Chamber of deputies as well as that of the emperor to stay in power. There were times when the chamber forced the council of ministers to change its composition. But the emperor held on to a considerable power through this ability to moderate, and this is what made the imperial system less than totally parliamentary, even between 1850 and 1889. The emperor exercised his moderating prerogatives when the Chamber did not support the cabinet he preferred. On those occasions, after hearing form the council of state, he would use his power to dissolve the Chamber and call for new elections.

The monarchy was overthrown in 1891.

Bulgaria, 1887–1918: Ferdinand (1887–1918), who succeeded Prince Alexander following the latter's abdication in 1886, appointed governments, if need be dissolved the parliaments (in 1889, 1901, 1902, and 1913), and then held elections to confirm his choice. Partisan alternations were engineered by agreements and followed by elections in 1894, 1899, 1902, 1908, 1911, and 1913. In 1913, the newly appointed government did not secure a majority and needed a second election in 1914. According to Crampton (2005: 121), "Elections by the turn of the century . . . were more often carried out simply to provide a newly appointed cabinet with a dependable majority in the assembly. And by 1900 it was the prince who determined when the composition of a government should be changed and an election held." According to Kostadinova (1995: 27), "By appointing governments the Monarch indirectly dictated the results of the elections, providing the executive authority the opportunity to 'elect' the legislature."

Japan: The constitution of 1889 did not provide for parliamentary responsibility. According to Scalapino (1968), between 1892 and 1937,

> a party in power never lost an election during the entire period … power did alternate by means of elections, but only when "neutral," non-party governments presided over such elections … alternation in power between parties took place as a result of the *genro* system, with the senior Japanese statesmen selecting prime ministers when, in their opinion, conditions necessitated a change. These prime ministers then proceeded to use elections to ratify their power.

Ramseyer and Rosenbluth (1995) maintain that although at various moments the ruling oligarchs found it difficult to maintain control over parliaments, every recalcitrant parliament was either bribed or dissolved. When antigovernment majority threatened to revise the budget in 1890 and again in 1898, several members were bribed to vote with the government. An antigovernment party was co-opted into a government coalition in 1895. The parliament was dissolved in 1892, 1893, 1894, 1898, 1903, 1916, 1930, 1936, and 1937. In the early stages of parliamentary rule, nonpartisan prime ministers were common: Between 1890 and 1906, the only partisan prime minister held office briefly in 1898 (Sims 1991: 87–88). In 1906, a second partisan prime minister took office. Elections in 1908, 1912, 1914–1915, 1920, 1930, and 1931–1932 ratified partisan changes that preceded them (Sims 1991). In 1917, elections were held under a nonparty prime minister, but the government-supported party won largest share of seats. In 1924, elections resulted in a change from a neutral to a partisan prime minister, and in 1928, elections produced a draw. Nonpartisan governments held office under military tutelage from 1932 to 1946, and the 1947 constitution did not grant the executive power to the emperor.

Portugal: The first constitution was adopted in 1822 (in force between 1822 and 1826), followed by new ones in 1826 (in force between 1826 and 1828 and again between 1842 and 1911), and 1838 (in force until 1842). After 1851, a system of alternation between two parties has developed. However, this alternation was orchestrated from above. "Elections usually occurred after a change of government, not before, and were then won by the incoming administration which manipulated the patronage of the party bosses among the provincial electors" (Birmingham 1993: 132). In 1907, King Carlos had bypassed parliament to appoint his own prime minister. He was assassinated in 1908, and monarchy was abolished in 1910.

Spain: The constitutional history of Spain is convoluted, with six monarchical constitutions following the first one, adopted in Cádiz in 1812, and several periods of nonconstitutional rule. None of these constitutions restricted the freedom of the monarch to appoint and dismiss ministers. Between 1844 and 1868, "the

Crown became the decisive factor of political changes, above the Parliament.... What mattered was the confidence of the Palace. Electoral falsification generated the rest. Crises and conflicts were resolved by naming a new government, independently whether or not it enjoyed parliamentary majority. The new chief of government called elections and tried to fabricate the Cortes of his convenience" (Bahamonde and Martinez 1998: 285). Dissolutions occurred in 1839, 1843, 1852, 1853, 1854, 1863, and 1865. In 1868, "a parliamentary monarchy of a democratic nature" (Darde and Estrada 1998: 148) was established, under the reign of Amadee of Savoy, but in fact, this constitution (Article 68) still granted the king the power to choose governments at his discretion. This monarchy lasted only two years because of the lack of consensus between the monarchist political parties. The Cortes were dissolved again in 1869, 1871, and 1872. After a short-lived republic, a new monarchy was established in 1874. Between 1874 and 1923, two parties, Conservative and Liberal, alternated in office, but this alternation was a result of an explicit agreement between them (Jacobson and Luzón 2000). No dissolution occurred during this period. In 1923, King Alfonso XIII supported the coup that established the dictatorship of Primo de Rivera. Monarchy was abolished in 1931. It was restored in 1978, but the king was not granted executive power in the 1978 constitution.

Suppress, Dynasty Deposed or Monarchy Abolished

The instances of suppression that follow are italicized.

Austria: The newly elected parliament was dissolved in 1849 and *no elections were held until 1861*, when a new constitution of the Austria-Hungarian Empire created a joint parliament. In 1867, a separate constitution was adopted for the Austrian part of the Dual Monarchy (May 1968). According to this constitution, the ministry was responsible to the emperor, who also had the power to promulgate decrees when the parliament was not in session, and to dissolve it. Although until 1900, ministries relied on parliamentary support, prime ministers were chosen by the emperor and partisan alternations occurred before elections. The first prime minister (Auersperg, a German Liberal) of the parliament elected in 1867 enjoyed support from the German majority in parliament. However, according to Taylor (1948: 139), the constitutional laws of 1867 and the appointment of Auersperg did not signify true parliamentary government: "This was not a true responsible ministry, where the leader of the party is appointed Prime Minister and then chooses his colleagues. The ministers were chosen by Francis Joseph on the advice of Beust [prime minister preceding Auersperg]." Thereafter, Francis Joseph appointed prime ministers from alternating factions of German Liberals in 1868, 1871, and 1873, when the faction already in power since 1871 won elections, and in 1879, when the newly appointed faction won. There were elections again in 1885 and 1891, but another partisan change did not occur until 1893, when Prime Minister Taaffe, in office from 1879 to 1893, was dismissed. Taaffe had proposed universal suffrage and opposition against the bill had grown in parliament. According to Taylor (1948: 164–68), Francis Joseph feared that if the opposition "maintained itself, it would impose on him a 'parliamentary' ministry. The sole reason for Taaffe's existence was to prevent a parliamentary ministry; he was failing to do so, and Francis Joseph had to employ other means." In 1895, a prime minister appointed by Francis Joseph failed to obtain support in parliament. The emperor then appointed a new prime minister, who won the subsequent election. There were a few other shifts until 1900, when Francis Joseph chose Koerber, the parliament was dissolved, and new elections were held in 1901. The Koerber ministry (1900–1904), unable to command a majority, *ruled by emergency decrees*. In 1904, Koerber was replaced, followed by more changes in 1906 and an important franchise reform in 1907. Elections held in 1907 altered the composition of parliament. After the entry of a new prime minister in 1908, *emergency decrees were used to pass essential legislation*, and in 1911, parliament was dissolved again and new elections were held. After the elections, the prime minister resigned because he was unable to command a majority. Parliament was dissolved yet again in 1914 and monarchy was abolished in 1918.

Bulgaria, 1878–1886: Bulgaria became self-governing in 1878 and adopted the first constitution in 1879. According to Black (1943: 308), Article 152 provided that ministers are appointed or discharged by the prince, but Article 153 stated that ministers are responsible to the prince and to the National Assembly collectively for whatever measures they take in common, and individually for the administration of the department entrusted to them. It is not clear, however, whether the constitution provided for a procedure of nonconfidence – that is, whether the "responsibility" of Article 153 was political or only criminal.[2] In any case, when the Liberals won the first elections in September 1879 and formed a cabinet, Alexander dissolved the assembly. New elections in 1880 were won again by the Liberals, who formed a ministry. In 1881, Alexander *suspended the constitution* (reinstated in 1883). In 1886, he was forced to abdicate.

Bulgaria, 1918–1946: During King Boris's rule (1918–1943), the Agrarian Party had come to power after the elections in 1919. The parliament was dissolved in 1920 and *a military coup, presumably with Boris's support*, ousted Prime Minister

[2] Wikipedia provides for a link to the Bulgarian text of the 1879 Tarnovo Constitution, but this link is broken and we could not find the text in any language.

Stambolinski in 1923. The oppositional People's Bloc had won the elections in 1931 (Kostadinova 1995: 66–68). A military coup in 1934 was followed in 1935 by a countercoup that established the *royal dictatorship* (Crampton 2005: 159). Until 1938, there was no legislature and the constitution was suspended; elections were held in 1938 and 1939, with appointments of nonparty prime ministers. Monarchy was abolished in 1946.

Egypt: The first constitution was adopted in 1882. The provisions concerning parliamentary responsibility stipulated that the parliament (Council of Delegates) was to be automatically dissolved if it could not resolve a conflict with the government, but if the newly elected Council maintained the same position, its will was binding. A precedent was immediately set when the khedive Tawfiq dismissed a prime minister under the pressure of the parliament. Yet the constitution went into oblivion when Great Britain occupied Egypt the same year (Brown 2002: 27–28). Egypt became a constitutional monarchy again in 1923, under King Fuad. According to Bentwich (1924: 49), the constitution of 1923 granted the king the right to nominate and dismiss ministers but governments, as well as individual ministers, were subject to vote of nonconfidence of the lower chamber. Botman (1998), however, emphasizes the king's prerogative in appointing and dismissing governments without mentioning the role of the parliament. In any case, throughout the entire period, kings appointed governments without considering results of elections. In the election of 1924, a party opposed to the king, Wafd, won the election and formed the government under Sa'ad Zaglul, but was forced to resign under British pressure the same year, the parliament was dissolved, and the king appointed a provisional government headed by Ahmad Ziwar Pasha (Federal Party). New elections were held in 1925 and 1926. Both were won by Wafd. After the first election, *the King locked the deputies out of parliament*, dissolved the lower chamber again, and called for new elections. After the 1926 election, the British opposed Sa'ad Zaglul taking office, and the monarch agreed. Wafd was forced to coalesce with the Liberal Constitutional Party (LCP), but Sa'ad Zaglul was vetoed as prime minister and Adli Yakan Pasha (Liberal Party) took his place. In 1931, Isma'il Sidqi, a monarch loyalist, who had been prime minister since June 1930, *dissolved Parliament and drafted a new Constitution strengthening the monarchy*. Wafd boycotted the election of 1931. Sidqi won and remained in office until 1933, when the king forced him to resign. Parliament was dissolved again in 1934. Until 1936 elections, different governments, all appointed by the king, succeeded one another. In December 1935, the British allowed the restoration of 1923 constitution, and new elections were called for in May 1936. Wafd won and Al-Nahhas was elected prime minister. One and a half years later, in December 1937, the new monarch, King Faruq (his father had passed away before May 1936 elections) removed Al-Nahhas, dissolved the parliament, and called for new elections, boycotted by Wafd (which still won twelve seats). The Liberal Party formed the government under Mohamed Mahmud. One year later, Mahmud was deposed by the king in favor of Ali Mahir (independent), who formed a nationalist government. The British forced the king to replace him in June 1940. The parliament was dissolved again in 1944, and the monarchy was abolished after the military coup of 1952.

France, 1815–1830: The 1814 constitution did not provide for parliamentary responsibility. In 1815, after an electoral success of ultra-royalists, the government of Talleryand resigned and Louis XVIII accepted the resignation: “J'ai reçu mes ministres, qui m'ont apporté leurs démission. Ils me l'ont donnée à l'anglaise, je l'acceptée de même” (cited in de Wasquerel and Yvert 2002: 160). Yet this change of government did not emanate from the parliament, but rather was a unilateral tactical move by the king. Dissolutions in 1816 and 1824 resulted in victories of the government. After de Villèle failed to pass an important law and his majority progressively diminished, the *Chambre* was dissolved again in 1827. Elections in November 1827 were catastrophic for the ministry. The opposition was about to win an absolute majority. Popular unrest erupted and was brutally repressed. Charles X resisted abandoning de Villèle. A new ministry was formed, but it was continuist. This incident did not change Charles X's views. He is reported to have said: “It [parliamentary responsibility] would be an absurdity and an injustice in France. In England ... the ministers govern and should be responsible. In France, the King governs and the ministers cannot be punished for obeying him. It is their duty” (de Wasquerel and Yvert 2002: 411). Prime Minister Montignac, speaking in the *Chambre*, emphasized that ministers govern only in the name of the king. He governs, they execute. “We are accused of going from concession to concession. Certainly, if to concede is to give, grant, award (*donner, octroyer, accorder*), in virtue of his right and his power, the Kings of France did not cease going from concession to concession. But if one would want to understand by this word the abandonment of a prerogative useful to the Crown, we would like to declare, the throne will never make such concessions” (de Waresquiel and Yvert 2002: 414). Montignac fell in May 1829, having lost a vote on local administration. The king used this occasion to get rid of him. Complex and secret negotiations ensued. The king decided to impose himself. The *Chambre* passed a resolution demanding a change of government. Charles refused and suspended the parliament. On May 16, the *Chambre* was dissolved. The Minister of Interior expected the government to win a majority in the ensuing elections. Polignac, the new prime minister, declared that in case of victory of the opposition, the king would be obliged to rule by decrees: “It is thus up to the voters to make it so that the majority of the new *Chambre* would not be such that the King would be obliged ... to take strong measures.” In the election, the opposition won 274 seats against 145 for the ministry. The king, on July 7, decided to *rule by ordinances*,[3] and a revolution ensued.

Greece: According to the constitution of 1844 (article 24), "The King appoints and removes his Ministers," a phrase that was repeated verbatim the constitution of 1864. Nevertheless, in 1875, "the King accepted the principle that he would invariably call upon the party leader enjoying the support of a majority of deputies in parliament to form a government." In his Crown Speech, King George I expressly declared, "I demand as a prerequisite, of all that I call beside me to assist me in governing the country, to possess the manifest confidence and trust of the majority of the Nation's representatives. Furthermore, I accept this approval to stem from the Parliament, as without it the harmonious functioning of the polity would be impossible" (http://www.parliament.gr/english/politeuma/default.asp). It was not until 1881, however, that Kharilaos Trikoupis was able to secure parliamentary support for his New Party. For much of the remaining two decades of the century, a two-party system operated, with Trikoupis alternating with his archrival, Deliyannis (Clogg 1992: 67). Yet in 1910, *the King dissolved the parliament even though the parliament voted confidence in Venizelos*. The new election was won by Venizelos. Another dissolution occurred in 1915, two parallel governments were formed, a civil war ensued, and Konstantin abdicated in favor of his younger son. Monarchy was abolished in 1924, reestablished in 1935, to be abolished again in 1974.

Note that this is the only case in which parliamentary responsibility was practiced for an extended period of time yet subsequently the monarch attempted to override the parliament.

Hungary: The constitution of 1867 did not provide for parliamentary responsibility. The Liberals had originally come to power through elections of August 1875, which gave them a majority and represented a change away from Conservatives. This event may have indicated the acceptance of parliamentary responsibility, but subsequent events showed the emperor's dominance over the parliament. After the budget could not be passed in 1903, the election of January 1905 brought the first defeat of the Liberals. They won only 159 mandates, whereas the National Coalition (opposition) elected 235 deputies. The emperor was willing to appoint the Coalition government but not to accept its platform. In June, Francis Joseph appointed a non-parliamentary caretaker government under the Minister of Defense General Fejervary. The

3 Charles X invoked article 14 of the Constitution as granting him the right to rule by decree. But this article does not seem to give this power. Here is the text:

Article 14. – Le roi est le chef suprême de l'Etat, il commande les forces de terre et de mer, déclare la guerre, fait les traités de paix, d'alliance et de commerce, nomme à tous les emplois d'administration publique, et fait les règlements et ordonnances nécessaires pour l'exécution des lois et la sûreté de l'Etat.

Coalition-led majority in parliament protested "by calling for nationwide passive resistance including the non-payment of taxes and the refusal to send recruits to the army.... On February 19, 1906, the army, violating the constitution, occupied Parliament, and a royal commissioner read a rescript dissolving the legislature without setting the date for new elections" (Jeszenszky 1990: 280–81). Only after a tacit agreement that they would not pursue their original course, Francis Joseph agreed to let the Coalition form a government, which subsequently won an absolute majority in the May election (Macartney 1962: 99–100; Jeszenszky 1990). The emperor continued to choose prime ministers until monarchy was abolished in 1918.

Iran: The first constitution was adopted in 1906–1907. According to the Article 67 of the Supplementary Fundamental Laws of October 7, 1907, "If the National Consultative Assembly or the Senate shall, by an absolute majority, declare itself dissatisfied with the Cabinet, or with one particular Minister, that Cabinet or Minister shall resign their or his ministerial functions." In 1907, however, the reigning Shah *bombed the Majlis building* and dissolved the parliament. He was deposed one year later and the parliament was reinstated.

From 1911 to 1914, the legislature was closed again and *the constitution was suspended.* In 1914, the legislature was reconvened, to be closed again in 1915. In 1921, the parliament was reconvened and met under a government that commanded its confidence. Ahmad Shah (who ruled from 1914 to 1923) of the Qajar dynasty established the practice of never appointing a premier unless the parliament had indicated its preference by vote. According to Farmanfarma (1954: 244), the last time "this constitutional custom" was exercised under the Qajar dynasty was in 1923 with the Mustofi cabinet. Between this cabinet and the accession of Reza Pahlavi in 1925, there was one other cabinet. A formal vote of preference was not obtained, "presumably because only a few days were left of the 4th session and the person appointed was particularly favored" (Farmanfarma 1954: 244). Ahmad Shah was overthrown in 1924.

From the accession of Reza Shah Pahlavi in 1925 to his deposition in 1941, there was no formal vote of confidence in the parliament and Pahlavi appointed and dismissed ministers as he pleased. During this period, parties were not allowed to operate, although elections continued to be held regularly. In 1941, Reza Khan resigned in favor of son, Mohammed Reza Pahlavi. From 1941 to 1949, no prime minister took office without a vote of preference, unless the parliament was not in session. In 1949, the young Shah made a first attempt to consolidate his power, *by declaring martial law and convening a Constitutional Assembly that introduced a Senate and gave the Shah the right to dissolve Parliament.* For two years, the practice of asking parliamentary approval for appointment of the prime minister was not followed, but it was reestablished in 1951 when Mosaddegh came to power as prime minister against the will of the Shah. Mosaddegh persuaded the Iranian parliament to grant him extraordinary powers and demanded that the Shah act as a constitutional monarch. He organized a plebiscite for the dissolution of the Majlis, claimed a massive vote in favor of the proposal, and dissolved the legislature. In August 1953, *Mosaddegh was overthrown* and Shah's power was restored. Elections were held, but parties were banned. In 1957, the Shah allowed for the creation of two government-sponsored parties that competed in elections in 1960. The first election, in which the government party won a majority, was annulled in the face of accusations that it was unfair. The government again won a majority in the election that followed in 1961. In response to protests, the Shah dissolved the parliament and gave the premier the right to *rule by decree*. After 1963, elections were held and the parliament was open, but opposition parties never gained even close to a majority of seats. The monarchy was overthrown in 1979.

Lesotho (Basutaland): The first constitution was adopted in 1959 and the second in 1966, when the country became independent. When the royalist Basutaland National Party seemed to be heading toward electoral defeat in the first post-independence elections in 1970, *the incumbent prime minister nullified the election, proclaimed emergency, dissolved the parliament, and suspended the constitution*. In 1986, a military coup transformed all the executive and legislative power to the king who, however, was supposed to act on the advice of the Military Council. King Moshoeshoe was exiled by the military in 1990, but a countercoup in 1991 brought him back. In 1993, a new constitution took all executive power from the king. In 1994, King Letsie III *staged a countercoup*, but constitutional government was restored within a month.

Nepal: In 1959, the king granted a constitution that provided for a cabinet responsible to the lower house. Elections were held in 1959, in which the Nepal Congress party won a majority. A cabinet led by B. P. Koirala, who led the Congress, was formed. In 1960, the king dismissed the government and *suspended parliament, appointed his own cabinet, and ruled directly*. The 1962 constitution contained a stronger and more explicit statement of royal authority than did previous constitutions. The king was the sole source of authority and had the power not only to amend the constitution, but also to suspend it by royal proclamation during emergencies. The Council of Ministers during this period were appointed by king at his own discretion. The constitution abolished all political parties. In 1977, King Birendra Bir Bikram Shah Deva broke a seventeen-year tradition when he appointed Kirti Nidhi Bista as prime minister on the recommendation of the National Assembly. Political parties were banned since 1960, however, so it is difficult to tell whether this appointee was a member of the "opposition." Still, it was the first time since 1960 that a Nepalese king waived his authority to appoint the leader of the government. A 1980 amendment to the constitution formally reinstated cabinet responsibility to the parliament, but partisan elections occurred only in 1990, when the ban on parties was officially lifted. King Birendra dissolved Nepal's national assembly, accepted the resignation of his Prime Minister Lokendra Bahadur Chand, and appointed a leading opposition figure of the Nepali Congress Party to lead Nepal's first government in thirty years not set up by the monarch. In the subsequent elections, the NCP won a majority and continued in office until the elections of 1994, which it lost. Between 1994 and 2002, with another elections intervening in 1999, several governments were removed by votes of nonconfidence. In 2002, King Gyanendra unilaterally changed the government and in 2005 he staged a royal coup and, although he agreed to reconvene the parliament one year later, the monarchy was abolished in 2008.

Ottoman Empire: Article 7 of the Basic Law of 1876 provided that the Sultan makes and cancels appointments of ministers. When some deputies elected in 1877 and, after the dissolution of the first parliament, in 1878 criticized the government and sought to impeach some ministers, the *Sultan dissolved the parliament sine diem*. The 1876 constitution was restored as a consequence of a military revolt in 1908, and elections for parliament were held for the first time in thirty years. In 1909, the Sultan Abdul Hamid II *attempted a coup* against the parliamentary regime and was deposed by the army in favor of his brother. The constitutional revision of 1909 stated in Article 30 that "Ministers shall be responsible to the Chamber of Deputies collectively for the general policy of the Government and personally for the affairs of their respective departments," but did not provide for a procedure of nonconfidence. In 1912, the ruling party, CUP, dissolved the parliament. Elections that year produced a CUP majority – the majority was secured through violence as a result of which only "a handful" of opposition party members were elected. Although the Chamber gave the CUP prime minister a vote of confidence, he resigned and was replaced by an anti-CUP cabinet that dissolved parliament again. In 1913, the old CUP prime minister returned as a result of a military coup; upon his assassination, a new CUP prime minister was appointed. Because the opposition did not participate, the CUP dominated elections held in 1914. Parliament was dissolved in 1918. Elections were held in 1919, but the chamber did not meet until January 1920 and prorogued itself in April of the same year (Zurcher 1997).

Romania: Constitutional monarchy was established in 1866. Articles 92 and 93 gave the king the right to choose and revoke his ministers. It was customary for the monarch to appoint governments, dissolve the parliament, and hold elections in which the new government would produce a majority in the legislature. Partisan alternations followed this pattern in 1876, 1888 (when the parliament was dissolved), 1895,

1899, 1901, 1905, 1907, 1911, and 1914. Hitchins (1994: 94) summarizes this period as follows:

> The King played a key role in determining the outcome of elections through his constitutional authority to appoint the incoming Prime Minister. By the final decades of the century the procedure for changing governments had been perfected. The process began with the resignation of the sitting government, consultations between the King and leading politicians, and the selection of one among the latter to form a new government. The first task of the newly designated Prime Minister after he had chosen his cabinet was to organize elections for a new Chamber and Senate. That was the responsibility of the Minister of the Interior … to make certain that the opposition would be overwhelmed in the coming elections. Between 1881 and 1914 … no government designated by the King was ever disappointed at the polls. The "rotation" of parties also became the rule during this period. It became customary for the King to alternate the two major parties in office.

In 1919, for the first time, elections did not result in an absolute majority for the (Liberal) party in power; the National Party, which had secured the largest share of seats, formed a government. However, opposition from the king forced the National Party out of office in 1920, parliament was dissolved, and elections held in that year gave the king's newly appointed prime minister's (People's) party a majority (Hitchins 1994). Thereafter, the previous tradition of alternation followed by election was reestablished, as evidenced in 1922, 1926, 1927, 1928, 1931, 1932, and 1933. Under the new constitution of 1923 (Articles 87, 88), the king "could choose his ministers even from outside parliament and he could dismiss them as he thought best" (Hitchins 1994: 378).

In 1937, elections did not produce a majority for the incumbent Liberal Party. The prime minister resigned, and King Carol appointed the head of the National Christian Party (merely the fourth-largest party in parliament) to form a government, intending "to show that the elections … had not really changed the way things were done and that it was, after all, his will that counted" (Hitchins 1994: 420). *A new constitution was adopted in 1938, and non-parliamentary rule was imposed in 1940.* Monarchy was abolished in 1947.

Russia: The organic laws of 1906 established a parliament, the Duma, leaving the prerogative to appoint and dismiss governments to the Tsar. The first Duma was elected in 1906 and dissolved after two months. The second Duma was elected in 1907 and also dissolved. *Electoral laws were then changed by Nicolas II to assure that no more electoral defeats would ensue.* Moreover, contrary to the Manifesto of October 1907, after June 1907, the Tsar could and did *issue edicts, bypassing the Duma* when it was not in session. Monarchy was abolished in 1917.

Serbia: According to Dragnich (1978), the 1869 Constitution did not make clear if ministerial responsibility was legal or political. According to Stead (1909: 58), however,

> [the] Constitution of 1869 represented the type of constitutional and parliamentary monarch of the English model. The direct representatives of the supreme authority exercising this authority were the Prince and the National Skupchtina. The responsible Ministerial Cabinet existed between them as their common organ as the expression of their common desire. This was appointed and dismissed by the Prince, but could only continue and act if supported by the confidence of the majority in the Skupchtina.

Political responsibility was recognized in practice in 1874: Liberals formed governments from 1869 until 1873, but when Prince Milan appointed a Conservative prime minister, Marinovic, and when the elections in 1874 did not produce a Conservative majority, Marinovic resigned despite having won two votes of confidence.[4] In 1875, Liberals returned to office having won the election. In the early 1880s, however, when the Radical Party won a majority, Prince Milan appointed a technocratic cabinet under a Conservative. Milan eventually appointed a Radical cabinet in 1887 and Radicals won nearly all the seats in the ensuing elections. A new constitution was adopted in 1888, providing again for a vote of nonconfidence: According to Stead (1909: 64), "The executive power is in the hands of a ministerial cabinet, appointed and dismissed by the king, but which cannot retain its position if it does not enjoy the confidence of the legislature, the assembly possessing all the necessary constitutional means for controlling the cabinet, and for obliging it to resign as soon as it can no longer command confidence." A Radical cabinet was formed and elections followed. Radicals governed until 1892, when Pasic (Radical) resigned and a Liberal prime minister was appointed. Elections in 1893 gave the Liberals a narrow majority, but in the same year Milan – who abdicated in the meantime – *staged a coup and returned in 1894*. A number of semi-party or nonparty cabinets ensued until Radicals returned to power in 1903 after a coup that ousted Alexander (Milan's son) and the Obrenović dynasty. The 1888 constitution was restored, subsequent elections were competitive, and the winners assumed office, but the country was incorporated into Yugoslavia in 1918.

Yugoslavia: In the early period, governments served with parliamentary support. Radicals (1918) and the Democratic Party (1919) headed cabinets in the provisional assembly. Elections for a constituent assembly in 1920 did not produce a majority for any party. A constitution adopted in 1921 did not provide for a vote

[4] Except as noted, this section is mainly based on Dragnich (1975; 1978: 52–93).

of nonconfidence. Elections in 1923, 1925, and 1927 gave Radicals a plurality. In 1928, there was a partisan alternation after a crisis where deputies were killed. King Alexander attempted federalist reforms, but when they failed, on January 6, 1929, he *abolished the 1921 Constitution, dissolved the parliament, and introduced a personal dictatorship*. The king revived parliament with the constitution of 1931, according to which ministers were responsible solely to the Crown. Elections held that year were not competitive, whereas elections held in 1935 and 1939 did permit some opposition, but cabinets formed in 1935 and 1939 were drawn from the official government party. Monarchy was abolished in 1945 (Seton-Watson & Laffan 1966.)

Yield, Survive

Belgium: Lorwin (1966: 119) asserts that "[t]he Belgian state was born parliamentary," but the Constitution of 1831 did not differ from the standard of the time – that is, the king was the chief executive, governed through his ministers, who had to cosign all acts and were only individually responsible. According to the Article 65, "Le Roi nomme et révoque ses ministres." From 1831 to 1847, King Leopold presided over unionist governments, most of which were mixed cabinets of Catholics and Liberals. In 1840, he made an issue of reinstatement in the army of an exiled colonel a matter of confidence. Defeated in both chambers, the government resigned. In 1841, the parliament refused to adopt the budget (van Beyme 2000: 21). The king appointed a purely Liberal government, which was defeated in the Senate and resigned, but the king refused to dissolve the parliament and appointed another unionist government. Liberals made electoral progress in 1845 and the prime minister resigned. But the king was not ready to accept the end of unionism and kept the prime minister in office while searching for a successor. The king appointed a government headed by a nonpartisan civil servant, who in turn resigned in 1846 because of internal dissensions within the ministry. "On the resignation of M. Van der Weyer, King Leopold recognized that the day of Unionism was over, and that it would be necessary to employ homogeneous ministries instead of mixed" (Boulger 2005: 295). The king was prepared to appoint a Liberal, M. Rogier, but the latter demanded the right to dissolve the chambers, and the king declined. The king appointed an exclusively Catholic administration, but the majority of the chamber was Liberal. When Liberals won the election after the parliament had been dissolved in 1847, the king appointed Rogier. In 1852, Catholics made electoral progress, Liberals were divided, and the king appointed a government of experts. In 1854, Catholics won a clear majority, first time ever. The expert government of de Brouckere survived one more year, but in 1855, it was replaced by a Catholic ministry. When a school bill advanced by this government passed the parliament but met with popular protest demonstrations, the king appointed a Liberal government and authorized it to dissolve the chambers. Liberals won the subsequent election, in 1857 (Boulger 2005). Subsequent dissolutions occurred in 1864, 1870, and 1892.

The current version of the constitution (Article 96) has an explicit article about parliamentary responsibility. It repeats the phrase "Le Roi nomme et révoque ses ministres" but then goes on:

> The Federal Government offers its resignation to the King if the Chamber of Representatives, by an absolute majority of its members, adopts a motion of disapproval, proposing to the King the nomination of a successor to the Prime Minister, or proposes to the King the nomination of a successor to the Prime Minister within three days of the rejection of a motion of confidence. The King names the proposed successor as Prime Minister, who takes office the moment the new Federal Government is sworn in.

We cannot trace the date of this article but we guess it must have been in 1892. Hence, parliamentary responsibility was not included in the constitution of 1831, it was practised as of 1847, and consitutionalized in (presumably) 1892.

Denmark: In 1848, the king yielded to mass pressure, led by Liberals, to dismiss his cabinet, but he appointed another Conservative government. This incident occurred, however, before Denmark had a constitution, which was adopted in 1849 and was followed by another one in 1866. In 1872, the opposition party, *Venstre*, won an absolute majority in the *Folketing* (the lower house), but the government continued to be Conservative. The right-wing party, *Højre*, continued to govern in spite of left majorities until 1901, when it won only eight out of 114 seats in the *Folketing*. Fearing that *Venstre* would be driven into the arms of radical Socialist Workers who were winning ever more seats since 1884, on July 24, 1901, Christian IX appointed the first *Venstre* government. "From that point on, parliamentarism was adopted as political practice in Denmark" (Jespersen 2004: 69). In 1920, Christian X attempted to impose his government but failed. The principle was codified in 1953.

Hence, parliamentary responsibility was not in the constitutions of 1849 or 1866, it was practised as of 1901, and consitutionalized in 1953.

Netherlands: Parliamentary responsibility was not provided for in the constitution of 1815. In 1840, when the government introduced some constitutional amendments, the First Chamber declined to consider the budget so long as the government had not brought in a bill for amending the constitutions by ministerial responsibility. "Reluctantly the government consented. The budget was passed as well as government's other constitutional amendments. But the King did not plan to continue his reign under this constitution." (Blok 1970: 443). He abdicated a few months later. In 1848, there was a comprehensive constitutional revision. Count Schimmelpennick asked the king to appoint him as "cabinet former" for the formation of a definitive "homogeneous and responsible" ministry. The king consented to preparing a constitution "in the main like the British. ... The ministerial responsibility fully introduced had bound the execution of authority to the cooperation of the ministers" (Blok 1970: 461–62; note, however, the plural of "ministers"). The ministry of De Kamenaer collectively resigned in 1849. "A Thorbecke (Liberal leader) ministry was desired by the majority [of the Second Chamber]. All attempts to escape it failed one after another. At the end of October the King yielded to the pressure. ... Thus the path of parliamentary government was finally entered upon" (Blok 1970: 465). But the Thorbecke government fell in 1853, "not by a parliamentary defeat but apparently by the King's will." The parliament was dissolved and the election was won by Conservatives. In 1856, Conservatives became a minority but continued to form governments, facing parliamentary defeats. In 1866, a motion of disapproval of the government was passed by the chamber, and the ministry proposed to the king the dissolution of the Second Chamber. "Before the elections set for October 31st the government induced the King to issue a proclamation urging the voters to choose representatives, who would agree with the administration and put an end to the 'constant change of responsible counselors.' The proclamation was sent with the ballots to the voters. The purpose was evident to use the attachment to the house of Orange against the liberal party" (Blok 1970: 482). The result was a slight defeat of Liberals. In 1867, the parliament refused foreign affairs budget, the ministry resigned, and the Second Chamber was dissolved again. The government was defeated in the elections of 1868. At the Liberal instigation, the chamber passed a motion declaring that "no national interest had required the dissolution." The government was again defeated over foreign affairs budget. In the 1869 elections, Conservatives were defeated again. "An antiliberal government was not possible against the liberal majority," and Thorbecke took office again in 1871. Alternation as a result of election occurred in 1877. There was a dissolution in 1886 over religious issues, in which the government was defeated. A dissolution in 1887 was required for the constitutional reform to become valid.

Parliamentary responsibility was not in the constitution of 1815. Everyone takes 1868 to be the turning point, and it is true that since 1871, governments alternated according to parliamentary majorities, but 1840 and 1848 are also possible dates. It seems that the principle was never explicitly constitutionalized: The constitution of 1983 still says (article 42, paragraph 1) that "The Government shall comprise the King and the Ministers" and (article 43) that the ministers are appointed and dismissed by Royal Decree, without mentioning any role of the parliament.

Norway: The Norwegian constitution of 1814 does not provide for parliamentary responsibility. In 1836, a prime minister kept his position despite having been impeached and convicted by the *Storting* (Storing 1963: 52). In 1869, however, Charles XV (Swedish King) had to accept the *Storting*'s request for a change of ministry (Verney 1957: 132). There is general agreement that the date when parliamentary responsibility was accepted as a principle was 1884, when the parliament successfully brought charges against the government of Selmer (Elster 2007a, Storing 1963: 30). In 1882, the Liberal party won sweeping victories at the polls. When Selmer was impeached, Oscar II did accept the verdict as well as the resignation of the Selmer government, but attempted to rule with an opposition ministry without conceding the principle. This tactic failed, and the king was forced to accept a Liberal ministry. Hence, although the procedure utilized was penal, the consequences were political. Lavaux (1998: 200) comments that "[t]he confirmation of the principle of governmental responsibility was very rapid. From 1888, the right, which had been in favor of maintaining the separation of powers, used the motion of censure and in 1891, while it was in power, the motion of confidence." However, in 1893, Oscar II appointed a government against an expressed lack of confidence in the *Storting*. According to Storing (1963), this was the only use of the vote of nonconfidence. This government lasted two years.

According to Elster (personal communication):

> After an impeachment case in 1926–27 showed deep ambiguities in the idea of the responsibility of the government to the parliament, a parliamentary committee was appointed in 1927 to clarify the matter. In its report (1929) it stated explicitly that a vote of no confidence was legally binding for the government. In the meantime (1928), the Hornsrud government (Labor) has stepped down after receiving a vote of no confidence, the first unambiguous case in recent times. Although the committee report did not lead to legislation, it was generally accepted among politicians and jurists that the principle of parliamentarism has now acquired constitutional status so that its violation could trigger impeachment.

Note, however, that the current version of the constitution says nothing about parliamentary responsibility. According to Article 3, "Executive power is vested in the King, or the Queen," whereas Article 12 still maintains that "[t]he King himself chooses his Council."

Sweden: Neither the Instrument of the Government of 1719, which ushered in the first period of constitutional monarchy (Roberts 2002), nor the one of 1809 provided for parliamentary responsibility. In 1868, *Storting* refused for the first time to grant the defense budget. Some ministers wanted to resign, but Charles XV did not accept it, declaring that such a resignation would imply parliamentary control over the ministry and, therefore, that there must be no suggestion of resignation. An opposition party, Farmers, first won in 1880, and Oscar II called on Count Posse, the leader of the party, to head the government. He was not fully supported, however, by his party and ended up forming a government that had the highest proportion of nobles of any such government during this period (Verney 1957: 103). His defense bill was defeated and Posse resigned. First collective resignation of the government occurred in 1905. In 1906, the first Liberal government, under Staaff, came into office because it had the plurality in the lower chamber. In 1907, an opposition leader referred to a "hypothetical vote of no confidence," but still no such vote could be taken. When Staaff resigned, a Conservative government came into office, and because of their majority in the upper chamber, they could muster as much support as Liberals. When Liberals won the election of 1911, they were returned to office again. In 1914, a stalemate ensued: Social Democrats won a one-vote plurality over the Conservatives, and Liberals were badly defeated. However, Social Democrats were not ready to enter a government, and a Conservative government was formed. In 1917, Social Democrats won the plurality, followed by Liberals, and a coalition of these two parties took office.

It is generally agreed that "[i]t is the 1917 Government which is regarded as the 'breakthrough of parliamentary government'" (Verney 1957: 232). In the constitution of 1974, the king no longer had the executive power and the government was made explicitly responsible to the parliament.

Thailand: After a series of coups and countercoups, a constitution was adopted in 1932. This constitution stipulated that the cabinet would be responsible to the legislature. King Prajadikhop left for Europe on the pretext of seeking medical treatment, refused to sign legislation, and abdicated in 1935. For the next sixteen years, Thailand had no resident monarch (Baker and Phongpaichit 2005: 116–23). Subsequent history of Thailand witnessed repeated conflicts between civilian and military factions, always claiming support of the monarch: Between 1932 and 2000, there were nine instances in which the parliament was dissolved and nine coups, yet none directed against the king. An appointed upper house was introduced in 1968, and votes of confidence had to be passed by both houses. Between 1976 and 1977, the legislature was fully appointed. However, the principle of cabinet responsibility was never reversed in the sense that the king never appointed a cabinet that did not enjoy the support of the majority of the legislature.

United Kingdom: The first instance may have been 1695, when the cabinet for the first time fully corresponded to the parliamentary majority or 1701 when the Tories, previously in opposition, won a majority and the king incorporated them into the cabinet (Schmitt 1993: 468). Lavaux (1998: 190) takes 1729 – the Walpole's cabinet – as the first incidence of a government that enjoyed the confidence of the parliament. Hume, writing in 1742, noted that the approval of the cabinet by the king was "but a formality." Yet in 1741, Walpole refused to resign when he was demanded to do so by the Commons. The government of Lord North was the first to resign collectively in 1782. In 1834, the Whig government of Lord Melbourne was dismissed by William IV and was replaced by a government headed by Peel, who was the Tory leader in the Commons. The Parliament was dissolved, and when Peel lost the election, the king recalled Melbourne. In 1858, however, Queen Victoria replaced Liberal Palmerston with a minority Tory government under Derby; the Tories lost the elections in 1859, the queen reappointed Derby, and only when he could not pass legislation, she accepted Palmerston and subsequently Gladstone.

Yield, Overthrown

Italy: The government was responsible only to the king in the Statuto Albertino of Sardinia, adopted in 1848, which became the constitution of Italy after unification in 1861. Nevertheless, the practice of parliamentary responsibility was recognized from the onset. There was a period when parties agreed to govern together, so the issue was moot. Although never recognized legally, the practice was so entrenched that in 1925, Mussolini had to pass a law explicitly stating that the government is not responsible to the parliaments. Monarchy was abolished in 1946.

Parliamentary responsibility was never constitutionalized but always practiced. The monarchy was abolished nevertheless.

Suppress, Survive

Jordan: The Constitution of 1952 provided for the principle of parliamentary responsibility (article 51) and the procedure of nonconfidence (article 53). After the election of 1954, King Hussain removed the prime minister, with eight governments appointed by him following until the elections of 1956. In early 1956, a previous dissolution was declared illegal and the previous government was restored. The parliament was dissolved in June 1956 and the ensuing elections resulted in a victory of the opposition parties. A few days after the election, King Hussein asked Suleiman Nabulsi, the leader of the National Socialist Party, which gained eleven seats in the elections, to form the government. After an attempted coup against the monarchy in 1957, however, the king, reassured of the army's backing, forced Prime Minister Nabulsi to resign and appointed a government of his own choice. The elections in 1961 were rigged, but those in 1962 were relatively free, although parties were banned (Robins 2004: 109). The incumbent government received the confidence of the new assembly but with some dissenting votes. Soon after, however, King Hussain replaced Prime Minister Tall with Samir al-Rifai, who for the first time in the history of Jordan was brought down by a vote of nonconfidence. In response, the king appointed an interim prime minister, and the lower house elected in 1963 proved to be more malleable. The parliament was dissolved sine diem in 1974, to be restored only in 1983. First elections after 1967, with parties still banned, were held in 1989, and parties were legalized in 1992. In November 1991, Prime Minister Tahir al-Masri lost his support in parliament and resigned in anticipation of losing a confidence vote. In 1992, parliament brought down a government, although not by directly using its power to withdraw confidence (Brown 2002: 118). Before the elections of 1993, however, the king dissolved the parliament and changed the electoral rules. Royalist forces won all the subsequent elections, some of which were boycotted by the opposition.

Kuwait: The first constitutional experiment occurred in 1938 and was short-lived. When the assembly attempted to exercise its fiscal prerogatives, the amir dissolved it and called for a new election. When the assembly failed to modify the constitution in amir's favor, the constitution was abandoned (Brown 2002: 30–31). A new constitution was adopted in 1962 after the country became independent in 1961. Although the parliament could censure individual ministers, it could not withdraw confidence from the prime minister, who was always the crown prince (Brown 2002: 57). In 1964, the amir conceded to the objections of some parliamentarians to the composition of the government. Yet in 1976, the amir disbanded the parliament and transferred its legislative authority to the government, which "required suspending parts of the constitution without the consent of the parliament, something specifically forbidden by the constitution" (Brown 2002: 57–58). The parliament was reconvened in 1981, but in 1986, the constitution was again suspended. After the Iraqi invasion of 1990, the parliament was reopened again in 1992. The parliament was dissolved in 1999, but this time constitutional provisions were observed.

Morocco: Morocco became a constitutional monarchy in 1962 and held first elections one year later. According to the Constitution of 1962 (Article 24), the king appoints and dismisses the ministers, but (Articles 80 and 81) the House of Representatives can dismiss the government by a vote of nonconfidence. When the opposition UNFP won the election, in 1965, the King suspended the parliament and served as his own prime minister during two years. The constitution was slightly revised in 1970 and again in 1972, increasing the power of the king to appoint and dismiss governments. Two more constitutions were adopted in 1980 and 1992, while another dissolution occurred in 1983. Yet another constitution was adopted in 1996, providing again for parliamentary responsibility and a procedure of confidence. The opposition won the plurality election in 1998 and formed the government, but this event is generally considered to have been engineered by the king. In 2002, Mohammed VI reverted to the practice of naming the prime minister regardless of election results (Ottaway and Riley 2006).

Swaziland: The first constitution was adopted in 1968, when the country became independent. It did not provide for parliamentary responsibility. When an opposition party won 20 percent of the vote and three out of twenty-four seats in 1972, King Sobhuza II dissolved the parliament, repealed the constitution, and assumed all powers. A new parliament was partly elected and partly appointed by the king in 1979. A new constitution was adopted in 2005, providing for governments responsible to the king.

ACKNOWLEDGMENTS

We appreciate the assistance of Gonzalo Rivero, Didac Queralt, and Kong-Joo Shin in collecting the data. This work was supported by a grant from the National Science Foundation.

REFERENCES

Bahamonde, Ángel and Jesús A. Martinez, *Historia de España Siglo XIX* (Madrid: Catedra, 1998).

Baker, Chris and Pasuk Phongpaichit, *A History of Thailand* (Cambridge: Cambridge University Press, 2005).

Barbosa, Silvana Mota, "O Conselho de Ministros no Império do Brasil," *Revista de História* 13 (2007) 52–62.

Bentwich, Norman, "The Constitution of Egypt," *Journal of Comparative Legislation and International Law* 6 (1924) 41–49.

Birmingham, David, *A Concise History of Portugal* (Cambridge: Cambridge University Press, 1993).

Black, C. E., *The Establishment of Constitutional Government in Bulgaria* (Princeton: Princeton University Press, 1943).

Blok, Petrus Johannes, *History of the People of the Netherlands. Part V: Eighteenth and Nineteenth Centuries [1898–1912]* (New York: AMS Press, 1970).

Blokker, Paul. 2003. "Modernity in Romania. Nineteenth Century Liberalism and Its Discontens," EUIWorking Paper SPS No. 2003/2, http://hdl.handle.net/1814/335

Botman, Selma, "The Liberal Age, 1923–1952," *The Cambridge History of Egypt, vol. 2, Modern Egypt from 1517 to the End of the Twentieth Century* (Cambridge: Cambridge University Press, 1998) 285–308.

Boulger, Demetrius C., *The History of Belgium, Part 2: 1815–1865, Waterloo to the Death of Leopold I [1909]* (Elibron Classics, 2005).

Brown, Nathan J., *Constitutions in a Nonconstitutional World: Arab Basic Laws and the Prospects for Accountable Government* (Albany: State University of New York Press, 2002).

Bury, J. T. P., *France 1814–1940* (New York: A.S. Barnes, 1962).

Carr, William, *A History of Germany, 1818–1945* (New York: St. Martin's Press, 1969).

Cheibub, José Antonio, Adam Przeworski, and Sebastian Saiegh, "Government Coalitions under Parliamentarism and Presidentialism," *British Journal of Political Science* 34 (2004) 565–87.

Christie, Emerson B., "The New Albanian Constitution," *American Political Science Review* 20 (1926) 120–23.

Clogg, Richard, *A Concise History of Greece* (Cambridge: Cambridge University Press, 1992).

Collier, Simon and William F. Sater, *A History of Chile, 1808–1994* (Cambridge: Cambridge University Press, 1996).

Congleton, Roger D., "From Royal to Parliamentary Rule without Revolution: The Economics of Constitutional Change within Divided Governments," *European Journal of Political Economy* 23 (2007) 261–84.

Crampton, R. J., *A Concise History of Bulgaria*. 2nd ed. (Cambridge: Cambridge University Press, 2005).

da Silva Soares, Carlos Dalmiro, "Evolução Historico-Sociológica dos Partidos Políticos no Brasil Imperial," undated, http://www1.jus.com.br/doutrina/texto.asp?id=1503

Dardé, Carlos and Manuel Estrada, "Social and Territorial Representation in Spanish Electoral Systems," in Raffaele Romanelli (ed.), *How Did They Become Voters? The History of Franchise in Modern European Representation* (The Hague: Kluwer, 1998) 133–54.

de Lolme, J. L., *The Constitution of England [1776]* (Delanco, NJ: The Legal Classics Library, 2002).

de Oliveira Marques, A. H., *História de Portugal. Volume III: Das Revoluções Liberais aos Nossos Dias* (Lisboa: Editorial Presenca, 1998).

Deveraux, Robert, *The First Ottoman Constitutional Period* (Baltimore: Johns Hopkins Press, 1963).

Dragnich, Alex, "Leadership and Politics: Nineteenth Century Serbia," *Journal of Politics* 37 (1975) 344–61.

The Development of Parliamentary Government in Serbia (Boulder, CO: East European Monographs, 1978).

Elster, Jon, *Ulysses and the Sirens*. Rev. ed. (New York: Cambridge University Press, 1984).

"Unwritten Constitutional Norms," unpublished paper, 2007a.

"Whether and How Constitutions Matter," prepared for the Conference on Constitutions and Consequences, Harvard Law School, 2007b.

Farmanfarma, A., "Constitutional Law of Iran," *American Journal of Comparative Law* 3 (1954) 241–247.

Fausto, Boris, *A Concise History of Brazil* (Cambridge: Cambridge University Press, 1999).

Figes, Orlando, *A People.s Tragedy: The Russian Revolution 1891–1924* (New York: Penguin Books, 1996).

Fischer, Bernd Jurgen, *King Zog and the Struggle for Stability in Albania* (Boulder, CO: East European Monographs, 1984).

Garrido, Aurora, "Electors and Electoral Districts in Spain, 1874–1936," in Raffaele Romanelli (ed.), *How Did They Become Voters? The History of Franchise in Modern European Representation* (The Hague: Kluwer, 1998) 207–26.

Hardin, Russell, "Why a Constitution?" in Bernard Grofman and Donald Wittman (eds.), *The Federalist Papers and the New Institutionalism* (New York: Agathon Press, 1989) 100–20.

Herb, Michael, "Princes and Parliaments in the Arab World," *Middle East Journal* 58 (2004) 367–84.

Hitchins, Keith, *Romania, 1866–1947* (Oxford: Clarendon Press, 1994).

Huang, Fali, "The Coevolution of Economic and Political Development from Monarchy to Democracy," working paper, School of Economics, Singapore Management University, 2008.

Jacobson, Stephen and Javier Moreno Luzón, "The Political System of the Restoration, 1875–1914: Political and Social Elites," in José Alvarez Junco and Adrian Shubert (eds.), *Spanish History since 1808* (London: Arnold, 2000).

Jespersen, Knud J. V., *A History of Denmark* (New York: Palgrave Macmillan, 2004).

Jeszenszky, Géza, "Hungary through World War I and the End of the Dual Monarchy," in Peter F. Sugar, Péter Hanák, and Tibor Frank (eds.), *A History of Hungary* (Bloomington: Indiana University Press, 1990) 267–94.

Kayali, Hasan, "Elections and the Electoral Process in the Ottoman Empire, 1876–1919," *International Journal of Middle East Studies* 27 (1995) 265–86.

Kornhauser, Lewis A., "The Normativity of Law," *American Law and Economics Review* V1 N1/2 (1999) 3–25.

Kostadinova, Tatiana, *Bulgaria, 1879–1946: The Challenge of Choice* (New York: Columbia University Press, 1995).

Lavaux, Philippe, *Les Grandes Démocraties Contemporaines*. 2nd ed. (Paris: PUF, 1998).

Lehoucq, Fabrice, "Electoral Fraud: Causes, Types, and Consequences," *Annual Review of Political Science* 6 (2003) 233–56.

Linz, Juan J., "Presidential or Parliamentary Democracy: Does It Make a Difference?" in J. J. Linz and Arturo Venezuela (eds.), *The Failure of Presidential Democracy: The Case of Latin America* (Baltimore: Johns Hopkins University Press, 1994).

Lorwin, Val. R., "Belgium: Religion, Class, and Language in National Politics," in Robert A. Dahl (ed.), *Political Oppositions in Western Democracies* (New Haven, CT: Yale University Press, 1966).

Macartney, C.A., *Hungary: A Short History* (Chicago: Aldine Publishing, 1962).

May, Arthur J., *The Hapsburg Monarchy 1867–1914* (New York: W.W. Norton, 1968).

McFarlane, Bruce J., *Yugoslavia: Politics, Economics, and Society* (London: Pinter, 1988).

Meeüs, Adriende, *History of the Belgiums* (New York: Frederick A. Preager, 1962).

Mota Barbosa, Silvana, "O Conselho de Ministros no Império do Brasil," *Revista de Historia* 13 (2007) 52–62.

Ottaway, Marina and Meredith Riley, "Morocco: From Top-Down Reform to Democratic Transition?" Carnegie Papers, No. 71. (New York: Carnegie Endowment for International Peace, 2006).

Popperwell, Ronald G., *Norway* (New York: Praeger, 1972).

Ramsdell, Daniel B., *The Japanese Diet: Stability and Change in the Japanese House of Representatives, 1890–1990* (Lanham, MD: University Press of America, 1992).

Ramseyer, Mark and Frances M. Rosenbluth, *The Politics of Oligarchy: Institutional Choice in Imperial Japan* (Cambridge: Cambridge University Press, 1995).

Roberts, Michael, *The Age of Liberty: Sweden 1719–1772* (New York: Cambridge University Press, 2002).

Robins, Philip, *A History of Jordan* (Cambridge: Cambridge University Press, 2004).

Scalapino, Robert A., *Political Development in Modern Japan* (Princeton: Princeton University Press, 1968).

Schmitt, Carl, *Théorie de la Constitution*. Traduit de l.Allemand par Lilyane Deroche (Paris: Presses Universitaires de France, 1993).

Secker, Ineke, "Representatives of the Dutch People: The Smooth Transformation of the Parliamentary Elite in a Consociational Democracy, 1849–1998," in Heinrich Best and Maurizio Cotta (eds.), *Parliamentary Representatives in Europe 1848–2000* (Oxford: Oxford University Press, 2000) 270–309.

Seton-Watson, R. W., *A History of the Roumanians from Roman Times to the Completion of Unity* (Cambridge: Cambridge University Press, 1934).

Seton-Watson, R. W., and R. G. D. Laffan, *A Short History of Yugoslavia, From Early Times to 1966* (Cambridge: Cambridge University Press, 1966).

Sims, Richard L., *A Political History of Modern Japan, 1868–1952* (New Delhi: Vikas, 1991).

Skendi, Stavro, *The Political Evolution of Albania, 1912–1944* (New York: Mid-European Studies Center, 1954).

Albania (London: Atlantic Press, 1957).

Stead, Alfred, *Servia by the Servians* (London: William Heinemann, 1909).

Stokes, Gale, *Politics as Development: The Emergence of Political Parties in Nineteenth-Century Serbia* (Durham, NC: Duke University Press, 1990).

Storing, James A., *Norwegian Democracy* (Boston: Houghton Mifflin, 1963).

Suster, Zeljan E., "Development of Political Democracy and Political Party Pluralism in Serbia, 1903–1914," *East European Quarterly* 31 (1998).

Taylor, A. J. P., *The Habsburg Monarchy, 1809–1918; A History of the Austrian Empire and Austria-Hungary* (London: Hamish Hamilton, 1948).

Van Caenegem, R. C., *An Historical Introduction to Western Constitutional Law* (Cambridge: Cambridge University Press, 1995).

Verney, Douglas V., *Parliamentary Reform in Sweden, 1866–1921* (Oxford: Clarendon Press, 1957).

von Beyme, Klaus, *Parliamentary Democracy: Democratization, Destabilization, Reconsolidation, 1789–1999* (London: MacMillan 2000).

Wasquerel de, Emmanuel and Benoît Yvert, *Histoire de la Restauration 1814–1830* (Paris: Perrin, 2002).

Zurcher, Erik, *Turkey: A Modern History* (London: I.B. Tauris, 1997).

6

Social Foundations of China's Living Constitution

Randall Peerenboom

The chapter examines the social foundations of constitutionalism in China, focusing on constitutions as a historical response to particular events. The goal is to move beyond an analysis of the constitution as a formal text to shed light on the de facto constitutional order in China, on China's living constitution and its social, historical, cultural, economic, political, and legal foundations. The first section begins with a brief historical overview of China's constitutions. The second section discusses the current constitution, passed in 1982, and its four subsequent amendments. The third section explores the main functions of the constitution in China today and how the constitutional order actually operates. The fourth section discusses China's living constitution. The fifth section concludes with some thoughts about the future of constitutionalism in China and the possibility of a party-state alternative to liberal democratic constitutionalism.

FROM THE QING TO NEW CHINA TO NEW NEW CHINA: QING, REPUBLICAN AND SOCIALIST CONSTITUTIONS, AND BEYOND

The contemporary Chinese term for constitutions – *xianfa* – existed in premodern times but assumed its present meaning when the idea of constitutions in the modern sense was introduced in the late nineteenth century from Western countries and via Japan. Since 1908, there have been twelve officially promulgated constitutions (and several drafts), including four socialist constitutions in 1954, 1975, 1978, and 1982, the last of which has been amended four times.[1] The constitutions differ in important ways in terms of certain formal features, reflecting the different social, political, and

[1] The Common Program, a quasi-constitutional document and the organic law adopted in 1949, served as the constitution from 1949 to 1954. The Common Program and all four socialist-period constitutions (both English and Chinese versions) are available at http://www.e-chaupak.net/database/chicon/

economic contexts in which they arose (Nathan, 1986). Nevertheless, on the whole, they share key characteristics.

First, the constitutions were based on Western models. They were drafted by jurists with training abroad and familiar with the constitutions and constitutional practices of the dominant powers at the time. Accordingly, despite some distinctive features, the constitutions look familiar and seem broadly consistent with constitutions elsewhere in terms of general principles such as popular sovereignty, state institutions and their powers, and fundamental rights.

To be sure, the four socialist-era constitutions reflect their socialist heritage and the moderation or radicalism of politics at the time of drafting. Drafters of the 1954 constitution drew heavily on the 1936 Stalin constitution of the USSR. The Soviet influence is evident in concepts such as democratic dictatorship of the people and democratic centralism, in institutions such as the procuracy, and in the inclusion of an expansive list of social, economic, and cultural rights. Some of the features of the socialist constitutions, including the reference in the preamble to the 1982 constitution to the Four Cardinal Principles,[2] coexist uneasily with many of the typical features of constitutions in liberal democracies.

Second, as true everywhere, China's constitutions were meant to serve a variety of purposes. In general, the constitutions have served to energize the people to better serve the state and contribute to a stronger China; symbolize national unity; affirm the policies of those in power; and set forth the ideals and goals for society to achieve. Different historical circumstances led to differences in emphases among these goals as well as to differences in how these broad purposes were understood. For example, in 1908, three years before the collapse of the Qing dynasty, the first of China's constitutions sought to establish a constitutional monarchy. One of the main goals in passing the constitution was to defuse the rising Han nationalism that was challenging the ruling Manchurian regime. Like subsequent constitutions during the Republican period, the Qing constitution was also intended to strengthen China as a nation and ward off encroachment from foreign powers.

Whereas all of the constitutions have announced broad goals, the socialist-era constitutions have had a more pronounced ideological and programmatic quality, particularly with respect to civil and political rights (Cohen, 1978; Edwards 1986; Nathan, 1986). The 1975 constitution – a Cultural Revolution product intended to consolidate Mao's power – was the most ideological of all with its repeated denunciations of foreign imperialists and the endorsement of continued revolution to fend off foreign aggression and combat class struggle at home. Nevertheless, all four

[2] The Four Cardinal Principles, enunciated by Deng Xiaoping as topics not open for challenge as part of a broader attempt to liberalize political discussion, refer to the need to adhere to the socialist path, maintain the people's democratic dictatorship, uphold the leadership of the CCP, and follow Marxist-Leninist-Mao Zedong thought.

socialist constitutions begin with a lengthy preamble that sets forth basic goals. The preamble to the 1982 constitution, for instance, traces the long and glorious history of China; laments the national humiliation at the hands of foreign powers from the mid-nineteenth century until Mao Zedong and the Chinese Communist Party (CCP) were able to defeat the collective historical forces of imperialism, feudalism, and bureaucratic capitalism to unify the nation and establish New China; and sets out some of the major achievements under the CCP in defending the nation against foreign aggression, developing the social and economic order, and improving the lives of citizens, before turning to major challenges.

Third, one of the key constitutional issues has been the strength of the executive relative to the legislative branch, or more fundamentally the extent to which state powers will be concentrated in the hands of a single person. Thus, debates in 1913 centered on the relative power of the executive and the legislature in the Temple of Heaven draft constitution. Liang Qichao and the Progressive Party favored giving more power to the president. The Nationalist Party favored a stronger parliament, which they controlled as a result of elections in 1912–1913.

Fourth, on the whole, judicial power and independence have been limited both formally and in practice. The 1946 constitution was the only one of China's constitutions to provide for judicial review of laws for their constitutionality. However, it was never implemented due to the civil war between the Kuomingtang (KMT) and the communists. Even though the powers and independence of the courts varied in the four socialist constitutions, the courts have never enjoyed the broad powers of judicial review as they do in the United States. Rather, courts' powers have been limited, as traditionally the case in civil law and parliamentary-supreme systems. Today, there is no constitutional court or constitutional review body. The NPC Standing Committee is charged with reviewing lower-level legislation for consistency with the constitution. Although the courts may review the legality of specific administrative acts or decisions, they do not have the power to review, and thus to strike down or quash, abstract acts (i.e., generally applicable rules).

The 1982 constitution provides for the independence of the courts in handling cases. However, both formally and in practice, the courts are subject to a variety of party and state mechanisms to ensure accountability, including supervision by the people's congress, procuracy, and party organs. In recent years, the courts have also been subject to increased scrutiny by the media and public (Peerenboom 2010).

Fifth, concerns about concentration of power in the hands of a strong leader have proven well founded. Leaders who have become too powerful have reverted to authoritarian rule, sought to undermine or dismantle the legislature, judicial organs, or other competing sources of power, and imposed extensive restrictions on individual rights in the name of social stability. Thus, once elected president, Yuan Shikai dissolved parliament in 1914 before declaring himself emperor in 1915. This usurpation of power resulted in an uprising by provincial warlords that forced Yuan to abolish the monarchy in 1916. Later, in April 1948, the KMT essentially gutted the constitution by passing the Temporary Provisions Effective during the Period of Communist Rebellion. These provisions, along with the declaration of Martial Law in 1949, allowed the KMT in Taiwan to halt parliamentary elections, pass administrative regulations restricting civil and political rights, and nullify provisions that would have imposed a term limit on the president.

Meanwhile, on the mainland, the four socialist constitutions have reflected struggles over the concentration of power, although key developments have also been influenced by the CCP constitution and constitutional conventions. The 1954 constitution limited the term of the head of state. Although Mao relinquished the head-of-state position to Liu Shaoqi, he maintained his positions as head of the Party and the military. However, the split in the trinity of powers (state, party, and military) proved unstable, and Mao used the Cultural Revolution to reunite the powers. The 1982 constitution distributed powers among different branches of the government to avoid the excessive concentration of power, with the Party constitution also being amended under Deng Xiaoping to achieve a similar purpose. However, the split of power led to political discord and competition among the political leadership, which erupted into public view over how to respond to the crisis in Tiananmen in 1989. This led to the reintegration of party, state, and military power under Jiang Zemin. When Hu Jintao assumed power, he first became general secretary of the Party in 2002, state president in 2003, and chairman of the Central Military Commission of the CCP in 2004. However, Jiang Zemin remained head of the Central Military Commission of the PRC until 2005, when Hu assumed that post as well, completing the reintegration of power. In resigning his last post, Jiang Zemin endorsed the constitutional convention concentrating power: "[T]he three offices, general secretary of the Party, state chairman and chairman of the Central Military Commission, are integrated into a trinity system of rule. Such a leadership regime and a leadership model is not only necessary, but also most appropriate for a party and a country as large as ours" (Jiang 2010).

Sixth, in addition to the horizontal checks and balances among the different branches and struggles over the concentration of power in the executive, another key issue has been vertical power relations between the central government and provincial and local governments. For instance, after Yuan's death, the Progressive Party and the Nationalists sought to draft a new constitution, with debate centering on whether the constitution should only set out central powers or try to delineate the powers of local and provincial governments as well. Some feared that local warlords would undermine the constitutional order through violence if the new constitution tried to limit their powers; others worried that the failure to rein in the powers of the warlords would simply perpetuate the current political chaos. Between

1917 and 1923, a federalist movement arose in which many provinces enacted their own constitutions. Federalists hoped that the issue of national unity could be addressed after autonomous provinces had established their own governance systems. Provincially elected representatives would then meet to create a national constitution. The movement failed when local warlords resisted limits on their powers and the need for national unity became more pressing.

Today, central-local relationships continue to be a major concern, which is not surprising given the size and complexity of China and the wide regional variation in terms of ethnicity, levels of wealth, strength of institutions, and, increasingly, the nature of the local economy. In general, the eastern region is much more economically developed and urbanized than the western region, which is more dependent on agriculture.

Seventh, every constitution after 1908 has expressly or implicitly provided for popular sovereignty (albeit with restrictions based on class or political status in some cases). On the whole, however, elites have been skeptical about the masses and their capacity for governance. Sun Yat-sen, for instance, believed the masses lacked the education and political competence to govern directly. Accordingly, he endorsed a three-stage transition to a constitutional state. During phase one, an autocratic military government would unify the country. Phase two was a period of tutelage where people would be allowed to exercise political control over basic-level government. This would lead to full-blown constitutional democracy in phase three.

Thus, although most constitutions provided for popular sovereignty, none provided for its effective exercise by the people. As Nathan (1986) notes: "In no constitution was the executive directly elected. The national legislature was always elected either indirectly or by a limited electorate and had very limited authority in government affairs. The influence of the citizen over state policy was so buffered and checked as to be negligible in practice." In addition to limits on the number and choice of candidates and who could participate in the voting, some elections have been marred by fraud. During the Republican period, some political factions that lost at the polls carried out coups, committed political assassinations, or engaged in military resistance. China's limited experience with elections then is that they are no panacea – a lesson current leaders and citizens are likely to take from the experience of other developing countries in East Asia and elsewhere (Peerenboom, 2007).

Eighth, despite the limits on elections, citizens have played a role in the constitutional process. Constitutions have generally been subject to public debate. In general, as elsewhere, the drafting process itself has been dominated by elites,[3] although with some avenues for citizen participation mainly through organized interest groups

[3] Although formally the power to amend the constitution belongs to the NPC, in practice, the CCP initiated constitutional revisions and determined their scope.

or associations. The public has usually then been given an opportunity to comment on published drafts. For instance, although the CCP clearly controlled the drafting of the 1954 constitution, a wide range of elites participated, including legal scholars who had studied in Japan and the United States, who were not Party members. The draft constitution was circulated to leading cadres in local government for comment and then opened up to the public for three months of public comment, resulting in more than one million questions, comments, and suggestions. The process of deliberation and discussion led to numerous revisions, including significant changes regarding the authority and independence of the courts (Tiffert, 2009). The National People's Congress (NPC) has ratified each new constitution or amendment, usually by unanimous or nearly unanimous vote.

In recent years, academic and public discussion of constitutional amendments has increased in breadth and intensity. In the run-up to the 2004 amendment, academics advocated a number of far-reaching revisions. However, once the leadership had settled on the topics to be addressed and the basic principles, they put an end to further discussion, resulting in the cancellation of academic conferences and the harassment of some academics who continued to push for additional reforms (Chen, 2008).

Ninth, all constitutions failed to take root or function in the way constitutions have functioned in the more fully developed constitutional orders of wealthy Euro-American liberal democracies. There are two main explanations. The period from the end of the Qing through much of the socialist period has been a turbulent one, punctuated by military struggle against foreign aggressors, civil war between the KMT and CCP, as well as battles between the central state and provincial warlords; political struggle among competing factions both at the central and local levels; and major changes in the economic, legal, and political systems, particularly during the socialist era with the Anti-Rightist Movement of the 1950s, followed by the Great Leap Forward, the Cultural Revolution, and then the transition to a market economy beginning in 1978. Xiao-Planes captures the difficulties in a neat summary of the Republican period equally applicable to the socialist era until the reform era: "The national entity imploded: political life became militarized; and power relations became personalized and fragmented" (Xiao-Planes, 2009).

An alternative but complementary explanation emphasizes the difficulty of transplanting Western liberal democratic institutions to the very different context of China. The constitutions were based on values and ideas that challenged core sociopolitical and cultural values and practices in China. Effective implementation of the constitution therefore required a radical transformation of local institutions, practices, and values that had existed for thousands of years. Today, the liberal democratic origins of the constitution are being tested by an increasingly confident CCP committed to developing its own form of constitutional order consistent with China's national conditions.

THE 1982 CONSTITUTION AND ITS AMENDMENTS: FROM A CENTRALLY PLANNED ECONOMY TO A SOCIALIST MARKET ECONOMY, FROM A REVOLUTIONARY PARTY TO A GOVERNING PARTY

Like the previous constitutions, the 1982 constitution was both backward-looking and forward-looking, and reflected both international practices and China's own circumstances. Whereas the 1954 constitution celebrated the recent victory of the CCP and China's close relations with the Soviet Union, the 1975 constitution consolidated Mao's power and displayed the radicalism of socialist ideology during the Cultural Revolution, and the short-lived 1978 constitution manifested the tension between continued endorsement of revolutionary politics and the need for stability, the 1982 constitution reflected Deng Xiaoping's rise to power, the shift from radical politics to modernization and economic development, and the Party's transformation from a revolutionary party to a governing party.

Zhu Suli has observed that whereas in many countries, the modern state preceded the rise of political parties and democratic constitutional orders, in China, the rise of political parties preceded the modern nation state. As a result, both the CCP and KMT were elitist revolutionary parties that mobilized and led the masses from above: "[B]oth the CCP and the KMT ... have had to be much more proactive and aggressive in mobilizing China's fragmented and premodern political and social forces into a modern unified state – and through this attain the national independence, and related capacities for social and economic development, that political parties in the West have been able to largely take for granted" (Zhu, 2009). The revolutionary nature of the CCP is also attributable to the shortage of qualified professional and educated elite, many of whom left with the KMT to Taiwan, although no doubt the Anti-Rightist Movement, the Cultural Revolution, and other ideologically driven purges contributed to the shortage and curtailed the development of a professional judiciary and bureaucracy. In any event, the Party remained revolutionary for too long rather than transforming into a governing party, relying on party organization and leadership – including an emphasis on ideology and discipline – to govern, rather than creating effective state institutions.

The transition to a market economy required more effective governance, including a more effective legal system. Thus, the preamble declares that the central goal of the 1982 constitution is to "steadily improve socialist institutions, develop socialist democracy, improve the socialist legal system and work hard and self-reliantly to modernize industry, agriculture, national defense and science and technology step by step to turn China into a powerful and prosperous socialist country with a high level of culture and democracy."

Since 1982, the amendment process has been used to codify, rather than signal, significant steps in the transition to a socialist market economy. Indeed, the amendments read like a play-by-play of China's ongoing efforts to shift from a centrally planned to a more market-based economy with their increasing support for a more robust private sector, deregulation, and the restructuring of state-owned enterprises (SOEs). The first amendment in 1988 hesitantly announced that the "State permits the private sector of the economy to exist and develop within the limits prescribed by law. The private sector of the economy is a complement to the socialist public economy." The 1999 amendment then upgraded the status of the private economy, which was acknowledged to be a "major component" of the socialist market economy. Other amendments reflected developments with respect to the autonomy and management of SOEs; changes in collectives and communes as a result of the rise of the rural household contract responsibility system; and the clarification of, and need to better protect, land use rights.

The amendment process has also sanctioned major ideological shifts resulting from leadership changes and the evolving nature of the economy, rather than signaling future policies. Thus, a 1993 amendment sought to reconcile socialism with the transition to a market economy and the rise of a capitalist class by introducing the notion of socialism with Chinese characteristics and announcing that China was in the primary stage of socialism. The basic idea was that China would first have to pass through a capitalist phase before a true socialist state could be realized. In 1999, the constitution was again amended, this time to acknowledge that China will remain in the primary stage of socialism "for a long time." The 1999 amendments also added Deng Xiaoping thought to Marxist-Leninist-Mao Zedong thought as the guiding ideology, reflecting the by then firmly established ideological shift from radical politics to economic development.

The constitution was amended once more in 2004 to add the "important thought" of the "Three Represents" associated with Jiang Zemin. The Three Represents refer to the CCP's role as representative of the development needs of the advanced productive forces, of the progressive direction of China's advanced culture, and of the fundamental interests of the broad majority of citizens. Their main import is to realign the CCP from a proletariat-based party to a more broad-based party that tracks changes in the economy and society by incorporating the new class of capitalists and entrepreneurs within the CCP, even though the 1982 constitution, like previous socialist constitutions, continues to describe China as a democratic dictatorship of the people led by the proletariat and based on an alliance of workers and peasants.

Given the historical pattern, the constitution will presumably again be amended to reflect the emphasis of the current administration of Hu Jintao and Wen Jiabao on the establishment of a *harmonious society*. The Deng-Jiang emphasis on aggregate growth led to rising inequality and severe environmental degradation. While pumping money into infrastructure development needed to support rapid growth, the government was ignoring other pressing social needs. The government's public spending on education and health as a percentage of GDP has been among the lowest in East Asia. The reduced spending, combined with a turn toward market forces in education and health and the underdevelopment of the welfare system, have exacerbated the plight of the most vulnerable members of society and heightened social tensions. With greater rights consciousness and higher expectations, Chinese citizens were turning to the courts, government agencies, and Party organs to address their needs. When those channels proved inadequate, they took to the streets in increasing numbers. There were 538,941 multiparty suits in 2004, up 9.5 percent from 2003.[4] The number of petitions to government entities rose dramatically until 1999, before starting to decline. Even with the decline, in 2005, the letters and visits offices received a total of 12.7 million complaints (Fu and Cullen, 2008). According to one survey, 63.4 percent of those who eventually brought their complaints to the central authorities in Beijing had first sought resolution in the courts (Yu, 2007). The number of mass protests and large-scale demonstrations also rose rapidly, from 58,000 in 2003, to 74,000 in 2004, to 85,000 in 2005, to more than 100,000 in 2008. According to the state media, more than 1,800 police were injured and 23 killed during protests in the first nine months of 2005 alone.

The government viewed these protests as a threat to social stability, and thus a threat to sustained economic growth. The CCP's legitimacy is based to a large extent on its ability to ensure social stability and improve people's living standards. Understandably, the Hu-Wen administration announced a major new policy initiative.[5]

The new policy turned away from the single-minded focus on aggregate growth, emphasizing instead high-quality sustainable growth, social justice, and the creation of a harmonious society. The goal is now efficient resource use, environmentally friendly development, and "green GDP" (although efforts to create a green GDP measure have been put on the back burner in light of the global economic crisis, technical difficulties, and normative controversies).[6] The harmonious society platform also pays more attention to income inequality, with greater efforts to stimulate growth in less developed regions through reallocation of state assets and new incentive programs as part of the Go Inland Campaign, the Great Western Development Strategy, and the Revitalize the Northeast Campaign. In addition, the government

4 Supreme People's Court's 2005 Work Report, available at http://www.court.gov.cn/work/200503180013.htm

5 These measures were set out in the Harmonious Society platform and Eleventh Five-Year Plan.

6 The global economic crisis has also called into question the export-driven model of development favored by China and other East Asian states. China could switch to a more consumption-driven development path without amending the constitution as the constitution did not endorse the export-driven model.

has sought to address the plight of farmers by eliminating the agriculture tax, promised more affordable medical care in rural areas, and vowed once again to eliminate school fees that prevented children from poor families from attending public school. The 2004 amendment reflected to some extent the switch in development goals in announcing "the promotion of the co-ordinated development of the material, political and spiritual civilizations."

The greater number of amendments addressing major changes in the economy compared to the number of amendments addressing political reforms testifies to the more limited nature of the latter since 1978. Elections remain limited to the township level, although there have been a few experiments at the county level as well as other elections for low-level administrative positions and for posts on neighborhood committees. Similarly, political participation remains limited in effectiveness, notwithstanding the emergence of an ever-growing civil society and more aggressive media, the passage of national and local access-to-information acts, and significant reforms to provide citizens with increased opportunities to participate in the law and rule making and implementation processes.

Nevertheless, the shift from revolutionary politics to effective governance is evident in a 1999 amendment endorsing rule of law – albeit a socialist variant of rule of law – where the country is governed in accordance with law. The amendment reflects the growing importance of the legal system for economic growth, a different concept of law where law is also understood to apply to state actors and limit state power, and the considerable progress made in improving the legal system since 1978. Although not reflected directly in constitutional amendments, there have been many measures to rationalize and professionalize administrative agencies, the judiciary, the procuracy, police, the legal profession, and other judicial and government actors (Peerenboom, 2002; Chen, 2004, 2008).

The increased salience of human rights, both internationally and domestically, is also reflected in China's constitutional history. The 1954 constitution contained a broad list of civil and political as well as social, cultural, and economic rights, albeit some of them to be realized gradually as China developed economically. The 1975 and 1978 constitutions were more restrained in their treatment of rights and restricted their enjoyment by requiring citizens to support the leadership of the Party and the socialist system. The 1982 constitution once again set forth an expansive list of rights and signaled the growing global importance of rights by moving the rights section to the front ahead of the section on the structure of the state. In 2004, the fourth amendment of the constitution added a paragraph announcing that "[t]he State respects and preserves human rights."

The meaning, purpose, and practical import of the 2004 amendment have been much debated. Although China signed the International Covenant on Civil and Political Rights (ICCPR) in 1998, it has yet to ratify it, which is not surprising given the restrictions on civil and political rights (Peerenboom, 2007). The 2004 amendment may have been intended to fend off international pressure to ratify the ICCPR or at least demonstrate a greater commitment to the protection of (civil and political) rights. Indeed, the amendment breaks new constitutional ground in referring to "human" rights, as opposed to rights of workers, citizens, or people. On the other hand, China has increasingly become more assertive in resisting foreign pressure on human-rights issues. Thus, the amendment may have been intended more for domestic consumption. The amendment may seem like a return to the tradition of programmatic statements of rights, a feature of many early Chinese constitutions and a pronounced feature of socialist constitutions more generally (Nathan, 1986). Yet, as we have seen, most amendments have been backward-looking, ratifying economic and political developments and ideological changes that already occurred. It is possible that the amendment was intended to ratify or acknowledge significant changes over the last several decades with human rights, as was arguably the case for the 1999 rule-of-law amendment, which both announced a distinctive socialist variant of rule of law and also reflected decades of progress in rebuilding legal institutions and in legal reforms. Although many would dismiss this possibility given China's record on civil and political rights, in fact, there has been a considerable shift in thinking from the time when rights were dismissed as a capitalist tool to induce false consciousness. Perhaps more importantly, China outperforms the average in its income class on most indicators of rule of law, good governance, human rights, and human well-being, with the notable exception of civil and political rights (Peerenboom, 2007). Moreover, the amendment may have been sought by those in China who were beginning to explore the possibilities of constitutional litigation and adopting more aggressive litigation strategies to protect rights.[7] Although the constitution is not directly justiciable, and in any event the provision is too broad to provide a meaningful basis for resolving rights claims, the amendment may indirectly support better protection of rights both through litigation and other noncourt means by signaling a more receptive attitude.[8]

At the same time, another amendment was added providing that "[t]he State establishes a sound social security system compatible with the level of economic development." On the one hand, this provision reflects ongoing efforts to create a viable welfare system. On the other hand, it reflects growing concerns about the broad commitment to social and economic rights typically found in socialist constitutions,

[7] Xu Xianming and Li Buyun, two well-know academic advocates for human rights, apparently played a role in promoting the provision.

[8] A group of thirty leading legal scholars recommended eighteen constitutional reforms to make good on the commitment to human rights. See He Weifang et al., "Suggestions for the Improvement of Constitutional Protection of Human Rights in Our Country," www.law-thinker.com/details.asp?id=2078

the global trend to make social economic rights justiciable and to judicialize socioeconomic claims, and the difficulty China's courts have had handling such claims given the lack of adequate resources and the relative weakness of the courts (Peerenboom 2008). Thus, the provision highlights the more programmatic or aspirational nature of social and economic rights, seeks to lower expectations, and suggests that welfare rights will be treated as an obligation of the government rather than a justiciable right for individuals.

THE FUNCTIONS OF THE CONSTITUTION AND THE OPERATION OF THE CONSTITUTIONAL ORDER

The constitution has clearly served a signaling function, reflecting major changes in ideology, the nature of the economy, governance, and also, by negative implication, the slower pace of fundamental political reform. However, to what extent has the constitution played a functional role as the most fundamental law of the country? From a functional legal perspective, constitutions serve several broad purposes. Most fundamentally, constitutions authorize, delineate, and limit political (and military) power and the power of the state, state organs, and state actors. More specifically, constitutions, constitutional law, and constitutional litigation serve three functions: addressing division of power issues among state organs; resolving conflicts between the central and local government, including inconsistencies between lower-level regulations and the constitution; and protecting individual rights.

Horizontal Power Issues

The main role of the constitution to date has been to provide an initial distribution of power among state organs. This then provides the backdrop against which legal reforms, which frequently affect the balance of power among key state actors, are negotiated. For example, the constitution now gives the procuracy the power to supervise the courts. In recent years, the procuracy has interpreted this power to mean that it has the authority to supervise final judicial decisions. As expected, the judiciary has argued that the procuracy's power of supervision should be eliminated, or at least limited to general oversight of the court or investigation of particular instances of judicial corruption. According to most judges, the procuracy should have no power to supervise individual cases. The courts have also come into conflict with the legislative branch over similar powers of individual case supervision and with administrative agencies over the power of judicial review of agency decisions.

As in all legal systems, the judiciary has acted strategically in defending and promoting their interests vis-à-vis other branches. Historically, the courts have been relatively weak compared to the government agencies (particularly the Ministry of

Public Security), the procuracy, and even the legislature. In recent years, they have adopted various strategies to improve their position. One strategy, reflected on a policy level under former SPC President Xiao Yang but much more pronounced under the current president Wang Shenjun, has been to embrace populism. Thus the judiciary has adopted a number of measures to become more user-friendly, cheaper, and more efficient, more accessible, and transparent. The goal has been to better meet the actual demands of Chinese citizens who use the courts.

After years of emphasizing litigation in courts as the main means of resolving disputes, beginning in the early 2000s, the SPC began to emphasize once again mediation of disputes. The renewed interest in mediation is, in part, the attempt of the judiciary to enhance its legitimacy by responding to the needs of citizens, many of whom – particularly in rural areas – want decisions that reflect local customs and norms rather than the formal central laws promulgated by national legislators in far-off Beijing. The increasingly popular practice of senior judges meeting with parties in potentially incendiary large collective suits to explain the legal issues is another example.

Still another example is found in what Stephanie Balme and Michael Dowdle refer to as "popular constitutionalism." As they point out, post-Mao constitutionalism "is not and cannot be the exclusive product of elite intellectuals" (Balme and Dowdle, 2009). Debates about the constitution and the constitutional order reflect different views, both elite and popular, about how to envision the state and what type of polity China is to become. Now that the authorities have let the genie out of the bottle by endorsing rule of law and attributing normative, legal, and political significance to the constitution, the meaning and role of the constitution have become part of public discourse and open to political contestation, with state and nonstate actors appealing to the constitution to pursue their (often conflicting) goals and agendas.

In one manifestation of popular constitutionalism, judges in local courts have taken on socially controversial cases as a way of enhancing their professional stature and gaining support by responding to citizen demands for social justice. They decide such cases by adopting a more purposive approach that emphasizes the spirit of the constitution and a sense of popular justice rather than on the basis of a strict positivist analysis or formalist interpretation of textual rules (Balme, 2010).

Other courts have adopted a different strategy to increase their stature and maintain the legitimacy and reputation of the judiciary. He Xin shows that lower courts in Guangdong province have effectively resisted pressure from Party and government organs to take on socioeconomic disputes, raising questions about the extent to which they are controlled by superior political powers (He, 2009). Citing legal barriers and enforcement difficulties, the courts resisted the global trend to judicialize these disputes, pushing them back to political and administrative channels. However, the courts then demonstrated their strategic sophistication by claiming the right to review the government's decisions in administrative litigation. In so doing, the courts retain an advantageous position in the power relationship with the governments. Moreover, as these cases inevitably leave some groups dissatisfied, the court is able to avoid public displeasure by forcing the government to make the difficult decision. He concludes that Chinese courts are capable of deliberating about and transforming their situation by strategically interpreting the law and negotiating with superior powers. He cautions that judicial independence in China is far more complicated than is often recognized, and that judicial behavior cannot be adequately explained without thick descriptions of the legal arguments, resource constraints, and strategic interpretations open to the courts in a particular context.

In the absence of a constitutional court, however, most issues involving the balance of power between state organs, such as whether the procuracy and people's congress should be able to review court decisions, have been left to the political process, with the Party being the ultimate arbitrator when the conflicts become too intense or there appears to be a deadlock.

Vertical Power Issues

Constitutional law also provides the basis for addressing conflicts between the central government and lower-level governments, which is a form of principal-agent conflict. The rapid pace of legislation and an incentive structure that rewards local officials for achieving high growth rates have led to numerous inconsistencies between lower-level regulations and higher-level laws and the constitution. Rather than relying on the courts to strike down lower-level laws that are inconsistent with the constitution, the main way for addressing inconsistent regulations is through a filing and review system, with the review performed by the administrative superior agency.

The 2000 Legislation Law granted citizens and other entities the right to propose to the National People's Congress Standing Committee (NPCSC) that lower regulations were inconsistent with the constitution or laws. The government has now established an NPC committee to perform this task, and is in the process of working out the details of how this mechanism will work in practice. This has provided an opportunity to push for changes to protect citizens' constitutional rights and advance constitutional claims.

For example, after Sun Zhigang, a university student from Hubei, was beaten to death while detained in a form of administrative detention known as Custody and Repatriation, several young scholars filed a proposal challenging the legality and constitutionality of the Custody and Repatriation Measures. One of the key arguments was that the Measures were passed by the State Council. However, the Legislation Law required all restrictions of personal liberty to be based on a law passed by the NPC or its Standing Committee. The case was widely reported in the media and resulted in the State Council repealing the Measures, thus avoiding the need for the NPCSC to strike down the regulation.

In another well-known case, Peking University law professor Gong Xiantian published two open letters arguing that the draft Property Law violated basic principles of socialism and a constitutional provision declaring that state property is inviolable (Hand, 2006). NPC spokespersons, including NPCSC Chairman Wu Bangguo, issued public statements defending the constitutionality of the draft law and noting that the draft had been amended to provide greater protection to state property and avoid the fraudulent sale of state assets. Although delayed for a year, the Property Law was passed in 2007.

To what extent this new review mechanism will empower citizens remains to be seen. Citizens have submitted at least thirty-seven requests for review (Hand, 2006). However the NPCSC has yet to respond formally to a citizen proposal for review. Moreover, although the NPCSC issued two circulars setting out detailed procedures for handling proposals for NPCSC review of administrative regulations and judicial interpretations, these circulars do not provide much transparency into how the decisions are actually made.

More generally, although the NPCSC review creates a constitutional mechanism for dealing with one type of principal-agent problem, for the most part, principal-agent issues such as inconsistent regulations, abuse of power, and corruption are dealt with through other administrative and political mechanisms, including Party mechanisms such as the nomenklatura system of appointments, the Party-endorsed incentive structure for the promotion of government officials, the Party discipline committee, and *shuanggui*, a form of detention and investigation for Party members suspected of corruption.

Constitutional Litigation and the Protection of Individual Rights

Constitutional litigation to protect individual rights is only just beginning, and future progress is likely to be slow. As noted, there is no dedicated constitutional review body, the constitution is generally not considered to be directly justiciable,[9] and many rights have a programmatic or aspirational flavor. The Supreme People's Court did rely on the constitution in reaching its decision in a civil case involving the right to education. However, that case did not involve enforcing the constitution against the government. The case was also extremely controversial, with proponents

9 This is more a matter of interpretation and convention than formal constitutional provision. See "Letter of Reply by Supreme People's Court Regarding the Inappropriateness of Quoting the Constitution as the Basis for Deciding a Criminal Case and Imposing Penalty," *Collected Laws of the PRC* 120 (Jilin People's Press ed., 1990).

of expanded constitutional litigation drawing hyperbolical comparisons to *Marbury v. Madison*, and critics arguing that decision was at odds with the constitutional structure or unnecessary to provide relief in the particular circumstances. Since then, there have been no cases where a court has cited a constitutional right as the sole basis for its holding (although courts do sometimes cite specific constitutional provisions along with other laws and regulations to support their decisions).

The constitution has, however, been invoked in a series of discrimination cases. In one case that combined the right to education with a discrimination claim, three students from Qingdao sued the Ministry of Education for its admissions policy that allowed Beijing residents to enter universities in Beijing with lower scores than applicants from outside Beijing. In another case, a person infected with hepatitis B won an administrative litigation suit when he was denied a post as a civil servant because of his disease.[10] The court did not reach the constitutional issues raised in the case but held that the application of the standard on the plaintiff was wrong (Kellogg, 2009). Other employment discrimination cases have challenged height, gender, and age restrictions.

Rural residents have also appealed to the constitution to protest discriminatory treatment. In one well-known case, three students were killed in a traffic accident. In China, compensation is based on average income, which differs significantly between rural and urban areas. Thus, the families of two of the victims who were urban residents received more than twice the compensation of the family of the victim who was a rural resident. The family of the rural victim brought a lawsuit to challenge the discriminatory compensation, arguing the standard violated the principle in Article 33 of the constitution that all citizens are equal before the law. But the court held that the compensation was in accordance with existing law.

Citizens have also drawn on constitutional principles to uphold privacy claims. In a much publicized case, a Shaanxi couple was awarded damages after police stormed into their bedroom while they were watching an adult movie and a scuffle broke out between the husband and police, resulting in injuries to the husband (Peerenboom 2007).

To be sure, most of these cases have been dismissed on technical grounds, including lack of jurisdiction, failure to apply to the proper court, or the lack of authority to overturn an abstract administrative act. Moreover, in most cases, relief came in the form of a change in the laws, not a favorable court judgment, and was the result of a fortuitous conflux of circumstances, including media attention. For instance, the civil servant's hepatitis B case arose after a man in Zhejiang, after being denied

[10] Even though the plaintiff won the suit in that the court quashed the act to deny him employment, the court could not order the defendant to provide a job as the post had already been filled. See Hand (2006).

a civil service position because he was a hepatitis B carrier, killed a local official and seriously injured another. Although the man was eventually sentenced to death, his case attracted much sympathetic media attention. At the time, a proposal had also been submitted by a group of hepatitis carriers to the NPCSC on the discrimination issue. In the wake of these events, several provinces announced that they will not exclude noninfectious hepatitis carriers from public employment. And in 2004, the NPC revised the Law on the Prevention and Control of Infectious Diseases, banning discrimination against the disease carriers.

Similarly, the rural resident's compensation case arose at a time when the Hu-Wen administration was announcing the new policy to create a harmonious society and address social injustice, including rising rural-urban inequality. After the case, which was again widely reported in the press, several provinces adopted a uniform compensation standard for urban and rural residents.

These quasi-constitutional cases generally have involved economic issues. They do not involve political dissidents or the right to free speech. Parties who invoke the constitution to criticize the government or call for greater democratization have been notably unsuccessful.[11] Further, most of the successful cases raised discrimination claims. Discrimination is less politically sensitive, and equality claims are easily understood and generally supported by the public.

The recent arrests of activist lawyers and the closure of a leading public-interest organization suggest that judicialization of two types of disputes in particular have not been successful and will be looked on unfavorably in the future: (1) political disputes that challenge, or are perceived to challenge, the ruling regime; and (2) certain socioeconomic disputes, particularly involving a large number of plaintiffs.[12]

[11] For instance, Wang Zechen was sentenced to six years for subversion for attempting to establish a Liaoning branch of the banned China Democratic Party, attacking the Party as a dictatorship, and advocating the end of the single-party system and the establishment of a multiparty system with separation of powers. In court, Wang did not contest the facts but argued the acts were legal. Peerenboom, *China Modernizes*.

[12] Xu Zhiyong and Zhang Lu were detained, and Open Constitution Initiative (*Gongmeng*), shut down, for failing to pay taxes on a $100,000 gift from Yale University. Both were released on bail, along with a Xinjiang political activist, the day after the new U.S. ambassador arrived in Beijing. Although some commentators have speculated that the arrests were a temporary precaution in the run-up to the sixtieth anniversary of the PRC on October 1, it would appear that the detentions were part of a much broader crackdown that reflects structural concerns about social and political activism. According to reports, more than fifty activist lawyers lost their license to practice law. In addition, a number of nonlawyer activists have been detained, most notably Hu Jia and Liu Xiaobo. Both have been prominently involved in a wide range of issues, and were signatories of the Charter '08 petition, a manifesto calling for democracy, human rights, and the end to CCP dominance, which was modeled on Charter 77, a petition written in 1977 by Czech intellectuals and artists that helped undermine the Soviet empire in Eastern Europe. See generally "China Human Rights Defenders," *China Human Rights Briefing*, August 3–9, 2009; "Chinese legal activist held for tax evasion," *Associated Press*, August 4, 2009; "China's Lonely Heretic," *The Australian*, July 3, 2009.

The limits on political cases reflect the nature of the regime and the limits of political cause lawyering in China – and in effectively single-party authoritarian states generally[13] – the current state of sociopolitical stability, the dominant conception of law/rule of law, China's model of development, and the political contract between central and local governments (Fu and Peerenboom, 2010). The second type of socioeconomic case reflects the realities in a lower-middle-income country such as China, and the fact that in many cases, the courts are not able to provide parties with legitimate complaints an effective remedy for various reasons – most notably resources are insufficient and institutions such as the social welfare system are too weak.

Notwithstanding these qualifications, the increased reliance on litigation signals and growing willingness on the part of plaintiffs, lawyers and courts to look to the constitution as the basis for norms and principles that may be applied in particular cases to expand protection of the rights of individuals, subject to current doctrinal, jurisdictional, and political limitations.

CHINA'S LIVING CONSTITUTION: SOCIALIST CONSTITUTIONALISM WITH CHINESE CHARACTERISTICS

As is clear from the previous section, China's constitution is not the only authoritative source for political order in China. Anyone who only looked to the formal constitution would not be able to understand how key decisions are made and power is exercised.

Indeed, many scholars and commentators have dismissed the constitution as irrelevant or unimportant, with little political or legal impact. On this view, China is a single-party authoritarian state. At best, like other socialist constitutions, the current constitution is programmatic or aspirational; at worst, it is simply a sham, an ideological smokescreen to conceal the tyranny of personal rule or rule by a small clique of elites while appearing to conform to international standards and practices. There is a constitution without constitutionalism. Real power lies elsewhere, in the Party apparatus, which is governed by its own constitution, practices, and norms.

Proponents of this view often add that what is needed is liberal democracy. The political, economic, and legal order must comply with international standards: a WTO-compliant market economy rather than the admittedly hitherto successful East Asian Model of a developmental state focused on export-driven growth; genuine competitive multiparty democracy rather than socialist democracy and the

[13] Political lawyering emphasizes first-generation civil and political rights – the negative rights of freedom of speech, thought, religion, movement, and association – and the political institutions of (primarily economically advanced Western) liberal democracies that protect these rights.

notions of democratic centralism and a democratic dictatorship of the people under the leadership and guidance of the CCP; liberal democratic rule of law rather than statist socialist rule of law; and a liberal interpretation of human rights that emphasizes individual autonomy and expansive civil and political liberties (evidenced by ratification of and compliance with the ICCPR) rather human rights policies and practices based on subsistence as the most fundamental right, the reduction of poverty, and restrictions on civil and political rights in the name of social stability and economic growth.

Others approach the constitution more instrumentally. They seek to use the constitution where possible to support individual rights and other reforms. Many adopt this approach because they believe that there simply is no hope for a more radical rapid transition to liberal democracy at this point. Others believe that such a transition would be unwise at this point. Still others may disagree on substantive normative grounds with the notion that liberal democracy as a whole or particular aspects of the liberal democratic agenda are appropriate or desirable. Indeed, there is widespread disagreement over fundamental issues relating to the economy, regime type, legal reforms, and human rights in China. The range of opinion and the depth and intensity of disagreement are much greater than in Euro-American liberal democracies, and not easily reduced to the simultaneously overinclusive and underinclusive categories of (New) Right and (New) Left, liberals and conservatives, or reformers and hardliners.

A more recent approach has been to take the differences between the formal constitutional order and the actual operation of power as an invitation and opportunity to explore China's living constitution.[14] This approach highlights the fact that constitutions everywhere are more than just a piece of paper or a set of formal rules. The actual constitutional order consists of related legal rules, conventions, and institutions, as well as formal and informal practices and norms (Pettys, 2008; Young, 2008). The living constitution depends on how the constitution is interpreted, with theories and methods of interpretation varying widely, including original intent and positive and purposive approaches (Balkin, 2009). Constitutional practice may

[14] See, e.g., Backer (2009); Jiang (2010); Zhu Suli, "Judicial Politics." Many other scholars have also implicitly called attention to China's living constitution by noting the "gap" between the formal constitution and actual constitutional practices and the de facto constitutional order. See, e.g., Yu (2009), noting that the Chinese constitution is very Western at first glance but operates quite differently. In an article first published in 1996 and reprinted in 2006, Andrew Nathan (2006) suggested that "the constitutionalist scenario gains credibility from the improbability of the alternatives." Yet his canvassing of the proposals to develop constitutionalism simply invoked the standard features of liberal democratic constitutionalism: empower the NPC, expand elections, strengthen constitutional supervision, enhance judicial independence, improve the protection of human rights, etc. In focusing on the process of constitutional development rather than the substance or content of a stable or mature constitutional order in China, Michael Dowdle (2002) was one of the first Western scholars to entertain the possibility that China may develop its own variant of constitutionalism.

change dramatically through interpretation even if there are no formal amendments to the constitution. Notable examples from the United States include the establishment via interpretation and convention of a robust and decentralized system of judicial review that allows all courts to strike down federal or state laws at odds with constitution; the discovery of the right of privacy; and changes in the interpretation of what constitutes unreasonable search, due process in criminal trials, or cruel and unusual punishment.

This approach is also motivated by the realization that relative to the rather dismal results for most developing countries, China's reforms have been extremely successful, even though – or perhaps *because* – they did not comport to Western models for promoting democracy, rule of law, human rights, or the neoliberal prescriptions of the Washington Consensus for economic growth. Although some commentators continue to portray China as on the brink of collapse (Chang, 2002), the dominant view among most scholars is that China is reasonably stable (Shambaugh, 2000). Rather than seeing reforms as stalled (Pei, 2006), many scholars now see the CCP as responding effectively to crises and capable of sustaining the momentum of reform and deepening the reform agenda (Cheng 2001; Nathan, 2003; Yang 2004, Liu and Dittmer 2006).[15] Moreover, poll after poll show that Chinese citizens overwhelmingly continue to support the Party, take pride in the growing power of China, and are optimistic about their own future and the future of the country. Thus, the current system enjoys considerably more legitimacy than often acknowledged abroad.

Just as the failure of many third-wave democracies led commentators to reject the assumption that countries were in transition to liberal democracy and to focus on developing new descriptive and analytical categories, theories, and models that better captured and explained reality in these countries and better predicted where they may be heading (Carothers, 2002), so too China's success and the seeming durability of the current form of government has led to a search for new categories, theories, and models to better capture the current situation in China and predict where it might be heading.[16] There is growing recognition that China has not mimicked, and

[15] See also the articles by Yang, Barry Naughton, Jacques deLisle, Joseph Fewsmith, Dowdle, and Peerenboom – all of which take issue with the central claim that China is trapped in transition – in Randall Peerenboom, ed., *Is China Trapped in Transition?, available online at [http://fljs.org/section.aspx?id=1939]*. It bears emphasizing that all these scholars are considerably more cognizant of the challenges China faces going forward than the more hyperbolic reports in the popular media that suggest we are now living in an era dominated by the G2, and soon to be living in an era dominated by the G1 – China. See, e.g., (Shirk 2007).

[16] Landry (2009) notes, "The unorthodox institutional arrangements that symbolize China's legal system compel social scientists to think seriously about the micro-foundations of these arrangements, as well as their consequences. It is no longer tenable to dismiss the unexpected outcomes as transitional simply because we regard them as temporary 'out-of-equilibrium' phenomena" [by liberal democratic or Marxist-Leninist standards]).

need not simply mimic, Western liberal democratic constitutionalism, and cautious attempts to articulate the main features of a new form of constitutionalism – socialist constitutionalism with Chinese characteristics – or state-party constitutionalism.

The two most salient features of this new constitutional order reflect the two most significant differences between a liberal democratic order and contemporary Chinese socialism. First is the absence of genuine multiparty elections. Despite the existence of nominal non-CCP parties and institutions like the Chinese People's Political Consultative Committee, China remains an effectively single-party state where the CCP claims to represent all viewpoints. As a result, there is greater emphasis on inner-party democracy and the CCP as representative of all interests. As Zhu Suli notes:

> The Party has long been aware that national modernization cannot be accomplished by the party's political elite alone. The task of social integration requires that the party enjoy some significant degree of voluntary support from other social forces in China. This requires, in turn, that it be able to comprehend and appreciate the different interests that underlie these different societal factors. The CCP has responded to this by adopting a certain degree of democracy *within* the party. In this sense, the party itself becomes a quasi-constitutional structure – a structure whose own internal democracy can supplement or even compete with (and through such competition improve) the more formal constitutional apparatus of the state. (Zhu, 2009)

Political contestation is internalized within the Party, with inner-party democracy serving as a less politically volatile and potentially destabilizing form of democracy. As Backer observes:

> Party membership [serves] as the functional equivalent in the West of political citizenship. The holders of political citizenship – Party members – then serve *within* the Party as the forces for social cohesion … and *outside* the Party in a fiduciary capacity to all people in the political community who are holders of social and economic rights, but who lack political rights. Political citizenship, then, though limited, is open to those who would adhere to and further the political and rule of law values of the Party within the governance structures of the state set up for that purpose. (Backer 2009)

The second most salient feature of the living constitutional order is the relationship between the Party and the state, including the relationship between the Party constitution and the state constitution, and between Party practices, norms, and conventions and the practices, norms, and conventions of state institutions.

Whereas the 1975 and 1978 constitutions acknowledged the leadership role of the party in their operative clauses, the 1982 constitution deliberately relocated leadership of the party to the preamble, announced in the preamble for the first time that the constitution was the fundamental law, and provided in Article 5 that "[a]ll state organs, the armed forces, all political parties and public organizations and all enterprises and institutions must abide by the constitution and the law. All acts in violation of the constitution or the law must be investigated. No organization or individual is privileged to be beyond the constitution or the law."

Countless books and articles have been written to try to reconcile the tension between the leadership role of the party and these constitutional provisions. To be sure, in any constitutional order, there are tensions between the ultimate source(s) of power and the institutions, rules, and practices for limiting that authority. In liberal democracies where the courts are charged with constitutional and judicial review, the issue is the democratic deficit of the judiciary. In parliamentary-supreme systems, the issue is the independence and authority of the judiciary and how to entrench and protect fundamental rights from being overridden or restricted by parliament. Forests have been felled trying to grapple with these issues as well.

There is no theoretical or practical way in any legal system to resolve completely the tension between ultimate political power and the need to impose restraints on such power. In all systems, the restraints will be a matter of degree and will represent the combined result of market, legal, political, military, and social forces, reflected in formal and informal institutions, codified rules, and noncodified conventions and practices.

In China, the need to constrain Party power while still allowing the Party to play a positive role in leading the country in the mission to modernize is well accepted in general, although the specifics are contested in practice. As Deng Xiaoping stated:

> We uphold the Party's leadership, but the problem is whether the Party is doing a good job of leading. It should give effective leadership and not intervene in too many matters. The Central Committee should take the lead in this regard. What I am proposing will not weaken the Party's leadership. On the contrary, its leadership will be weakened if it tries to take responsibility for too many areas. (Deng 1986)

There is a line between the party and state, but the line is determined largely by convention. For both practical and ideological reasons, some matters are left to the state. As noted in the previous section, the general trend during the reform era has been to rely more heavily on state organs to govern. The main role of the Party is to determine major policies, which are then transformed into state laws and regulations and interpreted and implemented by state actors, subject to supervision by a combination of Party and state (and, increasingly, nonstate) mechanisms.

THE FUTURE OF CONSTITUTIONALISM IN CHINA

Early Chinese constitutions were largely Western imports, used to fend off foreign aggression and strengthen the Chinese state's claim to legitimacy and sovereignty. Even the 1982 constitution is predominantly Western in origins. The liberal democratic origins of the constitution are difficult to reconcile with the actual constitutional order and a rising, increasingly confident China firmly under the leadership of the CCP.

After thirty years of economic and legal reforms, it is now abundantly clear that China is neither a traditional Marxist-Leninist regime nor a liberal democracy. It is equally clear that China has been extremely successful in achieving economic growth, improving living conditions, and maintaining social stability, particularly in comparison with the rather dismal results in most developing countries. If we are to understand how China has achieved these results, better appreciate the challenges China faces and its prospects, and better predict the possible development paths in the future, we can no longer afford to dismiss the results and the development model in China as temporary out-of-equilibrium phenomena. We must develop, and take seriously, new conceptual and analytical categories that better capture reality in a non-liberal-democratic, non-Marxist-Leninist country with a "socialist market economy" and party-led "socialist rule of law."

How then might constitutionalism in China develop in the future? There appear to be four possibilities. The first two involve providing a more solid constitutional foundation for the role of the Party by amending the constitution.

Option one would be to amend the constitution, moving the general provision about the leadership role of the Party from the preamble back to the operative clauses,[17] and leaving the specifics of how that general provision should be operationalized to be dealt with through some combination of state and Party regulations, policies, practices, and conventions.

Option two would be to amend the constitution not only to provide for the leadership of the Party, but to delineate with more specificity how Party leadership is to be operationalized in practice. Of course, there would still be room for further clarification and development via state and Party laws, regulations, practices, conventions, and so forth.

The main benefit of these amendments would be to provide a firmer legal foundation for the role of the Party, thus reducing – but by no means eliminating – the tension between the leadership role of the Party and the constitution as the fundamental law of the land.

However, the political cost would be high. Both of these options would encounter fierce opposition at home and abroad. They would be seen as entrenching the Party's role, enhancing the Party's power, and thwarting efforts to separate the Party

[17] Constitutional-law scholars are divided about the legal effectiveness of the preamble: Some hold that entire preamble has legal effect, some that it has no legal effect, and some that only certain clauses have legal effect. Even if all or part of the preamble has legal effect, there are debates about the nature of that effect in general and with respect to particular issues.

and the state, and thus at odds with the historical trend toward liberal democratic constitutionalism. Granted, formal incorporation of a broad provision in the constitution does not need to result in any substantive changes in how the constitutional order currently operates. Like other constitutional amendments that reflected major changes in the nature of the economy or ideology, its main impact arguably would just be to ratify the constitutional order that has arisen and become more stable and delineated in its main features. Moreover, the second option could, at least in theory, result in both the clarification and limitation of the Party's role vis-à-vis other state actors.

A third option would be to overcome the gap between China's socialist constitutional order and the transplanted liberal democratic constitution on which it is based by becoming a liberal democracy, or at least more closely approximating one. This is the hope of liberal reformers pushing for gradual or piecemeal change, as well as the hope of those wishing for a more rapid and radical transition to liberal democracy.

None of these three options appear to be likely at present or in the near future. Thus, the most likely outcome is a fourth approach of continuing to muddle through, setting aside ideological tensions, jurisprudential puzzles, and technical inconsistencies while adopting a results-oriented pragmatic approach that adjusts the multifaceted relationship between the Party and state on an ongoing basis through a combination of formal and informal rules, conventions, and practices.

In the longer term, it is possible that China will democratize and adopt the main features of liberal democracy, although, as with other Asian states, constitutional democracy in Asia is likely to be less liberal than in Euro-America (Peerenboom, 2006). It is also possible that the economy will continue to grow and the CCP will become increasingly confident that the current arrangements suit China's particular circumstances, at which point options one or two may become more attractive. It is certainly true that the central leadership has been more adamant in stressing the leadership of the Party, issuing white papers on human rights, democracy, and rule of law, all of which endorse distinctly socialist variants. Government spokespersons, including Zhou Yongkang, the head of the Political-Legal Committee and former head of the Ministry of Public Security, as well as the newly appointed President of the Supreme People's Court Wang Shengjun, have been adamant in insisting that Chinese courts and the legal system more broadly will not mimic those in Western liberal democracies. Whether these statements reflect a growing sense of confidence and triumphalism about the rise of China or growing insecurity about "color" revolutions, the Arab Spring, rising domestic instability, and structural weaknesses is debatable. However, should China remain stable and prosperous, it is possible that there will be another white paper, this time articulating and defending a non-liberal-democratic, socialist variant of Party-state constitutionalism.

REFERENCES

Backer, Larry Catá, "The Party as Polity, the Communist Party, and the Chinese Constitutional State: A Theory of State-Party Constitutionalism," *Journal of Chinese and Comparative Law* 16 (1), (2009).

Balkin, Jack, "Framework Originalism and the Living Constitution," *Northwestern University Law Review* (2009), available online at http://ssrn.com/abstract=1290869

Balme, Stephanie and Dowdle, Michael, "Introduction: Exploring for Constitutionalism in 21st Century China," in Balme and Dowdle, ed., pp. 1–22, *Constitutionalism in China*. New York: Palgrave Macmillan, 2009.

Carothers, Thomas, "The End of the Transition Paradigm," *Journal of Democracy* 13, pp. 5–21 (2002).

Chang, Gordon, *The Coming Collapse of China*. New York: Random House, 2002.

Chen, Jianfu. *Introduction to the PRC Legal System*. Hong Kong: Butterworths, 2nd ed., 2004.

Chinese Law: Context and Transformation. Leiden and Boston: Nijhoff, 2008.

Cohen, Jerome, "China's Changing Constitution," *China Quarterly* 76, pp. 836–37 (1978).

Deng Xiaoping, "Help the People Understand the Importance of the Rule of Law," in *Selected Works of Deng Xiaoping*. Beijing: Foreign Languages Press, 1986.

Selected Works of Deng Xiaoping. Vol. III (1982–1992). Beijing: Foreign Language Press (1994).

Dowdle, Michael William, "Of Parliaments, Pragmatism, and the Dynamics of Constitutional Development: The Curious Case of China," *NYU Journal of International Law and Politics* 35, pp. 1–125 (2002).

Edwards, R. Randle. "Civil and Social Rights: Theory and Practice in Chinese Law Today," in *Human Rights in Contemporary China*, edited by R. Randle Edwards, et al. pp. 41–69, New York: Columbia University Press, 1986.

Fu Hualing and Richard Cullen, "From Mediatory to Adjudicatory Justice: The Limits of Civil Justice Reform in China," (November 25, 2008), available online at http://ssrn.com/abstract=1306800

Fu Yulin and Randall Peerenboom, "A New Analytical Framework for Understanding Judicial Independence in China," in Randall Peerenboom, ed., *Judicial Independence in China*, pp. 95–133, New York: Cambridge University Press, 2009.

Hand, Keith, "Using Law for a Righteous Purpose: The Sun Zhigang Incident and Evolving Forms of Citizen Action in the People's Republic of China," *Columbia Journal of Transnational Law* 45, pp. 114–47 (2006).

He Xin, "The Judiciary Pushes Back: Law, Power, and Politics in Chinese Courts," in Randall Peerenboom, ed., pp. 180–95, *Judicial Independence in China* (2010).

Jiang Shigong, "Written and Unwritten Constitutions: A New Approach to the Study of Constitutional Government in China," *Modern China*, 36 (1), pp. 12–46 (2010).

Jiang Zemin Wenxuan [Selected Writings of Jiang Zemin], vol. 3, p. 603 Beijing: People's Publishing Co. (2006).

Kellogg, Thomas, "Constitutionalism with Chinese Characteristics? Constitutional Development and Civil Litigation in China," *International Journal of Constitutional Law* 7, pp. 215–46 (2009).

Landry, Pierre et al., "Introduction: Markets, Courts and Leninism," *The China Review* 9 (1) (2009).

Li, Cheng, *China's Leaders: The New Generation*. Lanham, MD: Rowman and Littlefield (2001).

Liu, Guoli **and** Ditmmer, Lowell, "Introduction: The Dynamics of Deep Reform," in Dittmer and Liu, eds., pp. 1–24, *China's Deep Reforms: Domestic Politics in Transition*, Lanham, MD: Rowman & Littlefield (2006).

Nathan, Andrew, "Political Rights in the Chinese Constitutions," in R. Randle Edwards et al., eds., pp. 77–124, *Human Rights in Contemporary China* (1986).

"Authoritarian Resilience," *Journal of Democracy* 14 (1), pp. 60–17 (2003).

"China's Constitutional Option," in Dittmer and Liu, eds., pp. 177–190, *China's Deep Reforms: Domestic Politics in Transition* (2006).

Peerenboom, Randall. *China's Long March toward Rule of Law*. Cambridge : Cambridge University Press (2002).

"An Empirical Overview of Rights Performance in Asia, France and the USA," in Randall Peerenboom, ed., pp. 1–64, *Human Rights in Asia*, New York: Routledge (2006).

China Modernizes: Threat to the West or Model for the Rest? Oxford: Oxford University Press (2007).

"More Law, Less Courts: Legalized Governance, Judicialization and Dejudicialization in China," in Tom Ginsburg and Albert Chen, eds., pp. 175–202, *Administrative Law and Governance in Asia*. London: RoutledgeCurzon (2008).

ed., *Judicial Independence in China: Lessons for Global Rule of Law Promotion*. New York: Cambridge University Press (2010).

Pei, Minxin, *China's Trapped Transition: the Limits of Developmental Autocracy*. Cambridge, MA: Harvard University Press, 2009.

Pettys, Todd, "The Myth of the Written Constitution," *Notre Dame Law Review* 84, 991 (2008).

Shambaugh, David, ed., *Is China Unstable?* Armonk, NY: M. E. Sharpe (2000).

Shirk, Susan, *China: Fragile Superpower*. New York: Oxford University Press (2007).

Tiffert, Glenn, "Epistrophy: Chinese Constitutionalism and the 1950s," in Stéphanie Balme and Michael Dowdle, eds., *Building Constitutionalism in China*, pp. 66–70 New York: Palgrave Macmillan (2009).

Wan, Ming, "Democracy and Human Rights in Chinese Foreign Policy," in Yong Deng and Fei-Ling Wang, eds., pp.279–304, *China Rising*, (2005).

Xiao-Planes, Xiaohong "Of Constitutions and Constitutionalism: Trying to Build a New Political Order in China, 1908–1949," in Balme and Dowdle, eds., *Constitutionalism in China*, pp. 37–58. New York: Palgrave Macmillan (2009).

Yang, Dali, *Remaking the Chinese Leviathan: Market Transition and the Politics of Governance in China*. Stanford, CA: Stanford University Press (2004).

Young, Ernest, "The Constitution Outside the Constitution," University of Texas Public Law Research Paper No. 119 (2008).

Yu Jianrong, "Dui 560 mingjing shangfangzhe de diaocha [An Investigation on 560 Petitioners to Beijing," *Falü yu senghuo* [Law and Life] 5, 14 (2007).

Yu Xingzhong, "Western Constitutional Ideas and Constitutional Discourse in China," in Balme and Dowdle, eds., *Constitutionalism in China*, pp. 111–124. New York: Palgrave Macmillan (2009).

Zhu Suli, "'Judicial Politics' as State-Building," in Balme and Dowdle, eds., *Constitutionalism in China*, pp. 23–36. New York: Palgrave Macmillan (2009).

7

The Political Economy of Constitutionalism in a Non-Secularist World

Ran Hirschl

Contrary to what many liberals predicted or wished for, not only has religion not vanished, but instead it has gained a renewed momentum worldwide. From the fundamentalist turn in predominantly Islamic polities, to the spread of Catholicism and Pentecostalism in the global south, to the rise of the Christian Right in the United States, it is hard to overstate the significance of the religious revival in late-twentieth and early-twenty-first-century politics. Hundreds of millions of people – perhaps as many as a billion – now live in predominantly Muslim polities or subnational units that feature core elements of what may be classified as "constitutional theocracies" where religion and its interlocutors are enshrined as "a" or "the" source of legislation, and at the same time core ideals and practices of modern constitutionalism are adhered to (Hirschl 2010). In countries such as Israel (Judaism), Malaysia (Islam), or Sri Lanka (Buddha Sasana), religious affiliation is closely entangled with definitions of ethnicity, nationality, and citizenship. A further two billion people live in countries such as India, Turkey, or the Philippines where no particular religion is granted formal status, but where religious affiliation is a pillar of collective identity. The de facto boundaries of religion and state in these countries can be described as being blurred at best and are continually contested in both the political and the judicial spheres.

The constitutional domain in virtually all these religion-laden polities have become bastions of relative secularism, pragmatism, and moderation, thereby emerging as effective shields against the spread of religiosity and increased popular support for principles of theocratic governance. Various constitutional strategies have been developed by those who wield political power – and represent the groups and policy preferences that defy principles of theocratic governance – to hedge or mitigate the impact of religiosity on politics and public policy in these countries. Meanwhile, universalists and modernists increasingly turn to constitutional jurisprudence to block, delay, or mitigate the impact of religion in public life. And they know why. Constitutional courts in religion-laden polities have emerged as key secularizing agents, skillfully "delivering the goods" for antireligious stakeholders (Hirschl 2010).

Why, however, are constitutional law and constitutional courts so appealing to secularist, modernist, cosmopolitan, and other antireligious social forces in polities that face deep divisions along secular/religious lines? What makes the domain of constitutional law so attractive to such groups, with their well-defined worldviews, cultural propensities, interests, and policy preferences? Several broad rationales come to mind: (1) co-optation; (2) jurisdictional advantages; (3) the very nature and characteristics of constitutional law, its epistemology, and its interpretive logic; (4) constitutional delegitimation of radical religious association; and (5) political control of constitutional courts and judges.

In this chapter, I draw on various examples from the non-secularist world to address each of these dimensions of constitutional law's secularist appeal. I argue that, counterintuitively, the constitutional enshrinement of religion is a rational, prudent strategy that allows opponents of theocratic governance to talk the religious talk without walking most of what they regard as theocracy's unappealing, costly walk. Many of the jurisdictional, enforcement, and co-optation advantages that gave religious legal regimes an edge in the premodern era are now aiding the modern state and its laws in its effort to contain religion. Turning to constitutional law and courts to bring religiosity under check or defuse its potentially radical edge is a rational choice of action by secularists and moderates. Despite occasional and inevitable setbacks, it is a prudent, judicious gamble.

CO-OPTATION

The formal enshrinement of a specific religion as the sole "state religion" of a given polity does not only grant religion status, prestige, and protection from possible competitors; it also subjects certain aspects of religious affairs to monitoring by the state. With state recognition and funding comes statutory regulation and monitoring, judicial or otherwise. Akin to the legalization of otherwise unregulated and unauthorized norms and practices, the constitutionalization of religion may help prevent the development of an "underworld" of religious authority and institutions. Such "legalization" also entails tighter government influence over appointments to key religious leadership positions. In other words, one of the main strategic impulses that may push anti-theocratic stakeholders to endorse constitutionalism is *co-optation*.

The limiting effect of establishment on religious autonomy is evident in a variety of forms. At the most basic of levels, constitutional enshrinement of a state religion facilitates state interference in, if not control over, the appointment of religious leaders. As the famous circumstances that brought about the creation of the Anglican

Church by Henry VIII show, ensuring the loyalty of religious authorities is not something besieged political leaders can take lightly. An archetypal example from the emerging world of constitutional theocracies is the 1996 appointment by Egypt's president Hosni Mubarak of the moderate Muhammad Sayyid Tantawi as the Grand Imam of al-Azhar Mosque and Grand Sheikh of al-Azhar University, one of the (some say "the") highest spiritual authorities for nearly a billion Sunni Muslims. Until his death in 2010, Tantawi issued numerous moderate fatwas that counter rigid, conservative interpretation of *shari'a* precepts. He continuously angered radicals by supporting organ transplants, denouncing female mutilation, and ruling that women should be appointed to senior judicial and administrative positions. In 2009, to pick one example, Tantawi issued a fatwa suggesting that female students may not wear the *niqab* (Islamic face veil) in universities, including on al-Azhar premises. To reiterate, the head of al-Azhar issues a typically moderate edict on a hotly contested symbolic issue that has been at the core of the struggle between the Egyptian state and Islamic fundamentalism. The benefits of co-optation are quite clear here. The appointment of Tantawi, to be sure, is merely one episode in a much longer and deeper institutional and historical process of "nationalizing" al-Azhar by state elites in postcolonial Egypt. Since the 1961 formal nationalization of al-Azhar by Nasser, the control of al-Azhar by the military has been tight until the 1970s, and became somewhat more relaxed at times after that (Zeghal 1996, 1999).

In Saudi Arabia, Wahhabi discourse is channeled through the ulama (learned Muslim high clergy), who are largely state-appointed and historically loyal to the royal family. Rare attempts (most notably in 1992) by groups of conservative ulama to criticize the king or the royal family have resulted in severe sanctions or dismissal of senior clergy members from their official position. The carrot? "Today state ulama travel abroad for medical treatment, live in luxurious villas, receive substantial sums of money for their noble services to political authority. … The image of the blind, miserable and poor scholar living on a meagre income in return for religious services, has given way to wealthy guardians of the tradition, who are seen on television screens greeting princes and international delegations visiting the country" (Al-Rasheed 2007, 55).

A different twist on the co-optation logic in a religion-infused setting seems to be at work in Chechnya, one of Russia's federal subject regions in the Northern Caucasus. As is well known, the war in Chechnya has taken a significant toll on the Russian army as well as on the Chechen people, virtually all of whom are devout Muslims. Islam has also made major inroads in neighboring Ingushetia and Dagestan. To contain the spread of Islamic fundamentalism in the region, Moscow threw its support behind Ramzan Kadyrov – a young local Chechen "big man," a former rebel and the son of assassinated former Chechen president Akhmad Kadyrov. Young Kadyrov's pertinent track record in terms of respect for human rights, along with the legality of some of his other habits, is very much in question. But a co-optation impulse quickly cleared these dark clouds, for only an "insider" can effectively tame fundamentalism. Because Islamic impulse in Chechnya is widespread, neither Moscow nor Kadyrov can govern the region effectively without allowing some accommodation of Islamic values and traditions. And so, as the president of Chechnya, Kadyrov, talks the talk of Islamic values and advances religion-infused views concerning revisions to public moral standards, personal-status laws, and the penal code. At the same time, Kadyrov and his Russian patrons cannot live with the fundamentalist Wahhabism. And so, a rigid dichotomy has been erected by Kadyrov's administration between Sufism – consistently portrayed as the "right," "proper," and "traditional" form of Islam in Chechnya – and Wahhabism, portrayed as the "wrong" or "evil" form of Islam, often equated with terrorism (Raubisko 2009). This allows the regime to express its commitment to Islam but reject the less pleasant aspects of it.

The potential "disarming" of threatening forms of religion by co-opted interpreters makes religious communities ambivalent, even suspicious, toward formal state recognition. An interesting twist on the conventional First Amendment's separationist vision is told by Stephen Feldman in *Please Don't Wish Me a Merry Christmas* (Feldman 1997). In this version, the First Amendment's disestablishment element is a product of a certain strand of Protestant theology that saw the state as a potential corruptor of religion. The First Amendment, from this perspective, is not a secularist declaration, but, at least in part, a reflection of a religious principle and, perhaps, interests. American society during the revolutionary era was profoundly Protestant, and would become even more so in the nineteenth century. In fact, it would be difficult to identify any American in the Revolutionary era who could be classified as a secularist in any robust sense of the term. And it is fairly easy to draw a straight line from a Lockean aversion to "priestcraft" to the similar feelings voiced by Jefferson and Madison as indicated in both of their writings on religion, including Madison's later-life correspondence on the subject and the Detached Memoranda. We need to consider, in this vein, how Madison goes on at great length in his Remonstrance about how establishment is both inconsistent with and subversive of Christianity. Disestablishment, therefore, may be as much a consequence of religious principles or interests as the triumph of the secular over the religious.

And so, religious institutions and authorities, not secular elites or the modernist state, may have an interest in maintaining the public/private distinction and in keeping religion within the confines of the private sphere, much like the business sphere, to shield it from state interference, manipulation, and co-optation. From religion's standpoint, formal recognition by the state, let alone establishment through state funding, may be seen as a sacrifice of autonomy in exchange for support. An argument of that nature was made by certain religious voices embroiled in the famous

Kiryas Joel case decided by the U.S. Supreme Court in 1994.[1] As is well known, the issue at stake was whether a law that created a separate school district for a village populated exclusively by a Satmar Hasidic community violated the Establishment Clause. The stated goal of the law was to provide accommodation for the Satmar children with special needs. The majority of the Court struck down the law on the basis that it violated the neutrality principle. Three judges (Scalia, Rehnquist, and Thomas) dissented, holding that the Court's precedent of prohibiting religious accommodation was improper. Within the Hasidic religious community itself, a spilt emerged. Whereas some argued that a separate, state-created school district would indeed cater to the community's special needs, others argued that any such move would only allow the state and its regulatory agencies to cross the public/private lines, penetrate the religious community, and, over time, transform its beliefs and worldviews. This is not a far-fetched concern; the modern state and its regulatory agencies are often driven by this logic. Consider, for example, why legislatures may choose to legalize morally questionable practices (e.g., the sex industry or euthanasia); legalization means formal recognition of less-than-ideal practices, but it also allows for close state monitoring and regulation of these practices. Such pragmatic considerations brought Dutch legislators in the early 2000s to legalize certain aspects of euthanasia, to pick one example.

Another pro-cooptation rationale echoes Adam Smith's treatment of religions as if they were firms developing products and competing for customers (Smith 1994). The official establishment of a religion may turn religious authorities into inefficient and lazy monopolists who try to please government officials and elites interested in theology rather than attract potential "customers." Formal establishment, alongside government support and privileges, is likely to discourage the monopoly clergy from engaging in any type of dissident social activism. And it is here that the pacifying co-optation impulse and the insight that official establishment can promote inefficacious complacency within that "state religion" may come together to explain why, quite counterintuitively, countries facing increasing support for principles of theocratic governance may elect to constitutionally enshrine such principles as their "state religion."

By contrast, disestablishment of religion creates a "free market" in which religions, new and old, can compete for the attention of particular believers (Finke and Stark 2005). As Roger Fink and Rodney Stark suggest, sect-like religions, which tend to be populist and demanding of their followers, will generally fare better in unregulated, disestablishment markets than church-like religions, which tend to be hierarchical and more accommodating of mainstream lifestyles. In their terminology, sects emphasize "salvation," whereas churches specialize in "theology."

[1] *Board of Education of Kiryas Joel Village School District* v. *Grumet*, 512 U.S. 687 (1994).

Most consumers, they argue, prefer salvation. The remarkable development and growth of African-American churches from the early nineteenth century onward may be explained by America's free marketplace of religion. Like other "upstart sects," these churches competed for adherents and drew on American norms of religious freedom to construct organizational havens with little outside intervention. Likewise, under monopolistic conditions, the Catholic Church in Latin America lacked an incentive to advance the religious and social needs of the poor, rural communities. But when confronted by the expansion of mainline Protestantism emanating from the United States, the Catholic clergy had to fight for support and thus became major institutional promoters of rural indigenous causes, and even adjusted its theological teachings and symbolism to reflect this new indigenous-rights agenda (Trejo 2009).

The "legalization" point has another centralizing aspect to it. Historically, in most places, religious law has operated primarily as private law. Its traditional location was in non-centralized religious institutions in which the judgment of individual jurists was autonomous and final, and certainly not subject to appeal (Shapiro 1981). Cases were voluntarily brought to religious tribunals by private parties, not by a public prosecuting authority, and there was no state enforcement mechanism. The whole enterprise was run as an informal, yet socially and morally binding, arbitration system. This is essentially what Max Weber and later Martin Shapiro referred to as non-appellate "*kadi* justice" that reflects the absence of central political authority (Shapiro 1981; Zubaida 2003). In fact, it was not until the latter days of the Ottoman Empire that appeal courts began to emerge in the Islamic tradition, possibly because judicial appeal procedures require some political and administrative centralization (Laitin 1986).

By contrast, formal codification of Islamic law transfers the locus of authority to interpret it from *kadi* justice settings to the state-appointed judges. More broadly, the change of religious law from an uncodified and locally administered set of legal practices to a codified, state-centered system of laws and tribunals allowed colonial authorities – and later state administration in postcolonial Africa and Asia – to revise and redefine certain aspects of religious law in ways they deemed essential to their interests. The Tanzimat legal reforms and the codification of Islamic law in the late days of the Ottoman Empire transformed *shari'a* from being the product of perpetual and dynamic processes of interpretation to a more static and delineated set of rules. Perhaps even more importantly, it moved authority over the law from the scholars to the state. Judges not rigorously trained as Islamic scholars were appointed by the state to administer the law in all areas but family law. The fact that law now emanated from the state and not God translated into judges' reluctance to treat organs of the state as subordinate to religious directives (Feldman 2008). A similar logic applies to modern constitutionalism; the formal constitutionalization of religion brings religious law to the fore of the public-law domain, where the state with its central political authority, regulatory hierarchies, and appellate procedures has always been a key stakeholder.

JURISDICTIONAL ADVANTAGES

Another reason for why constitutional law and courts appeal to antireligionists is state law's *jurisdictional advantage* – both prescriptive and adjudicative – over religious law and tribunals. In the secular/religious context, state law and courts, whether religion-infused or not, often enjoy the edge over religious law and tribunals.

To begin with, state law is centrally legislated, standardized, and catches the activities of most or all private and public entities. It is uniformly enforced and applied throughout the territory and over members of the polity. The effective jurisdictional dominance of state law and courts has proven instrumental in the secularist bid to tame religion. The Supreme Court of Pakistan, for example, has been successfully protecting its overarching review authority vis-à-vis the pro-religious jurisprudence of the Shari'at Appellate Bench. The Federal Court of Malaysia has drawn on constitutional principles of federalism to block the implementation of religious legislation at the state level. And while making concessions with regard to civil/religious court jurisdictional boundaries, it has effectively asserted its exclusive authority as the ultimate interpreter of the constitution. Similarly, the Supreme Court of Nigeria has relied on principles of federalism and the constitutional supremacy of federal laws over laws of subnational units to limit the spread of religious law in the predominantly Muslim northern states. A pinnacle of the Supreme Court of Israel's liberalizing jurisprudence in matters of religion and state is its subjection of the religious courts' jurisprudential autonomy in matters of personal status to the general principles of due process and gender equality. The Court's reasoning has been that religious tribunals in Israel are statutory entities, created by Israeli state law, funded by the government, and therefore are subject to the state's enabling as well as limiting functions, administrative law norms, and overall constitutional principles. The newly established UK Supreme Court has drawn on a similar logic in applying general principles of equality to religion-based admission criteria employed by denominational schools.[2] The Supreme Court of India has drawn on the "basic structure" doctrine to maintain and advocate a secularist vision of the Indian Constitution amid increased political presence of Hindu and Muslim religiosity.[3] Its well-known jurisprudence on personal-status law has sounded a clear voice for uniformity and standardization in that domain, currently dominated by legal regime of multiple

[2] See, e.g., *R(E) v Governing Body of JFS* [2009] UKSC 15.

[3] See, e.g., *S. R. Bommai v. Union of India*, A.I.R. 1994 S.C. 1918.

jurisdictional enclaves and marred by zealous debates. Even courts in two of the world's most diversity-accommodating polities – Canada and South Africa – have made every effort to maintain the overarching supremacy of constitutional law and institutions vis-à-vis claim for autonomy by religion law or customary law.[4]

Ironically, the uniformity and standardization aspect was initially one of the main reasons why the Church gained an edge over its nonreligious competitors in Medieval Europe. In fact, the initial streamlining and unification of religious law under what is known as canon law, and the expansion of its territorial applicability throughout much of medieval Europe, planted the seeds of modern law (Berman 1983). This is worthy of consideration when one seeks to fully grasp the current jurisdictional advantage of state law over religious law. Canon law is internal ecclesiastical law governing the Roman Catholic Church, the Eastern Orthodox churches, and the Anglican Communion of churches. It deals mainly with matters of faith, morals, and discipline, although these areas have been generously interpreted by church authorities to encompass numerous material aspects of life. The way that such church law is legislated, interpreted, and at times adjudicated varies widely among these three bodies of churches. In all three traditions, however, a canon was initially a rule adopted by a central council or religious authorities. It was imposed over vast territory by regional and local agents who were part of a hierarchical structure of authority. Its ontological and epistemological structure, modes of adjudication, and application resembled in many respects our perception of modern law today. Over the years, the study of canon law became a major scholarly discipline, and, through a continual process of precedent accumulation, elaboration, and interpretation, canon law was refined into an internally consistent code (Ekelund 1996; Gilchrist 1969).

Before this process of codification occurred, and until the eleventh century, most law was customary and very little of it was in writing. There was no professional judiciary, no professional class of lawyers, and no distinct "science" of law. As Berman notes, there was "no independent, integrated, developing body of legal principles and procedures clearly differentiated from other processes of social organization and consciously articulated by a corps of persons specifically trained for that task" (Berman 1983: 50). But in the late eleventh century and early twelfth century, a wave of legalism spread throughout Europe. The main driving force behind this sudden transformation was the assertion of papal supremacy over the entire western church and a push toward the independence of the church from secular control. This has

4 For a detailed elaboration of this argument and examination of pertinent Canadian and South African rulings, see Ran Hirschl and Ayelet Shachar, "The New Wall of Separation: Permitting Diversity, Restricting Competition," *Cardozo Law Review* 30 (2009): 2535–60. Two clear illustrations are: *Bruker v. Marcovitz*, [2007] 3 S.C.R. 607 [Canada] and *Shilubana & Others v Nwamitwa* 2009 (2) SA 66 (CC) [South Africa].

come to be known as the Papal Revolution, marked by the formal declaration to that extent by Pope Gregory VII in 1075. Of course, neither monarch nor civil authorities conceded without a fight. Bloody wars took place throughout Europe between the emperor party and the papal party, with the latter eventually emerging triumphant toward the end of the twelfth century. Canon law, and with it modern law, was born.

As Berman notes, from that moment on, the "folklaw" of peoples of Europe disappeared almost completely and was replaced by sophisticated legal systems, first for the Church and then for the secular political orders – canon law, urban law, royal law, mercantile law, feudal and manorial law. Studies of concrete legal practices – for example, Marianne Constable's account of the English "mixed jury" doctrine from the Middle Ages to the nineteenth century – also reveal the disappearance of "law as practice" and a process whereby law rooted in actual practices and customs of communities was replaced by law determined by officials (Constable 1994). Eventually, a series of great political and economic revolutions further transformed the Western legal tradition and established it in professional form it has taken over the last century. Its origins, however, may be traced back to the successful papal attempt to establish a uniform church-based legal authority over a vast territory and an array of subject matters, and in so doing to minimize the impact of competition such as local customary law or secular political orders. Today's state-backed secular law's advantage is merely a mirror image of religious law's edge in the premodern era.

By being more or less universal, internally coherent, and cumulative, the church's canon law – administrated by ecclesiastic courts overseen by bishops – enjoyed an organic advantage over its possible competitors. Ecclesiastical courts claimed jurisdiction over a wide array of subject matters, from all matrimonial and testamentary cases, to all civil and criminal cases involving clerics and church property, to cases involving issues the church considered crucial such as heresy, blasphemy, sorcery, usury, defamation, fornication, homosexuality, adultery, violation of oath and perjury (effective jurisdiction over much of contract law of the day), or injury and assault to clerics or religious places (Berman 1983). "As far as canon law was concerned, any case involving any of these matters could be instituted by filing a complaint in the court of the appropriate archdeacon or bishop, and an appeal could be taken by the losing party to the court of the appropriate archbishop and thence to the court of the pope in Rome" (Berman 1983: 261). The resemblance to today's secular/religious jurisdictional wars and especially to both parties' "imperialist," expansive conceptualization of subject matter jurisdiction is striking.

The similarity does not end there. Another clear advantage that canon law had over secular counterparts in premodern Europe, but which it no longer enjoys in today's nation-state, is cheaper enforcement costs. With the omnipresence of the church in most avenues of life in Middle Ages Europe, conviction or faith were effective substitutes to police forces (Ekelund 1996: 64). The threat of hell or an otherwise doomed afterlife was an effective deterrent. As a result, canon law in medieval Europe was nearly self-enforcing. By contrast, not all secular entities at the time possessed the fiscal means to establish effective deterrence or enforcement mechanisms, thereby ceding authority to the church. In fact, there is some evidence suggesting that secular courts in medieval Europe "free-rode" on the effective excommunication mechanisms developed by the church to enhance enforcement of punishments for "secular" offenses (Berman 1983: 266). Excommunication became a common punishment for offenses such as failure to appear in court when summoned, civil debts, property disputes, and so on. The modern state's enforcement edge over religion – a mirror image of religious law's jurisdictional advantage in the premodern era – is one of the reasons, alongside co-optation, for why those who are not keen on excessive religiosity turn to courts in their fight against theocracy.

The state's jurisdictional advantage over religious authorities is also reflected in a move in countries that enshrine a given religion, its sacred texts, and interpretations in their constitutions, to enact laws that "carve out" and insulate certain areas of the law, most notably economic law, from the influence of religious law. Secular jurisdictional enclaves of several sorts exist in many predominantly Muslim countries, ranging from Qatar, Dubai, and Saudi Arabia to the Maldives and the Comoros. Such jurisdictional enclaves allow lucrative industries that require departure from religious directives (e.g., finance, commerce, or tourism) to mitigate much of the non-business-friendly implications of Islamic restrictions on usury, insurance, and non-workmanship enrichment more generally. In some instances, certain geographical regions are insulated or partly exempted from religious precepts, such as the so-called free-trade zones in Iran, or the emergence of regional free-trade blocs such as the Gulf Cooperation Council.

Jurisdictional reforms are not limited to economic law. Several countries in the Middle East (e.g., Egypt in 2000, Morocco in 2004, Algeria in 2005) have embarked on family-law reforms that involve the codification of legal amalgams of moderate Islamic sources and secular legal principles such as gender equality and procedural justice. The reform in the Moroccan Personal Status Code (*Mudawwana*), for example, declares that husband and wife are jointly responsible for the family, and that women are not subject to the "guardianship" of a male family member, can institute a divorce, and have the right to demand a monogamous commitment from their husbands as a condition for the acceptance of a marriage. A National Women's Day was established in 2008 to commemorate the adoption of the family-law reform. In a similar vein, Israel has adopted a system of civil family courts that adjudicate all matters of personal status except marriage and divorce, thereby curtailing the jurisdictional autonomy of religious tribunals. However protracted their implementation may be, these legal reforms erode the jurisdictional and interpretive stature of religious authorities and make the modernized areas of law justiciable by the ordinary courts.

THE EPISTEMOLOGY OF CONSTITUTIONAL LAW

The very logic of modern constitutional law with its embedded notion of overarching objectives and conceptual supremacy, state-driven legitimacy and authority, separation-of-powers structure, procedural rules of engagement, methods and styles of reasoning, and often measured approaches to politically charged questions seems intrinsically appealing to those advocating a moderate approach to matters of religion and state.

By definition, constitutional supremacy means that the constitution is the highest law of the land. The constitution's supremacy entails not only that all constituencies and political institutions must abide by it, but also that all other sources of law or legal authority are placed lower than the constitution in a given country's legal hierarchy. It also means that in principle, all other laws, policies, and practices must conform with, or at least not unjustifiably and disproportionally infringe on, principles enshrined in the constitution. So at the simplest, most obvious of levels, the overarching and all-encompassing supremacy of the constitution brings together everything that moves under its jurisdiction, thereby making it a potentially effective framework for taming antiestablishment forces, religious or otherwise.

There is, however, much more to the invisible force of constitutionalism that makes it attractive to antireligious interests. To begin with, constitutionalism shares the core elements of what may be termed the modernist narrative. Destiny may be averted and passions controlled, for man has the ability to tame nature and shape and reshape reality through rational, goal-oriented data gathering, planning, and implementation. And although nature is fearsome and possibly chaotic, careful institutional engineering can introduce order, help overcome challenges, solve problems, and ultimately create better opportunities to serve the public good. At the most abstract level, constitutionalism suggests that desirable social and political outcomes may be accomplished through optimal institutional planning and implementation. Akin to most other "design sciences" – the many disciplines, domains, and activities from urban planning to space exploration that rely on design to accomplish big, noble goals – it rests on utterly optimistic (albeit not always empirically substantiated) predispositions toward order over chaos, reason over passion, formal authority over informal custom, collective good over individual whims, and evidence-based planning over improvisation and instincts. These goals may be accomplished through careful institutional design, which is assumed capable of changing human behavior, by enlightenment and education, deterrence and enforcement, or by creating meaningful incentives for people (or groups) to behave in a desirable way.

Constitutionalism is said to provide a rational, effective way of organizing public life; this involves balancing common good and individual freedoms; fundamental democratic governing principles with realities of very large numbers of participants and inputs; serious disagreements among participants on values, worldviews, identities, policy goals, and methods; and inevitable gaps between aspirations and realities.

More specifically, most modern constitutions establish a nexus of governing institutions and state organs whose legitimacy and *raison d'être* do not derive from celestial authority. Constitutions are man-made law, adopted by mere mortals, politicians and legal innovators who often purport to represent the authentic public will. And so constitutions, in essence, are political and earthly, not divine. Although religious and aspirational statements are common in many constitutions, a practical, pragmatic aura surrounds many or all of the governing structures they create. By its very nature, a constitution – an entrenched, special piece of legislation – advances the rule of law, often in lieu of and at times in tandem with the rule of God.

Perhaps more importantly, most modern constitutions, including those of most Middle Eastern, African, and Southeast Asian countries, contain some form of constitutional catalog of rights, individual freedoms, formal equality, and procedural justice, including basic due-process rights, freedom of expression, freedom of religion, and in some cases the right to privacy. By their very nature, these rights and liberties are much closer friends of liberalism and secularism than of theocratic governance. Granted, not all countries, theocratic or otherwise, take an across-the-board endorsing approach toward such rights. However, no matter how weak or tentative these rights provisions are in practice, they still provide a potentially favorable anti-theocratic legal platform for universalists and cosmopolitans alike. Either way, Western-style individual rights fare better under constitutionalism than under most systems that engage with either exclusionary or hierarchical discourses of divine authority.

There seems to be another, deeper aspect to this point, namely the conceptual affinity between the prevalent conception of rights as essentially protecting the private sphere from state interference and the pervasive small-state social and economic thought. Prevalent rights discourse is far more individualistic in its focus than religious law. It assumes that the individual is the ultimate source of meaning, and that individual autonomy is an absolutely indispensable and essential *sine qua non* of any just moral order. Religious (or state) coercion disrespects individual's dignity and autonomy.

Overarching belief or meaning systems (except, of course, the secularist, liberal, constitutionalist faith itself) are often treated by contemporary rights discourse as failing to recognize the elevated, "higher than the universal" (as Danish philosopher Søren Kierkegaard put it) moral status of the individual. In fact, no sacred law, association, or religious group identity can fully capture the "true" essence of the individual. And so, prevalent rights discourse has an a priori secularist tilt to it.

What is more, constitutional courts' very conception of the rule of (state) law, with its deep-rooted orientation toward the European legal tradition and what Max Weber characterized as formal and rational reasoning, consistent application leading to certainty and predictability, necessarily weakens the potential accommodation of alternative hierarchies of traditional or religious interpretation, supposedly less rational or formal, in Weber's terminology. Modes and methods of constitutional deliberation and reasoning are more hospitable to adversarial argumentation and counterargumentation than to an unquestioningly obedient "*Na'aseh Ve'nishma*" (Hebrew for "All that the Lord has spoken we will do, and we will be obedient").[5] They reflect the atheistic (or at least agnostic) predisposition to the power and logic of human-made law over that of an unseen creator-god. And, at a more abstract level, constitutional discourse is often understood as a relatively value-neutral domain that emphasizes a procedural, quasi-Rawlsian, justice-as-fairness approach over substantive perceptions of the good. Akin to its antagonism toward any other intolerant, substantive, or holistic perception of the good, this kind of constitutional discourse is not a natural companion to principles of theocratic governance.

A systemic judicial antipathy toward religion and its pre- and extralegal authority and morality resembles – and perhaps to some extent even stems from – what James Scott describes as the modern state's aversion to "local knowledge," and its drive to "cultivate" and domesticate nomads, register and monitor the movement of people, and to assert its authority over the entire polity. More generally, the modern state aspires to control things in a "rational" or "planned" manner, often cleverly disguised as a high modernist ideology, with a firm belief that progress *can* and *will* make the world a better place (Scott 1999). By its very nature, the modern state seeks to establish a centralized, one-rule-fits-all governance schema, with a monopoly over the historic national meta-narratives that constitute the body politic as such. The modern state is thus at best agnostic and often hostile toward alternative or competing systems of collective identity. This very difference between commitment to diversity as inclusion, and judicial antipathy toward nonstate law viewed as competition, explains much of the religion-and-state jurisprudence in contemporary multicultural jurisdictions, ranging from India to Canada to South Africa. When one comprehensive doctrine collides with another, the challenge for courts is fitting one doctrine within another.

As long as legal claims for accommodation are not seen by courts as challenging the lexical superiority of the constitutional religion itself (call it "diversity as inclusion"), they stand a fair chance of success. Contrast that with the unyielding

5 Israelites' (Bnai Yisrael) response to Moses' (Moshe's) presentation of the Divine Covenant, according to the Torah (Exodus, 24:7), has become a symbol for a rule-following, "first we obey and perform, and then we ask questions" approach.

reluctance of legislatures and judiciaries to accept as binding or even cognizable any potentially competing legal order that originates in sacred or customary sources of identity and authority. This pattern of clamping down and refusing to accept any alternative sources of regulation becomes particularly visible where the legal challenge at issue is interpreted as raising doubts regarding which set of norms and institutions, or what set of high priests, should have the final word in authoritatively resolving legal disputes within a given society (or "non-state law as competition"). This is a challenge that no secular legal order, no matter how tolerant and otherwise open to providing exemptions and accommodations to religious believers, can accept with indifference. For what is perceived to be at stake here is the very authority and source of legitimacy of the accepted civil religion (Hirschl and Shachar 2009).

Indeed, as Charles Taylor observes, early societies with a holistic, omnipresent religion have often been described as "stateless." No monopoly over interpreting God's will was present. But once something like state power arose – with, for example, Pharaohs in Egypt, or Stewards of the God in Mesopotamia – the unlimited presence and diffused, communal nature of religion started to break down. "States concentrate power and exercise control; by nature they cannot be entirely guided by preexisting law or custom.... The sacred web of order now mutates to hierarchy. There are now people, or strata, that are closer to the invisible order than others. The Steward of the God, or the divine king, is the link by which the higher power of the God makes connection with society" (Taylor 1997).

A constitutional court's reluctance to grant support to radical religious views may also derive from its interest in retaining its status as the one and only legitimate interpreter of laws vis-à-vis the perceived menace of alternative interpretation systems (e.g., religious interpreters and authorities that are well established within the circles of supporters of theocratic governance and have been steadily gaining support among new crowds). The legal arena here functions much like Pierre Bourdieu's concept of a *field* – a professional arena in which people maneuver and struggle in pursuit of desirable symbolic resources. (Think of how professional guilds, e.g., lawyers' bar associations, are concerned with monitoring the credentials of their members.) Much like conventional medicine's predispositions against alternative treatment methods (sometimes portrayed as mostly unproven, nonscientific, lacking in supportive empirical evidence, even superstitious, etc.), the judges' *habitus* (in Pierre Bourdieu's terms) reflects embedded predispositions for the rule of law and against alternative interpretive systems. Bourdieu's *doxa* – the fundamental, deep-founded beliefs, taken as self-evident universals – inform the judges' actions and thoughts within the legal domain. And as Bourdieu famously noted, the combination of habitus and doxa – certainly in this context – tends to favor the particular social arrangement of the field, thus privileging the dominant and taking their position of dominance as self-evident and universally favorable. Therefore, the categories of understanding and perception that constitute a habitus, being congruous with the objective organization of the field, tend to reproduce the very structures of the field. This "reproduction of the modes of production" process is made transparent by legal discourse that not only "brings into existence that which it utters," but is also "the divine word, the word of divine right, which, like the *intuitus originarius* which Kant ascribed to God, creates what it states, in contrast to all derived, observational statements, which simply record a pre-existing given" (Bourdieu 1991: 42). There is little wonder why the deep, near-organic reluctance of constitutional courts to recognize the legitimacy of alternative, primarily religious interpretation systems is one of the main reasons for their near-universal appeal to secularist circles.

Dominant interpretive methods in constitutional law – the "living-constitution" (or "living-tree") doctrine and the "proportionality" (or balancing) approach – are two prime examples of how structures of reasoning tend to reinforce courts' centrality in the process of interpretation and norm creation. They also make constitutional law and courts a very appealing domain to pragmatic worldviews and to relatively moderate or secular elites. According to the living-constitution doctrine, a constitution is organic and must be read in a broad and progressive manner so as to adapt it to changing times. Specifically, it should be regarded and interpreted as continually evolving in accordance with pertinent changes in the value system of the society within which it operates. The pragmatist view of the living-constitution doctrine suggests that interpreting the constitution in accordance with long-outdated views leads to arcane and practically unacceptable policies that will thus be rejected by society. For a constitution to remain relevant and applicable, an evolving interpretation is necessary. What is more, proponents of the living-constitution approach contend that most constitutions were intentionally written in broad and flexible terms so as to accommodate, and indeed encourage, a dynamic, "living" document. Without getting into a detailed account of the virtues and vices of the doctrine, one can say that it certainly lends itself more easily than most other interpretive approaches to an injection of the personal values of those who interpret the constitution, and it is a much more practical and effective, if admittedly less principled, way of introducing constitutional change than, say, the process of constitutional amendment. In any case, secular, modernist views in contested areas such as gender equality, reproductive freedoms, nonorthodox sexual preference, or even principles of modern economy are likely to fare distinctly better under such a living-constitution interpretive approach than under any originalist or ultraorthodox approach to interpreting religious or constitutional provisions.

The living-tree approach is complemented by the emergence of *proportionality* as the prevalent interpretive method in comparative constitutional jurisprudence. It has become the lingua franca of constitutional jurisprudence virtually anywhere beyond the United States, most notably throughout Europe, as well as in India,

Canada, New Zealand, Israel, and South Africa, and it is making its way into the jurisprudence of many higher courts in the developing world, from Latin America to Asia, Africa, and the Middle East. This interpretive method, commonly used throughout the world of new constitutionalism, is based on judicious balancing of competing claims, rights, and policy considerations. What is proportionality? It is a practical solution (although its avid proponents insist that it is principled) to the tension between rigidity and flexibility in interpretation of constitutive texts; a quasi-scientific, ideology-free weighing of competing claims, where the "spirit" or "purpose" of the law matters more than its words, and where no principle is absolute, although some are more important than others. Hence infringement on core principles – say, basic rights and liberties – may be allowed, but only to the extent that it is deemed necessary, serves a worthy or just goal, and represents the least drastic violation required to accomplish that goal. A limitation of rights must not go beyond the minimum required under the circumstances; deviation from basic principles of human dignity during wartime should be proportional to the level of threat or "necessity"; and so on. There is another pseudosophisticated element to proportionality: The degree of infringement on core principles reflects the relative significance, principled or practical, the balancer assigns to a competing value or argument. So the more worthy a claim against a core principle is regarded as being, the more willing an interpreter should be to accommodate it, and the deeper the encroachment on the core principle may be. And vice versa: claims deemed of little worth or of too high a cost will be weighed against core principles, but their accommodation will be minimal, in a way that is reflective of their questionable worth. State-appointed courts and judges are to serve as the forum of ultimate wisdom and to determine what constitutes such a proportional balance and what is the "worth" or "weight" of a given claim in the overall balancing matrix.

By its very nature, proportionality epitomizes moderation and conciliation and favors middle-of-the-road, balanced, or pragmatic solutions to contested issues. It also allows judges to consider nearly any factor, principled or practical, real or hypothetical, in weighing and balancing competing claims. This is a consequentialist, compromise-oriented interpretive method. Extreme or radical positions are not likely to fare well under proportionality. In that respect, the appeal of proportionality resembles the triumph of catchall liberalism over narrower, less flexible ideologies. The more absorbent a sponge is, the more liquid it can contain; and the larger a tent is, the more people can find refuge under it. A high-culture product or a specialty food store is not going to attract nearly as many customers as a mainstream news show or a large shopping mall. Likewise, more accommodating, permissive, eclectic, or elastic worldviews enjoy an inherent advantage over strict doctrinal worldviews. Not only do flexible worldviews require less sacrifice from their followers, but their lax boundaries can also appeal to or contain a wider array of preferences. By contrast, rigid doctrinal ideologies – say, religious fundamentalism or radical Maoism – are distinctly more demanding and less accommodating. Regardless of their substantive message, then, they appeal to far fewer people. Thus, much like the "median-voter" or catchall party logic in electoral politics, proportionality enjoys an a priori broader appeal base than more principled or overtly ideological interpretive approaches.

Constitutional jurisprudence in the early twenty-first century is also quite open to foreign influence. Given other broad economic, technological, and cultural convergence processes, let alone the dramatically improved availability of, and access to, comparative constitutional jurisprudence, jurisprudential cross-fertilization – and the globalization of constitutional law more generally – seem inevitable (Tushnet 2009). In a transnational age, even bastions of insular parochialism cannot avoid certain degree of international impact (Jackson 2010). However idiosyncratic or rooted in local traditions and practices a given polity's constitutional law may be, it is unavoidably open to liberalizing global influences. Constitutional courts worldwide increasingly rely on comparative constitutional law to frame and articulate their own position on a given constitutional question. This has given rise to what may be termed *generic constitutional law* – a supposedly universal, Esperanto-like discourse of constitutional adjudication and reasoning, primarily visible in the context of core civil rights and liberties (Law 2005). This phenomenon is particularly evident with respect to constitutional rights jurisprudence – a perennial bone of contention in constitutional theocracies.

Within this emerging comparative constitutional law enterprise there is an embedded tilt toward cosmopolitanism. In practice, comparative constitutional law is often used for purposes of self-reflection through analogy, distinction, and contrast. The underlying assumption here is that whereas most relatively open, rule-of-law polities face essentially the same set of constitutional challenges, they may adopt quite different means or approaches for dealing with these challenges. By referring to the constitutional jurisprudence and practices of other presumably similarly situated polities, scholars and jurists might be able to gain a better understanding of the set of constitutional values and structures inherent in their own systems. These references also enrich, and ultimately advance, a more cosmopolitan or universalist view of constitutional discourse. This is aided by the rise of supranational human rights regimes and the spread of their norms and jargon to their respective member states.

Constitutional law is a modernist enterprise. The very structure, predisposition, epistemology, and contemporary practice of constitutional law make it a more hospitable domain for secularist worldviews and policy preferences than for religious ideology and social order, or for rule-of-God-based perceptions of the good.

CONSTITUTIONAL DELEGITIMATION OF RADICAL RELIGIOUS ASSOCIATION

As several shrewd observers note, democracy is beneficial to its participants mainly in cases where political divisions do not cut that much deeper than the marginal issues on which the polity's constituents can achieve democratic compromise (Hardin 1999). But when the stakes are very high, democracy loses much of its appeal, particularly for the projected losers. Constitutional provisions that prohibit political association based on religion are one of the common weapons (their questionable effectiveness notwithstanding) used by regimes to contain the tremendous popular following that religious parties in these polities have gained. Algeria and Tunisia are obvious examples.

As is well known, a vicious decade-long civil war between the French-backed Algerian army and religious militants erupted after the Islamic Salvation Front party gained tremendous support among Algerian voters. In reaction, the historically hegemonic National Liberation Front party cancelled the first multiparty election in Algeria after the first round (December 1991). A military coup introduced a state of emergency, which suspended all electoral processes. Under the state of emergency, impunity for past wrongdoing against Islamists is guaranteed. In 1996, a revised constitution was introduced, which remains in effect today. Article 2 of Algeria's constitution states that: "Islam is the religion of the State." Article 42 allows for the formation of political parties. However, it also states that the right to form political parties "cannot be used to violate the fundamental values and components of the national identity ... as well as the democratic and Republican nature of the State. Political parties cannot be founded on religious, linguistic, racial, sex, corporatist or regional basis." Furthermore, political parties are prohibited from resorting to partisan propaganda based on any of these grounds. No political party can resort to any form of violence or constraint of any nature. And if some threat to the National Liberation Front party's hegemony appears on the horizon, the constitution has been amended to address it. In November 2008, parliament approved a constitutional amendment that ended presidential term limits. This allowed President Abdelaziz Bouteflika of the National Liberation Front to run for a third five-year term in the spring of 2009.[6]

In a similar fashion, Article 1 of the Tunisian constitution establishes Islam as the state religion. Article 38 further states that the President of the Republic must be a Muslim. Article 8 of the constitution guarantees the right to form political parties, but states that "political parties must respect the sovereignty of the people, the values of the republic, human rights, and the principles pertaining to personal status.

[6] See *Human Rights Watch World Report 2009*, 444.

Political parties pledge to prohibit all forms of violence, fanaticism, racism and discrimination. No political party may take religion, language, race, sex or region as the foundation for its principles, objectives, activity or programs. It is prohibited for any party to be dependent upon foreign parties or interests." So whereas Islam is the official state religion and must be the religion of its leader, no political party may take Islam as the basis of its principles. A similar set of provisions exists in other predominantly Muslim countries – the Egyptian constitution's blatant restrictions on political participation by the Muslim Brotherhood is merely one example.

Another form of constitutional exclusion of radical religion is closely related to the co-optation aspect discussed above. Controlling the provision of religious services by co-opting religious leaders may also facilitate state control of unregistered religious organizations, even if such organizations view themselves as subscribing to the majority or state religion. Indonesian law officially acknowledges six religions: Buddhism, Catholicism, Hinduism, Islam, Protestantism, and, as of 1998, Confucianism enjoy equal status as state-recognized religions. The country's controversial 1965 Blasphemy Law prohibits religious interpretation and activities that deviate from the basic (read: "state-endorsed") teachings of any of these denominations. This has been used to clump down on "unofficial" Islamic voices ranging from the Ahmadiyah sect (whose members have been persecuted in parts of the Islamic world) to militant Wahhabism. In a recent challenge to the constitutionality of the Blasphemy Law, proponents of Western-style rights argued that the law in its current form infringes on basic individual and group rights and violates the International Covenant on Civil and Political Rights. Drawing on a "war on terror" impulse (Bali and other parts of Indonesia have been targets of bombings tied to Islamic militants), the government argued that the law must be upheld to avoid interpretation-at-will by keeping the process of religious interpretation under official check – a position that the Indonesian Constitutional Court endorsed in full in its 2010 ruling on the matter.

A similar dynamic is evident in other countries. In Tajikistan and Uzbekistan, to pick two examples, Muslim followers of non-state-approved religious organizations may be arrested for holding "unsanctioned gatherings" or may be labeled "extremists" by state courts and by leaders of registered religious organizations. In 2007, for example, the Supreme Court of Tajikistan declared a dozen such unregistered organizations, including the Islamic Movement of Turkestan, "extremist." The practice is by no means confined to predominantly Muslim countries. Most Vietnamese, for example, follow Mahayana Buddhism. Vietnamese law requires that religious groups register with the government. Those groups that do not join one of the officially authorized religious organizations, the governing boards of which are under government control, are considered illegal. This has led to effective infringement on religious freedom of various Christian and non-state-controlled Buddhist sects.

POLITICAL CONTROL OF THE JUDICIARY

Political power holders in virtually all countries have some control over the personal composition of national high courts. As Robert Dahl observes with regard to the U.S. Supreme Court, "it is unrealistic to suppose that a Court whose members are recruited in the fashion of the Supreme Court justices would long hold to norms of rights of justice that are substantially at odds with the rest of the political elite" (Dahl 1957). A *fortiori*, it does not require a major leap of imagination to understand the scope of political control, direct or indirect, on judicial appointment processes in polities that feature distinctly lesser degree of judicial autonomy than in the United States. Accordingly, it is hardly surprising that Maher Abdel Wahed, the Chief Justice of Egypt's Supreme Constitutional Court (SCC) from 2006 to 2009, served as Egypt's Attorney General prior to his appointment to the Court, and was appointed to the top judicial position via a presidential decree. His appointment was supported by members of the ruling National Democratic Party as well as by the police, military, and prosecutors who all regarded Abdel Wahed as a tough "law and order" type. Some individuals pass from judgeship to civil service with the same ease. Mamdouh Marei, the Chief Justice of the SCC in the early 2000s, was appointed in August 2006 by President Mubarak as Minister of Justice. In July 2009, Farouk Sultan – a distinctly "system friendly" jurist – was appointed as the new Chief Justice of the SCC. In Egypt and elsewhere, seldom have law and politics been so unified since the days of Carl Schmitt.

Consider, for example, the professional biography of Zaki Tun Azmi, who has been, since October 2008, the Chief Justice of Malaysia's Federal Court (the highest court of the land). Zaki's father, Tun Azmi Mohamed, was also Chief Justice (then Lord President) from 1966 to 1974. Like father like son: Zaki received an elite legal education in both English and Malay. For years he served as legal adviser to the ruling United Malays National Organization party before becoming the first lawyer directly appointed as a judge of the Federal Court on September 5, 2007. Three months later, on December 11, Zaki Tun Azmi was appointed president of the Court of Appeal, and on October 21, 2008, following the end of Datuk Abdul Hamid Mohamed's term due to mandatory retirement, Zaki was appointed Chief Justice. Ascertaining whether Zaki's personal background and close ties to the ruling party are linked to his rapid ascent to positions of judicial power is beyond the scope of this work, but that seems like a reasonable working hypothesis.

In yet other countries, the antireligious military is a significant actor in appointments to the constitutional court. As Hootan Shambayati explains (Shambayati 2008: 105), the Turkish military has historically been involved in judicial appointments in that country, with the outcome being rather homogenous and technocratic, courts composed of like-minded judges who display little diversity of thought. It remains to be seen whether and how the recent attempts by the moderately religious AKP-led government to transform the Turkish judiciary will pan out.

Boualem Bessaih, as of September 2005 the president of Algeria's Constitutional Council, is a distinguished member of the Algerian revolutionary movement of the early 1960s, a former professor of literature, a prolific author and film director, who served as ambassador to several European and Arab capitals, as well as in several ministerial posts. His latest book, *L'Algérie belle et rebelle, de Jugurtha à Novembre*, published on the occasion of the fiftieth anniversary of the revolution, is prefaced by Algeria's President Abdelaziz Bouteflika.

At the other end, "noncooperative" judicial figures have been removed or otherwise tamed. A paradigmatic example is the replacement of the Supreme Court chief justice in Afghanistan. Following more than two years of conservative jurisprudence in religious matters by the newly established Afghan Supreme Court, President Hamid Karzai opted for a shake-up of the Court's composition. In 2006, Karzai appointed several new, more moderate members to the court. In addition, the reappointment of the conservative Chief Justice Faisal Ahmad Shinwari – a conservative Islamic cleric with questionable educational credentials – did not pass the parliamentary vote. Karzai then chose his legal counsel, Abdul Salam Azimi – a former university professor who was educated in the United States – to succeed Shinwari. The new, distinctly more moderate Court was sworn in in August 2006.

Looking now at the broader composition of constitutional courts in the Near and Middle East, as well as in North Africa, many judges have received some general legal education and are familiar with some of Western law's basic principles and methods of reasoning. More often than not, the judge's educational background, cultural propensities, and social milieu are closer to those of the urban intelligentsia and top state bureaucrats than to any other social group. Constitutional courts are established and funded by the state and their judges are appointed by state authorities, often with the approval of political leaders. Consequently, the judge's record of adjudication is well known at the time of their appointment. In an increasing number of countries in the region, judges are required to attend courses on the role and functions of the judiciary for several years where they are exposed to international human rights standards and other legal concepts that are not easily compatible with traditional views, pious authority, and sacred texts.

Likewise, government ministries and state bureaucracies have tightened their control over the appointment of judges to religious tribunals and require new appointees to have some formal training or background in general legal principles, in addition to their mastery of religious law. A good illustration is the quiet revolution in the early 2000s that took place during the process of appointing *kadis* to Israel's *shari'a* courts. Although historically the process had been controlled by the Ministry of Religious Affairs, the entire *shari'a* court portfolio was transferred in

2004 to the Ministry of Justice. This was coupled with the requirement that new appointees to religious tribunals have extensive formal legal education. The process of tightening political control over judicial appointments to religious tribunals has symbolic manifestations too; in 2008, and for the first time in Israel's history, three new Great Rabbinical Court judges (*dayanim*) were sworn in a ceremony held at the official residence of the President of Israel, and took the same oath of office that is taken by civil court judges. Until 2008, appointees to the rabbinical court system had been sworn in at the Chief Rabbinate.

Another telling example is the religious court reform in Indonesia – the country with the largest Muslim population in the world (more than 200 million). During the 1980s, the hitherto non-standardized Islamic court system was integrated into the national judiciary, with all the government supervisory powers that such incorporation entails (Cammack 2007). The Religious Judicature Act of 1989 established municipal and provincial *shari'a* courts' jurisdiction over Muslim litigants in certain civil matters specified by the Act, mainly marriage, inheritance, and charitable foundations (*waqf*), generally subject to ordinary (nonreligious) civil procedure norms. Alongside the formal recognition of Islamic courts' power, however, educational requirements and judicial appointment procedures were introduced so as to transfer the locus of power from local "strongmen" to government officials. Whereas in the past, judges were recruited locally, under the current system, judges are hired through a nationwide recruitment and undergo a process of training and socialization in Jakarta before being sent into the field (Cammack 2007, 162). As a result, judges appointed under the new standards have very different training and backgrounds from their predecessors. The vast majority of judges on Islamic courts – almost 90 percent by one count – have degrees from one of Indonesia's State Islamic Institutes, and many also possess a university degree. Moreover, the number of religious court judges with both university training and graduate training has been consistently increasing as additional education is a major factor in promotions (Cammack, 2007, 161). The reform also increased the number of female judges serving on Islamic courts from roughly 5 percent in the early 1980s to roughly 20 percent today.[7]

In other countries, judicial reform brought about the appointment of women to influential judging positions. In 2003, Tahani al-Gibali became the first woman to be appointed to Egypt's Supreme Constitutional Court. In a major follow-up move in 2007, Egypt's then- president Mubarak appointed thirty-one female judges to serve on courts throughout the country. In 2010, Egypt's Supreme Constitutional

[7] Women have served as Islamic court judges in Indonesia since the 1960s. Indonesian religious scholars concluded that women may serve as Islamic court judges in all but criminal cases, which in any event are not tried in the Islamic court system.

Court dismissed attempts to question the legitimacy of these appointments. The pertinent legislation stipulates that members of the Council of State must be "Egyptian," a word that in Arabic is specific to the male gender. However, the Supreme Constitutional Court ruled that in this context, the word means "citizen," which includes both genders.

Such oversight over judicial appointment and training procedures has practical implications on judicial outcomes. At least until 2011, Turkey's Constitutional Court was a bastion of historically powerful Kemalist secularist-statist interests against the backdrop of increasing popular support for political Islam in that country. Bound by Article 2 of the Egyptian Constitution (*shari'a* is "the main source of legislation"), Egypt's Supreme Constitutional Court has developed its own liberalizing "interpretation from within" of religious rules and norms. The Kuwaiti Constitutional Court issued a series of liberalizing rulings (including, most recently, concerning women dress code in the Kuwaiti parliament), made all the more important when they come from a court that operates within a constitutional framework that designates Islam as the state religion and enshrines its principles as "a main source of legislation." To remain relevant and to maintain their public legitimacy, national high courts in polities that have witnessed increasing popular support for theocratic governance do occasionally side with religious authorities and tribunals, mainly those formally recognized and funded by the state (Hirschl 2010, 160). And when the political stakes are high, and the costs of an antireligious ruling seem too high, the courts find creative ways to minimize the risk for themselves and to avoid swimming against the current. However, these more conservative rulings are the exception.

Extrajudicial determinants of judicial decision making are significant here. To begin with, judges in centralized and overly politicized court systems controlled by a dominant political force are likely to support the government position – especially in politically charged cases – to avoid harsh reaction by influential political power holders (Helmke 2002; Newberg 1995; Ramseyer and Rasmusen 2001). In some cases, self-censorship may be exercised by court leaders who push all judges to avoid confrontations with the interests of the executive to protect the institutional autonomy of the court (Hilbink 2007). Tightened political control over judicial appointments suggests that an "attitudinal" approach to judicial behavior is likely to manifest itself with most (or, indeed, all) apex court judges adhering to ideological preferences, worldviews, and values that are not in line with the fundamental tenets of theocratic governance. Most judges belong to the very same social stratum that, by and large, has the most to lose through the spread of religious radicalism. Likewise, judges seem to care about their reputations within their immediate social milieu, court colleagues, and the legal profession more generally, and will therefore likely seek to advance notions of collective identity that are popular among these epistemic communities of reference (Baum 2006; Posner 2008). It may also be argued that judges' policy preferences grow in part from their training and practice in the law, and that existing legal doctrines and analytic frameworks help shape those preferences. And lest we forget, alongside these attitudinal factors, other calculative, extrajudicial determinants of judicial behavior may be at play. As the strategic approach to judicial decision making has established, courts and judges may engage in strategic decision making either because of the variety of costs that judges as individuals or courts as institutions may incur as a result of adverse reactions to their unwelcome decisions, or because of the various benefits that they may acquire through the rendering of strategically tailored decisions (Epstein and Knight 2000; Spiller and Gely 2008).[8]

When political pressure, tacit or explicit, on the courts does not achieve the intended objectives of those who appoint and promote judges, these actors may take harsher measures. As the recent history of comparative constitutional politics shows us, the recurrence of unsolicited judicial intervention in the political sphere in general and unwelcome judgments concerning contentious political issues in particular have brought about significant political backlashes, targeted at clipping the wings of overactive courts. These assertive means may range from executive override of controversial or unwelcome rulings to political tinkering with judicial appointment and tenure procedures, and from court-packing attempts by those who hold political power to the introduction of serious jurisdictional restrictions that put boundaries on and limit powers of judicial review (Hirschl 2008). In some instances, such a backlash has ended in constitutional crisis, leading to the reconstruction or dissolution of the high courts. Such political responses to unwelcome activism or interventions on the part of the courts, or even the credible threat of such a response, can have a chilling effect on judicial decision-making patterns. Constitutional courts, then, are "constrained actors ... who must be attentive to preferences and likely actions of other relevant players" (Epstein 2001, 117).

Given all these factors, it is hardly surprising that in a number of Middle Eastern polities that lack established traditions of judicial activism, judicial reform has been instigated to create and empower state-controlled courts in an attempt to counterbalance the spread of religious fundamentalism. Saudi Arabia, for example, has recently embarked on a comprehensive modernization of its judicial system. Part of the rationale for the overhaul is the creation of courts specialized in dealing with criminal, commercial, labor, and family issues to replace the existing general judge-made *shari'a*-based interpretation in these matters that has prevailed for many years. Additionally, the judiciary council that used to act as the highest court and was controlled by some of the most reactionary clerics in the kingdom has been relegated to an administrative role. A new ten-member Supreme Court was established in

[8] This in a nutshell is the take-home message of the "strategic" approach to judicial behavior.

2009, staffed mostly with royal appointees, not merely with religious clerics, thereby allowing the kingdom to extend a more pragmatic, flexible application of *shari'a* to various aspects of public life. This is modeled in part on the experience of neighboring Bahrain, where a two-tier court system exists – civil courts that adjudicate commercial, civil, and criminal-law issues (as well as personal-status laws of non-Muslims) and a *shari'a* court system that handles personal-status issues of Muslims. More importantly, the constitution of 2002 established a Higher Judicial Council with full oversight over the entire court system, as well as an appointed constitutional court to rule on the constitutionality of both civil and *shari'a* court rulings. In short, even in the least likely settings, constitutional courts and tribunals have been established, or reformed, so as to hedge or mitigate the tension between political interests, modern-day needs, and principles of theocratic governance.

CONCLUSION

Regimes in dozens of countries worldwide have been struggling to contain the popular resurgence of religious principles, forced to navigate between modernist ideals and religious injunctions, contemporary governance and ancient texts, judicial and pious interpretation. These conflicting pressures, opinions, and interests have led to intense constitutional maneuvering and interpretive innovation in polities facing deep rifts along secular/religious lines. From these rifts, the constitutional domain has emerged as a secularist shrine in the non-secularist world. Universalists and modernists increasingly turn to constitutional law and courts to block, delay, or mitigate the impact of religion in public life. And they know why. As we have seen, there are important reasons – epistemological and ideological alongside more instrumentalist, strategic, and practical – for why constitutional law and constitutional courts are so appealing to secularist, modernist, cosmopolitan, and other antireligious social forces in such polities.

Of the several key secularist appeals of constitutionalism, co-optation seems a most attractive and effective one. Formal establishment of religion may be portrayed as surrender to religion, but in reality it helps to limit the potentially radical impact of religion by bringing it under state control. Granting religion a formal constitutional status is not only a legitimacy-enhancing move that appeases popular pressures; it also neutralizes religion's revolutionary sting and co-opts its leaders. This process allows for significant state input in the translation of religious precepts into guidelines for public life, helps mutate sacred law to serve powerful interests, and, above all, brings an alternative, even rival order of authority under state control and supervision. Statutory regulations, selective funding, and promotion incentives encourage moderate or state-dependent voices within religion to curtail the impact of extremism.

In addition, the very structure and logic of constitutionalism, with its very reasoned set of core tenets, modernist predispositions, and prevalent modes of interpretation, make it an attractive enterprise to those who wish to contain religiosity and assert state or civil society authority over religious texts, worldviews, and interpretive hierarchies. Effective political control over, as well as better access to, the constitutional arena also make it attractive to political power holders who seek to keep religious authority under check. Restrictive constitutional provisions have been drawn on to delegitimize and exclude radical religion. As a result, the jurisprudence of constitutional courts, even if formally "religious" in some sense, will inevitably reflect a less militant view of religious identity. Consequently, constitutional law and courts have become the natural companions of these groups and their political representatives in their struggle against the spread of principles of theocratic governance.

ACKNOWLEDGMENTS

An earlier version of this chapter was presented at a comparative constitutional design conference held at the University of Chicago School of Law, October 16–17, 2009. I am grateful to the conference participants, in particular Tom Ginsburg and Malika Zeghal, for their helpful comments and suggestions.

REFERENCES

Al-Rasheed, Madawi. *Contesting the Saudi State: Islamic Voices from a New Generation* (Cambridge University Press, 2007).
Baum, Lawrence. *Judges and Their Audiences: A Perspective on Judicial Behavior* (Princeton University Press, 2006).
Berman, Harold J. *Law and Revolution: The Formation of Western Legal Tradition* (Harvard University Press, 1983).
Bourdieu, Pierre. *Language & Symbolic Power* (Harvard University Press, 1991).
Cammack, Mark E. "The Indonesian Islamic Judiciary," in R. M. Feener and Mark E. Cammack eds., *Islamic Law in Contemporary Indonesia* (Harvard University Press, 2007), 146–69.
Constable, Marianne. *The Law of the Other: The Mixed Jury and Changing Conceptions of Citizenship, Law, and Knowledge* (University of Chicago Press, 1994).
Dahl, Robert. "Decision-Making in a Democracy: The Supreme Court as a National Policy-Maker," *Journal of Public Law* 6 (1957): 279–95.
Ekelund, Robert B. et al. *Sacred Trust: The Medieval Church as an Economic Firm* (Oxford University Press, 1996).
Epstein, Lee and Knight, Jack. "Towards a Strategic Revolution in Judicial Politics: A Look Back, a Look Ahead," *Political Research Quarterly* 53 (2000): 625–61.
Epstein, Lee et al. "The Role of Constitutional Courts in the Establishment and Maintenance of Democratic Systems of Government," *Law & Society Review* 35 (2001): 117–63.
Feldman, Noah. *The Fall and Rise of the Islamic State* (Princeton University Press, 2008).

Feldman, Stephen. *Please Don't Wish Me a Merry Christmas: A Critical History of the Separation of Church and State* (NYU Press, 1997).

Finke, Roger and Stark, Rodney. *The Churching of America, 1776–2005: Winners and Losers in Our Religious Economy* (Rutgers University Press, 2005).

Gilchrist, John T. *The Church and Economic Activity in the Middle Ages* (St. Martin's Press, 1969).

Hardin, Russell. *Liberalism, Constitutionalism and Democracy* (Oxford University Press, 1999).

Helmke, Gretchen. "The Logic of Strategic Defection: Court-Executive Relations in Argentina Under Dictatorship and Democracy," *American Political Science Review* 96 (2002): 291–303.

Hilbink, Lisa. *Judges beyond Politics in Democracy and Dictatorship: Lessons from Chile* (Cambridge University Press, 2007).

Hirschl, Ran. "The Judicialization of Mega-Politics and the Rise of Political Courts," *Annual Review of Political Science* 11 (2008): 93–118.

Constitutional Theocracy (Harvard University Press, 2010).

Hirschl, Ran and Shachar, Ayelet. "The New Wall of Separation: Permitting Diversity, Restricting Competition," *Cardozo Law Review* 30 (2009): 2535–60.

Jackson, Vicki. *Constitutional Engagement in a Transnational Era* (Oxford University Press, 2010).

Laitin, David. *Hegemony and Culture: Politics and Change among the Yoruba* (University of Chicago Press, 1986).

Law, David. "Generic Constitutional Law," *Minnesota Law Review* 89 (2005): 652–742.

Newberg, Paula. *Judging the State: Courts and Constitutional Politics in Pakistan* (Cambridge Univerity Press, 1995).

Posner, Richard A. *How Judges Think* (Harvard University Press, 2008).

Ramseyer, Mark and Rasmusen, Eric. "Why Are Japanese Judges So Conservative in Politically Charged Cases?" *American Political Science Review* 95 (2001): 331–43.

Raubisko, Ieva. "Proper 'Traditional' versus Dangerous 'New': Religious Ideology and Idiosyncratic Islamic Practices in Post-Soviet Chechnya," *Journal the Anthropological Society of Oxford* (online) 1 (2009): 70–93.

Scott, James C. *Seeing Like a State* (Yale University Press, 1999).

Shapiro, Martin. *Courts: A Comparative and Political Analysis* (University of Chicago Press, 1981).

Shambayati, Hootan. "The Guardian of the Regime: The Turkish Constitutional Court in Comparative Perspective," in S. A. Arjomand, ed., *Constitutional Politics in the Middle East* (Hart Publishing, 2008), 99–121.

Smith, Adam. *The Wealth of Nations* (Random House, 1994 [1776]).

Spiller, Pablo T. and Gely, Rafael. "Strategic Judicial Decision-Making," in Keith Whittington et al. eds., *The Oxford Handbook of Law and Politics* (Oxford University Press, 2008), 35–45.

Taylor, Charles. "Foreword," in Marcel Gauchet, ed., *The Disenchantment of the World: A Political History of Religion* (Princeton University Press, 1997), xi–xii.

Trejo, Guillermo. "Religious Competition and Ethnic Mobilization in Latin America: Why the Catholic Church promotes Indigenous Movements in Mexico," *American Political Science Review* 103 (2009): 323–42.

Tushnet, Mark. "The Inevitable Globalization of Constitutional Law," *Virginia Journal of International Law* 49 (2009): 985–1006.

Zeghal, Malika C. Gardiens de l'Islam: Les oulémas d'al Azhar dans l'Egypte contemporaine (Presses de Sciences Po, 1996)
"Religion and Politics in Egypt: The Ulema of al-Azhar, Radical Islam, and the State (1952–1994)," *International Journal of Middle East Studies* 31 (1999): 371–99.
Zubaida, Sami. *Law and Power in the Islamic World* (I. B. Tauris, 2003).

PART III

Issues in Institutional Design

8

Constitutional Amendment Rules

The Denominator Problem

Rosalind Dixon and Richard Holden

Formal procedures for constitutional amendment play a number of important functions in a constitutional democracy. In cases of major constitutional change, they help ensure that change occurs via legal, rather than extralegal, means (Griffin 1998). In other cases, they provide legislatures with the means to alter or "update" specific constitutional rules, or to engage in "dialogue" with courts about the interpretation of more open-ended constitutional provisions (see Dixon 2010; and compare also Denning & Vile 2002; Forbath 2003).

Over time, there may also be increasing demand for constitutional amendment procedures to play both this kind of rule-updating and dialogic function. Changing social circumstances and understandings will often make specific constitutional rules outmoded, yet in most countries, courts do not respond to this by changing their interpretation of such rules (Dixon 2010). Courts also tend over time to engage in more interpretation in aggregate (Samaha 2008) in a way that invites greater scope for legislative disagreement – or dialogue. As an empirical matter, there is certainly evidence that older constitutions tend to be amended more frequently than newer ones (see Lutz 1995: 253; Ferejohn 1997: 524; Elkins, Ginsburg, and Melton 2009).

At the same time, as constitutions age, they may also become more difficult to amend. One reason for this is that in most jurisdictions, the population tends to increase over time in a way that directly raises the costs of, or hurdles to, successful constitutional amendment.[1]

A number of authors have suggested the possibility of this kind of a "denominator problem" in the context of constitutional amendment rules (see, e.g., Samaha 2008). James Buchanan and Gordon Tullock, for example, have argued that "[e]veryday experience in the work of committees of varying size confirms... [the] direct functional relationship between the individual [bargaining or decision] costs

[1] See United Nations (2007, p. vii). Another reason is that constitutions may become more venerated over time, in ways that increase the political costs of proposing amendments: see, e.g., Griffin (1998).

of collective decision-making and the size of the group required to reach agreement" (Buchanan and Tullock [1962] 2004: 55). Because there is greater uncertainty in larger decision-making bodies about what others will do, and therefore in the benefits of cooperation, they have also posited a direct relationship between the size of a collective decision-making body and holdout costs, or the "opportunity cost of bargains that are never made" (Buchanan and Tullock [1962] 2004: 65–66). In other works, we have also suggested that successful constitutional amendment may be more difficult in larger decision-making bodies, simply as a result of *the law of large numbers* (Holden 2009; Dixon 2010, 2011).

In this chapter, we provide the first empirical test to date of these hypotheses, by gathering and analyzing a unique year-by-year data set on constitutional amendment rates at a state constitutional level in the United States. Using this data set, we show a clear, statistically significant negative relationship between the size of legislative voting bodies and the rate of constitutional amendment in various states, under various specifications. We further suggest that this finding has potentially important – yet hitherto overlooked– implications for the design of constitutional amendment rules.

The chapter is divided into four sections. The first section briefly sets out the existing theoretical arguments about the relationship between the size of constitutional decision-making bodies and the costs, or hurdles, to constitutional amendment. The second section sets out the basic empirical findings of this work. The third section discusses possible implications for constitutional design, including the role mechanisms, such as (1) sliding-scale constitutional amendment rules; (2) a low, as compared to high, constitutional supermajority rules; and (3) constitutional convention could play in addressing the denominator problem identified, along the potential disadvantages, as well as advantages, of each mechanism. The final section offers a brief conclusion.

CONSTITUTIONAL AMENDMENT, DIFFICULTY AND SCALE: THEORETICAL ARGUMENTS

The size of a particular voting body will have the potential to influence the effective difficulty of constitutional amendment for two interrelated reasons: one having to do with the *decision costs* associated with the process of constitutional amendment; and another with the statistical *likelihood* that (at least quasi-) independent decision makers will ultimately favor a particular proposed amendment.

In most constitutional settings, there will be some practical limit on the number of constitutional amendments that will be feasible for a legislature, or population as a whole, to adopt. The higher the decision costs are, for any given successful constitutional amendment, the fewer the amendments there will therefore be, overall. According to almost all theories of constitutional decision making, the decision costs associated with a successful process of constitutional amendment will also have a clear capacity to increase, along with the size of the relevant constitutional voting body.

For many constitutional theorists, a key function of constitutional amendment rules is to ensure that adequate deliberation occurs about the potential advantages and disadvantages of any proposed constitutional change, before such change occurs (see, e.g., Michelman 1986; Ackerman 1991). In most countries, this means that the process of constitutional amendment requires some degree of legislative, not just popular, involvement. Where this is the case, the time – and therefore also opportunity cost – of debating proposed constitutional amendments will have a clear relationship with the size of the relevant voting body. The more members there are in a given decision-making body, the more time it will take to hear from each member. Because deliberation involves an exchange of ideas, adding new members to a legislative body will also increase the time taken for existing members to absorb and respond to the arguments of new members, and also to debate with one another, about those new arguments. As the size of the legislature increases, deliberation-based decision costs ("deliberation costs") therefore have the potential not only to increase but also to do so exponentially.

For other constitutional theorists, constitutional amendment rules embody a more outcome-oriented trade-off from the perspective of individual citizens, between, on the one hand, the danger of "external costs," and on the other, the likely magnitude of "bargaining" – and also "hold out" – costs (see, e.g., Buchanan and Tullock [1962] 2004). External costs are those that individuals must bear as "a result of the actions of others over which he [or she] has no direct control," or in a constitutional context, the costs to an individual of constitutional changes that he or she does not favor (Buchanan and Tullock [1962] 2004: 43). Bargaining costs are the costs individuals must occur in seeking to bargain, or negotiate, collective agreement in favor of a proposed constitutional amendment they favor; and holdout costs the "opportunity cost of bargains that are never made" (Buchanan and Tullock [1962] 2004: 65–66). According to scholars such as James Buchanan and Gordon Tullock ([1962] 2004), both forms of decision cost may also increase significantly with the size of a collective decision-making body. "Everyday experience in the work of committees of varying size confirms," Buchanan and Tullock suggest, the "direct functional relationship between the individual [bargaining] costs of collective decision-making and the size of the group required to reach agreement" (Buchanan and Tullock [1962] 2004: 55). Holdout costs will also tend to increase, along with the size of a collective decision-making body, because greater uncertainty about what others will do, and therefore the benefits of cooperation, may make individuals "more reluctant to grant concessions" (Buchanan and Tullock [1962] 2004: 55).

Decision costs aside, we have argued that successful constitutional amendment may also be more difficult in larger polities, simply as a result of the law of large numbers

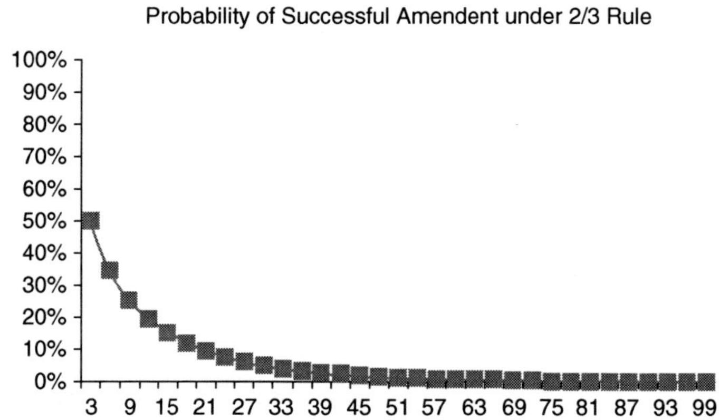

FIGURE 8.1. Scale and probability of amendment given supermajority rule.

(Holden 2009; Dixon 2010, 2011). The reason for this is that, in larger voting bodies, there will tend to be less idiosyncratic variation in the distribution of voter preferences, relative to the underlying views of the median voter, and therefore less likelihood of there being a supermajority position in favor of a change to the status quo.

Assume, for example, that the median voter in a given polity is more or less indifferent when it comes to whether or not to amend the constitution; that the views of the median voter on this question do not tend to change radically with the scale of the polity; and that the views of a particular representative voting body – such as the legislature or a subsection of voters who choose to vote at a particular election – are drawn at least semi-randomly from the voting population as a whole. Under a supermajority voting rule, the law of large numbers means that, even absent any change in decision costs, it is far less likely in a large decision-making body than in a smaller such body that there will be an idiosyncratic draw of preferences or types in favor of amendment.

Consider the probability, shown in Figure 8.1, of obtaining a majority vote in favor of ratifying a constitutional amendment by way of a coin toss – "heads" being a vote in favor of changing the status quo and "tails" being a vote for the status quo. For a voting body with, say, three or six members, the probability of successful amendment is 50 percent or 34 percent, respectively, whereas for a voting body of even twelve or twenty-four members, the probability is as low as 19 percent or 8 percent, respectively. For a voting body with 100 members, the probability of successful amendment falls below 1 percent.

As one of us has shown elsewhere, this effect is also quite general and does not depend on the binary nature of outcomes in the coin-toss setting (see Holden 2009). Rather, it applies even where there is a continuum of voter preferences and policy choices. The only limitation on this effect is that it is likely to apply most strongly at the lower, rather than higher, ranges of population size – that is where the law of large numbers is yet to apply.

In a legislative setting, both decision costs and the law of large numbers suggest that, after controlling for other factors, such as the relevant constitutional amendment rule, there should be quite clear negative relationship between the size of a legislative voting body and the effective rate of constitutional amendment (hypothesis 1).

In a popular setting, by contrast, it seems much less likely that there will be a statistically significant relationship between the scale of a polity and the rate of amendment, considering that, in such a setting – where there is both limited opportunity for deliberation and bargaining and sufficiently large population from the outset – a principle of diminishing returns (to the law of large numbers) is likely to apply. However, to the extent that there is any relationship found between the size of the overall population and the effective rate of constitutional amendment, in states with a popular ratification requirement (i.e., all states other than Delaware), both theories would also predict that the relationship should be negative rather than positive (hypothesis 2).

THE DATA ON AMENDMENT RATES AND DENOMINATORS

To test the two relevant hypotheses empirically, we collected data for forty-one states on state population size, legislative size, the formal requirements for constitutional amendment, and the annual amendment rate, for each state constitution, from the time of adoption of the present constitution to the present.[2] This generated 4,372 observations. For each constitution in our data set, we also obtained data on the length of the relevant constitution, its life span or number of years in existence, and its coexistence with other constitutional restrictions such as a single-subject rule and a double-passage requirement.

The key advantage of obtaining year-by-year data of this kind, rather than simply aggregate data such as that used by Donald Lutz (1995) in his pioneering earlier work in this area, is that it allowed us to test state-level types of constitutional heterogeneity.[3] Because there have been several changes to amendment rules within

[2] These data were collected from the text of the state constitutions, the National Bureau of Economic Research (NBER) state constitutions project, the U.S. Census Bureau, and numerous copies of *The Book of the States*, The Council of State Governments, Lexington, KY. The states for which data were not available were: Alabama, Georgia, Illinois, Indiana, Maryland, Minnesota, Missouri, Tennessee, and Wyoming. For these states, data were available on amendment rates, but not on the size of the state legislature for relevant time periods.

[3] On the more general advantages of longitudinal count data such as those assembled here, see, e.g., Neyman (1965); Hausman, Hall, and Griliches (1984) (in the context of patents/research and development). For an excellent overview and extension to more general stochastic processes, see King (1989). As Hausman, Hall, and Griliches (1984) pointed out in their pioneering work, there are certain additional complications involved in the analysis of panel count data. The two main issues are how to allow for

TABLE 8.1. *Panel summary statistics*

Variable	Observations	Mean	Standard deviation	Min	Max
vap	5285	2156768	5498174	10698.28	1.29E+08
amendts	4535	1.822933	6.148128	0	130
amend	4535	0.322161	0.4673558	0	1
legbuck	5198	2.192959	0.8885848	1	4
init	5315	0.5629351	0.8033729	0	2
doublepass	5315	0.2957667	0.4564296	0	1
limit	5315	0.1047977	0.3063214	0	1
exposure	5315	66.8984	46.86321	1	226
house	5315	118.6591	73.25775	31	749
singsub	5315	0.2425212	0.4286481	0	1
length	5315	36117.12	47408.06	9200	340136
vapsquared	5285	3.49E+13	4.87E+14	1.14E+08	1.66E+16

various states, over time, the use of all state constitutions, both past and present, also provided us with useful additional variation in testing our hypotheses. As John Ferejohn (1997) has shown in a closely related context, using all the available variations in the data has significant advantages in this context, and can even lead to different conclusions. Table 8.1 presents summary statistics of these variables.

VAP is the voting-age population in a given year, and VAPSQUARED is the square of this. INITIATIVE is a categorical variable measuring the possibility of popular initiatives, which takes the value 0 if initiatives are not possible, 1 if the requirement is less than 10 percent of the voting population (usually measured as the percentage of those who voted in the last gubernatorial election), and 2 if 10 percent or more such signatures are required. DOUBLEPASS is a dummy variable that takes the value 1 if amendments must pass the legislature in two successive sessions, and 0 otherwise. LEGBUCK_n is a series of dummy variables that measure the voting rule for passage in the legislature: It is denoted 1 (i.e., LEGBUCK1) if the rule is 50 percent, 2 if it is 60 percent, 3 if there is a two-thirds requirement, and 4 if there is a three-quarters requirement.[4] EXPOSURE is the number of years the current constitution has been in place. HOUSE is the number of members of the lower house of the state legislature in a given year. LENGTH is the length of the constitution in words.[5] SINGSUB is a dummy variable that takes the value 1 if the constitution has a single-subject rule for constitutional amendment.

persistent state effects (i.e., fixed or random effects), and how to allow for disturbances in the equation for a discrete probability distribution. The negative binomial specifications we use address these issues.

4 For all fifty states, the current voting rule is the same in the upper and lower houses of the state legislature, and hence we do not separate upper and lower house voting rules.

5 We do not have this data available on a year-by-year basis, and thus use the current length for all years.

TABLE 8.2. *Aggregate summary statistics*

Variable	Observations	Mean	Standard deviation	Min	Max
proposed	49	215.42139	209.3933	8	1063
passed	50	13.52	140.8594	8	766
conbuck	50	3859319	5.003019	1	20
vagepop	50	1.378804	3905686	360316	2.00E+07
rate	50		1.277779	0.2465116	7.158878
popadopt	50	1039159	1879353	10698.28	7865581
housenow	50	110.24	55.58614	40	400
legbuck	49	2.204082	0.9124051	1	4
adopted	50	1899.32	52.96762	1780	1986
intitiative	50	0.56	0.8121526	0	2
doublepass	50	0.24	0.4314191	0	1
limit	50	0.1	0.3030458	0	1
singsub	50	0.26	0.4430875	0	1
length	50	35985.08	47816	9200	340136

We also assembled data on the aggregate number of amendments for each of the fifty state constitutions, since adoption. Table 8.2 presents summary statistics of these variables.

Many of the variables are the same as those in the panel data, but there are some differences. PASSED is the total number of amendments to a constitution since its inception. ADOPTED is the year in which the constitution was adopted. RATE is the number of amendments per annum. HOUSENOW is the number of members of the lower house in each state, whereas HOUSEADOPT is the number of members when the constitution was adopted. VAGEPOP is the voting-age population of the state. Finally, CONBUCK is a measure of the difficulty of constitutional amendment, with 1 representing the lowest level of difficulty and 20 the highest.[6] CONBUCK is an aggregate measure of the overall difficulty of constitutional amendment, and includes

6 This measure is similar to the measures used by Lutz (1995), Lijhpardt (1999), and Elster (2000), but different in some respects. Lutz (1995) considers seventy possible different amendment requirements in three general categories: legislative majority, double-passage requirements, and referendum requirements. He then assigns cardinal values to different requirements. For example, he assumes that if an amendment must pass two houses of parliament, this is twice as hard as if it had to pass only one house. In contrast, we take an ordinal approach to remain agnostic about the exact *degree* of difficulty. Lijhpardt (1999: 219) focuses solely on the voting rule (simple majority, 50% to two-thirds, two-thirds plus). Elster (2000: 101) focuses on four categories: legislative supermajority requirements, parliamentary quorum requirements, state ratification, and referendum requirements. Our measure ranks (from easiest to hardest) lexicographically popular initiative requirement, then legislative majority rule, then popular majority rule.

consideration of legislative voting rules, voting rules for popular ratification, and the presence and level of difficulty for the proposal of amendments by popular initiative. It is constructed by ordering states lexicographically: first on the popular initiative rule (i.e., the percentage of voters required to initiate an amendment), second on the legislative rule, and finally on the popular rule.

The fact that we are dealing, in this context, with count data – that is, a situation in which the number of amendments over a particular time frame is the dependent variable – means that careful treatment is required to acknowledge that both negative outcomes are impossible (i.e., a state cannot have -7 amendments) and only integer outcomes are possible (i.e., a state cannot have 2.2 amendments in a year). In this setting, Ordinary Least Squares (OLS) estimates are statistically inefficient, do not have consistent standard errors, and can produce the impossible prediction that a negative number of events (here, constitutional amendments) may have occurred. We also found that for a poisson regression, there was a problem of overdispersion in our data. [7] We thus ran a fixed-effects panel negative binomial regression, and used a random-effects specification as a robustness check.

Table 8.3 presents the results of this negative binomial regression for *aggregate* data on the rate of amendment in each state in our data set, controlling for various measures of the difficulty of amendment and the number of members of the legislature. Given that this is, by necessity, so-called rate data, it also controls for the number of years each constitution has been in effect by including log (EXPOSURE) on the right-hand side.

Consistent with our first hypothesis, although the relationship was not particularly statistically significant (it had a p-value of 0.166), we found that an increase in the number of members in the house led to fewer amendments, or for a one standard deviation change in the number of house members (compared to an overall average rate of amendment of 1.37 per annum), approximately 0.143 fewer amendments per annum. Conversely, contrary to our second hypothesis, we found that states with a larger population tended to have *more* amendments.

The other variables we found to be statistically significant were LENGTH, LIMIT, VAP, and LEGBUCK2. As authors such as Lutz (1995) and Ferejohn (1997) have previously found, longer constitutions were amended with greater frequency (Lutz 1995: 249; Ferejohn 1997: 524). Formal limits on the number of amendments permissible in a given year, and a two-thirds supermajority requirement for legislative passage of a constitutional amendment, also led to there being fewer amendments.

7 The unconditional variance of many variables of interest is greater than the mean, as can be seen from the summary statistics table. A poisson specification imposes a parametric assumption that assumes that mean to be equal to the variance, which may lead to misleading results (Hausman, Hall, and Griliches 1984).

TABLE 8.3. *Amendment rates using aggregate data*

VARIABLES	Rate
Vagepop	1.53e-07**
	(7.70E-08)
Housenow	−0.00255
	(0.00184)
legbuck_1	−0.408
	(0.292)
legbuck_2	−0.549**
	(0.222)
legbuck_3	−0.215
	(0.283)
doublepass	−0.597
	(0.427)
limit	−1.039***
	(0.22)
init_1	−0.043
	(0.361)
init_3	−0.206
	(0.401)
singsub	0.0016
	(0.295)
length	5.58e-06***
	(1.30E-06)
vagepopsq	0
	(0)
Constant	−4.157***
	(0.419)
Observations	49

However, while these aggregate results are informative, they do not use the full amount of variation available in the data, and therefore we also ran panel data count regressions to obtain more efficient estimates. Table 8.4 reports the results of a negative binomial regression using the full panel structure of our data (i.e., year-by-year amendments rather than total amendments).

Most notably, it shows that the size of the lower house of the state legislature – that is, number of house members – is negative and statistically significant at the 1

TABLE 8.4. *Panel negative binomial results*

VARIABLES	amendts	amendts
	(1)	(2)
	Fixed effects	Random effects
doublepass	0.0974	0.0598
	(0.107)	(0.102)
limit	−0.00878	−0.0614
	(0.127)	(0.120)
legbuck_2	−0.603***	−0.516***
	(0.135)	(0.130)
legbuck_3	−0.243**	−0.218**
	(0.105)	(0.0998)
legbuck_4	0.275	0.338
	(0.425)	(0.381)
init_1	0.168	0.159
	(0.132)	(0.123)
init_2	−0.455***	−0.413***
	(0.136)	(0.130)
singsub	0.185	0.147
	(0.118)	(0.110)
house	−0.00363***	−0.00377***
	(0.000695)	(0.000671)
exposure	0.00756***	0.00708***
	(0.000702)	(0.000692)
length	1.45e-05***	1.46e-05***
	(2.00e-06)	(1.93e-06)
vap	−3.90e-09	2.08e-09
	(9.59e-09)	(9.36e-09)
vapsquared	−0	−0
	(0)	(0)
Constant	−2.179***	−2.152***
	(0.153)	(0.146)
Observations	4390	4390
Number of stateid	41	41

Standard errors in parentheses *** p<0.01, ** p<0.05, * p<0.1

percent level, and therefore provides strong confirmation of our first hypothesis. The magnitude of this effect is also quite significant. For example, a one standard deviation in the number of house members is associated with 0.27 fewer amendments per annum – or 2.7 fewer per decade. This represents a 14.6 percent reduction in the number of amendments relative to the mean.

Contrary to our findings for the aggregate amendment data, it also shows that in this setting, there was no statistically significant relationship between VAP, or VAPSQUARED, and the rate of amendment, but that to the extent there was a relationship between the two, it was negative. This confirms our second hypothesis.

Also of note is the finding that neither the presence of a double-passage requirement nor a single-subject rule had a statistically significant effect on the overall rate of amendment. Other factors we did find to have a statistically significant effect were LEGBUCK2, LEGBUCK3, INTIATIVE2, EXPOSURE, and LENGTH. As panel 1 shows, compared to a 50 percent majority voting in a state legislature, a 60 percent supermajority rule reduces number of amendments by 0.603 per annum (compared to a mean number across all states of 1.823 per annum), and a two-thirds majority rule by 0.243 per annum. [8] These effects were also clearly statistically significant – at the 1 percent and 5 percent levels, respectively. EXPOSURE and LENGTH were also significant at the 1 percent level, indicating that, as Lutz (1995), Ferejohn (1997), and others have found in the context of aggregate data, both longer-lived and longer-in-length constitutions tend to be more prone to amendment (see Lutz 1995: 253, Ferejohn 1997: 524).[9]

The effect of an initiative provision on the ultimate rate of constitutional amendment appears more complex. Only in the case of a relatively demanding initiative requirement (i.e., INITIATIVE2) did we find that there was any positive and statistically significant effect on the overall rate of amendment. For less demanding initiative rules (i.e., INITIATIVE1), the presence of an initiative rule in a constitution had no statistically significant effect on the overall rate of amendment, most likely because it was possible for proponents of constitutional change to propose an amendment without first building a broad base of political support.

As panel 2 shows, the random-effects model also produced almost identical estimates for these findings, with no change in which variables are significant, and little change in magnitudes, under this model.

As an additional robustness check, we also considered the possibility that our results could be affected by the presence of multiple amendments in a given state

[8] Because LEGBUCK is a categorical variable, LEGBUCK1 (equal to 1 if and only if a state has a 50% legislative rule) is dropped from the regression for standard collinearity reasons. It is immaterial which of the four variables is dropped, but dropping LEGBUCK1 makes the interpretation easier.

[9] For similar findings in a global context, see Elkins, Ginsburg, and Melton (2009).

in a particular year, followed by few amendments in other years; [10] therefore, we recoded our data to include a variable AMEND, the value of which is set at 0 if no amendments are made in a particular year and 1 if the constitution is amended. Because this produced a binary dependent variable, we then ran three different econometric specifications: a linear probability, a logit model, and a probit model. Table 8.5 reports the results of these three regressions, with standard errors clustered by state.

Consistent with our results in Tables 8.3 and 8.4, it shows that for three of these specifications, we found that the size of the legislature had a clear negative relationship with the overall amendment rate – and again that this result was statistically significant at the 1 percent level. As before, it also shows that variables such as DOUBLEPASS, SINGSUB, LIMIT, and INIT1 had no statistically significant effect.

For a linear probability model, as panel 1 shows, the only major difference in our findings was that LEGBUCK2 and LEGBUCK3 were no longer statistically significant, and that the effect of INIT2 was both less statistically significant and reversed – none of which affected our core hypothesis or findings.[11] For a logit model, as panel 2 reports, the only change in the results is that LEGBUCK4 becomes significant at the 10 percent level, with a positive coefficient indicating that a 75 percent legislative rule makes it harder to amend. For a probit model, which panel 3 reports, EXPOSURE, LENGTH, and HOUSE were all significant at the 1 percent level. The interpretation of the coefficient on HOUSE is that a one standard deviation change in the number of house members leads to a 7 percent decrease in the probability of amendment in a given year (at the mean).

As a final check of robustness, we also considered the possibility of common shocks across states as an explanation for these findings, and thus reran our original year-by-year negative binomial regression for a number of time subsamples of the data.[12] One period in particular that we focused on was the 1960s, because this was a period in which there were both a relatively large number of observations in our data set and large-scale parallel changes across different states in the functioning of many state and local governments, and also in the recognition of various civil rights claims at a state as well as national constitutional level (see, e.g., Williams 1985: 1210–12). Not surprisingly, given the smaller number of observations in this

[10] This could reflect a mechanical effect where a change to the constitution requires multiple textual changes, or bundling of disparate changes as a result of legislative bargaining or other factors.

[11] One explanation for this increased difficulty of amendment in INIT2 states may have something to do with informal attitudes toward the legitimacy of amendment in such states: compare Vermeule (2006) and Sullivan (1995).

[12] Given that there was no variation within decade (or overall) in certain variables such as the legislative amendment rule, length, and, crucially, the number of house members, it was not statistically feasible to run our main specification including time dummies for each decade.

TABLE 8.5. *Estimates of amendment probability*

VARIABLES	amend	amend	amend
	(1) Linear probability	(2) Logit	(3) Probit
vap	9.79e-09	–0.0155	–0.0168
	(9.58e-09)	(0.245)	(0.150)
doublepass	–0.00933	–0.255	–0.149
	(0.0506)	(0.218)	(0.133)
limit	–0.0519	0.00600***	0.00361***
	(0.0451)	(0.00173)	(0.00106)
exposure	0.00117***	–0.00506***	–0.00277***
	(0.000376)	(0.00156)	(0.000845)
legbuck_2	–0.0605	–0.251	–0.161
	(0.0575)	(0.264)	(0.162)
legbuck_3	–0.0147	–0.0427	–0.0325
	(0.0422)	(0.202)	(0.123)
legbuck_4	0.0634	0.453*	0.251
	(0.0546)	(0.265)	(0.159)
init_1	0.0323	0.138	0.0840
	(0.0362)	(0.186)	(0.108)
init_2	–0.0637*	–0.335**	–0.195*
	(0.0375)	(0.170)	(0.105)
singsub	0.0361	0.122	0.0810
	(0.0316)	(0.147)	(0.0894)
length	3.78e-06***	4.58e-08	1.08e-05***
	(9.65e-07)	(4.62e-08)	(2.62e-06)
vapsquared	–0	–0	2.82e-08
	(0)	(0)	(2.63e-08)
house	–0.000742***	1.78e-05***	–0
	(0.000253)	(4.32e-06)	(0)
Constant	0.200***	–1.228***	–0.777***
	(0.0534)	(0.268)	(0.160)
Observation	4390	4390	4390
R-squared	0.064		

Robust standard errors in parentheses *** $p<0.01$, ** $p<0.05$, * $p<0.1$

subsample than our overall data set, we found that our result was somewhat weaker in this context. However, we found that it was nonetheless still present and statistically significant at the 9 percent level.

Thus, overall, we find quite clear support, at a state constitutional level in the United States, for the existence of a scale-difficulty trade-off in the process of constitutional amendment.

SCALE, AMENDMENT RULES, AND CONSTITUTIONAL DESIGN

For constitutional designers, this finding also suggests that there is a clear potential for a denominator problem to arise in the operation of constitutional amendment rules.

It is certainly possible that, in some contexts, a progressive increase in the difficulty of constitutional amendment could be beneficial. However, in most cases, the weight of opinion on constitutional amendment favors the idea that the difficulty of amendment should at least remain stable, if not actually decrease over time (for discussion of this more Jeffersonian view, see, e.g., discussion in Holmes 1995: 158–61).[13] This will also be especially true if, as noted at the outset, there are legitimate reasons why the demand to use constitutional amendment procedures may increase with time.

This part, therefore, considers three potential ways in which a constitutional designer might go about attempting to address this denominator problem – (1) sliding-scale constitutional amendment rule; (2) a low, as compared to high, constitutional supermajority rule; and (3) constitutional convention mechanisms – as well as the potential strengths and weaknesses of each when it comes to concerns about political party dominance, minority rights protection, and constitutional stability.

Three Possible Design Solutions

Sliding-Scale Voting Rules

In the European Union, as the size and membership of the Union have changed over time, so too have both the actual and proposed requirements for "qualified majority" voting in the Council of the European Union. In many instances, these changes have reflected a concern on the part of larger member states to prevent the progressive enlargement of the EU from unduly diluting their voting power (see, e.g., Dinan 2005: 253–54).[14] However, in more recent years, changes have also been

[13] Two reasons to avoid substantially decreasing the difficulty of amendment, over time, are the desire to protect successful constitutional experiments as well as the decision costs and uncertainty associated with whole-scale constitutional revision. Compare Strauss (1996: 910).

[14] For example, in 2004, in the wake of ten new members joining the Union, Article 205 of the Nice Treaty introduced new requirements for qualified majority voting requiring that proposed legislation

proposed to these rules that would make the requirements for EU voting *less* rather than more demanding, in the face of increases in the size of the relevant voting body (see Paris Treaty).

It also seems quite feasible to imagine that a similar model could be adopted at a national constitutional level so as to create a sliding-scale constitutional amendment rule, whereby the level of majority support required for a particular amendment decreased as the size of a relevant voting body increased (or potentially also vice versa). Such a sliding-scale rule could, for example, be derived by combining two separate findings in our data: one relating to the relationship between changes in the scale of the legislature and the difficulty of amendment, and the other concerning the relationship between the formal difficulty of amendment and effective rate of amendment. In our data, we find, for example, that in the first context, a one standard deviation increase in the size of the lower house of a legislature leads to a decrease in the rate of constitutional amendment of approximately 2.7 amendments per decade; and in the second context, that a one-step increase in the formal amendment rule (i.e., the move from LEGBUCK1 to LEGBUCK2, or from 50 percent to 60 percent) is associated with an increase in the amendment rate of approximately 6 amendments per decade. If one combines these findings, and also assumes linearity in respect of the effect of changes in the formal amendment rule, this would imply that the formal difficulty of amendment should decrease by 5 percent for every standard deviation increase in the size of a state legislature – at least up to a lower threshold of 50 percent.[15]

Lower Supermajority Rules

While they are far less common than supermajority voting requirements for constitutional amendment (see Elkins, Ginsburg, and Melton 2009), simple-majority rules apply in fifteen states in the United States in the context of legislative amendments to the constitution; and also in many national constitutions, particularly those influenced by the United Kingdom's noncodified constitutional model (see, e.g., Young 2007). In other countries, such as India, simple-majority requirements also apply to the amendment of a particular subset of constitutional issues.[16]

obtain the support not only of 50% of member states – or 72% of Council members – but also 62% of the total population of the EU, upon a request for such a count (Official Journal of the European Union [OJEU] 29.12.2006 C 321 E/136–137). Subsequent proposed reforms, such as those contained in the Treaty of Lisbon, have also attempted to go further in this same direction, by imposing a supermajority requirement of 55% of member states and 65% of the total EU population (OJEU 17.12.2007 C 306).

[15] This result is, of course, potentially highly sensitive to the assumption of linearity.

[16] Constitution of India, Article 368.

TABLE 8.6. *House-legislative rule interaction*

VARIABLES	Amendts
doublepass	0.0464
	(0.109)
limit	−0.0611
	(0.129)
legbuck_2	−0.0929
	(0.259)
legbuck_3	0.269
	(0.246)
legbuck_4	0.828*
	(0.488)
init_1	0.106
	(0.135)
init_2	−0.413***
	(0.138)
singsub	0.170
	(0.118)
house	−0.00419***
	(0.000744)
exposure	0.00799***
	(0.000728)
length	1.38e-05***
	(2.03e-06)
vap	−1.31e-08
	(1.05e-08)
vapsquared	0
	(0)
houserule50interact	0.00542**
	(0.00234)
Constant	−2.560***
	(0.226)
Observations	4390
Number of stated	41

Standard errors in parentheses *** $p<0.01$, ** $p<0.05$, * $p<0.1$

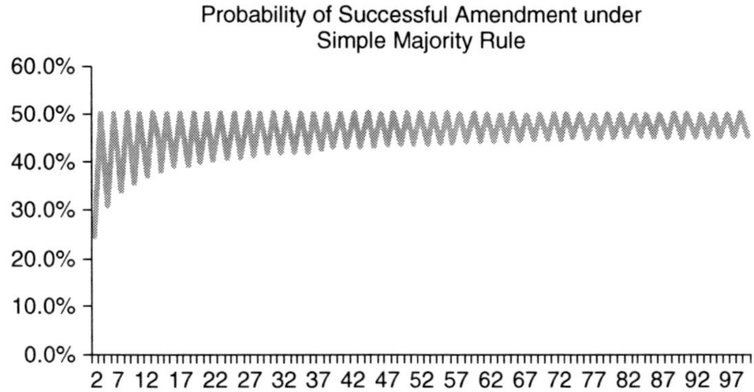

FIGURE 8.2. Scale and probability of amendment given simple-majority rule.

At an empirical level, we also found clear evidence to suggest that simple majority rules of this kind help counteract, at least to some degree, the effect of increases in scale in the legislature on the difficulty of constitutional amendment.[17]

As Table 8.6 shows, for example, when we reexamined the panel data reported in Tables 8.4 and 8.5 and included an interaction term between the number of house members and whether a state has a 50 percent legislative rule (interact HOUSE and LEGBUCK1), we found both that the previously estimated variables were essentially unchanged and that there was a clear positive interaction effect, statistically significant at the 5 percent level, between these two variables. The implication of this finding is that when there is an increase in the size of the legislature, the presence of a simple majority rule will tend, all else being equal, to lead to a clear increase in the number of successful constitutional amendments per year.[18]

At a theoretical level, one potential explanation for this, compared to more demanding supermajority voting rules, lower supermajority rules will tend to be more robust to changes in the size of the underlying voting population, particularly from the perspective of the statistical likelihood of there being independent support for a particular amendment. As Figure 8.2 demonstrates, if votes are drawn entirely randomly and independently, as they are in a coin-toss setting, the probability of successful amendment under a simple-majority rule will (subject to integer rounding considerations) remain constant at 50 percent.

[17] As a robustness check, we estimate the samples separately (i.e., those states with a 50% rule and the others) and find a significant difference between the coefficient of HOUSE in the two samples.

[18] Ibid.

Constitutional Conventions

In the United States, both Article V of the Constitution and most state constitutions explicitly provide for the possibility that constitutional amendments may be proposed by a constitutional convention rather than the legislature. Similar provisions also exist in the Swiss Constitution (see Tschaeni 1982), as well as more implicitly in the "small-c" constitutional framework of countries such as Australia (see Twomey 2008).

In most jurisdictions where actual conventions have been called, the practice has also been for conventions to be relatively small, at least compared to national or state legislatures. This, various scholars argue, both increases the likelihood of meaningful deliberation among members of a convention and reduces the costs of convening a convention, as a special legislative-like body (compare, e.g., Saunders 1997; Twomey 2008).

Therefore, provided a constitutional designer can ensure that a constitutional convention is, in fact, called where there is a demand for constitutional change, a convention mechanism will offer another potential way in which to respond to the denominator problem identified in the second section of this chapter.

There are also at least two ways in which a constitutional designer could overcome potential hurdles to a convention being called: first, by creating of a lower threshold for the calling of a convention than for the legislative approval of actual constitutional amendments; and second, by making a popular vote on the calling of a convention mandatory, at fixed points in time. Lower voting thresholds frequently apply in state constitutions in the United States, and also countries such as Switzerland, for the proposal of constitutional amendments, as compared to the ratification or approval of amendments (see, e.g., Swiss Federal Constitution 1999, Articles 138–42). At a state level in the United States, fourteen states also explicitly require a regular vote to be held on whether to call a constitutional convention (see, e.g., Twomey 2008).[19]

Comparative Dangers (or Disadvantages)

In assessing these three potential design solutions, it is, of course, important for a constitutional designer to consider a range of other constitutional structures and values – such as the structure of political parties (Issacharoff 2003), the protection of minority rights (see, e.g., Rawls 1993; Sager 2001), and the importance of constitutional stability – and not simply the effect of a denominator problem.

[19] The relevant states are: Alaska (every ten years), Connecticut (twenty years), Hawaii (nine years), Illinois (twenty years), Iowa (ten years), Maryland (twenty years), Michigan (sixteen years), Missouri (twenty years), Montana (twenty years), New Hampshire (ten years), New York (twenty years), Ohio (twenty years), Oklahoma (twenty years), and Rhode Island (ten years).

The strength and discipline of political parties, for example, will tend to have a major impact on the actual difficulty of constitutional amendment in almost all constitutional contexts. This impact may also be particularly pronounced for sliding-scale and simple-majority voting rules. (In the context of constitutional conventions, the influence of political parties will depend almost entirely on the mechanism adopted for the selection of convention delegates.)

Under such rules, the greater the dominance of a single party, for example, the greater the danger (at least in the case of sliding-scale rules, over time) that amendments will be passed without adequate deliberation and support from a diverse range of perspectives (compare Issacharoff 2003). By contrast, the stronger the degree of competition and discipline among two major parties, the more likely it is that political pressures will constrain the use of amendment procedures in a way that makes formally weak supermajority or even simple-majority voting requirements more than adequate to guard against the danger of overly flexible amendment.

The protection of minorities, and particularly "discrete and insular" minorities in the political process (see Ely 1980), will be another important factor for constitutional designers to consider when adopting various amendment mechanisms. One potential advantage to a constitutional convention mechanism, from this perspective, will be that it allows seats to be reserved for particular minority groups (such as, in Australia, indigenous groups: see Twomey 2008). Sliding-scale and simple-majority rules, on the other hand, may raise particular dangers. If they adopt such rules, therefore, constitutional designers may also wish to consider applying them to only some, rather than all, forms of constitutional amendment – that is, to only those amendments that do not touch on basic constitutional rights protections. Implicitly, this is the model adopted in the United States by state constitutions that have simple-majority amendment requirements, given that such amendments are also subject to the Fourteenth Amendment of the U.S. Constitution.[20] Several other countries have also adopted a similar approach by making certain fundamental rights guarantees either unamendable (see, e.g., the German *Basic Law* of 1949; and, as a matter of judicial interpretation, the *Constitution of India* 1950: see, e.g., Diwan and Diwan 1997, Neuborne 2003) or subject to higher-majority voting requirements (see Constitution of South Africa 1996, s. 74(1)).

The value of constitutional stability, and maintaining certain kinds of "internal" constitutional precommitment (see, e.g., Ferejohn & Sager 2003), will be another factor for constitutional designers to consider. One of the most serious objections against a constitutional convention mechanism, for example, is that it can empower a small subgroup of voters or representatives to propose whole-scale revisions to

[20] See, e.g., *Romer v. Evans*, 517 U.S. 620 (1996) (invalidating a Colorado constitutional amendment adopted by popular initiative for inconsistency with the Equal Protection clause).

a constitution, when the initial popular demand is for a much narrower form of constitutional updating or dialogue. Whatever the formal legal limits on a particular convention (and there has been a major debate in the United States in particular on this question: see, e.g., Dellinger 1979), as a political matter, most commentators agree it will be extremely difficult to restrain a "runaway convention" that exceeds the bounds of its mandate for constitutional change, and, therefore, the calling of such a convention always represents some threat to constitutional stability.

Compared to more demanding supermajority requirements or even-sliding scale rules, simple-majority voting rules can also pose a threat to constitutional stability. For sliding-scale rules, there will be an initial period in which amendment is more difficult and, therefore, also less likely; this, our findings in the second section suggest, can have a significant impact on the subsequent likelihood of actual constitutional amendment.[21] This is also another reason, beyond considerations of minority protection, why if they choose such a simple-majority rule, constitutional designers might wish to limit its use to more minor amendments, as opposed to more large-scale forms of constitutional revision (compare, e.g., Article XVIII of the California Constitution), or to certain subjects that do not touch on the "basic structure" of a constitution.

CONCLUSION

Political scientists and economists have long hypothesized that there is a connection between the size of a decision-making body and its output, in terms of constitutional amendment; in this chapter, we show that, at a state constitutional level in the United States, there is significant empirical support for this prediction. Our results show that for all states in the United States for which house size data is available, a larger house of representatives leads to a significantly lower probability of constitutional amendment: one standard deviation in the number of house members in a particular state, we found, was associated with 2.7 fewer amendments per decade – or a 14.6 percent reduction relative to the mean number of amendments. These results were also robust to the inclusion of a number of controls, as well to various different specifications in unreported robustness checks.

Our focus in the third section is on exploring the possible normative implications of this for the design of constitutional amendment rules, and in particular on the way in which three design mechanisms – namely sliding-scale voting rules, simple-majority voting rules, and constitutional convention mechanisms – may be able to

[21] In our data we found, for example, that if state amended its constitution in a given year, it was 2.8 times more likely than other states to amend it again 2 years later, and 1.9 times more likely to do so 4 years later. There was also a strong degree of persistence for this effect, with the odds ratio of amendment still standing at 1.4 after 10 years. These findings were also statistically significant at the 1% level.

help address potential denominator problems in amendment procedures over time. The empirical findings of the chapter, however, also have potential relevance to a range of other constitutional debates, including debates about the optimal size of legislatures (see Taagpera and Shugart 1989) and even nations (see, e.g., Alesina and Spolaore 2003). These are simply questions that, because of their complexity, are beyond the scope of this short chapter to address.

REFERENCES

Ackerman, Bruce, *We the People: Foundations* (Cambridge, MA: The Belknap Press of Harvard University Press 1991).

Alesina, Alberto and Enrico Spolaore, *The Size of Nations* (Cambridge, MA: The MIT Press 2003)

Alexander, Gregory S., *The Global Debate over Constitutional Property: Lessons for American Takings Jurisprudence* (Chicago: University of Chicago Press 2006).

Allen, Tom, "The Right to Property," in *The Research Handbook in Comparative Constitutional Law*, edited by Rosalind Dixon and Thomas Ginsburg (Northhampton, MA: Elgar Publishing 2011).

Amar, Akhil Reed, "The Consent of the Governed: Constitutional Amendment Outside Art V," *Columbia Law Review* 94 (1994), 457–511.

Ambwani, Justice Sunil, I. R. Coelho (deceased) by L. Rs. Vs. State of Tamil Nadu & Others: A Case Study. *Lecture Delivered at the Advocates Association Organized by SAMVAAD*, 2007.

Bearak, Barry, "Final Results Show Resounding Victory for ANC in South Africa," *The New York Times*, April 25 (2009).

Buchanan, James M. and Gordon Tullock, *The Calculus of Consent: Logical Foundations of Constitutional Democracy* (Indianapolis: Liberty Fund [1962] 2004), vol. 2.

Choudhry, Sujit, "Rethinking Comparative Constitutional Law: Multinational Democracies, Constitutional Amendment, and Secession," Paper presented at the annual meeting of the Law and Society Association (2007).

Dahl, Robert A. and Edward R. Tufte, *Size and Democracy* (Stanford, CA: Stanford University Press 1973).

Dellinger, Walter, "The Recurring Question of the 'Limited' Constitutional Convention," *Yale Law Journal* 8 (1979), 1623–40.

Denning, Brandon and John Vile, "The Relevance of Constitutional Amendments: A Reply to David Strauss," *Tulane Law Review* 77 (2002), 274–82.

Devans, Neal and Louis Fisher, *The Democratic Constitution* (New York: Oxford University Press 2004).

Dinan, Desmond, *Ever Closer Union: An Introduction to European Integration*. 3rd edition. (London: Lynne Rienner Publishers 2005).

Diwan, Paras and Diwan, Peeyushi, *Amending Powers and Constitutional Amendments: From First to the Latest Amendment* (New Delhi: Deep & Deep Publications 1997).

Dixon, Rosalind, "Creating Dialogue about Socio-Economic Rights: Strong v. Weak-Form Judicial Review Revisited," *International Journal of Constitutional Law* 5 (2007), 391–418.

"The Supreme Court of Canada, Charter Dialogue and Difference," *Osgoode Hall Law Journal* 47 (2009), 235–86.

"Updating Constitutional Rules," *Supreme Court Review* 2009 (2010), 319–46.

"Partial Constitutional Amendments," 13 *University of Pennsylvania Journal of Constitutional Law* (2011).

"Constitutional Amendment Rules: A Comparative Perspective," in *Comparative Constitutional Law*, edited by Rosalind Dixon and Tom Ginsburg (Northhampton, MA: Elgar Publishing 2011).

Dixon, Rosalind and Richard Holden, "Amending the Constitution: Article V and the Effect of Voting Rule Inflation," Working Paper, 2009.

Duclos, Jean-Yves, Joan Esteban, and Debraj Ray, "Polarization: Concepts, Measurement, Estimation," *Econometrica* 72 (2004), 1737–72.

Eisgruber, Christopher L., *Constitutional Self-Government* (Cambridge, MA: Harvard University Press 2001).

Elkins, Zachary, Tom Ginsburg, and James Melton, *The Endurance of National Constitutions* (Cambridge: Cambridge University Press 2009).

Elster, Jon, *Ulysses Unbound. Studies in Rationality, Precommitment, and Constraints* (Cambridge: Cambridge University Press 2000).

Ely, John Hart, *Democracy and Distrust: A Theory of Judicial Review* (Cambridge, MA: Harvard University Press 1980).

Epstein, Richard, "Executive Power in Political and Corporate Contexts," unpublished manuscript, University of Chicago Law School (2009).

Esteban, Joan-María and Debraj Ray, "On the Measurement of Polarization," *Econometrica* 62 (1994), 819–51.

Ferejohn, John, "The Politics of Imperfection: The Amendment of Constitutions," *Law and Social Inquiry* 22 (1997), 501–30.

Ferejohn, John and Lawrence Sager, "Commitment and Constitutionalism," *University of Texas Law Review* 81 (2003), 1929–63.

Flavelle, Lucinda and Philip Kaye, "Party Discipline and Legislative Voting," *Canadian Parliamentary Review* 9 (1986). Available online at http://www2.parl.gc.ca/Sites/LOP/Infoparl/english/issue.asp?param=117&art=665

Forbath, William. E. "The Politics of Constitutional Design: Obduracy and Amendability? A Comment on Ferejohn and Sager," *University of Texas Law Review* 81 (2003), 1965–84.

Friedman, Barry, "Dialogue and Judicial Review," *Michigan Law Review* 91 (1993), 577–682.

Gilbert, Michael D, "Single Subject Rules and the Legislative Process," *University of Pittsburgh Law Review* 67 (2006), 803–70.

Giovannoni, Francesco, "Amendment Rules in Constitutions," *Public Choice* 115 (2003), 37–61.

Griffin, Stephen M., "The Nominee Is...," in *Constitutional Stupidities, Constitutional Tragedies*, edited by William N. Eskridge and Sanford Levinson (New York: New York University Press 1998).

Guizan, Julia Anne, "Is the California Civil Rights Initiative a Wolf in Sheep's Clothing? Distinguishing Constitutional Amendment from Revision in California's Initiative Process," *University of Loyola Los Angeles Law Review* 21 (1997), 261–96.

Hausman, Jerry, Bronwyn H. Hall, and Zvi Griliches, "Econometric Models for Count Data with an Application to the Patents-R&D Relationship," *Econometrica* 52 (1984), 909–38.

Hirschl, Ran, "The 'Design Sciences' and Constitutional 'Success'," *University of Texas Law Review* 87 (2009), 1339–74.

Hogg, Peter W. and Allison A. Bushell, "The *Charter* Dialogue between Courts and Legislatures (or Perhaps the *Charter of Rights* Isn't Such a Bad Thing After All)," *Osgoode Hall Law Journal* 35 (1997), 75–124.

Holden, Richard, "Supermajority Voting Rules," unpublished working paper (2009).

Holmes, Stephen, *Passions and Constraint: On the Theory of Liberal Democracy* (Chicago: University of Chicago Press 1995).

Holmes, Stephen and Cass Sunstein, "The Politics of Constitutional Revision in Eastern Europe," in *Responding to Imperfection: The Theory and Practice of Constitutional Amendment*, edited by Sanford Levinson (Princeton, NJ: Princeton University Press 1995).

Issacharoff, Samuel, "The Enabling Role of Democratic Constitutionalism: Fixed Rules and Some Implications for Contested Presidential Elections," *University of Texas Law Review* 81 (2003), 1985–2012.

King, Gary, "Variance Specification in Event Count Models: From Restrictive Assumptions to a Generalized Estimator," *American Journal of Political Science* 33 (1989), 762–84.

Levinson, Sanford, "Designing an Amendment Process," in *Constitutional Culture and Democratic Rule*, edited by John Ferejohn, Jack M. Rakove, and Jonathan Riley (Cambridge: Cambridge University Press 2001).

Lijphart, Arend, *Patterns of Democracy: Government Forms and Performance in Thirty-Six Countries* (New Haven, CT: Yale University Press 1999).

Lutz, Donald S., "Toward a Theory of Constitutional Amendment," in *Responding to Imperfection: The Theory and Practice of Constitutional Amendment*, edited by Sanford Levinson (Princeton, NJ: Princeton University Press 1995).

Michelman, Frank L., "The Supreme Court 1985 Term, Foreword: Traces of Self-Government," *Harvard Law Review* 100 (1986), 4–77.

Neuborne, Bert, "The Supreme Court of India," *International Journal of Constitutional Law* 1 (2003), 476–510.

Neyman, Jezry, 'Certain Chance Mechanisms Involving Discrete Distributions," in *Classical and Contagious Discrete Distributions*, edited by Ganapati P. Patil (Calcutta: Statistical Publishing Society 1965).

Rawls, John, *A Theory of Justice* (Cambridge, MA: The Belknap Press of Harvard University Press 1971).

Political Liberalism (New York: Columbia University Press 1993).

Riley, Jonathan, "Imagining Another Madisonian Republic," in *Constitutional Culture and Democratic Rule*, edited by John Ferejohn, Jack M. Rakove, and Jonathan Riley (Cambridge: Cambridge University Press 2001).

Sadurski, Wojciech, "Judicial Review and the Protection of Constitutional Rights," *Oxford Journal of Legal Studies* 22 (2002), 275–99.

Sager, Lawrence, "The Birth Logic of a Democratic Constitution," in *Constitutional Culture and Democratic Rule*, edited by John Ferejohn, Jack M. Rakove, and Jonathan Riley (Cambridge: Cambridge University Press 2001).

Samaha, Adam M., "Originalism's Expiration Date," *Cardozo Law Review* 30 (2008), 1295–1368.

Saunders, Cheryl, "Why a Convention?" *Public Law Review* 8 (1997), 213.

Strauss, David, "Common Law Constitutional Interpretation," *University of Chicago Law Review* 63 (1996), 877–936.

"The Irrelevance of Constitutional Amendments," *Harvard Law Review* 114 (2001), 1457–1505.
Sullivan, Kathleen M., "Constitutional Amendmentitis," *The American Prospect* (September 1995), 21.
Sunstein, Cass R., "The Enlarged Republic – Then and Now," *The New York Review of Books* 56 (March 2009), 26.
Taagpera, Rein and Matthew Sobert Shugart, *Seats and Votes: The Effects and Determinants of Electoral Systems* (New Haven, CT: Yale University Press 1989).
Tschaeni, Hanspeter, "Constitutional Change in Swiss Cantons: An Assessment of a Recent Phenomenon," *Publius: The Journal of Federalism* 12 (1982), 113–30.
Tushnet, Mark, "The Whole Thing," *Constitutional Commentary* 12 (1995), 223–26.
"Some Skepticism about Normative Constitutional Advice," *William and Mary Law Review* 49 (2008),1473–95.
"Constitutional Workarounds," *Texas Law Review* 87 (2009), 1499–1516.
Twomey, Anne, "Constitutional Conventions, Commissions and Other Constitutional Reform Mechanisms," Sidley Law School Research Paper No. 08/38 (2008). Available online at: http://papers.ssrn.com/sol3/papers.cfm?abstract_id=1120628
United Nations. Department of Economic and Social Affairs. Population Division, *World Population Prospects: The 2006 Revision, Highlights* (New York: United Nations 2007). Available online at: http://www.un.org/esa/population/publications/wpp2006/WPP2006_Highlights_rev.pdf
Vermeule, Adrian, "Constitutional Amendments and Common Law," in *The Least Examined Branch: The Role of Legislatures in the Constitutional State*, edited by Richard W. Bauman and Tsvi Kahana (Cambridge: Cambridge University Press 2006).
Warhurst, John, "Conscience Voting in the Australian Federal Parliament," *Australian Journal of Politics and History* 58 (2008), 579–96.
Williams, Robert F., "Equality Guarantees in State Constitutional Law," *Texas Law Review* 63 (1985), 1195–224.
Young, Ernest, "The Constitution Outside the Constitution," *The Yale Law Journal* 117 (2007), 408–73.

9

Collective-Action Federalism

A General Theory of Article I, Section 8

Robert D. Cooter and Neil S. Siegel

INTRODUCTION

> The federal system was created with the intention of combining the different advantages which result from the magnitude and the littleness of nations.
>
> de Tocqueville, *Democracy in America*, 2003

Under the Articles of Confederation, Congress lacked the power to protect the states from military warfare waged by foreigners and from commercial warfare waged by other states. The states proved unable to solve these difficulties on their own. They acted individually when they needed to act collectively, and the Framers of the U.S. Constitution concluded that the states could not reliably achieve an end when doing so required two or more of them to cooperate. The solution lay with the establishment of a more comprehensive unit of government – a national government with the authority to tax, raise and support a military, regulate interstate and international commerce, and act directly on individuals. The Constitutional Convention thus instructed the midsummer Committee of Detail that Congress would possess the power to "legislate in all Cases for the general Interests of the Union, and also in those Cases to which the States are separately incompetent, or in which the Harmony of the United States may be interrupted by the Exercise of individual Legislation" (Farrand 1966). The Committee subsequently produced Article I, Section 8.

The Framers lacked the tools and language of modern social science, but they knew a collective-action problem when they saw it. When activities spilled over from one state to another, the Framers recognized that the actions of individually rational states produced irrational results for the nation as a whole – the definition of a collective-action problem. The federal government is the smallest unit that internalizes these spillovers. By internalizing the effects, the federal government is more likely than the states to solve the problem of interstate spillovers. So

Article I, Section 8 of the new Constitution gave Congress additional powers to address collective-action problems.

Interpretations of Article I, Section 8 since the Founding have not always focused on collective-action problems involving multiple states. Regardless of collective-action problems, many presidents and members of Congress throughout the nineteenth century doubted the constitutionality of internal improvements and disaster relief by the federal government. Moreover, the U.S. Supreme Court, in trying to distinguish the "truly national" from the "truly local" in the context of the Commerce Clause,[1] historically has gone back and forth between imposing essentially no limits on the scope of the commerce power and imposing a series of dubious formal distinctions. The crisis of the Great Depression ultimately exploded the *Lochner* Court's categorical differentiations between "manufacturing" and "commerce," "direct" and "indirect" effects on commerce, goods in the "flow" of commerce and goods not in the flow, and "harmful" and "harmless" goods in commerce (Brest et al. 2006: 447–49). More recently, the Court has distinguished "economic" or "commercial" activity, which Congress may regulate using its commerce power, from "noneconomic" or "noncommercial" activity, which Congress may not regulate.

A federal constitution ideally gives the central and state governments the power to do what each does best. Economic activity does not generally cause collective-action problems among the states, and noneconomic activity is not generally free from collective-action problems. Consequently, Congress is not generally better at regulating economic activity, and the states are not generally better at regulating noneconomic activity. Whatever its usefulness in defining the word "commerce," the distinction between economic and noneconomic activity is mostly irrelevant to the problems of federalism.

We propose a more promising constitutional foundation for American federalism in Article I, Section 8, one that may inform much of the Court's recent jurisprudence despite what it has tended to say. Our theory of collective-action federalism flows directly from the relative advantages of the federal government and the states: Much of what the federal government does best involves solving collective-action problems that the states cannot solve on their own. We will argue that the eighteen clauses of Section 8 are a coherent set, not a heterogeneous aggregation of unrelated powers. Coherence comes from the connection of the specific powers to collective-action problems impinging on the general welfare.

Section 8 begins in Clause 1 by granting Congress the power to "lay and collect Taxes … to pay the Debts and provide for the … general Welfare of the United States." Welfare is "general" (or "among the several States," in the language of

[1] United States v. Morrison, 529 U.S. 598, 617–18 (2000).

Clause 3) when the federal government can obtain it and the separate states cannot – that is, when spillovers pose a collective-action problem for the states. The theory of collective-action federalism interprets the clauses of Section 8 as authorizing Congress to tax, spend, and regulate when two or more states face collective-action problems. Conversely, governmental activities that do not pose collective-action problems for the states are "internal to a state" or "local."

Some concepts from economics help develop the theory of collective-action federalism. We show that the eighteen clauses of Article I, Section 8 mostly address two kinds of spillovers: interstate externalities and national markets.

Conscientious members of Congress and presidents should use the theory of collective-action federalism in assessing the scope of their own legislative or veto powers. Courts also should use the theory to the extent that they engage in judicial review of federalism questions. The theory of collective-action federalism addresses the constitutional meaning of Section 8, not the extent to which courts should declare its meaning in constitutional adjudication.

The first section of the chapter, on history, surveys past interpretations of Article I, Section 8, both outside and inside the courts. The second section, on theory, shows how interstate externalities and markets cause collective-action problems that affect the general welfare. The third section, on taxonomy, sorts the powers in Article I, Section 8 into analytical categories from economics, notably interstate externalities and national markets. Taken together, these sections demonstrate that the specific powers form a coherent group, one that defines a substantive constitutional conception of the "general Welfare."

The fourth section identifies substantial support for the theory of collective-action federalism in the U.S. Supreme Court's interpretation of Article I, Section 8 during the tenure of Chief Justice John Marshall and since 1937. We also identify two ways in which existing constitutional understandings of Congress and the Court would improve by taking greater account of the existence or nonexistence of collective-action problems involving multiple states. First, collective-action federalism differentiates interstate commerce from intrastate commerce by using the distinction between individual and collective action by the states, not the Supreme Court's distinction between "economic" and "noneconomic" activity. Second, collective-action federalism suggests that Congress possesses some power under Clause 1 to *regulate* noncommercial harms that spill over state boundaries, such as certain environmental problems and contagious diseases. We thus favor reconsideration of the Court's conclusion in *United States v. Butler* that the General Welfare Clause does not confer any regulatory authority.[2]

[2] United States v. Butler, 297 U.S. 1, 318–19 (1936).

The fifth section identifies one way of evaluating congressional judgments about the existence and seriousness of collective-action problems, and about the adequacy of Congress's response. The concluding section summarizes our argument.

PAST INTERPRETATIONS OF ARTICLE I, SECTION 8

We begin with previous interpretations of Article I, Section 8, both extrajudicial and judicial, over the course of American history. Although we will not rest our interpretation of Section 8 primarily on history, much of this history supports our structural and consequentialist approach. Moreover, the parts of the history that do not support our approach illustrate the problems that result when constitutional interpretation of Section 8 disregards collective-action problems and attempts to resolve federalism questions by using one or another variety of formal distinctions.

Section 8 Outside the Courts

Preratification

The structure of governance established by the Articles of Confederation often prevented the states from acting collectively to pursue their common interests (Rakove 1996). Solving these problems of collective action was a central reason for calling the Constitutional Convention (Kramer 1999: 616–23). These facts bear on the proper interpretation of the constitution that emerged from the Convention, as we show by beginning with the general welfare.

Like the Constitution that would replace it, the Articles of Confederation used the phrase "general welfare" to describe problems that a central government can solve better than the states. A particular understanding of this problem resulted in the Articles' assignment of taxing and spending powers: Congress was permitted to apportion taxes, but levying and collection were left to state governments.[3] The Articles thus required the national government to finance itself by requisitioning the states. State governments, however, failed to honor the requisition orders, which deprived the federal government of the resources it needed to protect the states both from external attack and from internal restraints on trade. The young nation subsequently experienced the failures of the Articles of Confederation, which changed many peoples' understanding of the problem of the general welfare and convinced them that the central government needed additional powers. As a result, the Framers retained the same phrase – the "general Welfare" – in the Constitution, but they enumerated many specific powers of Congress denied in the Articles. For example, to solve the problem of financing the national government, the General

[3] Articles of Confederation art. VIII.

Welfare Clause in the Constitution empowers Congress to levy taxes (Amar 2005: 46). The problems of collective action confronting America in 1787 "necessitated a government with many more powers than were possessed by Congress under the Articles – including the great powers to tax, to raise and support armies, and to regulate commerce" (Kramer 1999: 619). Facing these problems also "necessitated conferring authority to exercise these powers by acting directly on individual citizens" (Kramer 1999: 619–20).

The proceedings of the Philadelphia Convention confirm that, in thinking through the scope of congressional power that would eventually become Article I, Section 8, the delegates focused on collective-action problems involving multiple states. Specifically, the Convention instructed the midsummer Committee of Detail that Congress would be authorized to "legislate in all Cases for the general Interests of the Union, and also in those Cases to which the States are separately incompetent, or in which the Harmony of the United States may be interrupted by the Exercise of individual Legislation" (Farrand 1966). This language registers the need to overcome a series of collective-action problems facing the states. It was offered by Gunning Bedford of Delaware on July 17, 1787, to clarify the sixth resolution of the Virginia Plan, so named because it was drafted by the Virginia delegation before the Convention was ready to proceed (Rakove 1996: 177–78). Notably, when the Committee of Detail made its report ten days later, "[i]t had changed the indefinite language of Resolution VI into an enumeration of the powers of Congress closely resembling Article I, Section 8 of the Constitution as it was finally adopted" (Stern 1934).

This "radical change" wrought by the Committee of Detail was uncontroversial among the delegates; the Convention "accepted *without discussion* the enumeration of powers made by a committee which had been directed ... that the Federal Government was 'to legislate in all cases for the general interests of the Union ... and in those to which the states are separately incompetent'" (Stern 1934). The delegates apparently perceived the connection between the general propositions in Resolution VI and the specific powers conferred in Article I, Section 8. "If the Convention had thought that the committee's enumeration was a departure from the general standard for the division of powers to which it had thrice agreed, there can be little doubt that the subject would have been thoroughly debated on the Convention floor" (Stern 1934: 1340; Regan 1995). This history suggests that Section 8 is appropriately read as a coherent response to a series of collective-action problems. It suggests that Section 8 should be read as a unified whole, not as a list of unrelated powers.

Postratification

If key Framers were acutely mindful of collective-action problems facing the states, the need for collective action often seemed lost on constitutional interpreters during the Constitution's first full century. After the Constitution was ratified, national politicians continued to debate the scope of federal power in Section 8, particularly the meaning of the reference in Clause 1 to the "general Welfare." Because Congress seldom used its commerce power before the latter decades of the nineteenth century (Brest 2006: 176), and because presidential vetoes often prevented the constitutionality of spending bills from being litigated in court (Brest 2006: 450), the main participants in these debates tended to be presidents and members of Congress. Unfortunately for the young nation, many of these participants did not seem particularly interested in inquiring whether Congress or the states were better situated to address the problem at hand.

A major antebellum constitutional controversy concerned the extent to which the General Welfare Clause authorized Congress to spend money on "internal improvements." Members of the Federalist Party, heavily influenced by Alexander Hamilton, defended robust congressional power under Clause 1 to spend for the "general Welfare" regardless of whether the expenditure could plausibly be viewed as carrying out another enumerated power in Section 8.[4] Federalists were opposed by Democratic Republicans such as James Madison, who argued that Congress possessed no independent power to tax and spend in pursuit of the general welfare. Rather, Madison insisted that the constitutional meaning of the phrase "general Welfare" is defined and limited by the specific grants of authority in Clauses 2 through 17 of Section 8.[5]

It was on this constitutional ground that President Madison, in 1817, rested his veto of then-Representative John C. Calhoun's Bonus Bill, which would have funded internal improvements, including roads and canals. Calhoun believed that it would advance the "general welfare" of the nation as a whole "to perfect the communication from Maine to Louisiana," "to connect all the great commercial points on the Atlantic ... with the Western States," and "to perfect the intercourse between the West and New Orleans" (Brest 2006: 82). Madison conceded the policy virtues of the proposal but vetoed it because he was "constrained by the insuperable difficulty I feel in reconciling the bill with the Constitution of the United States" (Brest 2006: 83). Likewise, Madison's successor, President James Monroe, vetoed a similar internal improvements bill on constitutional grounds in 1822 (Brest 2006: 84), and President Jackson voiced constitutional objections in vetoing the Maysville Road bill in 1830 (Currie 2005). Subsequent Democratic presidents – specifically, Tyler, Polk, Pierce, and Buchanan – articulated increasingly narrow conceptions of congressional authority over internal improvements.

4 *See* Hamilton, Alexander. 1791 Report on the Subject of Manufactures (1791), *reprinted in* 10 Papers of Alexander Hamilton 230, 302–04 (Harold C. Syrett ed., 1966).

5 *See, e.g.*, The Federalist No. 41 (Madison); United States v. Butler, 297 U.S. 1, 65–66 (1936) (discussing Madison's restrictive view of the General Welfare Clause and Hamilton's expansive view).

"And thus on the eve of the Civil War," David Currie writes, "Congress found itself unable even to remove obstructions to naturally navigable waters, which Andrew Jackson himself had conceded it not only could but ought to do" (Currie 2005: 25).

In the decades after the Civil War, the same constitutional qualms about federal spending extended to disaster relief. There was substantial political precedent for federal spending to help the victims of disasters (Brest 2006: 451). People disagreed, however, on whether such spending was for the "general Welfare" as required by the Constitution rather than for the particular welfare of those who benefited from the expenditures. For example, some congressional supporters of federal funding to aid the victims of an Ohio River flood in 1884 argued, in effect, that necessity trumped the Constitution (Brest 2006: 451). Likewise, President Grover Cleveland signed certain disaster relief bills during his presidency, but in 1887 he vetoed on constitutional grounds a bill that would have provided relief to drought victims in Texas (Brest 2006: 452–53).

Section 8 Inside the Courts

The General Welfare Clause

The Supreme Court did not weigh in on this long-standing political debate over the scope of the federal taxing and spending powers until 1936. In *United States v. Butler*, the Court explicitly approved Hamilton's robust view of the scope of the taxing and spending powers as "the correct one."[6] Accordingly, the Court has held that Congress possesses broad authority to tax and spend for the general welfare, so long as Congress does not violate another constitutional provision. The Court reaffirmed this holding in subsequent cases. In *Steward Machine Company v. Davis*,[7] the Court rejected a constitutional challenge to the federal unemployment compensation system created by the Social Security Act ("SSA"). And in *Helvering v. Davis*,[8] the Court sustained the constitutionality of the SSA's old-age pension program, which had been funded exclusively by federal taxes.

Whereas the *Butler* Court approved broad congressional power to tax and spend according to its assessment of what the general welfare requires, the same Court rejected the possibility that the General Welfare Clause allows federal regulation in addition to taxation and spending. "The true construction [of the first clause]," the Court wrote, "undoubtedly is that the only thing granted is the power to tax for the purpose of providing funds for payment of the nation's debts and making provision for

[6] 297 U.S. 1, 66 (1936).

[7] 301 U.S. 548 (1937).

[8] 301 U.S. 619 (1937).

the general welfare."[9] The *Butler* Court reasoned that a contrary conclusion would allow a general federal police power and render the rest of Section 8 superfluous:

> The view that the clause grants power to provide for the general welfare, independently of the taxing power, has never been authoritatively accepted. Mr. Justice Story points out that, if it were adopted, "it is obvious that under color of the generality of the words, to 'provide for the common defence and general welfare', the government of the United States is, in reality, a government of general and unlimited powers, notwithstanding the subsequent enumeration of specific powers."[10]

Madison reasoned in much the same fashion in vetoing Calhoun's "internal improvements" bill (Brest 2006: 83). Neither seemed to consider the possibility that their concerns about a general federal police power were overstated – that the phrase "general Welfare" in Clause 1 might possess substantive content illuminated by considering the nature of the problems addressed in the balance of Section 8.

Instead, the *Butler* Court held unconstitutional the Agricultural Adjustment Act of 1933 (AAA), which sought to stabilize agricultural production and raise prices by offering farmers subsidies to limit their crops. The Court explained that the AAA "invades the reserved rights of the states" because its "purpose is the control of agricultural production, a purely local activity."[11] "It hardly seems necessary to reiterate," Justice Owen Roberts wrote for the Court, "that ours is a dual form of government."[12] The Court was unmoved by "the fact that," as one astute commentator noted contemporaneously, "no state has ever undertaken any serious exercise of such power, and ... could not possibly make any such regulation effective."[13]

The Commerce Clause

In contrast to judicial interpretation of the General Welfare Clause, the Court began construing the scope of Congress's "power ... [t]o regulate Commerce ... among the several States"[14] early in the nineteenth century. During that time period, the Court rarely but broadly interpreted the Commerce Clause. After generously construing the scope of congressional power in Section 8 as a whole in *McCulloch*

9 *Butler*, 297 U.S. at 64.

10 *Id.* (quoting Joseph Story, 1 COMMENTARIES ON THE CONSTITUTION OF THE UNITED STATES § 907 (5th ed. 1905) (originally published in 1833).

11 *Butler*, 297 U.S. at 63, 64. This part of the *Butler* Court's holding is no longer good law.

12 *Id.* at 68.

13 Friedman 2009: 204 (quoting Loeb, Isidor. *Constitutional Interpretation in a Transitional Period*, 21 ST. LOUIS L. REV. 105 (1936)).

14 U.S. CONST. art. 1, § 8, cl. 3.

v. Maryland,[15] the Court expansively read the scope of the commerce power in *Gibbons v. Ogden*.[16]

The *Gibbons* Court has held that the Commerce Clause authorizes Congress to regulate navigation. In reaching that conclusion, Chief Justice Marshall's definition of the phrase "among the several States" in Clause 3 was expansive but not limitless. "The word 'among,'" Marshall wrote, "means intermingled with. A thing which is among others, is intermingled with them. Commerce among the States, cannot stop at the external boundary line of each State, but may be introduced into the interior."[17] Yet Marshall took care to note that "[c]omprehensive as the word 'among' is, it may very properly be restricted to that commerce which concerns more States than one. ... The completely internal commerce of a State, then, may be considered as reserved for the State itself."[18] Although Marshall's language left a good many line-drawing problems unresolved, he did point the way toward a functional middle ground between very limited federal power on the one hand and effectively limitless federal power on the other.

Congress did not begin using its commerce power in earnest until the decades after the Civil War, in response to the rapid industrialization of the country. From the late 1800s until 1937, the *Lochner* Court, which was committed to a largely unregulated national economy, adopted a narrow view of the Commerce Clause and invalidated many federal statutes as beyond the scope of the commerce power. Sometimes the Court struck down acts that regulated "manufacturing" and not "commerce."[19] Other times the Court concluded that the commerce at issue was not "among the several States" because the effect on interstate commerce was "indirect," as opposed to "direct,"[20] or because the goods at issue were not in the "flow" of commerce,[21] or because the goods that Congress was attempting to regulate were "harmless," as opposed to "harmful."[22] In one of these decisions, the Court went out of its way to dismiss the "proposition, often advanced and as often discredited, that the power of the federal government inherently extends to purposes affecting the nation as a whole with which the states severally cannot deal or cannot adequately deal."[23]

15 17 U.S. (4 Wheat.) 316 (1819) (holding that Congress had Section 8 authority to create the Bank of the United States and that the states were prohibited by the Constitution from taxing the Bank).

16 22 U.S. (9 Wheat.) 1, 193–97 (1824).

17 *Id.* at 193.

18 *Id.* at 195–96.

19 *See, e.g.*, United States v. E.C. Knight Co., 156 U.S. 1, 12–13 (1895); Carter v. Carter Coal Co., 298 U.S. 238, 303–04 (1936).

20 *See, e.g.*, A.L.A. Schecter Poultry Corp. v. United States, 295 U.S. 495, 546 (1935).

21 *Compare, e.g.*, Swift & Co. v. United States, 196 U.S. 375 (1905), *with Schecter Poultry Corp.*, 295 U.S. at 543.

22 *See, e.g.*, Hammer v. Dagenhart, 247 U.S. 251, 271–72 (1918).

23 *Carter*, 298 U.S. at 291.

These formal distinctions proved difficult to apply consistently, nonarbitrarily, and (eventually) in a manner that was compatible with the widely perceived necessity for action by the federal government during the Great Depression. All of these distinctions abruptly exited constitutional law beginning in 1937, when Justice Roberts altered his view of the scope of the commerce power and became the fifth vote to uphold laws of the kind previously invalidated by the Court.[24] Perhaps he responded to a very popular president who was pushing a "Court packing" plan to overcome judicial invalidations of key components of his New Deal economic recovery programs. (Roosevelt registered quickly that "[i]f forty states go along with adequate legislation and eight do not … we get nowhere."[25]). Perhaps Roberts experienced a genuine change of heart. In any case, his "switch in time that saved nine" came to characterize this deferential era of Commerce Clause jurisprudence.[26] From 1937 until 1995, the Court did not invalidate one federal law as beyond the scope of the commerce power.

For example, in *Wickard v. Filburn*, the Court allowed Congress to use its commerce power to attempt to raise the price of wheat on the interstate market.[27] Specifically, the Court upheld the Agricultural Adjustment Act's wheat production quota as applied to a farmer who exceeded his quota but used the excess wheat exclusively for home consumption and livestock feeding. The Court reasoned that such home consumption constituted a substantial and varying percentage of national demand, and so had a significant effect on the price.[28] The Court also reasoned that Congress might rationally fear that excess wheat would end up being sold on the interstate market.[29] *Wickard* has long been considered controversial; many commentators have viewed it as an instance in which Congress pushed the outer limits of its commerce power.

Until the 1990s, conventional wisdom held that Congress could regulate essentially any activity under the Commerce Clause. In 1995, however, the Supreme Court started imposing some limits on the regulatory power of Congress. The Court's holdings created a new jurisprudence of the Commerce Clause. As discussed below, the Court has ostensibly placed decisive emphasis on its determination of whether the activity regulated by Congress is "economic" or "noneconomic" in nature, which also appears to determine whether that activity exists "among the several States" or instead is internal to one state.

[24] *See* NLRB v. Jones & Laughlin Steel Corp., 301 U.S. 1 (1937).

[25] Franklin Delano Roosevelt, *quoted in id.* at 208.

[26] *See, e.g.*, United States v. Darby, 312 U.S. 100 (1941); Heart of Atlanta Motel, Inc. v. United States, 379 U.S. 241 (1964); Katzenbach v. McClung, 379 U.S. 294 (1964).

[27] 317 U.S. 111 (1942).

[28] *Id.* at 127.

[29] *Id.* at 128.

The new epoch began with a constitutional challenge to the federal Gun-Free School Zones Act of 1990 ("GFSZA"),[30] which criminalized possession of a firearm within 1,000 feet of a school zone.[31] In 1995, in *United States v. Lopez*, the Justices considered whether Congress had exceeded its commerce power in enacting this law. Writing for Justices O'Connor, Scalia, Kennedy, Thomas, and himself, Chief Justice Rehnquist concluded that the law was unconstitutional on the ground that the presence of a firearm near a school did not substantially affect interstate commerce. In supporting this conclusion, the Chief Justice stressed that GFSZA "is a criminal statute that by its terms has nothing to do with 'commerce' or any sort of economic enterprise, however broadly one might define those terms."[32] He did not actually refute the government's empirical assertion that guns near schools substantially affect interstate commerce in the aggregate. Instead, he changed the subject, "paus[ing] to consider the implications of the Government's arguments,"[33] which were essentially that if Congress may regulate gun possession in schools, then Congress may regulate anything. Specifically, Rehnquist rejected the government's rationales because he could not "perceive [in them] any limitation on federal power, even in areas such as criminal law enforcement or education where States historically have been sovereign."[34] The Court did not – because it could not – provide a functional test for distinguishing substantial from insubstantial effects on interstate commerce. In *Lopez*, the Court's characterization of the regulated activity as noncommercial appeared decisive.

Likewise, Justice Kennedy, whose views are likely controlling for the time being, wrote in a concurring opinion that "here neither the actors nor their conduct has a commercial character, and neither the purposes nor the design of the statute has an evident commercial nexus."[35] While noting that "[i]n a sense any conduct in this interdependent world of ours has an ultimate commercial origin or consequence," he stressed that "we have not yet said the commerce power may reach so far."[36]

Five years later, the Court demonstrated that *Lopez* was not merely symbolic. The federal Violence Against Women Act ("VAWA") authorized victims of gender-motivated violence to sue their assailants for money damages in federal court.[37] *United States v. Morrison* concerned the constitutionality of this civil-damages provision; the question presented was whether the damages remedy fell within the scope of

[30] 18 U.S.C. § 922(q)(2)(a) (2000); *id.* § 921(a)(25) (2000).
[31] *Id.* § 922(q)(2)(a); *id.* § 921(a)(25).
[32] 514 U.S. 549, 561 (1995).
[33] *Id.* at 564–65.
[34] *Id.* at 564.
[35] *Id.* at 580 (Kennedy, J., concurring).
[36] *Id.*
[37] 42 U.S.C. § 13981.

congressional authority under either the Commerce Clause or Section Five of the Fourteenth Amendment. Splitting five-to-four, the same way as in *Lopez*, the Court invalidated the damages remedy as beyond federal power under both provisions. In analyzing the commerce power, Chief Justice Rehnquist again emphasized for the Court that Congress was regulating noneconomic activity traditionally regulated by the states: "Gender-motivated crimes of violence are not, in any sense of the phrase, economic activity." Rehnquist declined to impose "a categorical rule against aggregating the effects of any noneconomic activity in order to decide these cases," but he nonetheless insisted that "thus far in our Nation's history our cases have upheld Commerce Clause regulation of intrastate activity only where that activity is economic in nature."[38]

The Court rejected the government's submission that violence against women substantially affects interstate commerce, despite a voluminous legislative history documenting Congress's judgment to that effect.[39] According to the Chief Justice, "Congress' findings are substantially weakened by the fact that they rely so heavily on a method of reasoning that we have already rejected as unworkable if we are to maintain the Constitution's enumeration of powers."[40] Specifically, such reasoning "seeks to follow the but-for causal chain from the initial occurrence of violent crime (the suppression of which has always been the prime object of the States' police power) to every attenuated effect upon interstate commerce."[41]

The Chief Justice warned that the government's reasoning, if accepted, would allow Congress to regulate any violent crime "as long as the nationwide, aggregated impact of that crime has substantial effects on employment, production, transit, or consumption."[42] This rationale could "be applied equally as well to family law and other areas of traditional state regulation since the aggregate effect of marriage, divorce, and childrearing on the national economy is undoubtedly significant."[43] Again, the Court did not actually refute the government's empirical assertions. Instead, it denied "that Congress may regulate noneconomic, violent criminal conduct based solely on that conduct's aggregate effect on interstate commerce."[44]

In *Gonzales v. Raich*,[45] the Court clarified that the economic/noneconomic characterization attaches to the general *class* of activity at issue. The general class of activity must be economic in order to fall under the regulatory power granted to Congress by Clause 3, but some particular instances within the class may be noneconomic. In other words, regulation may encompass activity that the Court deems

38 529 U.S. 598, 613 (2000).
39 *Id.* at 614.
40 *Id.* at 615.
41 *Id.*
42 *Id.*
43 *Id.* at 615–16.
44 *Id.* at 617–18.
45 545 U.S. 1 (2005).

noneconomic if Congress rationally concludes that it is part of a general class of activity that the Court deems economic. For example, production of marijuana or wheat generally is an economic activity and thus is regulable by Congress under its commerce power. However, according to the Court, congressional regulation of this general activity also can cover marijuana or wheat grown and consumed at home, which may be noneconomic.

Raich arose when California created a medical exception to its marijuana laws. No such exception exists in the federal Controlled Substances Act (CSA).[46] The Court held six-to-three that the Commerce Clause allows Congress to prohibit the local cultivation and use of marijuana in compliance with state law authorizing such use. Writing for the Court, Justice Stevens relied on *Wickard v. Filburn*, which he read as "establish[ing] that Congress can regulate purely intrastate activity that is not itself 'commercial,' in that it is not produced for sale, if it concludes that failure to regulate that class of activity would undercut the regulation of the interstate market in that commodity."[47] Justice Stevens saw "striking" similarities between *Raich* and *Wickard*: Congress could have rationally concluded that leaving home-consumed wheat or marijuana outside the federal regulatory scheme would affect interstate price and market conditions.[48]

In these cases, the Court has sought to impose limits on the power of Congress in order to preserve the separation of federal and state powers established by Clause 3's grant of authority to "regulate Commerce ... among the several States." The Court has purported to find this limit by restricting regulatory power under the Commerce Clause in "substantial effects" cases to "economic" or "commercial" activity, no doubt in part because of the reference to "Commerce" in Clause 3. To clarify what it regards as "economic activity," the Court in *Raich* cited a dictionary definition of "economics" as "the production, distribution, and consumption of commodities."[49] Under the Court's jurisprudence, then, the economic/noneconomic determination appears dispositive because only economic activities may be aggregated for purposes of deciding whether the activity has substantial effects on interstate commerce, and every activity Congress might want to regulate has substantial effects on interstate commerce in the aggregate.

There is a basic problem with using formal distinctions to divide federal and state powers in Article I, Section 8: The main reason for separating powers is the relative advantages of the federal and state governments. Formal distinctions unrelated to relative advantages will fail to advance the general welfare when applied to federalism problems. To clarify the mismatch, we turn now to the economic theory of the general

[46] 21 U.S.C. § 801 *et seq*.

[47] *Raich*, 545 U.S. at 18.

[48] *Id.* at 18–19.

[49] *Id.* at 25 (quoting WEBSTER'S THIRD NEW INTERNATIONAL DICTIONARY 720 (1966)).

welfare. Later, we will show that a substantive conception of the general welfare has informed many of the Court's decisions construing the Commerce Clause or the General Welfare Clause, both during the tenure of Chief Justice Marshall and since 1937 – sometimes despite what the Court has said. We also will identify ways in which contemporary constitutional understandings would be improved by taking greater account of the distinction between individual and collective action by states.

THEORY OF THE GENERAL WELFARE

We will use modern economics to analyze problems in the Articles of Confederation and their amelioration by Article I, Section 8. We begin with concepts that are familiar to economists and positive political theorists, but that constitutional lawyers and judges may comprehend imperfectly.

Externalities

Economists use the term "public goods" to refer to goods supplied by the state whose technical characteristics require financing by taxes instead of prices. Two characteristics of public goods necessitate financing by taxes. First, pure public goods are *nonrivalrous*, meaning that one person's enjoyment does not detract from another's. Thus, the security from foreign invasion enjoyed by one citizen does not detract from the security enjoyed by another citizen. Similarly, when pollution abatement improves air quality, one person who breathes air does not detract from another person's breathing it. In contrast, private goods are rivalrous. The bite that I take out of a sandwich leaves one less bite for someone else, and the land where I build my house becomes unavailable for building by others.

Aside from being nonrivalrous, pure public goods are *nonexcludable*, which means that excluding individuals from enjoying the benefits generated by the goods is infeasible or uneconomical. For example, all residents of the United States during the Cold War enjoyed the benefits of deterring a Soviet missile attack, and no one could be excluded from enjoying these benefits. Likewise, when abatement improves local air quality, everyone in the locality enjoys breathing the improved air. Similarly, everyone enjoys free access to local streets because establishing toll booths on them is impractical. In contrast, private goods are excludable with help from the law. Thus, the owner and possessor of a sandwich can prevent others from eating it, and the owner of land can prevent others from entering it.[50]

[50] Using these two defining characteristics of public goods, Paul Samuelson provided a remarkably simple and powerful mathematical formulation of efficiency in demand and supply. *See* Paul A. Samuelson, *Diagrammatic Exposition of a Theory of Public Expenditure*, 37 REV. ECON. & STAT. 350, 350–56 (1955); Paul A. Samuelson, *The Pure Theory of Public Expenditure*, 36 REV. ECON. & STAT. 387, 387–89 (1954).

When exclusion is unfeasible or uneconomical, individuals have an incentive to free-ride by not paying for the benefits they receive. When beneficiaries do not pay, suppliers cannot earn a profit, and so the market undersupplies the good.[51] A free market will undersupply national defense, clean air, local streets, and other public goods. The state can prevent free-riding by collecting taxes to finance public goods. Because taxes are compulsory, people who try to free-ride break the law.

We have been discussing public goods, which convey benefits to people regardless of whether they pay for them. In general, "externalities" refer to unpriced benefits and costs. Public goods are positive externalities that the state produces intentionally. Similarly, a person who gets vaccinated benefits others by reducing their risk of exposure to contagious diseases, and an apiarist who keeps bees for honey also pollinates other peoples' orchards. These are positive externalities that individuals incidentally convey to others without their paying for it. Similarly, pollution is a negative externality that individuals and firms incidentally convey to others without having to pay for it. Dirty air is the by-product of burning fuel; congested streets are the by-product of commuting by car; and depleted stocks of fish are the by-product of overfishing. Households and firms pursue private goods and dump pollution in the public domain.

Some negative externalities affect only contiguous landowners, such as the tree that blocks the neighbor's light or the smell from a neighbor's barn. In law, many of these externalities are "private nuisances." Other negative externalities affect many people, such as pollution in the Los Angeles basin. Externalities that affect many people are called "public externalities" because they have the two characteristics of public goods: nonrivalry and nonexclusion.

Three propositions are analytically equivalent: (1) a free market will undersupply public goods; (2) a free market will undersupply positive externalities; and (3) a free market will oversupply negative externalities.

Internalization Principle

By definition, a *national public good or bad* is nonrivalrous and nonexcludable at the national level. Military defense is the standard example. Instead of being national, however, many externalities are mostly local. A local public good or bad is nonrivalrous and nonexcludable at the local level. Thus, Central Park in Manhattan mostly benefits the people who live or work nearby, and congestion on the streets of

51 Technical characteristics of goods can cause markets to fail. K. J. Arrow & F. H. Hahn, GENERAL COMPETITIVE ANALYSIS (1971). Market failure provides the conventional economic justification for state supply and regulation of goods. Stephen Breyer, REGULATION AND ITS REFORM 7–8 (1982). Economic theory has analyzed the forms of market failure and proposed remedies for them. *See* Charles L. Schultze, THE PUBLIC USE OF PRIVATE INTEREST 54 (1977) ("[A]n incentive-oriented approach [to market failure] has a very large potential role, and its absence is very costly.").

San Francisco mostly harms local people who drive or walk on them. An air quality basin, a city park, and a congested local street are standard examples of local public goods and bads.

All public goods and bads present a challenge for public policy. Economists have a simple prescription to meet this challenge. Compared to unaffected people, the people affected by a policy have more reason to inform themselves about it and to influence it. Thus the affected people are more likely to cast informed votes, monitor politicians, impose taxes on themselves, and perform the acts of citizenship that make democracy work. Considerations of information and motivation imply a prescription for allocating political power in a federal system called the *internalization principle*: *Assign power to the smallest unit of government that internalizes the effects of its exercise* (Baumol and Oates 1988).

To illustrate, the internalization principle suggests why the largest and finest parks in the United States are almost entirely the work of the federal government. Assume that establishing a large park in the mountains would attract visitors from all over the nation. The national government, not state or local governments, represents *all* of the beneficiaries. If most financing must come from taxes and not entrance fees, financing the national park from a national tax puts the burden on the beneficiaries. Federal officials have better incentives than state or local officials to build a large park that would attract visitors nationally. Responsibility for such parks should fall on officials who have a national perspective, which is mostly what we observe in fact.

Thus the internalization principle has this national application: When a public good is purely national, or nearly so, the central government should provide it. In other words, the central government should raise revenues and use them to supply national public goods, either directly by government production or indirectly by purchasing the good from a nongovernment producer. Equivalently, when a negative externality is purely national, or nearly so, the central government should control it. In other words, the federal government should abate the harm directly through government activity or indirectly by regulating the activities that cause the harm.

Conversely, assume that a city neighborhood needs a small park for local residents. In situating and scaling the park, local residents possess better information than nonresidents. Local residents also have stronger incentives than nonresidents to monitor the officials responsible for creating and maintaining the park. Thus, local officials have better incentives than central officials for supplying local public goods. Moreover, a local public good can be financed by a local tax, which primarily hits the beneficiaries and misses nonbeneficiaries. These facts favor assigning power over city parks to local governments. Thus the internalization principle has this local application: When a public good or bad is purely local, or nearly so, local government should provide or control it (Oates 1972).

The internationalization principle applies simply and immediately when the extent of the public good or bad corresponds to a government's jurisdiction. Many types of externalities, however, disrespect jurisdictional boundaries. Water and air circulate in regions formed by natural contours such as rivers and mountains, not political boundaries. Consequently, pollution spills over from one government jurisdiction to another. Spillovers create an incentive for each government to free-ride on pollution abatement by others. To avoid free-riding by localities, the government with primary responsibility for abatement should encompass the natural region affected by the pollution.

Sometimes special governments can be created to fit the boundaries of a natural region. The jurisdiction of a special government ideally extends as far as the effects of the public goods it supplies or the externalities it abates. A special district might provide clean water to several counties, or it might impose liability on local governments that pollute an air basin. Some jurisdictions rely more heavily on special districts than others. For example, the legal framework in California makes forming special districts relatively easy, and the state contains more than 5,000 special governments such as water districts, school districts, park districts, and transportation districts (Cooter 2000).

We use the phrase "interstate externality" to refer to a good or bad that is nonrivalrous and nonexcludable at the interstate level. Interstate externalities exist when significant benefits or costs from activities in one state spill over to another state without being priced. In practice, the federal government may be the only authority to solve the problem. To understand why, the next subsection explains the political foundation of the internalization principle.

Federal Coase Theorem

The internalization principle is grounded in the politics of federalism, which we will analyze abstractly. With interstate externalities, two or more states can gain by cooperating with one another. Economists have studied various obstacles that increase the time and effort needed for cooperation, or block it completely. The obstacles include unclear rights, incomplete contracts, lack of credible commitments, asymmetrical information, distrust, holdouts, and high communication costs.

The strategies that people use to respond to such obstacles are often complicated, and models of them in game theory often have indeterminate results. A remarkable simplification often gives determinancy: sweep all of the obstacles to cooperation into the encompassing term "transaction costs." A famous proposition in law and economics, which helped Ronald Coase win the Nobel Prize in economics, asserts that individuals bargain successfully unless transaction costs impede them. Applied to intergovernmental relations, this proposition implies that when transaction costs are low, bargaining among governments will correct any undersupply of public goods or oversupply of public bads. For example, when state governments can bargain easily with one another, they will cooperate in supplying the optimal amount of national defense and pollution abatement. These considerations lead to a proposition that we call the *Federal Coase Theorem*: *Assuming zero transaction costs, the supply of public goods and the control of externalities is efficient regardless of the allocation of powers to different levels of government.*

The Federal Coase Theorem describes a condition – zero transaction costs – under which the allocation of powers to different levels of government makes no difference to the efficient supply of public goods. In reality, the allocation of powers to different levels of government makes a big difference. The point of the Federal Coase Theorem is to isolate the cause of this difference, not to deny its existence. Following this lead, we compare the transaction costs of cooperation in centralized and decentralized states. We will explain why unanimity rule paralyzes organizations with many members and majority rule animates them.

In a decentralized system, states can cooperate with each other by forming compacts. In principle, compacts among states can supply interstate public goods and suppress interstate externalities without intervention by the federal government. When states compact, each one is free to join or not to join. Forming a state compact thus requires unanimity among the participating governments.[52] In contrast, Congress does not require unanimity among the states to pass a federal law. Instead of unanimity, Congress follows a majoritarian process – enacting legislation requires a majority of votes in both Houses of Congress and the president's signature.[53] We think of centralized and decentralized states as different ways to organize cooperation that affect transaction costs. Differences in transaction costs especially depend on the difference between unanimity and majority rule. We will contrast these two poles of intergovernmental relation – unanimity and majority rule – very abstractly, without a complicated discussion of the division of powers.

Unanimity rule quickly becomes unmanageable as the number of participants increases. To illustrate, assume that five local governments have jurisdiction over segments of a lake's shore. They want to use the lake for recreational swimming, which requires all of them to stop polluting. An agreement among any four governments is worthless without participation by the fifth government. The governments negotiate to distribute the abatement costs. If any four governments reach a tentative

52 In the United States, compacts also require congressional approval. U.S. CONST. art. I, § 10, cl. 3.

53 *See* U.S. CONST. art. I, § 7. It may be more accurate to describe Congress, especially the Senate, as operating under a supermajority rule than under a majority rule, but this fact does not change the analysis in the text. There is less of a difference between unanimity rule and supermajority rule than there is between unanimity rule and majority rule, but there is still a difference, and typically a significant one.

agreement, the fifth government can hold out. A holdout government may refuse to cooperate unless the others pay most of the abatement costs. Any of the five governments could be the holdout that shifts abatement costs to the others. In the worst case, all five governments hold out, so that abatement efforts never begin.[54]

In this example of lake swimming, cooperation among four jurisdictions has no value without cooperation by the fifth. The value of cooperation jumps from zero to a large number when the number of cooperators increases from four to five. This is an extreme case of increasing returns to the scale of cooperation. In general, a coalition has increasing returns to scale when the payoff per member increases with the number of members. Under unanimity rule, increasing returns to scale often causes a holdout problem. Sometimes people can overcome holdout problems by nongovernmental means, such as social norms (Ellickson 1991), but often they cannot. Because of the holdout problem, the probability of cooperation under unanimity rule usually falls with the number of actors who must cooperate.[55]

Economies of scale and scope generally create positive externalities that impose collective-action problems. Interstate infrastructure provides an example. Just think of what would happen if the states were responsible for the interstate highway system. North Carolina might plan a north-south highway in a different place from where South Carolina was planning a north-south highway. Coordinating their plans so that the roads meet in the same place involves a collective-action problem. The federal government solved this problem and created a coherent interstate highway system that far surpassed prior accomplishments by the individual states.

The same logic that applies to interstate externalities also applies to the legal foundations for interstate markets. Thus assume that an interstate market requires a highway (an "internal improvement") to pass through five states arranged in a line: A⇔B⇔C⇔D⇔E. Building the road through compacts requires all five states to agree. The road will benefit people in each of the five states, but each state may prefer to shift most of the construction costs onto the other states. As with the lake, the value of cooperation jumps from zero to a large number when the number of cooperators increases from four to five. Each state gains bargaining power by holding out and being the last state to join the compact.

[54] As a coalition grows, each member who joins demands a fraction of the resulting increase in the surplus from cooperation. With increasing returns to the scale of cooperation, the last member to join increases the coalition's value more than each previous member. The last member can thus demand better terms than each previous member for joining the coalition. Recognizing this fact, everyone has an incentive to hold out and join the coalition last. If everyone holds out, however, the coalition never forms.

[55] Equivalently, the transaction costs of bargaining under unanimity rule increase rapidly with the number of bargainers.

To reiterate, the holdout problem makes the probability of cooperation fall with the number of actors who must cooperate. We can illustrate these facts by using hypothetical numbers for a federal system. Imagine that the probability of cooperation is roughly 0.9 when interstate externalities affect two states. The probability of cooperation approaches zero as the number of states that must unanimously agree exceeds, say, ten. So the probability is very small that all fifty states would join a compact for common defense, create a unified post office, protect intellectual property, abolish internal tariffs, or allow the free mobility of capital and labor. Because unanimity rule paralyzes groups with more than a few members,[56] state compacts seem unpromising as means to solve interstate externalities and build interstate markets.

Having explained why unanimity rule paralyzes organizations with many members, now we will explain why majority rule animates them. Majority rule creates competition to become the decisive member in a majority coalition. Consider an assembly of 101 members. A coalition of fifty-one constitutes a majority. To form a majority coalition, a minority coalition of fifty members must attract one additional member. Any one of fifty-one persons could join the coalition and make a majority. Belonging to the majority coalition conveys power and advantages unavailable to the minority. Conversely, holding out risks exclusion from power and other advantages. Instead of holding out and risking exclusion, the fifty outsiders may stampede to join the majority coalition and share in the advantages of power.

Applying this logic to the example of the polluted lake, assume that five local governments form a council with the power to impose a pollution abatement program on its members by majority vote. A coalition of three local governments can impose an abatement plan that makes the other two bear a disproportionate share of abatement costs. A minority coalition with two members must attract an additional member to create a majority coalition. All three players outside this coalition may rush to join in order to avoid bearing a disproportionate share of abatement costs. In general, competition to become the decisive member of the majority coalition often prevents holdouts in large organizations.[57]

As an organization grows, it may switch from unanimity to majority rule to avoid paralysis. Thus, as more countries join the European Union, the Council of Ministers

[56] Unsurprisingly, the Framers provided that ratification by nine of the thirteen states would suffice to establish the Constitution, *see* U.S. CONST. art. VII, even though unanimity was required to amend the Articles of Confederation, *see* Articles of Confederation art. XIII.

[57] Note, however, that the same reason many people wish to join the majority coalition explains why it may be unstable: Anyone excluded from the majority coalition can offer to benefit all but one member of it by replacing one of its members on terms more favorable to the others. The technical name for this problem is the "empty core." *See* Tracey E. George & Robert J. Pushaw, Jr., *How Is Constitutional Law Made?*, 100 MICH. L. REV. 1265, 1270 n. 21 (2002); *see also* Cooter 2000: 58–60 (discussing majority-rule division of a fixed sum of money).

increasingly follows qualified majority rule rather than unanimity rule (Craig and de Burca 2008). Equivalently, a shift from unanimity rule to majority rule increases the optimal number of governments in a federal system. A federal system with majority rule can work effectively with more members than can a federal system with unanimity rule. Thus, as the European Union resolves more problems by majority rule and fewer problems by unanimity rule, it can accommodate more members.

Switching from unanimity rule to majority rule ameliorates the problem of holdouts, but it creates a new problem: minority exploitation. Under unanimity rule, anyone who stands to lose from collective action can veto it. The switch to majority rule removes this protection from the minority. If collective action creates more costs than benefits for the minority, then the minority suffers a net loss from federal action.[58] For this reason, governments that fear being in the minority (rightly or wrongly) may resist the centralization of power, as do the smaller countries in the European Union, as did delegates from the smaller states at the Constitutional Convention in 1787. They prefer risking paralysis under unanimity rule to exploitation under majority rule.

As more parties must cooperate, the transaction costs of cooperation increase, and so does the probability of failure. Consequently, the probability that federal power is required to solve an interstate externality increases as the number of affected states increases. When all states are affected, as with military defense and free trade, the advantages of federal power are overwhelming. Conversely, when two states are involved, the advantages of federal power are smaller.[59] When the number of parties shrinks to two, there is no majority or minority, so the difference between unanimity rule and majority rule disappears. Without majority rule, there is no holdout problem. Two-state externalities pose a problem of bargaining but not a problem of holdouts. Successful cooperation is much more likely when it involves a bargaining problem between two states than when it involves a holdout problem among many states. Even so, experience under the Articles of Confederation included important examples where two states failed to cooperate.[60]

58 This is one reason why Buchanan and Tullock stressed the advantages of unanimity rule in their classic book that revived contractarianism. James M. Buchanan & Gordon Tullock, THE CALCULUS OF CONSENT: LOGICAL FOUNDATIONS OF CONSTITUTIONAL DEMOCRACY 85–96 (1962); *see also* Mathias Dewatripont & Gerard Roland, *Economic Reform and Dynamic Political Constraints*, *in* 2 MONETARY AND FISCAL POLICY: POLITICS 421 (Torsten Persson & Guido Tabellini eds., 1994).

59 Even in the two-state scenario, the advantages of federal power are often significant, which helps explain why the Constitution extends federal judicial power "to Controversies between two or more States." U.S. CONST. art. III, § 2.

60 *See, e.g.*, THE FEDERALIST NO. 7 (Hamilton) (George W. Carey & James McClennan eds., 2001), at 28–31 (detailing land disputes between Connecticut and Pennsylvania and between New York and Vermont, and describing Connecticut's "disposition to retaliation" in response to Rhode Island's passage of laws violating private contracts).

In interpreting the Constitution, a rule is required to bound federal power. The Commerce Clause grants federal regulatory power over commerce "among the several states," which always has been understood to include two or more states.[61] Given experience under the Article of Confederation, two states was a natural boundary to draw as the lower limit for the power of Congress to regulate interstate commerce. As we show in the third section, the Framers wrote Section 8 to give Congress power over interstate externalities and interstate markets, regardless of whether they affect two states or many states. The fact that Congress possesses this power, however, does not mean that it should always exercise it. Rather, Congress should exercise its regulatory power only when two or more states fail to promote the general welfare because they cannot cooperate with one another.

Political Logic of U.S. Federalism

To review, benefits and costs that spill across state lines create an incentive for each state to free-ride on the efforts of other states. The incentive to free-ride exists if spillovers affect two states or many states. If the problem is not addressed, citizens will suffer from too few interstate public goods, too many harmful interstate externalities, and not enough interstate commerce. To overcome this problem, states may compact with one another. Compacts that require unanimity impose high transactions costs on collective action. Transaction costs increase sharply with the number of states that must cooperate together. If the compact encompasses many states, holdouts will paralyze it. The central government operating through majority rule can find solutions that elude states cooperating through unanimity rule. Empowering Congress animates collective action but risks exploiting states in the minority. Thus, majority rule ideally extends far enough to solve the problem of public goods, harmful externalities, and interstate markets, but no further in order to reduce the danger of exploitation. Balancing these considerations leads to the internalization principle: *Assign power to the smallest unit of government that internalizes the effects of its exercise.*

ANALYTICAL CATEGORIES OF ARTICLE I, SECTION 8

We have explained the political logic at the foundation of the internalization principle. The internalization principle grounds our analysis of the enumerated powers in Article I, Section 8, to which we now turn. In the system created by the U.S. Constitution, the federal government is the smallest unit of government that always internalizes the effects of interstate public goods, externalities, and markets. The internalization

[61] 22 U.S. (9 Wheat.) 1, 194 (1824) ("Comprehensive as the word 'among' is, it may very properly be restricted to that commerce which concerns more States than one.").

principle thus implies that Congress should have constitutional authority to solve these collective-action problems. This explanation, although incomplete,[62] is fundamental for understanding the allocation of powers in Article I, Section 8.

Analysis of Section 8

Figure 9.1 assigns numbers to the eighteen clauses of Section 8. The General Welfare Clause, which comes first, authorizes Congress to "lay and collect Taxes ... to pay the Debts and provide for the ... general Welfare of the United States."[63] A list of sixteen specific powers follows. The final clause authorizes Congress to use the means "necessary and proper" to achieve the previously authorized ends – the Necessary and Proper Clause.[64]

Using this enumeration, Figure 9.2 sorts the specific powers into three analytical categories that we will explain.

We begin with interstate externalities. Clause 1 authorizes Congress to "lay and collect Taxes ... to ... provide for the common Defence,"[65] and Clauses 10 through 16 confer specific powers of national defense. In economics textbooks, military defense is the standard example of a good with positive externalities that affect an entire nation. Without a federal army, each state would have to provide for its own defense. The benefits of defense in one state would spill over to people in another state. The provider would have no practical way to collect fees from out-of-state beneficiaries to pay for the costs of defense. So each state would have an incentive to free-ride on the security provided by other states, leaving each of the states insecure.

In general, a positive interstate externality exists when an activity in one state benefits people in another state who do not pay for it. Given the technical characteristics of the activity, the provider in one state has no practical way to collect fees from the beneficiaries in another state. Congress, which does not suffer this disadvantage, can provide for the common defense much more effectively than the states.

After the common defense, Clause 7 refers to the next power embodying positive externalities: the federal post office. The post office is a network that becomes more valuable for each user as it acquires more pickup and delivery points. If the

[62] A complete discussion would consider the separation and interrelation of powers at the national level, including such topics as the bicameralism and presentment requirements of Article I, Section 7; instability under majority rule, including the empty core of a game of redistribution by majority rule; and the agency problem of representation of citizens by officials, including lobbying. For a discussion, see Part III of Cooter, 2000.

[63] U.S. CONST. art. I, § 8, cl. 1.

[64] *Id.* art. I, § 8, cl. 18.

[65] *Id.* art. I, § 8, cl. 1.

The Congress shall have power

1. To lay and collect taxes, duties, imposts and excises, to pay the debts and provide for the common defense and general welfare of the United States; but all duties, imposts and excises shall be uniform throughout the United States;
2. To borrow money on the credit of the United States;
3. To regulate commerce with foreign nations, and among the several states, and with the Indian tribes;
4. To establish a uniform rule of naturalization, and uniform laws on the subject of bankruptcies throughout the United States;
5. To coin money, regulate the value thereof, and of foreign coin, and fix the standard of weights and measures;
6. To provide for the punishment of counterfeiting the securities and current coin of the United States;
7. To establish post offices and post roads;
8. To promote the progress of science and useful arts, by securing for limited times to authors and inventors the exclusive right to their respective writings and discoveries;
9. To constitute tribunals inferior to the Supreme Court;
10. To define and punish piracies and felonies committed on the high seas, and offenses against the law of nations;
11. To declare war, grant letters of marque and reprisal, and make rules concerning captures on land and water;
12. To raise and support armies, but no appropriation of money to that use shall be for a longer term than two years;
13. To provide and maintain a navy;
14. To make rules for the government and regulation of the land and naval forces;
15. To provide for calling forth the militia to execute the laws of the union, suppress insurrections and repel invasions;
16. To provide for organizing, arming, and disciplining, the militia, and for governing such part of them as may be employed in the service of the United States, reserving to the states respectively, the appointment of the officers, and the authority of training the militia according to the discipline prescribed by Congress;
17. To exercise exclusive legislation in all cases whatsoever, over such District (not exceeding ten miles square) as may, by cession of particular states, and the acceptance of Congress, become the seat of the government of the United States, and to exercise like authority over all places purchased by the consent of the legislature of the state in which the same shall be, for the erection of forts, magazines, arsenals, dockyards, and other needful buildings;—And
18. To make all laws which shall be necessary and proper for carrying into execution the foregoing powers, and all other powers vested by this Constitution in the government of the United States, or in any department or officer thereof.

FIGURE 9.1. The eighteen clauses in Article I, Section 8.

1. Provide for common defense and general welfare	
A. Interstate Externalities	
	1. Common defense 10. Suppress piracy 11. Declare war 12. Raise armies 13. Maintain navy 14. Make military law 15. Call militia 16. Govern militia
	7. Establish post office
	8. Make intellectual property law
B. Interstate Markets	
	3. Regulate interstate and foreign commerce
	4. Naturalization law
	4. Bankruptcy law
	5. Issue money
	5. Fix weights and measures
	6. Punish counterfeiting
C. Federal Administration	
	1. Taxes and duties
	2. Issue bonds
	9. Create lower federal courts
	17. Govern D.C. & federal buildings in states
	18. Make laws necessary & proper to execute these and other powers

FIGURE 9.2. Economic analysis of enumerated powers.

postal industry consisted of several private firms that cooperated, each firm's activity would expand the network and thus benefit the other firms. In this respect, the post office in the eighteenth century resembles the railroad in the nineteenth century and the Internet in the twentieth century. Modern legal scholars who observed positive externalities on the Internet called them "network effects."

Given network effects, the initial problem is to grow the industry enough so that costs fall to the point of economic viability. In this respect, the federal government's interest in promoting the post office in the eighteenth century resembles its concern with promoting the railroad in the nineteenth century and the Internet in the twentieth century.

Once such an industry is viable, competition often propels the market toward a single provider or a small number of very large providers, as with the railroads in the nineteenth century and Google in the late twentieth century. A large firm can internalize positive externalities and lower the transaction costs of coordination. Economists call this situation a "natural monopoly." With a natural monopoly at the national level, the federal government appropriately stands ready to constrain the dominant firm through antitrust laws and regulations, or to provide the service itself.

Proceeding down the rows of Figure 9.2, we turn to Clause 8, which empowers Congress to make intellectual property law. An inventor without a patent cannot prevent someone else from copying her invention, and an author without a copyright cannot prevent someone else from reprinting her book. Effective intellectual property law enables creators to collect fees from users of their creations, which provides an incentive for creativity.[66] Because the problem of unauthorized use extends across state lines, the problem is national and Congress is better placed than the states to solve it. Federal intellectual property laws enable creators to collect fees from users across the nation, which creates a unified national market for creative works.

Military defense, the postal service, and intellectual property affect the "general" welfare because of positive interstate externalities. Now our analysis turns from interstate externalities to interstate markets. The publication of Adam Smith's *Wealth of Nations* in 1776 systematically explained the advantages of free markets and free trade for a nation. In the same year, America declared its independence. Subsequently, the young nation's unhappy experience under the Articles of Confederation confirmed Smith's ideas about the disadvantages of fettered markets and trade barriers.[67]

[66] Scholars are now engaged in a lively debate about where intellectual property rights should expand and where they should contract. *See, e.g.*, James Boyle, THE PUBLIC DOMAIN: ENCLOSING THE COMMONS OF THE MIND (2008); William M. Landes & Richard A. Posner, *Indefinitely Renewable Copyright*, 70 U. CHI. L. REV. 471, 471–75 (2003); Lawrence Lessig, *The Creative Commons*, 65 MONT. L. REV. 1, 11 (2004).

[67] *See, e.g.*, Granholm v. Heald, 544 U.S. 460, 472 (2005) (emphasizing the "tendencies toward economic Balkanization that had plagued relations among ... the States under the Articles of Confederation").

In the eighteenth century, America faced the problem of creating a unified market for goods, capital, and labor. Legal obstacles to the movement of resources inhibit national markets. In contrast, a uniform regulatory framework lubricates national markets for some goods. Recognizing the federal government's decisive advantage over state governments, the drafters of the Constitution in 1787 gave Congress the power to create unified national markets in Clauses 3 through 6.

Congress used this power. Labor mobility increased as a result of uniform federal laws enacted pursuant to Clause 3, such as social security and civil rights, and as a consequence of naturalization laws passed pursuant to Clause 4. Stability and trust in capital markets increased following federal statutes enacted pursuant to Clause 3, such as federal deposit insurance, compulsory disclosure by issuers of stocks, registration of brokers, and uniform bankruptcy law passed pursuant to Clause 4. Federal statutes enacted pursuant to Clause 3 also provide the legal foundation for specific industries such as radio and television, in which the Federal Communications Commission prevents broadcasters from interfering with one another. The dormant Commerce Clause, which the Supreme Court has inferred from the grant of power to Congress in Clause 3, usually prohibits states from discriminating against interstate commerce or placing an undue burden on the interstate movement of goods and services.[68] The transaction costs of interstate trade fell because Congress created a common currency as authorized in Clauses 5 and 6, and established national standards for weights and measures as authorized in Clause 5. Taken together, these actions made the United States into the world's largest zone of unrestricted mobility of goods, capital, and labor for more than 150 years, which goes far toward explaining the country's remarkable economic performance.

Implementing the preceding powers requires federal administration. Clauses 1, 2, 9, 17, and 18 authorize robust means to achieve the ends in the other clauses.

In sum, the theory of collective-action federalism reads Section 8 as a unified whole, like a well-written paragraph. Clause 1 is the topic sentence that expresses the main idea of a federal government empowered to promote the general welfare. Clauses 2 through 17 provide illuminating instances of the idea that were most important at the time the Framers wrote the paragraph. And Clause 18, the Necessary and Proper Clause, concludes by underscoring the broad availability of means to realize both the main idea and specific instances of it.[69]

[68] For a cogent discussion of contemporary doctrine, see *Granholm*, 544 U.S. at 472–73. There are two exceptions to the dormant commerce principle: congressional approval and market participation by states. We do not discuss them here.

[69] In our account, the Necessary and Proper Clause is primarily a reminder. Similarly, Chief Justice Marshall already had decided *McCulloch* in favor of the federal government before he turned to the Necessary and Proper Clause. *See* 17 U.S. (4 Wheat.) at 411.

Collective-action Federalism and Constitutional Disagreement

When collective action problems harm all of the states, the justification of congressional power does not turn on the precise definition of externalities. Overlapping views about the nature of externalities suffice to justify congressional authority under Article I, Section 8. In other cases, however, the interests of the states diverge, so one can anticipate vigorous disagreements about the nature and extent of externalities. Our analytical framework for interpreting Section 8 encompasses robust disagreements about the appropriate scope of federal power. If the theory of collective action federalism gained general support, then hard cases involving the enumerated powers might resemble many environmental disputes. In such disputes, cost-benefit analysis is a basic method for focusing debates. Putting numbers on divergent values identifies the important areas where differences in values yield different policy decisions. Focus improves debate so much that the law often mandates cost-benefit analysis in environmental impact statements. Environmental impact statements thus illustrate our claim that externalities provide a useful framework within which parties can dispute legal questions, including the enumerated powers.

Disagreements about interstate externalities will follow predictable political lines. People who seek to reduce federal power will argue that, beyond national defense, interstate public goods are few in number. They will also articulate a narrow understanding of interstate externalities, and they will contend that national markets are self-regulating. Conversely, those who aim to expand federal power will argue that interstate public goods are numerous, including education, research, poverty relief, the arts, and the environment. They will also maintain that national markets often fail without federal regulation. And in addition to material externalities, they will point to psychological externalities, such as the concerns of people in one state for the health, education, environment, and physical or financial security of people in another state (Esty 1996; Sen 1977). Psychological externalities can be particularly large in the wake of a natural disaster, such as Hurricane Katrina or the recent earthquake in Haiti.[70]

If weak feelings that people in one state have for people in another count as interstate externalities, then collective action is a ubiquitous problem and our framework would impose no limits on federal action. In principle, unbounded expansion of the meaning of "externalities" would destroy the usefulness of the concept and vindicate the general complaint that collective-action federalism is too indeterminate for use in constitutional interpretation.

[70] An interstate externality refers to interdependence in the utility functions of individuals in at least two states. Mathematics can handle interdependence regardless of whether it is material or psychological. But the measurement of some kinds of externalities is easier than others, notably the traditional, material externalities. The history of cost-benefit analysis, however, is in part a history of learning to measure what was previously unmeasurable.

In fact, economists bound the concept of externalities sufficiently for cost-benefit analysis to become a basic tool for debating public policy. In the economics tradition, feelings count as costs and benefits only if people are willing to pay to vindicate them. Cheap talk does not suffice. Under this approach the concerns of people in one state for what happens in another state count as interstate externalities to the extent that they would be willing to pay to vindicate them.

Could the standard of "willingness to pay" achieve the same success in constitutional law by limiting the feelings that count as interstate externalities? Several difficult questions require answers. One question is whether willingness to pay is an appropriate measure of welfare effects when individuals care intensely but lack the ability to pay. "Ability to pay" refers to a person's income and wealth. The most common approach to cost-benefit analysis gives the same weight to how much people are willing to pay even though they differ in their ability to pay. A less common but familiar approach in economics gives more weight to the willingness of poor people to pay.[71]

We further note that the theory of collective-action federalism addresses the substantive meaning of Article 1, Section 8, not the institutional roles of Congress and the Court in constitutional interpretation and implementation.[72] Those who endorse vigorous judicial review of federalism questions will interpret our framework primarily in terms of how courts should restrain Congress. Those who favor judicial deference to Congress will interpret our framework primarily in terms of congressional self-restraint and the political safeguards of federalism.[73]

There is much to be gained from an analytical framework that encompasses disagreements. Theory directs research toward missing information that often advances policy debates and occasionally ends them. Collective-action federalism directs political disagreements into debates about the scope of public goods, externalities, and markets. Applying our framework requires extensive fact finding, which interacts with contestable normative judgments. Finding the scope of interstate externalities and market failures requires mathematical theory, econometrics, cost-benefit analysis, psychological surveys, behavioral experiments, and

[71] For an illuminating discussion, see generally Cass R. Sunstein, *Willingness to Pay vs. Welfare*, 1 HARV. L. & POL'Y REV. 303 (2007). Willingness to pay is also not an appropriate criterion in certain situations regardless of whether it accurately measures welfare, such as on matters of basic human rights.

[72] Similarly, Jack Balkin distinguishes questions of fidelity to the Constitution from questions of institutional responsibility. *See* Jack M. Balkin, *Fidelity to Text and Principle*, *in* THE CONSTITUTION IN 2020, at 20 (Jack M. Balkin & Reva B. Siegel eds., 2009).

[73] There is a robust and long-standing debate over the political safeguards of federalism in constitutional law and theory. *See, e.g.*, Herbert Wechsler, *The Political Safeguards of Federalism: The Role of the States in the Composition and Selection of the National Government*, 54 COLUM. L. REV. 543 (1954); Jesse Choper, JUDICIAL REVIEW AND THE NATIONAL POLITICAL PROCESS (1980); Andrej Rapczynski, *From Sovereignty to Process: The Jurisprudence of Federalism After Garcia*, 1985 SUP. CT. REV. 341; Larry Kramer, *Understanding Federalism*, 47 VAND. L. REV. 1485 (1994).

so on. Social scientists from across the political spectrum generally embrace these techniques, although they often reach different conclusions when using them. In cases where our framework does not end disagreement, it directs argument towards questions that matter to the general welfare, not towards formal distinctions that do not matter.

EXPLAINING (OR IMPROVING) CONTEMPORARY UNDERSTANDINGS

The preceding section showed that collective-action federalism provides a sound structural and consequentialist understanding of the division of powers between the federal government and the states in Article I, Section 8.[74] Collective-action federalism clarifies how members of Congress should interpret their constitutional powers – that is, when they should vigorously use the authority granted by Article I, Section 8 and when they should leave problems for the states to address. Sometimes state cooperation is likely to succeed, as when the need for cooperation involves only two states and they are disposed to cooperate. In such circumstances, Congress should *not* exercise its power. Rather, it should allow the affected states to solve the problem on their own. Other times, state cooperation is unlikely to succeed, as when the need for cooperation involves numerous states, or when states have historical or political obstacles to cooperation. In such situations, Congress should exercise its constitutional power.

Turning from Congress to the courts, we say nothing about whether courts should engage in judicial review of federalism questions. We argue, rather, that if courts do engage in such review, they should use the theory of collective-action federalism to understand the clauses of Section 8.

We now consider judicial interpretation of Article I, Section 8 by justices past and present. We will identify substantial support for the theory of collective-action federalism in the U.S. Supreme Court's interpretation of Article I, Section 8, both during the Chief Justiceship of John Marshall and since 1937. We further identify ways to improve existing constitutional understandings, including judicial doctrine, by taking more explicit account of the existence or nonexistence of collective problems involving more than one state.

[74] A collective-action approach does *not* explain the proper scope of federal powers authorized by the enforcement clauses of the Civil War Amendments. *See* U.S. CONST. amend. XIII, § 2; amend. XIV, § 5; amend XV, § 2. These amendments dramatically changed the balance of power between the federal government and the states by authorizing congressional regulation of certain subject matters – including, but not limited to, racial inequality. These amendments especially aimed to grant basic constitutional rights previously denied to minority groups. Minorities had been excluded because collective action had succeeded for the majority, not because it failed. We see no reason why the logic of collective action should guide interpretation of these provisions.

This section will focus on the two most important and controversial clauses of Section 8. First, our discussion of the Commerce Clause will identify the bases in case law for replacing the distinction between economic and noneconomic activity with the distinction between collective and individual choice by states. This discussion also encompasses the dormant Commerce Clause, whose justification we locate in the collective-action problems motivating each state to impede business competition from other states. Second, our discussion of the General Welfare Clause explains why it could bear some of the justificatory burden of federal regulation that courts currently assign to the Commerce Clause.

The Commerce Clause

Recall that Chief Justice Marshall upheld congressional power to regulate navigation between states in *Gibbons v. Ogden*. To reach this result, he read the word "among" in the phrase "To regulate commerce … among the several states" to mean "intermingled with," and he stated that navigation intermingled commerce in one state with commerce from another state.[75] Collective-action federalism supports this interpretation of the Commerce Clause. When commerce from different states intermingles, large economic advantages come from uniformity, access, and coordination in the channels and instrumentalities of commerce. Thus a road across one state is far more valuable if it connects to a road across another state; a flood control program upstream is more effective if it coordinates with a flood control program downstream; standardized electric plugs are more useful than heterogeneous plugs; and the Internet is more valuable than unconnected intranets. Instead of uniformity, access, and coordination, firms often seek diversity, closure, and noncooperation by state governments to protect against competition. Like exclusionary tariffs, such policies create modest individual advantages and massive collective costs. Marshall's decision gives Congress the power to solve this collective-action problem for the channels and instrumentalities of interstate commerce.

The theory of collective-action federalism is also consistent with many of the Court's post-1937 Commerce Clause decisions. For example, *Wickard v. Filburn*[76] is controversial because of skepticism that federal power to regulate interstate commerce could possibly extend to home production of wheat. The case looks different in light of collective-action federalism. Congress perceived a national problem of overproduction of wheat. A state could have ordered limits on production within its own jurisdiction, which would have disadvantaged its producers relative to

75 Gibbons v. Ogden, 22 U.S. (9 Wheat.) 1, 193–97 (1824).

76 317 U.S. 111 (1942).

unrestricted producers in other states. The states thus faced insuperable difficulties cooperating together to limit wheat production (the "holdout problem"). In contrast, national regulation could effectively reduce production of wheat. The main question posed by this case for collective-action federalism is whether home production undermines regulation of market production for wheat. This is a question of fact.

During this post-1937 period of deference to Congress, the Court often decided cases involving allegedly unfair economic competition among states. A central argument in these cases concerned whether an unfair practice in one jurisdiction conveyed a competitive advantage over another jurisdiction with a fair practice (Esty 1996; Stewart 1977, 1992). In national markets, competition favors the lowest-cost producers. Absent federal intervention, economic pressure will cause producers to adopt practices that lower costs, even when legislators and the public judge them to be unfair, such as paying low wages, permitting various forms of discrimination in the workplace,[77] or destroying the environment.[78]

The Court used this argument in the 1941 case of *United States v. Darby* when it sustained federal minimum-wage and maximum-hour regulations on manufacturers of goods shipped in interstate commerce:[79]

> [T]he evils aimed at by the Act are the spread of substandard labor conditions through the use of the facilities of interstate commerce for competition by the goods so produced with those produced under the prescribed or better labor conditions; and the consequent dislocation of the commerce itself caused by the impairment or destruction of local businesses by competition made effective through interstate commerce. The Act is thus directed at the suppression of a method or

[77] Antidiscrimination provisions that cover the workplace may increase the costs of doing business. Accordingly, states may be disinclined to impose such costs on employers that operate within their jurisdictions unless a certain number of sister states do the same. Moreover, local discrimination against potential providers or consumers of goods and services may impede the development or functioning of national markets in various ways. *Heart of Atlanta Motel, Inc. v. United States*, 379 U.S. 241 (1964), and *Katzenbach v. McClung*, 379 U.S. 294 (1964), both of which upheld a federal prohibition on racial discrimination in places of public accommodation, can be justified on this ground. When discrimination discourages (or encourages) the interstate movement of labor and capital, a collective-action problem exists.

[78] Note that this is a statement about national markets, not externalities. Competitive pressures favoring the lowest-cost practices operate through markets, not externally to them. The confusion in language stems partly from Tibor Scitovsky's description of market competition as a "pecuniary externality," which contradicts the idea that an externality is unpriced. *See* Tibor Scitovsky, *Two Concepts of External Economies*, 62 J. POL. ECON. 143, 146 (1954).

[79] Fair Labor Standards Act (FLSA), 29 U.S.C. § 201 (2000). *Darby* overruled *Hammer v. Dagenhart*, 247 U.S. 251 (1918) (the Child Labor Case) and embraced the dissent of Justice Holmes. The post-1937 Court repudiated the pre-1937 Court's insistence that "[t]here is no power vested in Congress to require the states to exercise their police power so as to prevent possible unfair competition." 247 U.S. at 532.

> kind of competition in interstate commerce which it has in effect condemned as "unfair."[80]

The *Darby* Court thus viewed Congress as concerned about the "race to the bottom" that might ensue among the states in the absence of federal intervention.[81]

The Court later used a similar argument from collective action to justify federal regulation of environmentally destructive practices. In *Hodel v. Virginia Surface Mining and Reclamation Association*,[82] the Court deemed significant a congressional finding that national "surface mining and reclamation standards are essential in order to insure that competition in interstate commerce among sellers of coal produced in different States will not be used to undermine the ability of the several States to improve and maintain adequate standards on coal mining operations within their borders."[83] The Court emphasized that "the prevention of this sort of destructive interstate competition is a traditional role for congressional action under the Commerce Clause."[84]

Rather than focusing on races to the bottom, the Rehnquist Court emphasized the distinction between economic and noneconomic activity. As we saw in the first section, the modern Court has sought to impose limits on the power of Congress in order to preserve the separation of federal and state powers established by Clause 3's grant of authority to "regulate Commerce ... among the several States." The Court has purported to find this limit by restricting regulatory power under the Commerce Clause to "economic" or "commercial" activity.

Although current doctrine formally emphasizes the economic or noneconomic nature of the regulated activity, a more functional logic may in fact have animated the Court in *Lopez*, *Morrison*, and *Raich*. Just as the Court offered collective-action problems as a reason to sustain congressional regulation in many of the Commerce Clause cases decided from 1937 until the early 1990s, so the Rehnquist Court implicitly has offered the absence (or presence) of a collective-action problem as a reason to prohibit (or sustain) congressional regulation. Almost appearing to anticipate *Raich*, and with *Wickard* surely in mind, Chief Justice Rehnquist wrote in *Lopez* that the Gun-Free School Zones Act "is not an essential part of a larger regulation of economic activity, in which the regulatory scheme could be undercut unless the intrastate activity were regulated."[85] This statement, particularly if one replaces the word "economic" with "interstate" (Brest 2006: 626), suggests that the absence of

80 312 U.S. 100, 122 (1941).

81 For the use of similar reasoning to defend the result in *NLRB v. Jones & Laughlin Steel Corp.*, 301 U.S. 1 (1937), see Regan, *supra* note ix, at 603–04.

82 452 U.S. 264, 281 (1981).

83 *Id.* at 281–82 (quoting 30 U.S.C. § 1201(g) (1976 ed., Supp. III)).

84 *Id.* at 282.

85 *Lopez*, 514 U.S. 549, 561 (1995).

regulation of guns near schools in one state would not undercut the effectiveness of regulations prohibiting them in other states. Justice Kennedy may have been getting at the same point when he stated in his concurring opinion that "[i]f a State or municipality determines that harsh criminal sanctions are necessary and wise to deter students from carrying guns on school premises, the reserved powers of the States are *sufficient* to enact those measures. Indeed, over 40 States already have criminal laws outlawing the possession of firearms on or near school grounds."[86] With independence rather than interdependence, the states do not face a collective-action problem.

The key constitutional question posed by these and related criminal cases is how much coordination among law enforcement personnel in different states is required to police the proscribed conduct at issue. The question is whether there is a spillover of welfare and whether the spillover causes a collective-action problem. The issue is not whether a crime is "economic" in nature. The general welfare is affected by the presence or absence of spillovers, not the formal category of the activity.

For example, enforcing a prohibition on guns within school zones seems the opposite of a problem requiring coordination among law enforcement officers in different states. It seems local: local officials presumably have better information concerning who might carry firearms near schools, and better incentives to do something about the problem. As we explained in the second section, these considerations are central to the internalization principle. By contrast, suppressing a market for guns is a national problem in light of the ease with which firearms can move across state lines. The failure to suppress such a market affects the ability of state law enforcement personnel to keep guns away from schools. The federal government in *Lopez* did not argue that the Gun Free School Zones Act addressed this national problem or was otherwise an integral part of a larger regulatory scheme.

Raich, by contrast, did involve a potential spillover problem. Given the inability to distinguish marijuana used for medicinal purposes from marijuana used for other purposes, and given that the market for marijuana disrespects state borders, California's authorization of marijuana use for medicinal purposes might make it more difficult for other states to ban marijuana use. If there is no spillover problem for state policing, then states and localities should be permitted to go their own way as far as constitutional federalism is concerned. But if there is a spillover – for example, medical marijuana use in California makes it more difficult to police drug traffickers on the Arizona border – then there is a rationale for federal intervention.

[86] *Lopez*, 514 U.S. at 581 (Kennedy, J., concurring) (emphasis added); *see* Regan, *supra* note ix, at 566 (arguing that this is one way to read the portion of Kennedy's opinion quoted in the text).

The distinction between individual and collective action, which collective-action federalism uses to draw the limits and expanse of congressional power, best explains why Congress may not ordinarily use its commerce power to regulate such crimes as assault or gun possession in schools, but may regulate a multistate market for guns or drugs.

Collective-action federalism also explains why the distinction between economic and noneconomic activity should not demarcate the boundary between federal and state power in Clause 3. The main reason for separating powers is the relative advantages of the federal and state governments. The economic/noneconomic distinction, however, does not systematically relate to the advantages of the federal and state governments. The federal government is not especially able in economic matters and the state governments are not especially able in noneconomic matters. This is because economic activities do not generally cause collective-action problems, and noneconomic activities are not generally free from collective-action problems.

By contrast, the distinction between individual and collective action by states relates to the advantages of the federal and state governments. It gives independent, sensible meaning to the phrase "among the several States" in Clause 3. On our account, the phrase "among the several States" references a problem of collective action involving at least two states. That is the key inquiry in determining whether "Commerce" is interstate and thus regulable under Clause 3 or intrastate and thus beyond the scope of the commerce power.

The power of Congress to "regulate Commerce … among the several States" given in Clause 3 is best understood in light of the collective-action problems that the nation faced under the Articles of Confederation, when Congress lacked this power. Interpreting this phrase requires a theoretical account of federalism. With such an account in mind, the economic/noneconomic categorization may suffice in a rough-and-ready way for defining "Commerce" in Clause 3; we have nothing to say about that subject. Without such an account, however, a dictionary definition of "economics" cannot yield the proper interpretation of Clause 3. Moreover, reading the enumerated powers to exclude the regulation of "noneconomic" problems will frustrate the animating purpose of Section 8, which is to give Congress the authority to solve collective-action problems. If interpretation of Clause 3 turns on the economic/noneconomic distinction, then pressure must mount to find authorization for regulatory powers elsewhere in the Constitution.[87]

87 If Clause 1 continues to be read to prohibit any federal regulation, then we share Akhil Amar's concern that "[w]ithout a broad reading of 'Commerce' in [Clause 3], it is not entirely clear whence the federal government would derive its needed power to deal with noneconomic international incidents – or for that matter to address the entire range of vexing nonmercantile interactions and altercations that might arise among states." Amar, *supra* note viii, at 107–08. *See* Jack M. Balkin, *Commerce*, 109 MICH.

Dormant Commerce Clause

In contrast to the post-1937 Court, which often (explicitly or implicitly) recognized the existence of collective-action problems among the states in upholding congressional regulation, the Rehnquist Court twice perceived the absence of a collective-action problem among the states as impugning congressional regulation. A third type of case – implicating the so-called dormant Commerce Clause – occurs when a collective-action problem allows a state to pass a law that harms businesses or individuals in other states. In these cases, a state regulation typically conveys a competitive advantage to in-state producers or users. The Court invalidates state laws that advantage in-state producers or users by impeding interstate commerce. The dormant Commerce Clause almost always prohibits states from discriminating against interstate commerce or placing an undue burden on the interstate movement of goods and services. In international trade, economists regard tariffs as favoring domestic producers at the expense of foreign producers and domestic consumers. This analysis of international trade applies to the behavior of states in most dormant Commerce Clause cases.

The Court has inferred the existence of the dormant Commerce Clause from the role that state protectionism played in inspiring the Constitutional Convention, as well as from the grant of legislative power to Congress in Clause 3. Although the idea that state and local governments are capable of violating the Commerce Clause is difficult to defend textually, such a constitutional principle is sound from a structural and consequentialist perspective. A collective-action problem is at the core of any regulation by a state that benefits its inhabitants less than it harms inhabitants of other states.

There are many examples in the *U.S. Reports* of these kinds of collective-action problems.[88] We will not attempt a comprehensive or historical treatment of the doctrine; rather, we will offer an illustration. In *H. P. Hood & Sons, Inc. v. Du Mond*, Justice Jackson wrote for the Court that "the established *interdependence* of the states only emphasizes the necessity of protecting interstate movement of goods against local burdens and repressions."[89] In that case, a New York law prevented a company from building an additional depot for receiving milk. The effect of the law was to retain more milk for consumption in New York at the expense of consumers in Massachusetts. The Court invalidated the law for lacking a permissible

L. REV. (2010) ("In the eighteenth century . . . 'commerce' did not have such narrowly economic connotations. Instead, 'commerce' meant 'intercourse' and it had a strongly social connotation. 'Commerce' was interaction and exchange between persons or peoples.").

88 *See, e.g.*, Granholm v. Heald, 544 U.S. 460 (2005) (prohibiting New York and Michigan from discriminating against certain out-of-state wineries).

89 336 U.S. 525, 538 (1949) (emphasis added).

nonprotectionist purpose. In general, collective-action problems justify the Court's distinction there and elsewhere between state protectionism, which is almost always unconstitutional (Regan 1995), and health and safety regulations, which are often permissible exercises of a state's police powers. States may not advantage their industries by protectionist regulations, but states may disadvantage their industries in interstate competition by imposing higher health and safety standards.

The General Welfare Clause

The Purposes for Which Congress May Tax and Spend

In *Steward Machine Company v. Davis*,[90] the Court upheld the federal unemployment compensation system created by the Social Security Act (SSA). In *Helvering v. Davis*,[91] the Court upheld the SSA's old-age pension program. In both cases, the Court based its decision in part on a collective-action problem involving more than one state, specifically the problem of destructive interstate competition discussed earlier. Justice Cardozo wrote for the Court in *Steward Machine Company*:

> But if states had been holding back before the passage of the federal law, inaction was not owing, for the most part, to the lack of sympathetic interest. Many held back through alarm lest in laying such a toll upon their industries, they would place themselves in a position of economic disadvantage as compared with neighbors or competitors. Two consequences ensued. One was that the freedom of a state to contribute its fair share to the solution of a national problem was paralyzed by fear. The other was that in so far as there was failure by the states to contribute relief according to the measure of their capacity, a disproportionate burden, and a mountainous one, was laid upon the resources of the government of the nation.[92]

As evidence for a collective-action problem, Justice Cardozo noted a Massachusetts bill that would remain inoperative unless the federal bill became law or eleven states from a list of twenty-one states "impose[d] on their employers burdens substantially equivalent."[93]

Justice Cardozo also wrote for the Court in *Helvering*, and again he pointed to a collective-action problem among the states:

> Apart from the failure of resources, states and local governments are at times reluctant to increase so heavily the burden of taxation to be borne by their residents for

[90] 301 U.S. 548 (1937).
[91] 301 U.S. 619 (1937).
[92] 301 U.S. at 588 (citations and footnote omitted).
[93] *Id.* at 588 n.9.

> fear of placing themselves in a position of economic disadvantage as compared with neighbors or competitors. We have seen this in our study of the problem of unemployment compensation. *Steward Machine Co. v. Davis*, supra. A system of old age pensions has special dangers of its own, if put in force in one state and rejected in another. The existence of such a system is a bait to the needy and dependent elsewhere, encouraging them to migrate and seek a haven of repose. Only a power that is national can serve the interests of all.[94]

Note that federal unemployment compensation and old-age pensions promote labor mobility among the states by creating rights that workers take with them when they move. In contrast to the United States, local provisions for unemployment and old-age pensions in Europe create impediments to labor mobility, so the European Union has not reached its goal of a single labor market.

Cardozo gave notice that the Court would defer to Congress's determination that taxing and spending advances the general welfare "unless the choice is clearly wrong; a display of arbitrary power, not an exercise of judgment."[95] Perhaps implicitly suggesting how the Court might make that determination, he returned to collective-action problems by insisting that "the concept of the general welfare" is not "static." On the contrary, "[n]eeds that were narrow or parochial a century ago may be interwoven in our day with the well-being of the Nation."[96] Cardozo's use of "interwoven" echoes Jackson's use of "interdependence," which echoes Marshall's use of "intermingled."

Regulation under Clause 1?

The theory of collective-action federalism conceives the "general Welfare" as substantively defined by collective-action problems involving more than one state. This interpretation suggests that it is time to revisit the *Butler* Court's rejection of the possibility that the General Welfare Clause allows some federal regulation in addition to taxation and spending. To begin with, the text of Clause 1 should not end the conversation; notwithstanding what generations of lawyers have been taught in law school, the Clause does not clearly include taxation and spending while excluding regulation. The relevant language grants Congress the power to "lay and collect Taxes … to pay the Debts and provide for the common Defence and general Welfare of the United States."[97] The clause thus ends the requisition practice that existed under the Articles of Confederation and authorizes Congress to use federal tax revenue to pay national

[94] *Id.* at 644 (footnote omitted).

[95] *Helvering*, 301 U.S. at 640. The Court has taken this approach ever since. *See, e.g.*, South Dakota v. Dole, 483 U.S. 203, 207 (1987).

[96] *Helvering*, 301 U.S. at 641.

[97] U.S. CONST. art. I, § 8, cl. 1.

debts and "provide for the common Defence and general Welfare of the United States." One way to "provide for the common Defence and general Welfare of the United States" is to spend federal money on public goods. Another way to achieve this objective is by spending federal money to enact, administer, and enforce federal regulations. Neither expenditures on public goods nor expenditures on regulations are explicitly mentioned in the text of Clause 1. It is not clear or obvious from the text that Clause 1 authorizes supplying public goods or prohibits imposing regulations.

Further, the theory of collective-action federalism ameliorates the long-standing concern about a general federal police power by imbuing the phrase "general Welfare" with substantive meaning. We offer a rationale for federal power to address problems of collective action among the states when the other clauses of Section 8 are unavailable. We do not provide a justification for Congress to regulate whatever it wants under Clause 1.

Moreover, under our approach, allowing regulation under Clause 1 does not render the rest of Section 8 superfluous. On the contrary, when Article I, Section 8 is interpreted according to the theory of collective-action federalism, the enumerated powers constitute a coherent response to a series of collective-action problems, not a diverse collection of unrelated powers. Coherence comes from the conceptual link between the specific powers and collective-action problems affecting the general welfare. It is the enumeration of the specific powers in the balance of Section 8 that imbues the inherently vague phrase "general Welfare" with definite meaning. That is the purpose of the enumeration; the purpose is not to exclude everything not enumerated.

Also relevant to the proper construction of Clause 1 is the fact that many economists advocate externality taxes as the most effective way to accomplish regulatory objectives. For example, a federal price on pollution could be construed as a permitted tax or a forbidden regulation under Clause 1 of Section 8. The tenuous economic distinction between taxes and regulations suggests that it does not make sense to allow one under Clause 1 but not the other.[98] Regulations often impose fines for their violation. Distinguishing a fine on forbidden behavior from a tax on permitted behavior can be difficult.[99] Confusion is especially likely insofar as policy makers heed the urging of economists to control behavior by relying more on taxes and less on regulations.[100]

[98] The Court at one point distinguished impermissible "regulatory" taxes from permissible "revenue raising" taxes. *See, e.g.*, Bailey v. Drexel Furniture Co., 259 U.S. 20 (1922) (Child Labor Tax Case). But the Court appears to have abandoned that doctrine as resting on a false distinction and as not grounded in the Constitution. *See, e.g.*, Sonzinsky v. United States, 300 U.S. 506, 513 (1937); United States v. Kahriger, 345 U.S. 22, 31 (1953).

[99] For a behavioral distinction, see Robert Cooter, *Prices and Sanctions*, 84 COLUM. L. REV. 1523 (1984).

[100] Economists have notably urged governments to scrap regulations and replace them with taxes for pollution, congestion, overfishing, accident risks, and energy consumption.

More concretely, when Congress wants to address a problem of collective action involving multiple states, the specific clause of Section 8 that it may use under our approach depends on the nature of the problem. If no clause in Section 8 authorizes Congress to address a problem of collective action involving more than one state, then the General Welfare Clause may be available to Congress. Collective-action federalism reads Section 8 as authorizing Congress to address problems of collective action that the states are unable to solve.[101]

To illustrate, consider situations in which Congress seeks to regulate arguably noneconomic activities that spill environmental harms across state borders. When the regulated activity crosses state boundaries, the federal courts are lax about its being "economic." Thus, environmental pollution and endangered species that cross state lines are apparently understood to fall within the commerce power, even though they are not commerce and may have very attenuated effects on commerce.[102] Congress may regulate the interstate movement of, say, naturally occurring arsenic in water that crosses state lines through an underground aquifer or nonnavigable stream.[103] And Congress may regulate activities just because they threaten the existence of a species that moves across state boundaries (Funk 2001). These examples are unequivocally interstate in the sense that material harms are spilling across state borders, but the nexus to commerce is attenuated or nonexistent. Decisional law endorses the principle that Congress may regulate interstate pollution and interstate endangered species as if they were commerce, and we know of none that casts doubt on it.

We have explained that when the regulated activity is interstate in the sense that it spills across state borders, the Court is undemanding about its being economic. Conversely, as we showed in the first section, when the regulated activity is deemed economic, the Court is undemanding about its being interstate. The Court simply presumes that economic activity has substantial effects on interstate commerce and that noneconomic activity does not. In short, the federal judiciary has construed the Interstate Commerce Clause in Article I, Section 8 as if it were the Interstate *or* Commerce Clause.

This could change, however, if the Roberts Court continues to build Commerce Clause jurisprudence on the economic/noneconomic distinction. What is presently

[101] It follows from our account that Congress need not invoke the Necessary and Proper Clause to justify federal regulation of noneconomic activity on the ground that it affects economic activity. Rather, the Necessary and Proper Clause serves as a reminder of the breadth of federal power in Section 8 to address collective-action problems, economic or otherwise. *See supra* note 69 and accompanying text.

[102] *See, e.g.*, Bradford C. Mank, *Protecting Intrastate Threatened Species: Does the Endangered Species Act Encroach on Traditional State Authority and Exceed the Outer Limits of the Commerce Clause?*, 36 GA. L. REV. 723, 724 (2002).

[103] The airshed is easier to defend as a channel of interstate commerce because air is undifferentiated and airplanes fly through it at nearly all altitudes.

uncontroversial may not always remain so. In time, the Court may find that Congress lacks the power to regulate interstate pollution and interstate endangered species unless they have a causal nexus with commerce. Environmental harms may spill across state borders, but their causes and effects may or may not be economic or commercial as the Supreme Court has conceived these terms.

Unlike the Commerce Clause, the General Welfare Clause does not require a distinction between economic and noneconomic welfare. Regardless of whether it is economic, air pollution, water pollution, and endangered species that move between states constitute an interstate externality. Under the theory of collective-action federalism, Congress may target them when they pose a problem of collective action.

For example, the touchstone of federal authority for five Justices in *Rapanos v. United States* was interstate navigable waters.[104] But lots of water that flows across state boundaries is *nonnavigable*, and some of this water presumably lacks a significant nexus to interstate navigable waters. Were federal authority triggered by an interstate externality, however, as it would be under our interpretation of the General Welfare Clause, the movement across a state line could justify federal action. The crucial fact would be a spillover of welfare and a collective-action problem, not a significant nexus to interstate navigable waters.[105]

To consider another example, the extinction of an endangered species harms the future well-being of people in all states where the species might otherwise live. Thus an activity in state A may extinguish a species in states A, B, and C. Moreover, whether the harmful activity is the construction of a housing development or the recreational use of land by local residents makes no difference for purposes of the general welfare. The same can be said of interstate drinking water that has been contaminated by naturally occurring arsenic instead of an industrial polluter. In either case, federal action can internalize the externality. The federal government, therefore, potentially enjoys a decisive advantage over the states in addressing the problem of preserving species or combating pollutants that move interstate. Justifying federal pursuit of the general welfare would extend federal regulation to instances of environmental degradation without notably economic character that involve collective-action problems.

[104] *Rapanos v. United States*, 547 U.S. 715 (2006), concerned a fight over wetlands endangered by economic development. The question presented was whether wetlands adjacent to nonnavigable tributaries of traditional navigable waters were part of "the waters of the United States" within the meaning of the federal Clean Water Act (CWA).

[105] Whereas it is important to distinguish between questions of statutory interpretation (for example, the meaning of "navigable waters" in the CWA) and issues of constitutional authority, it is also true that the former often takes place in the shadow of the latter. For example, the Justices in *Rapanos* were partially motivated by constitutional concerns.

The theory of collective-action federalism focuses the interpretive community on the issue that really matters to lawmakers and citizens: the environmental impact of the harmful activity on the general welfare, not the effect on interstate economic activity. In the environmental context, debate over whether a regulated activity is economic activity distracts attention from the central constitutional question of whether welfare is general or particular. So do arguments about whether Congress "really" wanted to regulate economic activity or whether its commerce justification is pretextual.[106] For example, the relationship between water pollution and economic activity distracts attention from the question of how clean water promotes the general welfare of the United States. A debate on that point should result in a more straightforward defense of federal authority, aligning better with commonsense reasoning.

The same could be said of the justification for federal regulation in other settings. Consider, for example, the control of contagious diseases. The federal government might want to impose regulations to prevent the spread of a contagious disease across state lines – say, by authorizing federal officials to quarantine infected individuals or to close local schools in defined and temporally limited circumstances. This would not qualify as a regulation of economic activity in any obvious or straightforward sense (even though here, as elsewhere, one could invoke substantial effects on interstate commerce in the aggregate). Yet in light of potentially large spillover effects impinging the general welfare, Congress ought to possess this power without having to condition related federal funds on compliance. The rationale for allowing federal regulation of this powerful noneconomic externality under the General Welfare Clause is straightforward and compelling.

In his biography of the Constitution, Akhil Amar criticizes the Supreme Court's "move[ment] toward reading the [Commerce Clause] paragraph as applicable only to economic interactions," arguing that "[w]ithout a broad reading of 'Commerce' in this Clause, it is not entirely clear whence the federal government would derive its needed power to deal with noneconomic international incidents – or for that matter to address the entire range of vexing nonmercantile interactions and altercations that might arise among states" (Amar 2005: 107–08). There may be an independent way: Under our interpretation of Article I, Section 8, Congress possesses at least some authority under Clause 1 to regulate noneconomic collective-action problems involving multiple states.

[106] Our concern is with the distracting quality of the "pretext" debate in many settings. We do not argue that Congress may regulate interstate commerce only for certain purposes and not others. *Compare, e.g.*, William Van Alstyne, *Federalism, Congress, the States and the Tenth Amendment: Adrift in the Cellophane Sea*, 1987 DUKE L.J. 769 (arguing for the invigoration of pretext doctrine in Commerce Clause cases), *with, e.g.*, Christopher H. Schroeder, *Environmental Law, Congress, and the Court's New Federalism Doctrine*, 78 IND. L.J. 413, 443–45 (2003) (critically analyzing Van Alstyne's view).

EVALUATING CONGRESSIONAL JUDGMENTS ABOUT COLLECTIVE-ACTION PROBLEMS

Because people disagree about the appropriate scope of federal power, they will disagree about how constitutional interpreters, particularly courts, should evaluate congressional judgments about the existence and seriousness of collective-action problems, and about the adequacy of Congress's response. Because Congress can always seek to justify legislation by asserting that a collective-action problem exists, that its effects are significant, and that the law it has enacted addresses the problem effectively, the evaluative question becomes what degree of proof courts should require of Congress before they will defer to its judgment. We do not seek to resolve disagreements over this question in this chapter, but we can illustrate one form that judicial review could take.

Many people believe that Congress possesses broad but not limitless authority to legislate under Section 8. This belief is reflected in the interpretive principle of loose construction first articulated by Chief Justice Marshall for the Court in *McCulloch v. Maryland*[107] and recently reaffirmed by a majority of Justices in *United States v. Comstock*.[108] One possible standard of review is whether Congress had a reasonable basis to believe that it was ameliorating a significant problem of collective action involving two or more states. If reasonable people could disagree (1) about the existence of a collective-action problem, (2) the seriousness of the problem, and (3) the efficacy of the congressional response, then courts should uphold the law. Congress would have to offer a basis for its judgments that there is a serious multistate problem of collective action and that the law addresses the problem to some extent. Courts would defer to plausible findings by Congress. Such an approach to judicial review would "cue" the political branches to take seriously those federalism questions that are worth taking seriously (Bednar and Eskridge 1995; Meltzer 1996; Young 1999), but it would not license federal courts to engage in *Lochner*-style invalidations of many federal laws and overrulings of precedent. A deferential approach to judicial review would also substantially address the objection that the theory of collective-action federalism tasks judges with making determinations ill-suited for them.[109]

[107] 17 U.S. (4 Wheat.) 316 (1819).

[108] 130 S. Ct. 1949 (2010). The Court stated that "in determining whether the Necessary and Proper Clause grants Congress the legislative authority to enact a particular federal statute, we look to see whether the statute constitutes a means that is rationally related to the implementation of a constitutionally enumerated power." *Id.* at 1956.

[109] In vetoing an internal improvements bill on constitutional grounds, Madison worried about "excluding the judicial authority of the United States from its participation in guarding the boundary between legislative powers of the General and State Governments, inasmuch as questions relating to the general welfare, being questions of policy and expediency, are unsusceptible of judicial cognizance and decision." Brest et al., 2006, at 83. *See, e.g.*, Ernest A. Young, *Protecting Member*

The preceding illustration leaves several critical questions unanswered or answered incompletely. To establish the existence of a collective-action problem among the states, does Congress need a plausible rationale, some evidence, or substantial evidence? Would it make sense to use a balancing test, such that greater intrusions on the regulatory autonomy of states would require greater evidentiary showings from Congress? What is the minimum threshold of harm to the general welfare that a collective-action problem must cross before Congress has the constitutional authority to act? When addressing a collective-action problem, does Congress need to adopt the least intrusive means of federal intervention?

To illustrate concretely, if the severity of punishment for the same crime differs between two states, then criminals have an incentive to commit their crimes in the state with milder punishment. Perceiving this fact, states might enact severe punishments to deflect crime away from themselves and onto others. This interstate externality could cause the states to race to severity, even though all states would benefit from lowering average punishments and reducing the burden on their prisons. Could Congress rely on this rationale to federalize all of criminal law? Or would it have to proceed crime by crime? Would it have to provide evidence that the race to severity exists and causes a large fall in the general welfare? Would it have to show that federalizing some or all criminal law is the least intrusive federal solution?

We can raise these questions but we cannot answer them in this chapter. Answers must await future developments and applications of the theory of collective-action federalism in different areas of law. We resist, however, the objection that the concept of a collective-action problem involving two or more states is indeterminate – that Congress can, with equal plausibility, justify regulating whatever it wishes on the ground that it is adequately addressing a serious problem of collective action. Some federal laws are substantially easier to justify on such grounds than others. Moreover, we are aware of no better alternative to understanding the division of power between the federal government and the states in Article I, Section 8. For example, the Court's distinction between economic and noneconomic activity is neither determinate nor sensible for all of the reasons we have identified.

Most importantly, the indeterminacy objection may presuppose that the Constitution is substantially more determinate than it in fact is – that the

State Autonomy in the European Union: Some Cautionary Tales from American Federalism, 77 N.Y.U. L. REV. 1612, 1647–48, 1677–82 (2002) (critiquing a collective-action approach to federalism as contrary to judicial role). The theory of collective-action federalism, whether or not it is used in judicial review, is similar in important respects to the European principle of "subsidiarity." *See, e.g.*, Mattias Kumm, *Democratic Constitutionalism Encounters International Law: Terms of Engagement*, *in* THE MIGRATION OF CONSTITUTIONAL IDEAS 256, 264–68 (Sujit Choudhry ed., 2007); Stephen Gardbaum, *Rethinking Constitutional Federalism*, 74 TEX. L. REV. 795, 831–38 (1996).

Constitution authoritatively resolves disagreements, as opposed to organizing and orienting them.[110] We offer the theory of collective-action federalism as the best, all-things-considered interpretation of what Article I, Section 8 means. Whether that meaning is fully determinate is a separate question. It is not fully determinate, but neither is it wholly indeterminate.

CONCLUSION

A federal constitution ideally gives the central and state governments the power to do what each does best. To secure these advantages, according to the internalization principle, a constitution should assign power to the smallest unit of government that internalizes the effects of its exercise. By definition, the costs and benefits of interstate public goods, externalities, and markets spill over from one state to another, which creates a collective-action problem for the states. The federal government is usually the smallest unit that effectively internalizes the benefits and costs of interstate public goods, externalities, and markets. Accordingly, the internalization principle assigns power over interstate externalities and markets to the federal government.

The theory of collective-action federalism interprets Article I, Section 8 in light of this principle; it views the enumerated powers as a coherent response to collective-action problems, not a heterogeneous collection of unrelated powers. Welfare is "general" when the federal government can obtain it and the states cannot. Article I, Section 8 empowers Congress to solve collective-action problems that predictably frustrate the states. In the language of Clause 3, interstate public goods, externalities, and markets are "among the several States." In the language of Clause 1, they are "general." Governmental activities that do not pose collective-action problems for the states are "internal to a state" or "local." The "general Welfare" is a substantive conception of interstate effects. Members of Congress, presidents, their supporters, and their critics should use this framework to understand and debate the constitutional scope of the Congress's powers to tax, spend, and regulate.

In 1995, the Court abandoned its long-standing willingness to allow the federal government to regulate almost any activity by invoking the Commerce Clause. The Court has purported to build a jurisprudence of federalism under Clause 3 on the

110 It is a mistake to view the Constitution or constitutional law as fully determinate. *Cf., e.g.*, H. Jefferson Powell, A COMMUNITY BUILT ON WORDS: THE CONSTITUTION IN HISTORY AND POLITICS 6 (2002) ("However counterintuitive it may seem, the integrity and coherence of constitutional law are to be found in, not apart from, controversy."); Robert C. Post & Neil S. Siegel, *Theorizing the Law/Politics Distinction: Neutral Principles, Affirmative Action, and the Enduring Insight of Paul Mishkin*, 95 CALIF. L. REV. 1473, 1501 (2007) ("[I]t is simply fantasy to imagine that law can be fully determinate or fully autonomous from popular beliefs.").

distinction between economic activity, which Congress may regulate, and noneconomic activity, which Congress may not regulate. Unfortunately, Congress is not generally better at regulating economic activity, and the states are not generally better at regulating noneconomic activity. However adequate it may (or may not) be for purposes of defining "Commerce" in Clause 3, the distinction between economic and noneconomic activity seems mostly irrelevant to the problems of federalism. A more promising foundation for the American federal system distinguishes between activities that pose collective-action problems for the states and those that do not pose such problems. We hope that Section 8 will eventually be understood as authorizing congressional power over activities that pose collective-action problems for the states, and as not authorizing congressional power over activities that do not pose collective-action problems for the states. With these changes, federal law would then be seen to rest on what often motivates its enactment: its promotion of the general welfare, not the economic character of the activity it regulates.[111]

REFERENCES

Amar, Akhil Reed. *America's Constitution: A Biography* (New York: Random House, 2005).

Baumol William J. &. Oates, Wallace E. *The Theory of Environmental Policy* (New York: Cambridge University Press, 2nd ed. 1988).

Bednar, Jenna & William N. Eskridge , Jr. Steadying the Court's "Unsteady Path": A Theory of Judicial Enforcement of Federalism, 68 *S. Cal. L. Rev.* 1447– 1491 (1995).

Brest, Paul, Sanford Levinson, Jack M. Balkin, Akhil Reed Amar, & Reva B. Siegel. *Processes of Constitutional Decisionmaking: Cases and Materials* (New York: Aspen Publishers, 5th ed. 2006).

Cooter, Robert D. *The Strategic Constitution* (Princeton: Princeton University Press, 2000).

Craig, Paul & Grainne de Burca. *EU Law: Text, Cases and Materials* 124 (New York: Oxford University Press, 4th ed. 2008).

Currie, David P. *The Constitution in Congress: Democrats and Whigs 1829–1861, at* 9–25 (Chicago: University Of Chicago Press, 2005).

[111] The recently enacted health care legislation, Patient Protection and Affordable Care Act, Pub. L. No. 111–148, 124 Stat. 119 (2010) (to be codified at 42 U.S.C. § 18001), has provoked renewed interest in the constitutional limits on the federal powers to tax and regulate. One question presently being debated in public discourse and constitutional litigation is whether the provisions in the statute requiring individuals either to obtain a minimum level of health insurance coverage or pay a yearly fee fall within the scope of the commerce power. Collective-action federalism provides a useful framework of analysis: The key federalism question is whether individual action by states suffices to address the cost shifting and adverse selection problems targeted by these provisions, or whether addressing them effectively requires collective action – for example, because of the likely movement to different state regimes of insurance companies, sick Americans, and healthy Americans. Another question currently in dispute is whether the exaction for remaining uninsured in the law qualifies as a tax or a regulation for constitutional purposes. Economic theories of federalism have a lot to say about taxes and regulations, including differences between them. A future article will extend our theory of collective-action federalism to this timely issue.

de Tocqueville, Alexis. *Democracy in America* 141 (Washington DC: Regnery Publishing, 2003).
Ellickson, Robert C. *Order Without Law: How Neighbors Settle Disputes* 123 (Cambridge, MA: Harvard University Press, 1991).
Esty, Daniel. Revitalizing Environmental Federalism, 95 *Mich. L. Rev.* 570, 638–48 (1996).
Farrand, Max. 2 *The Records of the Federal Convention of 1787* (New Haven: Yale University Press, 1966).
Friedman, Barry. *The Will of the People: How Public Opinion Has Influenced the Supreme Court and Shaped the Meaning of the Constitution* (New York: Farrar, Straus & Giroux, 2009).
Funk, William. The Court, the Clean Water Act, and the Constitution: SWANCC and Beyond, 31 *Envtl. L. Rep.* 10766 (2001).
Kramer, Larry D. Madison's Audience, 112 *Harv. L. Rev.* 611, 616–23 (1999).
Meltzer, Daniel J. The Seminole Decision and State Sovereign Immunity, 1996 *Sup. Ct. Rev.* 1, 63.
Oates, Wallace. *Fiscal Federalism* (San Diego: Harcourt Brace Jovanovich, 1972).
Rakove, Jack N. *Original Meanings: Politics and Ideas in the Making of the Constitution* (New York: Knopf Doubleday, 1996).
Regan, Donald H. How to Think About the Federal Commerce Power and Incidentally Rewrite United States v. Lopez, 94 *Mich. L. Rev.* 554 (1995).
Sen, Amartya. Rational Fools: A Critique of the Behavioral Foundations of Economic Theory, 6 *Phil. & Pub. Aff.* 317 (1977).
Stern, Robert. That Commerce Which Concerns More States Than One, 47 *Harv. L. Rev.* 1335, 1340 (1934).
Stewart, Richard B. International Trade and the Environment: Lessons from the Federal Experience, 49 *Wash. & Lee L. Rev.* 1329–71(1992).
Pyramids of Sacrifice?: Problems of Federalism in Mandating State Implementation of National Environmental Policy, 86 *Yale L.J.* 1196–271 (1977).
Young, Ernest A. State Sovereign Immunity and the Future of Federalism, 1999 *Sup. Ct. Rev.* 1–78(1999).

10

Personal Laws and Equality

The Case of India

Martha C. Nussbaum

Religious groups have made law throughout history. Virtually always, they make laws for their members in matters touching on ritual, questions of religious status and inclusion, and questions of morality. Very often, however, they go further, making laws about matters usually classified under "family law": marriage and divorce, the status and custody of children, and parents' rights over their children and responsibilities to them. These laws may or may not be recognized as law by the state in which they operate. At times their domain extends further yet, to matters of inheritance and property. Again, their laws in these domains may or may not be recognized by government. And of course, in many cases known to history, the domain is fully comprehensive: A religious system of law is the law of the land.

In many modern pluralist democracies, religious groups do not demand that their legal system be the law of the land – whether because they believe that this goal is out of reach or because they are convinced that this is not a good goal to pursue in a land of many religious and nonreligious views of life. Even in such cases, however, many religious bodies do still demand some degree of control over lawmaking, in some of the areas I have mentioned previously: They seek a delegation – usually constitutionally grounded – of certain spheres of lawmaking to religious officials and religious systems of law. These demands, and their occasional realization in the constitutions of pluralistic democracies, raise delicate questions of both respect and equality. This chapter proposes to investigate a single complex case of personal law and its history, the case of India, using this case as a lens through which to examine more general questions about the wisdom and the workings of such systems, the arguments both for and against them. The Indian system is a good one to study because it has been in operation for more than sixty years, and crucial problems have been confronted over time. It can offer insight bearing on other newer systems and systems still in prospect.

HISTORY

The Indian systems of personal law long predated independence.[1] The British thought it crucial to make commercial law and criminal law uniform throughout the whole of their Indian domain;[2] here they largely instituted British law of the time. The non-commercial part of civil law, however – personal property, inheritance, and family law – they allowed to remain controlled by the major religions.

It has been suggested that one motive for this concession – or at least one welcome effect – was to give the subject male a domain of rule. If Indian men could not control their destinies in politics or the economy, at least they could govern their own families as they pleased, meaning, in particular, that they could continue to exert control over women, resisting demands for reform by appealing to traditional religious authorities. Historian Tanika Sarkar has shown that the British repeatedly resisted indigenous calls for reform in areas such as marital age and marital violence, citing the importance of allowing Indians to determine their own destinies according to their own religious traditions (Sarkar 2000). Given that this appeal was used to resist protests by *Indian* men and women, not by foreigners, Sarkar's suggestion that the motive was not really respectful deference, but, instead, diversion of the subject's desire for power from political rebellion to domestic domination, seems quite plausible, although evidence for such things is hard to come by. Let us consider one case, to which Sarkar devotes much emphasis.

In 1890, Phulmonee, a girl of age ten or eleven, was raped to death by her husband Hari Maiti, a man of thirty-five. She died after thirteen hours of acute pain and continuous bleeding. Under existing law, he was not guilty of rape, because the age of marriage had been set at ten, and sex in marriage did not require the wife's consent. But indigenous Indian reformers took up the case, campaigning aggressively to raise the age of consent to twelve. Forty-four female doctors brought out lists of cases where women were killed or maimed by rape at a young age. The British judge, Wilson, chose to accept the husband's version that they had slept together consensually many times, so that he would have had no reason to fear bad consequences on this occasion – ignoring medical evidence that she had died of forcible penetration. Wilson said that he had to obey the strict letter of the law, despite the fact that family and reformers were firmly on the other side. The judge alluded to "the supreme importance of his marriage rules to the Hindu, and the inadvisability of external interference with them." He then continued: "[O]ur native fellow subjects

[1] For a comprehensive history of the personal-law systems, see Parashar (1992); see also Jaising (1996, 2005). For a general assessment of India's constitutional tradition in the area of sex equality, see Nussbaum (2000, chapter 3, 2005).

[2] Except for certain princely states, which they allowed to be largely self-governing.

must be allowed the fullest possible freedom in deciding when their children should be ceremonially married. That, in the constitution of Hindu society, is a matter with which no Government could meddle and no Government ought to meddle." Reformists then pushed for legislative change, but the British resisted, speaking of "a distinct tenderness towards ... the customs and religious observances of the Indian people." Notice, then, that the British position was not simply that Hari Maiti could not be convicted under a reform that had not been implemented at the time of his alleged crime; that would have been a reasonable stance. The position was, instead, that the proposed reform could not be seriously entertained, even for future cases, because it went against Hindu tradition – *even though* the call for reform came from Hindus themselves. Is this "tenderness" for the subject population, or is it something more sinister?

We should bear this history in mind in what follows: Personal laws may be represented as a way of respecting the religion of the subject, but they may have effects, and even purposes, that are far less savory. The British surely had other reasons for being deferential to indigenous religious traditions – the role of those traditions in generating the Sepoy Mutiny of 1857, for example[3] – but control over the bodies of women has been one very prominent effect of systems of personal law, and we may plausibly suppose, with Sarkar, that it is often among the purposes animating support for such systems.

As for the laws themselves: Islamic law, grounded in *shari'a*, was already in operation since the Moghul Empire of the seventeenth and eighteenth centuries, so the British simply took it over and made it official, adjusting it for uniformity. For example, the Shariat Act of 1937 substituted *shari'a* for a variety of customary laws that were still used in many regions. This law was supplemented by a 1939 law, the Dissolution of Muslim Marriages Act, which gave Muslim women a right to initiate divorce proceedings.[4] Parsi law was similarly taken over from existing precedents, and in 1864, the Parsi community was granted the right to be ruled by its own system of personal laws. The Christian communities of India are heterogeneous, including Roman Catholics from many different national origins and a wide range of Protestants, so here the British had more work to do, constructing a system out of the different materials to hand. By and large, they did not press for uniformity: Thus, the Roman Catholic Christians of Goa were governed, until very recently, by the

[3] The Sepoy Mutiny clearly had many causes, but one was a controversy about the grease needed for bullets in a newly introduced rifle. Because the bullet casing had to be bitten by the soldier, and because casings were greased with either pork or beef fat, both Hindu and Muslim soldiers worried that religious violation was being forced on them. The British attempted to address this question by guaranteeing that neither sort of fat would be used, but too late.

[4] This law occasioned considerable controversy, although some defended it as fully consistent with the Quran.

Portuguese Civil Code. Jews were numerous in southern India, but they never had a codified system of personal law: The British ruled that they were to be governed by the Indian Succession Act of 1865.

By far the largest job, however, was the codification of Hindu law, which, prior to the eighteenth century, was a set of regionally diverse oral traditions and practices loosely related to classic jurisprudential sources. The British gathered the source texts (which, on the whole, had previously been understood as jurisprudential reflections rather than positive legal injunctions) and set about turning them into a system of positive law, eventually formalizing these laws in a series of acts of Parliament. Hindu law as so codified is, then, a British construct.

At independence, the choice that confronted the constitutional framers was, therefore, not whether to construct anew, within the legal system of the new nation, a niche or niches for personal laws. It was whether to abolish with one stroke the laws that for decades had governed the lives of members of these four communities in matters of family law, inheritance, and property, substituting for them a uniform civil code.

For the majority Hindu community, little seemed at stake, because acts of Parliament passed under the Raj to govern the Hindu community could simply be replaced (or validated) by new acts of the Hindu-majority Indian Parliament. Not that the majority made reform easy. On caste they soon gave way, going along with Gandhi's insistence that discrimination on the basis of caste be outlawed in the Constitution itself.[5] On women's rights, they dug in their heels. Shortly after the new Constitution took effect, the Hindu Code Bill of 1950, which proposed to grant Hindu women a right to divorce, to abolish child marriage, and to grant women more nearly equal property rights, was ferociously resisted by traditional religious leaders. The resulting storm in Parliament caused the resignation from the Law Ministry of the great legal thinker, B. R. Ambedkar, a *dalit* who was a fierce champion of the oppressed. He commented, resigning, "To leave inequality between class and class, between sex and sex ... untouched and to go on passing legislation relating to economic problems is to make a farce of our Constitution and to build a palace on a dung-heap" (quoted in Nussbaum 2000, 171). (Shortly after his resignation, Ambedkar announced that he had embraced Buddhism.) The key provisions of the Hindu Code bill were eventually passed in 1954, 1955, and 1956 (Nussbaum 2000).

For the minority communities, however, and for Muslims in particular, the idea of the abolition of the personal laws seemed highly ominous. Earlier controversies over dietary violation during the Sepoy mutiny and over divorce after the 1939 law had convinced Muslims that their religious requirements were in a fragile position.

5 Article 15 prohibits discrimination on grounds of caste, and Article 17 abolishes untouchability, saying that "its practice in any form is forbidden."

Moreover, the violence of Partition was fresh in people's minds, and it seemed quite evident to Muslims who remained in India that they risked remaining second-class citizens. To surrender their autonomy in these areas of law was, in effect, to permit Hindus to make laws for them, at a time when Hindus harbored considerable animosity toward them. Muslims understood and trusted Gandhi's commitment to inclusion and equality, but the question was how stably this commitment would prevail. It was the official position of the Hindu Mahasabha, a Hindu right-wing political party, that Muslims and Christians *ought* to have unequal civil rights, and it seemed plausible that these ideas could gather a large following.[6] In 1948, a member of this party, and a devoted follower of its charismatic leader V. D. Savarkar, shot Gandhi at point-blank range. At his sentencing hearing, Nathuram Godse offered as "justification" for his murder the fact that Gandhi sought the full equality of Muslims in the new nation (Nussbaum 2007, chapter 5). It was, then, not surprising that many Muslims feared the future and saw the potential abolition of the personal laws as profoundly threatening.

At the time of the constitutional framing – immediately following Gandhi's death – there was some support for the introduction of a uniform civil code, but ultimately the abolition of Muslim personal laws proved too sensitive an issue, given the overriding importance of reassuring Muslims that India was a truly pluralistic nation and not a Hindu nation. The ideal of Indian "secularism" was always that of state neutrality among the religions, not that of the total separation of church and state (Sen 2005); therefore, it seemed in principle possible to combine a commitment to secularism with the maintenance, for the time being, of the separate systems of religious personal law. In consequence, the goal of a uniform civil code was included in the Constitution among the aspirational and unenforceable "Directive Principles of State Policy," as something that the state "shall endeavour to secure" in the future – the idea being that when things had calmed down and people were ready for it, this next step would be taken. It never has been taken, and by now it is further away than it was fifty years ago.[7]

The way the system operates is labyrinthine and uneven, and it is not easy to get two legal experts to agree on a description of what the system is. [8] But, to give a reasonable general description: At birth, a child is typically classified as a member of

6 The Mahasabha was openly political; by contrast, the RSS, which later became far more influential, represented itself, at the time, as an apolitical social movement.

7 For a forceful Muslim argument in favor of a uniform code – in the period prior to the *Shah Bano* case and the rise of Hindu fundamentalism – see Qureshi (1978).

8 The best account of the contemporary systems, with comprehensive detail and many discussions of legal challenges, is in Jaising (1996). The authors are members of the Lawyers Collective, a leading legal NGO founded by Jaising. Jaising was a senior advocate of the Supreme Court of India, and has argued some of the important sex equality cases in various parts of the country. In 2009, she became one of the Solicitors General of the nation and in 2011 she became chief Solicitor General.

some religious group. Usually it is that of both or one of the parents,[9] and usually some religion is chosen, although it is possible not to mention a religion at all. Children who are enrolled as members of some religion are henceforth governed by that system of personal law. Since the passage of the Special Marriage Act in 1954 (itself much opposed by various religious leaders as an infringement of their power), they may elect secular marriage and secular divorce (although secular laws are quite similar to the reformed Hindu laws). This is usually taken to mean that they will also be governed by secular inheritance law, but in 1975, the relevant law was amended under pressure from Hindu leaders so that two Hindus who elect a secular marriage will still be governed by the Hindu law of inheritance. Religious conversion typically results in a change of legal system, although cases in which Hindus who convert to Islam to contract polygamous marriage have been a source of legal controversy, and such "converts" may now be charged with bigamy if they do not secure a legal divorce from their first wife (Law Commission 2009). Conversions into Hinduism are extremely rare – in large part because it would be unclear what the caste of such a convert would be.[10] What makes mobility among systems especially difficult is the arrangement for hereditary property, which typically involves complex family consortia (called the "coparcenary" in the Hindu system), in which individuals have rights, but which are not transferrable should one individual within the family decide to switch to another system (Agarwal 2004). This discourages conversion, secular marriage and divorce, and the declaration of a secular identity for a newborn child.[11]

It is important to notice that personal laws in India are not laws passed by special religious courts. The personal laws are laws passed by Parliament like other laws, in consultation with the leaders of that religious community, but they apply only to members of a particular religious community. Typically the religious authorities consult with the Law Minister, a committee is formed, and eventually legislation is drafted, which then, after much delay and discussion, may eventually be passed by Parliament, meaning by a majority vote of Parliament, which always means a majority vote of an overwhelmingly Hindu body. Thus, laws for the tiny Christian community are passed, like all other laws, by a Parliament consisting of roughly 85 percent Hindus.

9 Interreligious marriage remains extremely rare in India today, even in liberal academic circles.

10 Converts out of Hinduism lose all caste, something that has large legal relevance, given the affirmative-action programs established for "scheduled castes." See Galanter (1989, part IV) for a discussion of legal cases involving converts from Hinduism to Buddhism who still tried to claim these benefits. For a comprehensive account of the affirmative action programs, see Galanter (1984).

11 It also gives heads of Hindu joint families a tax break: Under the laws pertaining to a Hindu United Family (HUF), the head of such a family can separate personal income from income pertaining to family land, and frequently pay much less income tax as a result of this division. When Hindus charge Muslims with having an unfair break in matters of plural marriage, the response is typically to point to Hindu advantages under the tax code.

The system makes delay almost inevitable. Christian women won the right to divorce on grounds of cruelty – a right Christian women in many nations of the world had long enjoyed – only in 2001. First the different types of Christian clerics had to be persuaded to listen to the voices of women. Then they had to be persuaded to agree among themselves. Then they had to approach and move Parliament, working out the details of the proposed legislation with the Law Minister, who could either facilitate or impede their progress. This process, which can remind one of the Circumlocution Office in Dickens's *Little Dorrit*, virtually guarantees that any significant reform will take decades. Even the majority community encounters large delays: Hindu women won equal shares in agricultural land only in 2005. But in their case, only sexism must be overcome; for the minorities, the multiple hurdles constitute further impediments to reform.

But what about the Fundamental Rights, as described in Section III of the Indian Constitution? Surely these are core entitlements that belong equally to all citizens, and they have teeth. Article 14 guarantees all persons the equal protection of the laws; Article 15 prohibits discrimination on the grounds of religion, race, caste, sex, or place of birth; Article 16 guarantees all citizens equality in matters relating to employment and prohibits employment discrimination on the basis of religion, race, caste, sex, descent, place of birth, and residence; Article 21 (the basis for privacy-right jurisprudence in cases involving marital rape and the forcible "restitution of conjugal rights") says that no citizen "shall be deprived of his life or personal liberty" without due process of law; Article 25 states that all citizens are "equally entitled to freedom of conscience and the right freely to profess, practice and propagate religion." The constitution itself makes very clear the fact that the abolition of caste is not inconsistent with these rights: Article 25 is qualified to permit the state to abolish caste discrimination, and untouchability is explicitly abolished in Article 17. Otherwise, however, it is left unclear how far the Fundamental Rights limit the religiously grounded personal laws.

One might think that Article 13 gives the answer: It renders invalid all "laws in force" that conflict with any of the Fundamental Rights and forbids the state to make any new laws that take away or abridge a Fundamental Right. In 1952, however, in *State of Bombay v. Narasu Appa Mali*,[12] the Supreme Court held that "laws in force" did not include the personal laws.

Supporting this failure to insist on individual rights regardless of the views of religious communities is the fact that the Constitution, in this very Fundamental Rights section, recognizes groups as having rights. The permissibility of group-based affirmative action is stated in Article 14; Article 29 gives linguistic and cultural rights to region-based groups; and Article 30 gives minorities, "whether based on religion or language," the right to "establish and administer educational institutions of their

[12] AIR 1952 Bom 84.

choice." There may certainly be a theoretical way of understanding these group-based rights that sees them as instrumental to individual rights, but the Constitution does not set things up that way. In that sense, the failure of individual rights to prevail in key instances over the group reflects a tension inherent in the constitutional framing.

That is the status quo, more or less, until just before the present day. In 1983, Mary Roy, a Syrian Christian woman, attempted to get the Travancore Christian Act declared unconstitutional on grounds of sex discrimination. (It allowed daughters to inherit only one-fourth of the amount that sons inherit, and guaranteed that a portion of each daughter's inheritance would go to the Church.) The Supreme Court ducked the issue of constitutionality, however, by saying that henceforth Christians in Kerala would be governed by the Indian Succession Act of 1925, which gave equal shares to daughters and sons and gave nothing to the Church.[13] (Christian clerics protested that the judgment would destroy "the traditional harmony and goodwill that exists in Christian families.") So the inequality was remedied, but the issue of constitutionality was evaded.

We now arrive at a case that has attracted attention all over the world, and which we follow throughout this chapter to its unlikely conclusion in 2001.

In Madhya Pradesh in 1978, an elderly Muslim woman named Shah Bano was thrown out of her home by her husband, a prosperous lawyer, after forty-four years of marriage, and divorced by the permitted form of the triple *talaq*. (The occasion seems to have been a quarrel over inheritance between the children of Shah Bano and the children of the husband's other wife.) As required by Islamic personal law, he returned to her the *mehr*, or marriage settlement, that she had originally brought into the marriage – Rs. 3,000 (less than $100 by today's exchange rates). Like many Muslim women facing divorce without sufficient maintenance, she sued for regular maintenance payments under Section 125 of the (uniform) Criminal Procedure Code, which forbids a man "of adequate means" to permit various close relatives, including (by special amendment in 1973) an ex-wife,[14] to remain in a state of "destitution and vagrancy." This remedy had long been recognized as a solution to the inadequate maintenance granted by Islamic personal law, and many women had won similar cases.

[13] *Mrs. Mary Roy v. State of Kerala and Others*, AIR 1986 SC 1011. Mary Roy is the mother of Arundhati Roy, but the family was very poor at the time.

[14] The recognition of ex-wives as included relations under Section 125 was itself controversial in 1973. When the amendment was discussed in the Lok Sabha, members of the Muslim League objected, claiming violations of free exercise. Initially the government denied that there was any religious issue: The purpose of the amendment was simply humanitarian. Later, however, the government changed its stand, adding yet a further amendment to exclude divorced Muslim women from the purview of the new amendment. Nonetheless, Muslim women continued to bring petitions to the courts, and the Supreme Court explicitly pronounced, in two prominent judgments, that they were entitled to do so: The purpose of the law was to help destitute women, and the text had to be interpreted in accordance with this social purpose. See *Bai Tahira v. Ali Hussain*, 1979 (2) Supreme Court Reporter, 75, and AIR 1980 Supreme Court 1930. Thus the conflict between the Supreme Court and the Muslim leadership was of long standing.

What was different about Shah Bano's case was that the Chief Justice of the Supreme Court of India, a Hindu, awarding her maintenance of Rs. 180 per month (about $4), remarked in his lengthy opinion[15] that the Islamic system was very unfair to women, and that it was high time that the nation should indeed secure a Uniform Civil Code, as the Constitution had long ago directed it to do. The Chief Justice wrote, "Undoubtedly, the Muslim husband enjoys the privilege of being able to discard his wife whenever he chooses to do so, for reason good, bad, or indifferent. Indeed, for no reason at all." Although of Hindu origin, the Chief Justice also undertook to interpret various Islamic sacred texts and to argue that there was no textual barrier in Islam to providing a much more adequate maintenance for women.[16]

A storm of public protest greeted the opinion. Although some liberal Muslims backed Chief Justice Chandrachud, he had made their task difficult by his contemptuous remarks and his zealous incursion into the interpretation of sacred Islamic texts. The Islamic clergy and the Muslim Personal Law Board organized widespread protests against the ruling, claiming that it violated their free exercise of religion. In response to the widespread outcry, the government of Rajiv Gandhi introduced the Muslim Women's (Protection of Rights on Divorce) Act of 1986, which deprived all

[15] *Mohammed Ahmed Khan v. Shah Bano Begum & Ors.* (AIR 1985 SC 945). The opinion opens as follows:

> This appeal does not involve any questions of constitutional importance but, that is not to say that it does not involve any question of importance. Some questions which arise under the ordinary civil and criminal law are of a far-reaching significance to large segments of society which have been traditionally subjected to unjust treatment. Women are one such segment. *Na stree swatantrama-rhati* said Manu, the Law-Giver: The woman does not deserve independence. And, it is alleged that the "fatal point in Islam is the degradation of woman." [Footnote reference is made to a British commentary on the Quran by Edward Lane.] To the Prophet is ascribed the statement, hopefully wrongly, that "Woman was made from a crooked rib, and if you try to bend it straight, it will break; therefore treat your wives kindly."
>
> This appeal, arising out of an application filed by a divorced Muslim woman for maintenance under section 125 of the Code of Criminal Procedure, raises a straightforward issue which is of common interest not only to Muslim women, not only to women generally, but, to all those who, aspiring to create an equal society of men and women, lure themselves into the belief that mankind has achieved a remarkable degree of progress in that direction.

From these words alone, one can get a sense of the strange combination of progressive courage with political obtuseness (referring to a *British* critic of Islam!) that characterize the opinion throughout.

[16] This famous case has been discussed in many places. The central documents are assembled in Engineer (1987); Das (1992, chapter 4); Kavita R. Khory, "The Shah Bano Case: Some Political Implications," in Baird, ed. (1993), 121–37; Sen (2005: 294–316); Parashar (1992: 173–89) (an unusually comprehensive account of different attitudes within the Islamic community); Zoya Hasan, "Minority Identity, State Policy and the Political Process," in Hasan, ed. (1994), 59–73; Danial Latifi, "After Shah Bano," in Jaising, ed. (1996), 213–15, and "Women, Family Law, and Social Changes," in Jaising, ed. (1996), 216–22 (criticizing Muslims who opposed the Supreme Court decision).See also Mahmood (1983).

and only Muslim women of the "protection" that consisted in a right of maintenance guaranteed under the Criminal Procedure Code. Women's groups tried to get this law declared unconstitutional on grounds of both religious discrimination and sex equality, but the Supreme Court (in rapid retreat from charges of religious intolerance and excessive activism) refused to hear such cases. Hindu activists, meanwhile, complained that the 1986 law discriminates against Hindus, giving Muslim men "special privileges." (Notice the truth in Sarkar's diagnosis: Men of the various religions tend to think of the systems of personal law as ways of ensuring their power over women, and they view any advance toward greater gender equality as an assault on the privileges guaranteed them by the system. It is as if a religion can measure its political strength by the extent to which its members have been able to avoid legal reform toward women's equality.)

Progress toward a Uniform Code had been stalled. Meanwhile, the Hindu Right had been rising to power. Mobs associated with the Rashtriya Swayamsevak Sangh (RSS) and Vishwa Hindu Parishad (VHP),[17] in December 1992, destroyed a mosque at Ayodhya called the Babri Masjid, which stands on a site that is alleged to conceal the remnants of a Hindu temple that is supposed to mark the god Rama's birthplace.[18] Shortly thereafter, the Bharatiya Janata Party (BJP), the political wing of the Hindu Right, rose to power as the leading party in a coalition government. They held the reins of power until 2004.

During this period, the cause of the Uniform Civil Code became a pet BJP cause, and sympathy to women allegedly oppressed by Islam became a BJP posture. Leaders of the BJP represented themselves as reformers, highly sympathetic to women. Remarkably, Arun Jaitley, then-BJP Law Minister and a man with deep RSS roots, a real hard-liner, left an emergency cabinet meeting (called after the attempted bombing of Parliament in 2001) to deliver the opening speech at a conference on sex equality and personal laws organized by feminist legal thinker and jurist Indira Jaising. (This was the conference that ultimately gave rise to the book *Men's Laws, Women's Lives* (Jaising 2005)). By this dramatic gesture, Jaitley let all present see how

17 The Rashtriya Swayamsevak Sangh (RSS) and the Vishva Hindu Parashad (VHP) are the two leading social organizations of what has come to be known as the Sangh Parivar, or "family of groups," the network of social and political organizations that compose the Hindu Right, of which the Bharatiya Janata Party (BJP) is the political wing. For the histories of these and other groups, see Nussbaum (2007, chapter 5).

18 By now it is clear from excavation that there is some structure underneath the ruins of the mosque, but whether the structure was a Hindu temple is deeply disputed, and the BJP-led coalition government did not allow access to the data on the part of independent archaeologists. Of course, the entire idea that Rama is the central god in the Hindu pantheon is a modern construct – Hinduism traditionally is plural and decentralized, and some regions do not even recognize Rama as a god at all; similarly, the idea that the modern city of Ayodhya is the place where Rama was born is a construct, with a distinct political purpose. Both of these myths were made popular through the ideological dramatization of the classic epic *Ramayana* on national television in the 1980s. See Nussbaum (2007, chapter 5).

important he thought the cause of sex equality was.[19] It was reasonable to wonder, however, whether his allegiance was to the cause of sex equality or to the anticipated subordination of Muslims and Christians. Because of this tarnished type of support, the cause of the Uniform Code languished, and is languishing until the present day.

PERSONAL LAWS AS ACCOMMODATION

All religiously plural societies must deal with the fact that majorities are apt to be insensitive to the needs of minorities. Even when religious liberty is protected, and nobody would dream of interfering with religious belief and even religious observance, minorities are apt to be burdened by heedless majority choices in matters that touch on their religion. Majorities set the calendar, determining which days will be work days and which holidays. They set the drug laws, determining what will be legal and what illegal. They set up laws about matters such as social security classification, military service, the uses of government land, and many other matters that may appear to have nothing to do with religion, but that actually turn out to touch on the core of some people's religion (Nussbaum 2008, chapter 4). Even so simple a matter as requiring a flag salute at the start of the school day, or requiring men to take off their hats when appearing in court, may prove profoundly burdensome to some minority.

Such laws restrict religious liberty. They do not remove it, but they make the liberty of minorities unequal to that of the majority. In nations where Sunday is the day off from work, mainstream Christians have an advantage over people whose holy day is Saturday or Friday. Majority Christian nations will usually make alcohol legal, at least for sacramental purposes, while restricting the sacramental use of peyote. Innumerable cases of this sort figure in the history of U.S. free-exercise law.

One response to the problem is that of John Locke: If the law is not malicious or persecutory in intent, it may stand, and the minority will just have to obey it, or they may choose to disobey and pay the legal penalty. Another tradition, associated in the United States with Roger Williams, holds that religious equality requires allowing minorities exemptions in such cases, unless there is a very grave reason on the other side (Nussbaum 2008, chapter 2). Already at the time of independence, most state constitutions allowed for such exemptions. A typical expression of the principle of "accommodation" – religiously grounded exemption – is a letter that George Washington wrote to the Quakers, who refuse military service on grounds of conscience, saying, " I assure you very explicitly, that in my opinion the conscientious scruples of all men should be treated with great delicacy and tenderness: and it is my wish and desire, that the laws may always be as extensively accommodated to them, as a due regard for the protection and essential interests of the nation may justify and

[19] I was present at this conference.

permit." He did not make them perform military service, and he did not, as Locke would have, make them pay a legal penalty. Similarly, Jews were not required to appear in court on a Saturday, and they were not fined either. Shortly after independence, in a memorable early court decision, a Roman Catholic priest was allowed to refuse to answer questions posed to him in a criminal case, when he protested that his information about the identity of the criminal came to him in the confessional. The judge, a Protestant, reasoned that to require a priest to divulge this information *or* to penalize him for not doing so would effectively abolish the sacrament of the confessional, and thus would impose a very severe burden on all Catholics.[20]

We can see that these practices of accommodation are already a kind of dispensation to be governed by religious law rather than the law of the state. The Jew who refuses to answer a subpoena on the Sabbath is refusing to obey the law of the state and is obeying Jewish law. By not fining him or her, the state is deferring to Jewish law. The priest who refused to testify was prompted by religious law concerning the sanctity of the confessional, and the state, by not jailing him for contempt, was deferring to religious law. Most accommodation involves, in this way, a statement by the state that in some matters a person may permissibly be guided by religious law rather than state law. Sometimes these accommodations are quite systematic: Quakers and Mennonites were exempted from military service as a rule. So one might say that we have, here, approaches to something like personal law.

Let us think now of the history I mentioned. Minorities had reason to fear not only the heedlessness, but also the hostility of the Hindu majority. They imagined that Hindus would deliberately trample on things of great importance to them. The personal laws were a refuge against that tyranny, protecting the equal worth of religious liberty. In this way, one might defend personal laws as a natural extension of the commonly accepted principle and practice of accommodation, and one might think that the Indian Constitution's guarantee of not just religious liberty but "equal religious liberty" is admirably fulfilled by the personal law system, and perhaps even requires it.

On the other hand, it has long been clear that accommodation is in considerable tension with a ban on religious establishment. India's constitution contains no ban on establishment as such, so at this point I shall analyze the issue from the point of view of political theory, asking what reflection on establishment can show us about the wisdom or lack of wisdom in extending accommodation that far.

PERSONAL LAWS AS ESTABLISHMENT

Right now, India's form of secularism involves a form of religious establishment, in the sense that four religions have been given privileges that other religions, along

[20] *People v. Philips*, N.Y. Court of General Sessions, June 14, 1813.

with agnosticism and atheism, do not enjoy, namely to organize systems of property and family law, subject to the approval of Parliament. When the BJP was in the ascendancy, it seemed possible that, winning an outright majority, the party might try to move India toward a one-religion form of establishment, declaring India a Hindu nation. We can pursue our inquiry into the personal laws, then, by asking what is wrong with religious establishment, and whether the objections to it apply only to the one-religion form or also to the plural form.

Scholars argue about the precise relationship between the idea of nonestablishment and the idea of free exercise of religion, but let me simply advance one plausible account (see Nussbaum 2008, chapters 3, 6, 7). What is wrong with establishing one religion as *the* religion of a nation is that it drastically limits (or usually does, or gravely risks doing) the equal opportunity of other people to exercise their own religion or nonreligion freely. Moreover – and of critical importance in explaining why a good constitution needs a nonestablishment provision in addition to a strong free-exercise provision – establishments, in addition to threatening liberty, also threaten equality. They limit the *equal* freedom of minorities to carry on their own religious life, and they compromise the equality of status of citizens as they enter the public square. Even when the majority religion is tolerant and behaves impeccably to minorities, tax money will be spent on it that limits the money people have to fund their own religions. As Madison said, this inequality in turn creates a civic in equality: Citizens do not all enter the public square "on equal conditions."[21] Even when financial inequalities do not obtain, the very declaration that the state is Christian, for example, announces a distinction of status: Others, once again, enter the public square on different conditions, at the sufferance of the majority.

The U.S. tradition pays close attention to the symbolic importance of the statements made by government, and I believe that this is wise (Nussbaum 2008, chapter 6). It is not enough that government does not penalize people for their minority status: The symbolic creation of an "in-group" and an "out-group" is problem enough. Establishments are worst when they threaten liberty, penalizing people for nonorthodox worship, forcing them to affirm orthodox sentiments that they might not believe, or attaching conditions of religious orthodoxy to a person's civil rights or ability to hold office. It was quickly understood by early U.S. thinkers, however, that even an apparently benign establishment fosters inequality by making a statement that the government of the nation endorses a particular brand of religion. This endorsement is at the same time, inevitably, a disendorsement, creating an in-group and an out-group. As James Madison said, "[A]ll men are to be considered as entering into Society on equal conditions,"[22] and even a noncoercive establishment violates

[21] Madison, A *Memorial and Remonstrance Against Religious Assessments*, 1785.
[22] Madison, *Memorial and Remonstrance*.

that equality. Madison was speaking, in 1785, in opposition to a proposal to tax all citizens of Virginia for the support of the established Anglican Church. According to the proposal, citizens who were not Anglicans would be permitted to divert their tax payments to their own churches; people who did not have a church could pay into a general fund for "teachers of religion"; and Quakers and Mennonites did not have to pay at all. Nonetheless, Madison thought that the bare announcement that the Anglican Church was the default option, the official state church, created ranks and orders of citizens. In 1984, discussing the U.S. Constitution's ban on religious establishment, Justice Sandra Day O'Connor recapitulated the long Madisonian tradition:

> The Establishment Clause prohibits government from making adherence to a religion relevant in any way to a person's standing in the political community.... Endorsement sends a message to non-adherents that they are outsiders, not full members of the political community, and an accompanying message to adherents that they are insiders, favored members of the political community. Disapproval sends the opposite message.[23]

According to Justice O'Connor's very helpful analysis, the right question to ask of any potentially problematic policy in the area of religious establishment is the following one: Would an objective observer, acquainted with all the relevant historical and contextual facts, view the policy in question as one that makes a public statement of endorsement or disapproval, sending a message of inequality?

In short: Establishments are bad because they threaten equal religious liberty and the equality of citizens.

In India, for these reasons, single-religion establishment would be a horrible idea. Even if it did not lead right away to curtailments of the rights and privileges of minorities, it would be very likely to do so down the line. And, as Madison saw, the very declaration that the nation's religious identity is that of one particular religion by itself sends a message of inequality to other citizens. The BJP-led coalition government's efforts to "Hinduize" textbooks used by all students, for example, sent a message of second-class status to others. The context made these Hinduizing statements more ominous still. It was not a question of introducing a benign establishment such as the Lutheran establishment of Finland; it was a question of redesigning the Indian nation in a form passionately advocated, for many years, by a Hindu movement many of whose members have long aimed at domination over others, even at the cost of violence. That proposal was, rightly, rejected at the time of independence, and its recent revival was rightly seen as ominous. The very declaration that India is a Hindu nation would send, in that context, not simply the message of unequal

[23] *Lynch v. Donnelly*, 465 U. S. 668 (1984).

status that any establishment would send, but a further message of domination and even of imminent violence.

What about India's current form of plural establishment? It is surely not a perfect system. Over time it has given rise to various problems, among which seven stand out as particularly severe.

The first and most obvious problem with plural establishment, the unequal treatment of groups who are utterly left out, has not created large-scale social unrest in India. We do not hear much about bad treatment of Jews *qua* Jews, or of Taoists and Confucianists as such, or even of atheists as atheists. Secular laws of marriage and property give these people a legal order to rely on, which, being relatively modern, is in general not worse than the religious systems; and atheists continue in most cases to be classified under the religious system of their origin. Nonetheless, social unrest is not the only problem caused by religious establishment. (Indeed, if we were to say that social unrest is the primary problem, we would disadvantage very small groups and privilege larger ones who have the potential to cause unrest.)[24] I have argued that the primary problem with religious establishment is one of equal respect: Establishments send a message of favor and disfavor, creating ranks and orders of citizens. The Indian system, which favors four religions and leaves others to the sidelines, involves a statement by the government that it will favor some groups and not others. Perhaps this problem offers part of the explanation for why the Jews of Cochin and Travancore have largely emigrated. But respect, in my view, is not a matter of subjective feeling: Even if the Jews of India did not feel the stigma involved in their omission from the list of established religions, the message of disendorsement remains.

A second related problem that has been too little studied is one of *voicelessness by inclusion*. Buddhists, Sikhs, and Jains are all classified under the Hindu system, and yet, by the numbers, they have little power to influence its shape. They are not omitted utterly, but their subsumption by the majority creates a similar difficulty: They are an unrecognized out-group within an in-group, and their distinctive views have little chance of gaining a hearing when laws relating to the group are formulated. Given that all these groups contest major traditions of Hinduism, this subsumption is, for them, a particularly unfortunate result.[25]

[24] This is one of my objections to Justice Stephen Breyer's use of the possibility of social unrest as a criterion of an Establishment Clause violation: See my discussion in Nussbaum (2008, chapter 7).

[25] Buddhism has been seen as an alternative to Hinduism at least since the second century B.C.E., when Emperor Ashoka converted from Hinduism to Buddhism; Buddhism was and is casteless, and it also has a wide concern for animal life, by contrast to Hinduism's focus on the cow: Ashoka wrote of his strenuous attempt to become a vegetarian. Jains are even more rigorous in their defense of all living things, even covering mouth and nose to prevent inadvertent killings of insects. The differences of Sikhs with Hindus are numerous and subtle, and have occasioned considerable violence.

Further grave problems arise when we consider the Indian systems of personal law themselves, both internally and in comparison to one another. We see – a third problem – many instances of discrimination on the basis of religion: A person gets a worse deal than another person, in maintenance, or property, or marriage, simply by the luck of belonging to a given religious community, when the other community has more favorable laws in the area. Thus Christian women lost out in the matter of divorce on grounds of cruelty, in relation to women of other religions, by being Christian. Before the Roy case, they also lost out, relatively speaking, in inheritance law. Hindu women lost out in the matter of shares in agricultural land, until the 2005 reforms. This defect, peculiar to the Hindu legal system, handicapped them in many ways.[26] Muslim women lost out in the matter of maintenance (after the Muslim Women's Act) by the luck of being Muslim. Such inequalities took a long time to correct because of the cumbersome structure inherent in the personal-law system.

Indeed, we may go further, introducing a fourth problem: The system encourages factionalism. One reason why reform is difficult is that the various religions are encouraged by the structure to compete with one another, and one way they always compete with one another is to resist change, particularly in the matter of control over women. In this sense, plural establishment may be worse than single establishment.

A fifth and closely related problem, already revealed by the preceding discussion, is that the system perpetuates and empowers a very undemocratic structure of decision making. Religious groups are typically not run democratically; they entrust a lot of power to clerics, who are unlikely to be representative of the community as a whole. (For one thing, the empowered clergy will usually all be male.) The way decisions are made disadvantages minorities, dissidents, and women within each community. We should have no objection to hierarchically organized voluntary associations within an egalitarian democracy. The problem begins, however, when they exert power over the making of law in ways that are not in the least voluntary. The result is that laws binding on an entire group of citizens are made in a manner that runs afoul of the basic political commitment of the democracy to principles of equal representation and voice. The reason Christian divorce reform took so long to pass was that all the different Christian denominations, Protestants and Roman Catholics from different original colonial powers, had somehow to be brought together, and all had to be convinced to listen to the voices of women. Given that all the denominations were dominated by male clerics, typically aging, this took a lot of doing. These clerics, of course, were not elected by all Christians to represent them; they were powerful because of their promotions within the churches, and

[26] See Agarwal (2004). Agarwal was involved in urging the recent reform legislation. See also Agarwal and Panda (2007), which shows that landownership is a very important variable in explaining how women manage to avoid domestic violence, insofar as they do.

all of this was quite undemocratic. Similarly, the Muslim Personal Law Board is a self-perpetuating nonelected body that is unaccountable to and unrepresentative of India's Muslims. The fact that laws relating to a community must be passed by Parliament does introduce a measure of accountability and democracy – but of an odd sort, because most of the people voting on any given such law will be members of the majority community. The voices of Christian women, for example, are unlikely to be prominent in the Lok Sabha.

If all the people affected by laws passed in this undemocratic way had made a choice to join the religious group in question, the undemocratic character of its procedures would be, at least, less objectionable (although it would still be unclear that an egalitarian nation should permit its members to give up the equal worth of their fundamental legal and political rights). We know, however, that voluntary choice is far from the norm in India. It is not only that children's lot is affected by the religious choices of their parents – a problem endemic to all nations that consider personal laws. In India, as I have mentioned already, people are classified in a religious group when they are born, and exit is very difficult. Conversions to Islam or Christianity are sometimes (albeit not always) legally recognized; but just try to drop out of being a Hindu, and you will find that the reach of the classification is tenacious – in part because of the fact that one's property is often entangled in that scheme. These difficulties of exit mean that most of India's people are trapped for life inside a system that they may not have chosen; under the personal laws, they are, like it or not, affected in major ways by the undemocratic decision procedures of those religious groups.

Religious groups typically argue that governmental deference to their own nondemocratic ways of making decisions is essential to ensure the health of their religious group. Just as churches cannot remain healthy unless they can manage their own affairs internally, choosing clerics and leaders by their own principles, so too they are likely to be threatened unless they are able to decide some crucial matters affecting the lives of their congregants in ways that respect their own chosen decision-making structure. Some such contention may well be correct in limited areas, such as the need for churches to be able to select their own leaders, to determine criteria of membership, and to own property. But when it is made into an argument for religion-based systems of law, the argument runs into historical and empirical difficulty. Entanglement of religion with state bureaucracy simply has not been an effective way of promoting the health of religion – a sixth problem with establishment. Ever since debates about religious establishment in the eighteenth century, it was frequently observed that establishment is bad for religion because it makes religion bureaucratic, lazy, and lacking in vitality.[27] This argument by now

27 This argument was commonly made against religious establishments in the eighteenth century: It can be found in Madison, Adam Smith, and many others.

has strong empirical backing. The United States is the most religiously active and zealous nation in the world, in large part because people are free to be religious in their own way, and no disadvantage attaches to them for this. People can and do go off and invent a new construction of their own religion, be it conservative or progressive. There are thousands of different types of Baptists, many different types of Jews, all kinds of small splinter religions. (One important military-conscription case even recognized a religion that was the creation of one person only and had no other members.[28]) Even the most centrally organized denominations, such as Anglicans and Roman Catholics, contain enormous differences. Feminists can thus feel free to join (or found) a feminist branch of their religion; racial minorities can join (or form) a branch that is focused on the needs of their group.

This flexibility is impossible in a system such as that of Israel or India, where there is substantial state entanglement of religion and religions are part of a political bureaucracy. Bureaucracies are slow-moving and cumbersome. It would have done feminist Christians in Kerala no good to organize a feminist Christian Church, although in principle they could have done so: The reins of power within the system of personal law were squarely in the hands of the traditional leaders, ergo males. For such reasons, religion in India is often identified, in the minds of sensitive progressive people, with reactionary views. (Much the same is true in Israel, where Reform and Reconstructionist forms of Judaism, which have led numerous progressive movements in the United States, can hardly exist and play no role in the religious bureaucracy of the state.) Establishment, in short, ensures not the health but the non-health of religion, by giving governmental power to entrenched power structures within each religion, which can then use their enhanced power to resist calls for change and reform, thus discouraging dynamism.

A seventh problem with the system of plural establishment – perhaps the gravest of all – is that it fails to grapple with the fact that religious groups, like all groups, contain internal hierarchies and often involve the subordination of some members by others. The nation came to grips with this difficulty in the case of Hindu caste: Untouchability, as we saw, is outlawed in the constitution itself, as is all discrimination on grounds of caste. The constitution also carefully states that affirmative-action policies to aid the scheduled castes and the scheduled tribes – groups long subjected to stigmatization and invidious discrimination – do not violate constitutional equality provisions. Thus the grant of power to Hindu clerics did not involve a permit to continue discriminating on grounds of caste.

The same cannot be said of gender, the issue over which Ambedkar resigned his law ministry. Although some of the reforms he favored were eventually adopted, and although the constitution prohibits discrimination on grounds of sex, this

[28] *U. S. v. Seeger*, 380 U. S. 398 (1963).

prohibition, as we have already seen, was immediately held by courts not to apply to the personal laws. Thus the power ceded to (male) clerics included a power to continue discriminating on grounds of gender. This problem arises directly from the existence of personal laws. In their absence, the equality rights that the constitution grants to women would simply trump other considerations.

Returning to our earlier discussion, we now see that even democracy, were it present, is not enough: We want a system of law to protect the equal entitlements of internal minorities, who might lose out even if there were a majority vote. (Women are, in fact, a minority in India, where the sex ratio is 92 women to 100 men, very likely on account of sex discrimination in basic nutrition and health care, plus sex-selective abortion. But even if they were not a numerical minority, they probably would constitute a minority of voters because of difficulties of mobility and access.)

In general, sex equality is surely easier to protect in a system of nonestablishment than in a system of plural establishment, because discriminatory laws will have to be changed multiple times in a plural system, and, as we have seen, one religious community often resents being forbidden to discriminate against women when others do not have similar requirements imposed at the very same time. Groups (or their leaders) can even come to define their power in the state in accordance with the degree to which they are permitted to continue subordinating women. Procedures for reform, being internal to each religion, do not permit simultaneity. So it might have been foreseen that reform would be difficult. What is most obvious, however, is that (given the exemption of personal laws from the scrutiny of Fundamental Rights) reform is simply not constitutionally required.

Recall the asymmetry between the treatment of women and the treatment of the scheduled castes and tribes. The equality of the *dalits* was taken seriously and given real force against Hindu religion and law. The equality of women was taken to be a matter that could be put on the back burner, constitutionally speaking: not a matter of basic citizenship in the nation, but a matter to be negotiated later, using the non-democratic and male-dominated procedures I have already described.

The idea that personal laws are inimical to sex equality derives support not only from the way the codes have operated in recent history, but also from the mode of their formation under the Raj. As we saw, there is reason to suppose that they were created, at least in part, precisely in order to be a bastion of male dominance.

ACCOMMODATION AND ESTABLISHMENT: AN APPARENT TENSION AND A PROPOSED RESOLUTION

Are there any merits of the system of plural establishment, which might possibly outweigh these difficulties and defects? A state with no religious establishment de jure can still be an establishment de facto. In the United States, despite the fact that people have been very vigilant about religious minority rights, we still have, right now, a Pledge of Allegiance that mentions God, currency that says "under God," a president who mentions God often and who sometimes mentions Jesus, a former president who did so even more aggressively and frequently, a former Attorney General (John Ashcroft) who begins every working day by singing Christian songs with his staff, and a military establishment who happily allow Christian soldiers to wear crosses but who try to stop Jewish, Sikh, and Muslim soldiers from wearing their characteristic items of dress. Christmas and Easter are national holidays; the holidays of other religions are not.

If these problems obtain even under a regime of nonestablishment, they are all the more likely to obtain when the largest religious group in a nation has a recent history of hostility toward minority religious groups, and when it makes up 85 percent of the population, as is the case with Hinduism in India. An India without plural establishment could well have become a de facto establishment, one might argue, imposing the customs and will of the majority on minorities in matters of deep importance to them.

That is the best rationale one can offer for India's current system of plural establishment: It gives religious minorities assurance that in some very important matters they can handle things as they want, without interference from the majority. The systems of personal law, we recall, were in existence already. There was no possibility of not starting them up in the first place. The only two possibilities were abolishing them and allowing them to continue. The latter choice was, whether right or wrong, at least defensible, on grounds that the abolition of a cherished sphere of control would be a grave injury to both the power and the self-respect of minority groups. The system has not worked perfectly. It also does not exactly promote minority autonomy, in that roughly half of each group are women, and the system is worse for their autonomy (as well as for the autonomy of other internal minorities, such as progressive reformers, atheists, etc.). But in some important ways, at the time of independence, the system gave a signal of full civic equality to vulnerable minorities, thus apparently serving a valuable constitutional purpose.

To return to my argument about accommodation: I suggested that the dispensation to govern one's own life with respect to property, inheritance, and family law might be called simply an extended form of the common constitutional practice of religiously grounded accommodation, or dispensation from laws of general applicability on religious grounds. It might be argued further that personal laws serve the same purpose that accommodation in general serves: to protect the equal worth of liberty. Muslims, the argument goes, could not rely on having fully equal liberty in matters of marriage, inheritance, and so forth in a Hindu-majority nation because the laws that would be adopted in any Uniform Civil Code would (even without malice aforethought) reflect the customs and needs of the majority, ignoring special religious needs of Muslims. Therefore, protecting fully equal liberty of religion requires giving Muslims, Christians, and Parsis a space within which to function in accordance with their conscience.

The general idea behind this argument is, I believe, sound: Protecting the equal worth of liberty for minorities requires accommodation from at least some laws of general applicability. In the United States, the practice has done real good in protecting the equal worth of liberty for minorities in matters such as unemployment compensation (when a worker refuses jobs that require Saturday work), sacramental drug use, and military service (Nussbaum 2008, chapter 4). However, there must be limits to this practice in any nation governed by the idea of equal rights for all citizens.

Typically in the United States, two types of limits have been observed. First, the minute accommodation tilts over into granting the religious body control over lawmaking, the accommodation issue becomes an establishment issue, and the grant of lawmaking powers to the religious group is declared impermissible on Establishment Clause grounds. In *Kiryas Joel v. Grumet*, the Supreme Court held that the Satmar Hasidim were not permitted to run their own school district, even though they had won the right to do so on the basis of a significant accommodation-based argument.[29] By "delegating the State's discretionary authority over public schools to a group defined by its character as a religious community," the state of New York had violated the important principle that "governmental power" should "be exercised neutrally." Similarly, the followers of the Baghwan Sri Rajnish were not permitted to establish a municipality, Rajnishpuram, that they would run according to their own lights: That too was regarded as an impermissible delegation of lawmaking power to a religious body.[30] The defendants argued that they could not practice their religion freely unless they were allowed to incorporate and run their own municipal government. The state denied this, however: The "joint exercise of legislative authority by church and state" was not necessary to the protection of religious freedom. The "potential injury to the anti-Establishment principle of the First Amendment by the existence and the operation of the City of Rajneeshpuram clearly outweighs the potential harm to defendants' free exercise of religion."

The second limitation that has traditionally been observed, when accommodation is allowed at all, is a more general and a vaguer one: Wherever a "compelling state interest" obtains, it may outweigh even a "substantial burden" to some individual or group's free exercise of religion. The classic compelling interests, under U.S. law, were peace and safety: Even before the Revolution, most state constitutions incorporated exceptions to religious freedom for that purpose. Over time, others have

[29] *Board of Education, Kiryas Joel Village School District v. Grumet*, 512 U. S. 687 (1994).
[30] *State of Oregon v. City of Rajneeshpuram*, 598 F. Supp. 1208 (D. Ore. 1984).

been recognized: administrative unworkability of an accommodation, for example; or government's interest in using its own property for the common good; or, in an interesting case concerning education, the governmental interest in educating young people to be respectful citizens of a pluralistic democracy.[31]

The notion of "compelling state interest" has never been given a systematic analysis. In my book, *Women and Human Development*, I have proposed that one useful analysis would be to think of a group of fundamental entitlements as always trumping claims of accommodation. In my case, it is the list of the ten Central Human Capabilities, conceived as core entitlements of all citizens founded on justice (Nussbaum 2000, chapter 3). But let us stick to India: We can find this idea of core entitlements in the section of the constitution entitled "Fundamental Rights," and we know already that the personal laws were exempted from the scrutiny of those Fundamental Rights. According to the view I am developing, that is a grave error. Accommodation can be permitted only within the constraints set by the Fundamental Rights. Within those constraints, some dispensation from laws of general application may be allowed. (For example, the use of marijuana during the Hindu festival of Holi is legal, and if a statute had not created this exemption, there would be a strong case to be made that the courts should create an accommodation, because no compelling state interest exists on the other side.) But if Muslims wish to claim that the right to polygamous marriage is a key part of their religion, and that they should therefore be exempted from generally applicable marriage restrictions, they will, on my view, need to show that polygamy does not run afoul of any constitutional constraint, such as the right to nondiscrimination on grounds of sex. If they cannot make that case, the dispensation will not be granted.

What I have just said presupposes a uniform civil and criminal code, envisaging exemptions from some elements of that for religious purposes. What about the systems of personal law? It should be unproblematic for religions to solemnize marriages in accordance with their own rules. State rules for marriage and divorce, however, should not be written or enforced by a religious body on the Establishment/equality grounds I outlined in my previous section. Thus, the personal laws should never have been permitted to persist. Once they were in place, however, what should have taken place? Probably selective invalidation of those provisions that offend against sex equality and religious equality would have been the best starting point. In the end, however, the delegation of major lawmaking powers to nondemocratic, nonaccountable groups is itself a problem, offending against the equal protection of the laws. Therefore, the entire system could, in principle, have been found unconstitutional, or the adoption by Parliament of a uniform civil code might have forestalled such a destabilizing decision.

[31] *Mozert v. Hawkins County Bd. Of Educ.*, 827 F. 2d 1058 (1987).

NEGOTIATION: *LATIFI V. UNION OF INDIA*

None of this happened. As we have seen, the political movement toward a Uniform Code that was well underway was abruptly derailed by the *Shah Bano* decision, which, taking place in a general atmosphere of growing anti-Muslim agitation, convinced many Muslims that a "Uniform Code" would very likely mean a "Hindu Code." They dropped their support for the Uniform Code and began to support the continued authority of the personal laws, even at the cost of denying an elderly indigent woman a living. The Muslim Women's Bill was a shocking result, albeit understandable under the circumstances.

For many years, progressives and feminists asked about the next move. As we saw in the first section of this chapter, after the destruction of the Babri Masjid in 1992 and the ensuing rise to power of the BJP in a coalition government, most progressive people dropped the tainted cause of the Uniform Code. Feminists have continued to press for uniform law in some areas not previously covered by law: The recent Domestic Violence Act is one example.

Meanwhile, many people began championing the cause of internal reform within the religions: If feminists and other egalitarians worked aggressively to promote such reforms, the differences among the codes would be ironed out over time, as all came around, more and more, to the constitutional equality standards embodied in the Fundamental Rights. So we would gain uniformity in the most important matters, without divisive takeovers, or the specter of Hindu hegemony. That course has been pursued with success in some areas: Christian divorce, Hindu property law. It is unsatisfactory, however, because of its cumbersome delays (as reformers still have to convince male clerics in each religion and then move Parliament) and its piecemeal character.

Still other people – for example, the legal NGO The Lawyers' Collective, which has worked on most major Supreme Court cases involving sex equality – have focused on overturning statutes that seem clearly violative of fundamental rights – thus allowing difference to flourish within the constraints of basic entitlements, the course I have been defending. In effect, they are asking the Court to reverse its earlier decision that the personal laws are exempt from the scrutiny of Fundamental Rights. This strategy is a piecemeal way of achieving the goal that I recommend: limiting religious accommodation in accordance with the compelling state interest of securing fundamental rights. In the wake of *Shah Bano*, however, such a strategy risks alienating groups who have learned to identify civic equality with the continued authority of the personal-law system.

A case from 2001, *Danial Latifi & Anr. v. Union of India*,[32] found a creative route out of this dilemma. The case concerned a challenge to the Muslim Women's

[32] 2001 7 SCC 740.

Act. The Court emphasized that, prima facie, the Act is unconstitutional, under three distinct articles. Article 21, which guarantees the right to life and liberty, and which has been interpreted to include the right to a life commensurate with human dignity,[33] is violated if the Act indeed deprives an indigent divorced Muslim woman of maintenance in such a way as to force her into a condition of vagrancy. Article 14, which guarantees equality before the law, is violated by an Act that gives Muslim women disadvantages that do not apply to women of other religions. Finally, Article 15, which forbids discrimination on the ground of religion, is also violated, "as the Act would obviously apply to Muslim divorced woman only and solely on the ground of their belonging to the Muslim religion."

On the other hand, a well-known (and international) principle of statutory interpretation, which the court goes on to cite, tells us that if there is an interpretation of a law according to which it is constitutional, that interpretation must be preferred to one under which it is unconstitutional. The Justices then go on – with many twistings and turnings involving the distinction between "provision" and "maintenance" and the precise meaning of the word "within" – to produce a rather unlikely but still possible reading of the Act, according to which Muslim women could claim the very same maintenance to which other women are entitled under the Criminal Procedure Code, and which the Bill had seemed to remove from Muslim women. The Act is upheld, but only under an interpretation according to which it means virtually the opposite of what most of its interpreters, including the politicians who sought its passage, took it to mean.

In the process, the Court advances a very interesting further interpretive principle. Statutes, the Justices hold, must always be interpreted in the light of current social conditions, which in this case prominently include male domination.

> In interpreting the provisions where matrimonial relationship is involved, we have to consider the social conditions prevalent in our society. In our society, whether they belong to the majority or the minority group, what is apparent is that there exists a great disparity in the matter of economic resourcefulness[34] between a man and a woman. Our society is male dominated both economically and socially and women are assigned, invariably, a dependant role, irrespective of the class of society to which she belongs.

How is this relevant to interpreting the statute? The Court goes on to say that anyone who knows these facts knows that women denied maintenance after divorce are thrust into a very vulnerable position. In consequence, such a person will understand

33 *Olga Tellis vs. Bombay Municipal Corporation*, 1985 (3)SCC545; cf. also *Maneka Gandhi vs. UOI*, 1978 (1) SCC 248.

34 *Sic*. The Court clearly means "access to resources," not the psychological characteristic of resourcefulness.

that a reasonable degree of maintenance that "partakes [of] basic human rights to secure gender and social justice is universally recognized by persons belonging to all religions and it is difficult to perceive that Muslim law intends to provide a different kind of responsibility." In other words, a reasonable person (that common legal fiction) will understand that women require a decent level of maintenance after divorce as a matter of basic human rights; it would be too discriminatory to suppose that Muslim law is not reasonable in this way. Therefore, an interpretation of the statute that comes to the conclusion that Muslim law provides for a woman's basic human rights is to be preferred over one that comes to the opposite conclusion.

What is so fascinating about this paragraph – and, I think, so splendid – is that it does, in effect, take my ideal solution, namely finding that Fundamental Rights trump religious accommodations, but it does so in such a devious way that the integrity and authority of Muslim law are preserved and the community is shown respect rather than offense. Rather than saying, "Muslim law here violates Fundamental Rights and must be overruled," the Court says, "Surely Muslims are reasonable people and must understand what all reasonable people understand about women's needs and women's rights. Therefore, the law must be interpreted in such a way as to grant them these rights. Any other interpretation would be an insult to the reasonableness of Muslims and Muslim law." How much better this is than the contemptuous utterances of the Court in *Shah Bano*.

The Court now recognizes that some authorities on Islamic law have argued that the Act does not grant women this generous maintenance. But, the Court now says, we do not need to defer to these particular religious authorities: "Solutions to … societal problems of universal magnitude pertaining to horizons of basic human rights, culture, dignity and decency of life and dictates of necessity in the pursuit of social justice should be invariably left to be decided on considerations other than religion or religious faith or beliefs or national, sectarian, racial or communal constraints." In other words, our argument, based on general considerations of human rights *and* on the reasonableness of Islamic law and Muslims, cannot be rebutted by this or that religious authority.

In my view, this opinion represents a balanced and reasonable solution to the problem of accommodation in today's India. On the one hand, the system of plural establishment is respected, up to a point. There is no aggressive attempt to undo every aspect of the control exercised by religious law over lawmaking. Indeed, throughout the opinion, Muslim law is treated with respect. On the other hand, the area of control by nondemocratically accountable Muslim leaders is seen as sharply bounded: It must not affect basic rights or matters of basic justice and human dignity. This protected sphere is understood to include the matter of sex equality, religious equality, and, generally, equality before the laws and a right to life with human dignity (thus, Articles 14, 15, and 21). In a brilliant argumentative move, this constraint is held to come not from an external imposition on Muslims or Muslim law, but from respect for the inherent reasonableness and decency of both.[35]

Another case of creative interpretation – in this case involving a partnership between legislators and courts – pertains to bigamy. It had become common for Hindus who wished to contract a new marriage without getting involved in potentially costly divorce proceedings to convert to Islam in order to add the new wife. Two decisions of the Supreme Court made clear that this practice makes a mockery of both religions and of the legal order, and is illegitimate.[36] Nonetheless, high-profile cases of remarriage in this vein, violative of the Court's decisions, kept surfacing.[37] The Law Commission of India therefore studied the question and issued a report recommending five specific legislative changes in the relevant personal laws and the Special Marriage Act, in order to make the decisions of the Court legally binding.[38] Like the *Latifi* decision, the Report emphasized the reasonableness of actual Islamic traditions, which permit bigamy only with the consent of the first wife and do not countenance the abandonment of a first wife to join a second.[39] They are highly critical of the Hindu Marriage Act's definition of monogamy, which "provides built-in devices for an easy avoidance" of the requirement of monogamy. They stress the fact that the conversions are usually sham, and thus a "fraud on Islamic law" and "repugnant to the Islamic religion and law." In this way they attempt to show that standing up for women's rights against abandonment without maintenance and without consent is not at all inimical to any genuine Muslim or Hindu tradition, but only to unscrupulous individuals who use loopholes in the law to pursue selfish ends.

If such a process of reinterpreting – together with findings of unconstitutionality where reinterpreting does not work – could be applied consistently across the whole range of the personal laws, would there be any reason to prefer a Uniform Code of civil law? Reasons still might exist, because the religious bodies themselves are often undemocratic and unrepresentative. Moreover, the whole system of classification

35 Problems still remain to be solved. In particular, Muslim women are still governed by the 1989 Dissolution of Muslim Marriages Act with respect to where they can initiate divorce proceedings: A woman must file either where she was married or where her husband lives. Corresponding provisions of the Hindu Marriage Act and the Special Marriage Act have been amended in 2001 to allow women to file divorce petitions where they live (Wajihuddin 2010).

36 *Sarla Mudgal v. Union of India*, AIR 1995 SC 1531; *Lily Thomas v. Union of India* (2000), 6 SCC 224.

37 See Law Commission (2009). One case they describe involved a prominent politician who abandoned his wife and family, disappeared, and turned up later with a new bride saying that he had converted to Islam; the other involved an army physician stationed in Afghanistan who converted to Islam to marry an Afghan girl who was his interpreter, concealing from her the fact of his prior marriage.

38 Law Commission (2009).

39 Law Commission (2009, chapter 5). The report emphasizes that Islam was a reform movement on this point in its original historical context: Polygamy was very narrowly circumscribed by the requirement of consent and equal treatment, and the Quran makes monogamy the default position. As they stress, bigamy is extremely rare among Muslims in India.

entrenches citizens within a system from birth, making it very difficult for them to exit from one system to another, especially if they hold shares in jointly owned property. Even in a regime of full legal equality in the areas touched on by Fundamental Rights, there is a religious-freedom problem when individuals cannot without sacrifice and difficulty extricate themselves from entanglement in a particular religious system. Nonetheless, these problems might themselves be eased by reform (especially in the law of property).

THE FUTURE OF PERSONAL LAWS

My argument has shown that there is an interesting moral and legal argument for the recognition of personal law, an argument from equal liberty that parallels standard arguments for religiously grounded accommodation. I hope I have also shown, however, that granting a religious body the right to make law involves a host of problems that suggest that the line drawn by U.S. constitutional law is a wise one: Religious bodies exceed reasonable accommodation when they ask for lawmaking privileges, and granting them these privileges creates an establishment problem that is closely linked to a variety of inequalities. The best way to avoid these problems is not to accede to the demand for personal laws in the first place. (I do not mean to say that religions cannot continue to decide matters internal to that religion, such as excommunication,[40] or religious marriage and divorce, where those are distinct from the public option and the public option is easily available to all.) This best course may not be politically feasible when, as in India, the systems are already in existence and have a long track record. The second-best course would then be to hold that the personal laws are understood in advance of particular cases to be always limited by the menu of fundamental rights of individuals that a nation has chosen to recognize.

If, however, one has not taken either of these sensible courses, one may make up for that error by exercising judicial ingenuity in the manner of India's Supreme Court in *Latifi*, which managed to show respect to the minority community and its legal tradition while standing up firmly for the equal rights of Muslim women, or in the manner of the Law Commission in its bigamy report, which stands up for Hindu women while showing respect for the genuine religious traditions of both communities.

ACKNOWLEDGMENTS

I would like to thank Tom Ginsburg for his encouragement and for creating such a stimulating event for interdisciplinary exchange. For helpful comments on an

[40] Such has not always been the position of champions of church-state separation: Moses Mendelssohn, in *Jerusalem*, argues that churches should not retain the power of excommunication, or be allowed to hold property.

earlier draft, I am grateful to Rajmohan Gandhi, Donald Horowitz, Eric Posner, and Adrian Vermeule.

REFERENCES

Agarwal, Bina 2004. *A Field of One's Own: Gender and Land Rights in South Asia*. Cambridge: Cambridge University Press.

Agarwal, Bina and Panda, Pradip 2007. "Toward Freedom from Domestic Violence: The Neglected Obvious," *Journal of Human Development* 8: 359–88.

Baird, Robert (ed.) 1993. *Religion and Law in Independent India*. Delhi: Manohar.

Das, Veena 1992. *Critical Events*. Delhi: Oxford University Press.

Engineer, Asghar Ali (ed.) 1987. *The Shah Bano Controversy*. Delhi: Ajanta.

Galanter, Marc 1984. *Competing Equalities: Law and the Backward Castes in India*. Delhi: Oxford University Press.

1989. *Law and Society in Modern India*. Oxford: Oxford University Press.

Hasan, Zoya (ed.) 1994. *Forging Identities: Gender, Communities, and the State in India*. Boulder, CO: Westview.

Jaising, Indira (ed.) 1996. *Justice for Women: Personal Laws, Women's Rights and Law Reform*. Mapasu, Goa: The Other India Press.

Jaising, Indira (ed.) 2005. *Men's Laws, Women's Lives: A Constitutional Perspective on Religion, Common Law and Culture in South Asia*. Delhi: Women Unlimited.

Law Commission of India 2009. *Preventing Bigamy via Conversion to Islam – A Proposal for Giving Statutory Effect to Supreme Court Rulings*. Government of India Report No. 227, August.

Mahmood, Tahir 1983. *Muslim Personal Law, Role of the State in the Indian Subcontinent*. Nagpur: Vikas.

Nussbaum, Martha C. 2000. *Women and Human Development: The Capabilities Approach*. Cambridge and New York: Cambridge University Press.

2005. "India, Sex Equality, and Constitutional Law," in Beverley Baines and Ruth Rubio-Marin (eds.), *The Gender of Constitutional Jurisprudence*. Cambridge: Cambridge University Press, 2005, pp. 174–205.

2007. *The Clash Within: Democracy, Religious Violence, and India's Future*. Cambridge, MA: Harvard University Press.

2008. *Liberty of Conscience: In Defense of America's Tradition of Religious Equality*. New York: Basic Books.

Parashar, Archana 1992. *Women and Family Law Reform in India: Uniform Civil Code and Gender Equality*. Delhi: Sage.

Qureshi, Mohammed A. 1978. *Marriage and Matrimonial Remedies: A Uniform Civil Code for India*. Delhi: Concept Publishing Company.

Sarkar, Tanika 2000. *Hindu Wife, Hindu Nation*. Delhi: Permanent Black.

Sen, Amartya 2005. *The Argumentative Indian*. London: Allen Lane.

Wajihuddin, Mohammed 2010. "Nikah," *The Times of India*, April 11. Online at http://timesofindia.indiatimes.com/home/Sunday-toi/special-report/Nikah/articleshow/5783043.cms

11

Constitutional Adjudication, Italian Style

John Ferejohn and Pasquale Pasquino

INTRODUCTION

We have written elsewhere of the rise of constitutional adjudication in the postwar period, especially in Europe (Ferejohn and Pasquino 2004, 2009). We emphasized in our previous work that the new institutions of constitutional adjudication were nearly always created following periods of authoritarian rule: initially in Germany and Italy following the World War II, then in Greece, Spain, and Portugal following the collapse of authoritarian regimes, and again in Eastern Europe and post-Soviet Russia after the fall of the communist regimes in those countries.[1] We distinguished among three ideal typical regimes, which we called the Italian, German, and French models. Of course, our discussion of the French case emphasized that it was special both because it was not an authoritarian regime prior to the establishment of the Fifth Republic and because the French *Conseil Constitutionnel* was not really established as a constitutional court, although it has effectively become one after the constitution was amended in 1974.[2] Nevertheless, we included this special case because it was established in a new constitution and because as of this writing,

[1] There are exceptions: The South African system of constitutional adjudication was instituted following the apartheid regime that may not have been authoritarian in the same way as those mentioned in the text. We discuss the French Conseil in the text. Recently, Wojciech Sadurski has expressed reservations about the "exceptionalist" thesis: "Judicial Review in Central and Eastern Europe: Rationales or Rationalizations?" Paper presented to the conference "Judicial Review: Why, Where, and For Whom?" May 31–June 1, 2009, Hebrew University of Jerusalem.

[2] The Conseil was established in the 1958 Constitution as a device to control the legislature by permitting the majority the right to appeal legislative decisions. Insofar as the conservative majority retained effective control in the legislature, this right of appeal was rarely used, except in one critically important case in 1971 when the majority fractured over a constitutional issue and the Conseil ended up overturning a government-backed law. In 1974, the government of Giscard D'Estaing obtained a *constitutional* amendment that permitted parliamentary minorities in either chamber the right to appeal against legislation. This right effectively gave the minority a right to appeal nearly any important governmental law, and it has been extensively employed to check governmental projects.

it plainly has demonstrated its potential to develop into a genuine instrument for constitutional adjudication.

Each of the three models exhibits a specialized constitutional court, which has prima facie a monopoly on constitutional adjudication – an institution that we and others have characterized as Kelsenian. Each of these courts is empowered to strike down legislation in certain circumstances. The chief differences among them have to do with the point in time when they can overturn a statute (or other legal order); whether they can control legislative or judicial (as in Germany) as well as parliamentary and executive actions; and what parties are able to gain access to them.[3] Roughly speaking, in the French model, the *Conseil* can overturn statutes prior to their promulgation, cannot review administrative or judicial actions, and can only be accessed by political actors, and mostly by the political minority in the parliament.[4] In the German model, the Federal Constitutional Court (*Bundesverfassungsgericht*) can review judicial and administrative final orders on appeal in constitutional complaint by an individual citizen, and can overturn parliamentary statutes in the judicial process. In the Italian model, the court can review statutes if it is asked to rule on them by the judge of an ordinary court.

Whereas our earlier work noted that the German model – which is open to ordinary citizens through the device of the constitutional complaint – was widely applied in the "third" surge of constitutionalism, which followed the collapse of the Soviet system, commentators have said relatively little about the Italian model in that context. As we explain, the two models have very significant political implications and need to be distinguished. In fact, there is recent evidence that what we are calling the Italian model may already be significant in postcommunist Europe. In a recent survey of postcommunist constitutional courts, Sadurski writes that, "The possibility of judicial review submitted through lower court referral channels exists in twelve of

3 The control has been so far only *ex ante* in France, meaning that it operates only after the bill has been approved by the Parliament but before its promulgation. Both the German and Italian Constitutional Courts can exert *ex post control*: In the Italian case, the Court can review a statute as soon as its application is challenged in a court, or immediately after the promulgation of the statute. In the German model, the Constitutional Court can conduct a constitutional review after the exhaustion of legal remedies. This question of temporality is very important and has never been clearly discussed in comparative analysis.

4 A minority of sixty members of the House (the *Assemblée nationale*) or of the Senate is required for a referral; de facto, it is only the parliamentary opposition that sends referrals to the Constitutional Court – we know only one exception, the first *saisine*, in 1975. Also the president of the republic, the prime minister, and the presidents of the House and the Senate are allowed to send referrals. The most important case was the referral by the President of the Senate Alain Poher in 1971, which is at the origin of the opinion that created the so-called *bloc de constitutionnalité*, making the *Preamble* of the Constitution of the Fifth Republic, the 1789 and 1946 Declarations of Rights, and the "fundamental principles of the republic" into constitutional texts that could serve as standards for the decisions of the Constitutional Council.

the twenty countries in the region. In Poland, for instance, so-called 'legal questions' addressed by regular courts to the Constitutional Tribunal ... constitute now by far the highest proportion of all initiations of the review of constitutionality: in 2008 there were 121 such cases, compared with 25 initiations of abstract constitutional review by authorized organs" (Sadurski 2009: 11).

Recently it has become clear that the recent efflorescence of practices of constitutional adjudication, in Latin America, has seen the appearance of what we call the Italian model – in which the constitutional court decides constitutional issues that arise in the course of ordinary litigation.[5] At one level this is surprising, because most of the Latin American countries have long had the *amparo* or constitutional complaint – which postpones the question of whether a person's rights have been violated until the litigation in civil or administrative courts is complete – which is also the most common instrument of the German system of constitutional adjudication. Although it is true that the specific form of constitutional review varies widely throughout the region, one might have thought that increasingly vigorous constitutional adjudication would have relied on existing legal instruments and specifically the constitutional complaint. As far as we can see, however, that has not really been the case everywhere. Rather, there has been experimentation with other forms of constitutional adjudication. Why? The idea we explore is this: Introducing effective constitutional review entails a shift in judicial-political relations, especially the relation between the ordinary judge and the institution that makes the final legal judgment on constitutional issues.

In our earlier papers, we suggested that the different models of constitutional adjudication effectively created "coalitional" partners in the political-constitutional system. The German model, focused on reviewing final rulings by ordinary or administrative courts, enlists citizens to challenge judges. The German Constitutional Court (GCC) is in this respect a kind of "popular" court – of course it is not at all similar to the Athenian popular courts (the *dikasteria*) that were made up of citizens sorted by lotteries – because it is a court open to the complaint of any citizen who feels that their

5 The recent increase of constitutional adjudication throughout Latin America is very complex, and there are many more "models" on display in the region than our very simple categorization can account for. Julio Rios-Figueroa has recently provided a very useful survey and analysis of Latin American practices using the traditional analytical categories (abstract vs. concrete; a priori vs. a posteriori, centralized vs. decentralized, *intra partes* vs. *ergo omnes*): "Institutions for Constitutional Justice in Latin America," in Gretchen Helmke and Julio Ríos-Figueroa (eds.) *Courts in Latin America* (New York: Cambridge University Press, 2011). These categories, while they may be useful in giving an overview of change over time, are difficult to fit with the Italian model that is, in various ways, both concrete and abstract. That is to say, a referral to the Italian Constitutional Court (ICC) is normally initiated in a concrete case. But the ICC does not decide the case, but only judges the statute (deciding to strike it down in whole or in part, or to rewrite it, or to restrict its interpretation), referring the case back to the judge to decide the concrete case.

rights have been violated in a judicial or administrative setting. [6] In the Italian model, by contrast, the court is not open to citizens but to judges: The Italian Constitutional Court (ICC) cannot act unless a judge appeals for a ruling so ICC is in that sense allied with ordinary judges, and its creation effectively empowered these judges to take a part in constitutional review. In the French model, since 1974, the alliance is between the *Conseil Constitutionnel* and the parliamentary minority, which has the power to effectively activate a constitutional review of a statute. The constitutional amendment passed in 1974 permitting minority appeals effectively gave the minority some power to control the majority through the Constitutional council.

While each of these new constitutional institutions created a new characteristic set of coalition partners, it also created characteristic opponents. In Germany, the opponents are ordinary or administrative judges whose work is being put under a microscope in the German Constitutional Court (GCC). In France, it is the parliamentary majority and nowadays the president of the republic, whose work is being evaluated. In Italy, while government legislation is being judged as in France, the

6 In this context, it is possible to speak of "constitutional patriotism." This expression was introduced in Germany by the political scientist Dolf Sternberger (1979: 13–16), who wrote notably:

> State authority is not concentrated in one place, neither at the top nor the bottom, neither on the left nor the right; instead, it is distributed widely. We participate in it in many ways, not only passively and enduringly but also actively. The constitution does not live only in the parliaments of the Federal Republic, not only in the states and local communities, not only in the governments and administrations. In addition, the courts serve as the "third power," particularly those that check and balance the legislature and the executive; they have proven amazingly effective in keeping political power within its limits. Social organizations, in all their diversity, exist and work as guaranteed by the basic freedom of association; they represent the powers of a living constitution, even if they are not aware of it. It is up to the political institutions to respect their rights and to keep their enthusiasms from running roughshod. Every collective bargaining session is part of the living constitution; and the autonomy of the bargaining agents, who require no intervention by the authorities, itself represents a piece of the state. Not to mention the simultaneous conversation between the many voices of so-called public opinion that grows out of the freedom of speech and information. Citizens' initiatives and demonstrations are also part of a living constitution: the state is present not only in the squads of police officers who escort them and assure the peacefulness required by the constitution. It is a good constitution that provides for all these things and for a powerful leadership. We do not have to be afraid to praise the Basic Law. At any particular moment we might censure the government, charge the opposition with being too weak, resent the flood of laws passed by the parliament, find spirit and imagination generally lacking in the parties, feel burdened by bureaucracy, and consider the trade unions too demanding and the reporters too intrusive – the constitution allows all of this to be improved; it advises and encourages us to improve it. A certain degree of moderate dissatisfaction serves to benefit the state. It doesn't diminish the loyalty that is due the constitution. But the constitution must be defended against declared enemies – that is a patriotic duty. (http://germanhistorydocs.ghi-dc.org/pdf/eng/Chapter14Doc6Intro.pdf)

Jürgen Habermas made the expression of constitutional patriotism popular in a variety of his writings (for instance: *A Berlin Republic. Writings on Germany* [Cambridge: Polity Press, 1998]). It is possible to argue that the constitutional complaints are an instrument by which the citizens participate in the defense of the constitution, playing an active role in the defense of their own rights.

other rivals were the traditional supreme courts (actually the two highest appellate courts in the Italian judicial system: the *Corte di Cassazione* and the *Consiglio di Stato*), which lost their monopoly over reviewing the work of lower court judges. Of course, insofar as all these are systems of constitutional adjudication, the parliamentary majority is in all cases a potential opponent. But which parliamentary majority is opposed depends on the point in time when judicial review takes place. In France, it is the sitting parliament at the moment of promulgation. In Germany and Italy, the legislation of old parliaments and old majorities is vulnerable and current legislation is much less so (especially in Germany, where normally all ordinary remedies at law must be exhausted prior to filing a constitutional complaint). Moreover, as we have observed elsewhere, the constitutional complaint is rarely against a piece of legislation, but is usually directed against a judicial ruling.

The first three waves of the institutionalization of postwar constitutional adjudication (first, Germany, Italy, and Japan in the late 1940s after World War II;[7] second, Spain, Portugal, and Greece from the late 1970s; and third, South Korea in 1988, Eastern Europe after 1989, and South Africa in 1994) were mostly established in newly adopted constitutions; the fourth wave (Latin America) has seen fewer new constitutions. Rather, older institutions and structures – generally intended for other uses – have been transformed in ways that permit them to achieve higher levels of constitutional adjudication.[8] This situation is perhaps similar in this respect to the unexpected evolution of the French *Conseil Constitutionnel* into a constitutional court in that a preexisting set of alliances had to be rearranged for the transformation to occur. In France, this was accomplished by a split among the conservatives (in 1971) and by the decline of the *gaulliste* majority, which may have produced a constitutional amendment (1974). In the Latin American countries, something similar may be happening, notably in Chile, which we discuss later in the chapter. That is at least what we conjecture.

7 We do not discuss Japan here because, unlike the other Axis powers, it did not adopt a specialized constitutional court, but rather was forced by the American framers of its constitution to keep constitutional-review powers inside the judiciary with a powerful Supreme Court at its apex. It stands as the one postauthoritarian nation to have adopted an American-style solution but with an even more institutionally powerful Supreme Court at the top.

8 A good example of this is Uruguay, which has not created a constitutional tribunal or court but authorizes its Supreme Court to receive referrals on constitutional questions from ordinary courts, as in the Italian model. It may be significant that Uruguay's Supreme Court is part of the regular judiciary because it gives to the judiciary the power to check the legislature, which is a very substantial departure from the notions of parliamentarism that have been widely accepted throughout those countries with some democratic experience, which requires judges to apply legislative texts quite literally. And as a cautionary note, we point out that constitutional review powers of the Uraguayian Supreme Court were swept away in the 1973 coup when the constitution itself was suspended in favor of a presidential/military dictatorship (and constitutional rule was not reestablished until the late 1980s).

There is an irony in the late evolution of constitutional adjudication in Latin America. Most of the Latin American countries have long had supreme courts empowered to undertake constitutional adjudication. And because nearly all of the Latin American legal systems had some form of the *amparo* (constitutional complaint), one might have thought that their courts would have been open to popular grievances about violations of fundamental rights. Typically, however, those courts and the lower judiciaries were dominated by very conservative legal professionals who were inclined to show a great deal of deference to whatever regime was in power, and especially to be highly protective of property interests. Moreover, the *amparo* was often restricted to having only *intra partes* effects, as perhaps seemed natural in civil-law systems. As in most of Europe, the lower courts tended to be staffed by judges recruited into the judicial career out of law school. Typically the supreme court exercised a great deal of control over the careers of ordinary judges and not merely their particular rulings. And often, membership on the supreme court was very dependent on the political regime (Argentina and Mexico are telling examples). This situation is in many ways similar to other political circumstances: The court system in contemporary Japan seems to present a similar picture. The Japanese, however, have not, so far, decided to reform their judicial institutions in the direction of any of the European models (as, for example, the Koreans have). So from our perspective, it is the postwar transformation in Italy that offers the most illuminating parallel.

A key aspect of that transformation was a breakdown of the traditional left opposition to judicial review. From the standpoint of the Italian Communist Party, conservative property protecting judges could not be trusted to review new legislation that they hoped and expected to issue from the new parliament. Surely some of that new legislation would seek to institute social legislation and to disturb traditional institutions of property.[9] As things transpired, the left was to be disappointed in short order because they were unable to win the legislative elections in 1948. Prior to that (unexpected) setback, the only way the left could have been persuaded to accept any kind of constitutional review was to keep it out of the hands of the judges, and especially those high-court judges who controlled the judicial institutions. That is the reason that the Kelsenian model of a Constitutional Court was politically required in Italy, since a Kelsenian Court is located mostly outside the judiciary.

But there are many ways that such a court could have been implemented, and it is necessary to ask how this new institution was supposed to work. The Cassation Court proposed to control referrals to the new ICC – thereby making it its political

[9] It is a sort of paradox that progressive legislation expropriating southern Italian *latifundia* was passed by the Christian-democratic governments under American impulsion at the end of the 1940s and at the beginning of the 1950s, to defuse the danger of a stronger control of the communists over the poor peasants of the south of the country.

dependent in a way. Proponents of the new court saw that this would weaken it, perhaps fatally, and proposed instead to permit any judge to refer questions to it. Because no single body could control access to the court, none could stop it from deciding a question if there was any judge in the whole country who could be persuaded that there was a constitutional issue at stake. In effect, ordinary judges were invited to compete with each other to play a role in the process of constitutional adjudication. This system made it very likely that constitutionally dubious statutes (and many of these would have been enacted during the quarter-century of Mussolini's government) would be examined in the ICC. And it no doubt liberated the ordinary judges from control by the higher judiciary (who rose to their posts during the fascist period).

We think some of the postwar "Italian" circumstances have been reproduced more recently: a conservative judiciary, inclined to defer to the executive, where both the judicial decisions and judicial careers are controlled by the higher courts, and where there is a felt political need to reconcile left and right to the transition. Such a circumstance may have held in several countries in Eastern Europe after the collapse of the Soviet-supported regimes. It also may have occurred during at least some of the transitions from authoritarian rule in Latin America, and specifically in Chile.

THE ITALIAN MODEL

The standard account of *constitutional adjudication* in continental Europe emphasizes its differences with the American mechanism of *judicial review*, an opposition based on three major structural differences: (1) it is *concentrated* in a specialized constitutional tribunal rather than *diffused* throughout the judiciary; (2) it permits a priori review rather than being confined to a posteriori adjudication of constitutional claims; and (3) the questions posed in a constitutional court are *abstract* – asking whether a legislative text is constitutional – rather than *concrete*.[10] Here we want to dwell on the last dichotomy to show why it is misleading.

The abstract-concrete dichotomy is actually based (as is much of the comparative analysis in this field) on the French case in which litigation could never trigger constitutional review and was therefore necessarily abstract for that reason. But the history of constitutional adjudication in France is exceptional in the European panorama. And in any case, the original French model is now in some question because of the recent reform that permits judicial referrals to the *Constitutional Council* that the French parliament passed in 2009 – a question we discuss later. We shall also say something on the first opposition, concentrated versus diffuse review. As to the second dichotomy, a priori versus a posteriori, it is also drawn from France where,

[10] Typical of this dichotomous approach is Favoreu (1990).

at least until the enforcement of the recent constitutional reform, no statute could be nullified, because only voted bills before their promulgation could be declared unconstitutional.

Narrowly rational choice (we would say, materialist) explanations of the origin of political institutions, such as constitutional courts (Ginsburg 2003), tend to focus on the *interests* of political actors. But one can seek a more general account that takes into account the way actors conceive of their interests, and specifically by considering two other factors, *ideology* and *myopia*. By ideology we mean the beliefs and values publically held by political actors – which may be different from their private opinions and intentions. These public attitudes are important because they represent ways that public actors are constrained to explain their activities. Myopia may also be seen as the "short-term interests" of public actors, specifically the necessity of taking account of periodic elections or, to put it otherwise, the election cycle. We may illustrate the consequences of this broader formulation in the following narrative.

At the end of two years of intense and very interesting debates, the Constituent assembly of the post–World War II Italian Republic decided in December 1947 to establish a Constitutional Court, for the first time on the European continent, patterned after the Austrian *Verfassungsgericht* (the experience of Portugal in 1911, of Czechoslovakia in 1920, and of Spain during the Republic were too short to allow us to say anything relevant about them), which was established in 1920 and which was dismantled after 1930, when the man who inspired it, Hans Kelsen, was removed from the Court by the conservative political majority in Vienna.[11] The debate that took place inside the Italian Constituent Assembly was extremely contentious and could not be resolved until the very last days of the constitution-making process because of the stubborn and long-standing opposition of the social-communists and of the pro-British liberals, who defended the model of absolute parliamentary democracy.[12] Probably because of these divisions, the text of the constitution only specified the competences of the new organ and not the details of its implementation.[13] Because of the contentious nature of this decision, nothing could be specified in the constitution as to the mechanism of access to the Court – evidently a crucial question because

[11] The pretext of this decision was that Kelsen declared as unconstitutional a statute that made divorce impossible. Growing antisemitism was another cause of his removal (even though he had converted to Catholicism in 1905 and was, in any case, an agnostic. In the atmosphere of Austria at that time, evidently such things were no barrier to antisemitic persecution).

[12] On those debates, see P. Pasquino, "L'origine du contrôle de constitutionnalité en Italie: Les débats de l'Assemblée constituante (1946–47)," in *Rivista trimestrale di diritto pubblico*, 1 (2006), 1–11.

[13] In February 1948, the Constituent Assembly itself enacted Constitutional Law No. 1/1948, which stipulates who can petition the Court and in which way. Other implementation statutes were not enacted for some years as the short-run interests and beliefs of party leaders shifted with political events, so the Court did not begin to function until the spring of 1956.

without it, nobody could have opened the door of the institution – so that question was left to be resolved by a parliamentary statute.

In the section of the fundamental law on *Constitutional Guarantees* (notice that in the Italian Constitution, the Constitutional Court is not part of the judiciary, so it is established in a special part of the Constitutional text: "Guarantees of the Constitution" Title VI, Part II) we read:

> Art. 134
>
> The Constitutional Court shall pass judgment on:
>
> – controversies on the *constitutional legitimacy of laws* and enactments having force of law issued by the State and Regions;
>
> – conflicts arising from *allocation of powers of the State* and those powers allocated to State and Regions, and between Regions;
>
> – charges brought against the President of the Republic and the Ministers, according to the provisions of the Constitution (emphasis added).

The constitutional provision seems to imply indeed that the Court would work a mechanism that can be described as a Kelsenian (or Marshallian) constitutional syllogism: If a statute law, a norm of inferior rank, contradicts a constitutional provision, then the first one has to be cancelled in order to maintain the strict hierarchy of norms, which is required for a legal system with a *rigid* constitution. The phrasing of Article 134 apparently does not say who is able to activate the Court by bringing a case or question to it. As a court, the Constitutional Court was, by definition, a "passive" organ that had to wait to be asked before giving answers. It may have seemed natural (to the constituent assembly) that the Court had to be a political actor (as was established in the 1958 French Constitution), given that it was introduced to protect the losers of the elections from the winners, which could threaten and dismantle the constitutional compromise. But this is not what was actually decided in January 1948 when the first constitutional law was approved regulating the access to the Court.

Notice that the Constituent Assembly was still active after the approval of the constitution until the end of January, and moreover that the government, run by the Christian-democratic leader Alcide De Gasperi, was very keen to pass immediately a statute regulating the referral. This was because he very much wanted to activate the Constitutional Court as soon as possible so it would be able to maintain the constitutional bargain after the upcoming legislative elections, because there seemed a real possibility that the Christian Democrats would be defeated!

> The text of the article 1 of the constitutional [*ratione materiae*] law No. 1/1948 reads: "The question concerning the constitutional legitimacy of a statute law or of a norm of the same rank of the Italian Republic may be sent to the Constitutional Court

> by the *ordinary judge during* a trial or by one of the litigants, *if the judge* doesn't consider the question *evidently lacking any justification*" (emphasis added).[14]

Before considering the effects of this crucial decision, let us step back and consider the possible reasons that explain the behavior of the political actors during the Constituent Assembly. This body was divided in two almost equal political groups: the Christian-democrats on one side and the social-communists on the other (a very important intellectual role was also played by few other representatives, notably by Piero Calamandrei, a law professor, and by members of a left non-Marxist party, the *Partito d'Azione*, favorable to constitutional adjudication). As we have emphasized, the outcome of the upcoming legislative elections, scheduled after the end of the Constituent Assembly (April 18, 1948) seemed particularly uncertain to everyone. One would think that actors motivated by simple material interests would have agreed on the introduction of an independent organ able to protect the constitutional agreement to avoid the possibility that the newly elected majority could abuse its powers. At that time, however, only the Christian-democrats supported that project; with the exception of the minuscule *Partito d'Azione*, the left strongly opposed that idea (as did the French left in 1946, 1958, 1974, and 2008!). Why?

Supporting this provision would have seemed prima facie in the interests of the communists given that they had no (objective) certainty of repeating their very good score in 1946.[15] The reason can be presented as a peculiar mix of self-interest, ideology, and myopia. In effect, the social communists held beliefs, shaped by their ideological understanding of political structures and motivations and thought, that gave them a powerful advantage in the upcoming election. In other words, they thought that, for various historical and material reasons, they were likely to continue to gain strength in new elections and that nothing should be put in place to limit the powers they would inherit once they formed a majority. The ideological background of the social-communist public discourse was the Jacobin version of Rousseau's political theory: Popular sovereignty is exercised by the parliament, the only governmental organ with democratic legitimacy, because its members are elected, and by an executive accountable to it.[16] This further tapped into a long tradition of French political thought, which was opposed to any institutional limitations on direct majority control, such as bicameralism, for example. Any obstacle to the exercise of parliamentary power – that is, to the power of the elected majority – was considered a reactionary

[14] http://legislature.camera.it/_dati/Costituente/Lavori/LEGGI/68nc.pdf, for the Italian text.

[15] In fact the DC (Christian democratic party) won the absolute majority in the first legislature, 1948–1953.

[16] In the French Constitution of 1793, Article 64, we read: "[The executive council] shall be renewed each half session of every legislature, in the last months of its session [the legislature last one year]." This is evidently an extreme and peculiar form of accountability.

attempt to make impossible the social and political reforms that the working class would have been able to implement after winning the upcoming elections.

From this ideological viewpoint, a constitutional court was seen by the social-communists not only as an anachronistic aristocratic institution, but its unelected and unaccountable members seemed likely to be a bunch of conservative bourgeois empowered to stop the social and political reforms that would be passed by a democratic parliament. This view was not intrinsically wrong but just, as we will see, slightly myopic in combining Jacobin institutional ideology with the Marxist belief that the rise of the left was both inevitable and immediate and pointed to a victory of the social-communists at the very next election. And what if they would have lost the race? Well, they could have answered, not wrongly so: "Was it not a certainty that a conservative aristocratic court would be antagonistic to the interests of the Italian working class?" So, as far as they were concerned, there was no need for a constitutional court that would inevitably be a body defending the interests of the Catholic and conservative social elites (the obsession with the elites in social-communist discourse is a well-known mania).

Moreover, independently of their different ideologies and interests, both the social-communists and the Christian-democrats were thinking in short-sighted perspectives, which seemed natural for election-driven politicians. Both the Christian democrats and the left were quite sure that the judges (here the members of the Constitutional Court) in Italy would always be conservative and indoctrinated in the French legal culture requiring the strict subordination of judges to the letter of the positive statute law. As regards the constitutional court, this proved to be completely wrong.

The experience of the opposition after the staggering victory of the Christian-democrats in the election of April 1948 and the transformation in the culture of the Italian judges – very relevant in this perspective is the final declaration of *Gardone*'s meeting of the Italian ordinary judges in 1965, when they declared their *subordination to the constitution* before the subordination to statute laws[17] – is at the origin of the radical change of the attitude of the social-communist vis-à-vis the Court. But we have to come back now to the constitutional law enacted before the first legislative election in February 1948. Thanks to this statute, the ordinary judges were established as the gatekeepers of the Court. It is not difficult to understand why. Catholic, conservative, and largely educated under the fascist regime that lasted in Italy more than twenty years, and always subservient to the political branches, the ordinary Italian judges of the end of the 1940s certainly did not represent a threat to the power of the elected majority. In case of victory of the left, they would have very likely kept the door of

[17] Associazione nazionale magistrati, XII Congresso nazionale. Brescia-Gardone 25–28-IX 1965. Atti e commenti, Arti grafiche Jasillo, Roma, 1966, pp 309–310. See also: L'ordinamento giudiziario, edited by Alessandro Pizzorusso, Il Mulino, 1974, p. 31 fn.; the final report by Giuseppe Maranini, ivi, p. 257.

the Constitutional Court just as well closed as they would in the case of a Christian-democratic government. So this "bizarre idea" of the Court, as Togliatti described it, seemed to be a perfectly conservative mechanism, in that it would probably not disrupt the normal operations of parliamentary government. In the short run, this seems right. From a longer perspective, however, as the composition of the ordinary judiciary evolved, the choice made in January 1948 by the political class had important systemic consequences on the Italian mechanism of constitutional adjudication.

During the constitutional debates and in Article 134, the central idea was to guarantee the hierarchy of norms introduced by the *rigid* constitution, which, the Constituent Assembly had decided, would replace the *flexible* constitution (*Statuto Albertino*) that governed Piedmont from 1848 and then Italy from 1861 for one century and was no obstacle at all[18] to the establishment of a fascist regime. In this perspective, the job of the Constitutional Court had to consist simply – so to speak – in making sure that no statute would contradict the constitutional norm. Notice by the way that the section 2 of Article 134 gives the Court a connected and major function: the one of being the judge of the conflicts not only among the central government and the regions, like in the original jurisdiction attributed by the American Constitution to the U.S. Supreme Court, but also of *conflicts among the branches of the central government*. If we do not believe in the (Madisonian) mythology of a self-enforcing equilibrium of the horizontal distribution of power and also reject the Bodinian-Jacobin idea of legislative sovereignty, an independent judge of this type of conflicts represents the only possibility of conceiving of a limited governmental power. The German Federal Constitutional Court assumes the same competence under the name of *Organstreit*. Indeed, the German law speaks of *abstrakte Normenkontrolle* when the court has to decide of the constitutionality of a statute law *facially* we could say [*ohne dass subjektive Rechte verletzt sein müssten*], meaning independently from its enforcement or application, because the consequences

[18] Evidently a rigid constitution is not at all a guarantee of its stability, nor of the respect of its provision by the elected majority; a dramatic case in point is the Weimar constitution that was rigid and still entirely disregarded by Hitler. Article 76 of the Weimar Constitution states:

> The constitution may be amended by legislation. Constitutional changes become valid only if at least two thirds of the members are present and at least two thirds of the present members vote in favor of the amendment.
>
> Decisions of *Reichsrat* regarding a constitutional amendment also require a two-thirds-majority. If, requested by referendum petition, a constitutional amendment shall be decided by plebiscite, the majority of the enfranchised voters is required in order for the amendment to pass.
>
> If *Reichstag* decided on a constitutional amendment against *Reichsrat* objection, the Reich president may not proclaim the amendment, if *Reichsrat*, within a period of two weeks, demands a plebiscite to be held.

But if there is a Constitutional Court, which was not the case in Weimar Germany, the violation of the constitution can at least be signaled. Pakistan was recently an example of what we have in mind.

of the statute are supposed to be clear and clearly unconstitutional or not. But the mechanism of referral invented in Italy in 1948 introduced a different function of the Constitutional court making it a proper *co-legislator* quite far away from the simple Boolean logic according to which a statute can just be constitutional or not.

More and more starting from the 1960s, ordinary judges, recognizing that they were subordinate to the constitution even more than to statute laws, have been active in sending questions to the Constitutional Court in Rome. These questions are posed either by the litigants in a trial and sent to the Constitutional Court, or by the judges acting on their own.[19] Sending a question is not costly for the judge given the modest precondition for sending the question: *non manifesta infondatezza* (evident futility). In any case, the condition for a question arises during the trial and is very often not connected with the *facial* unconstitutionality of the norm, with the exception of old fascist statutes still on the books (notably the criminal law), but with what we could call the effects of the statute in its concrete enforcement/application. This corresponds roughly to the American distinction between facial challenge to a statute's constitutionality and an applied challenge to the statute's application under specific factual circumstances. So beginning in the 1970s, the Italian judges were asking the Constitutional Court: "Please, what do I have to do with this statute which, if applied in this case, seems to produce unconstitutional (we may want to say: unjust) effects?" Thus, because of the specific access mechanism, the Constitutional Court was asked to do more and less than exercise a constitutional syllogism; it was asked to help the judges in their job of doing justice in the specific case, by means of the constitutional interpretation of the law in the light of the specific facts of the case itself.

This is the concrete origin of a type of very important decision of the Constitutional Court called *interpretative di rigetto* (in Germany, where there is a similar tradition of adjudication, it is called *verfassungsmäßige Auslegung* or constitutional interpretation). Through such a determination the Court may declare a statute *constitutional*, provided it is interpreted in a way that the Court specifies in its opinion (*sentenza*). A number of important consequences follow:

1. The Constitutional Court is no longer a merely negative legislator of the Kelsenian doctrine; it does much more than just nullifying statutes, it rewrites them (co-legislative function).
2. The Constitutional Court starts not from the "facial content" of the statute, but from the problems emerging from the concrete enforcement of the statute in a particular case.

[19] We cannot say "from her" since the beginning, for in Italy, the judicial career opened to women only in 1965(!), thanks, by the way, to some opinions of the Constitutional Court, see notably the *Sentenza* n. 33/1960.

3. This makes it possible to limit potential conflicts with the political branches, because the statute is not cancelled but only modified through interpretation.
4. It makes obsolete the dichotomy between countermajoritarian and deferential Court's opinions (in Italy, like in France and mostly in Germany, it is not possible to speak of the opinions of the justices because the decisions are collective and the vote, when and if it takes place, is covered by secrecy; justices in these countries are like the members of a good string quartet not soloists).
5. The opinion of the Constitutional Court cannot, therefore, be considered "abstract" *stricto sensu*. To be sure, the decision is about the law and not directly about the case at the origin of the *preliminary question* sent by the judge, and its effect as the Italian doctrine says are *erga omnes* (not very different from a *precedent* in the so-called common-law legal systems), but the decision originates in the context of problems emerging from the concrete enforcement of the statute.
6. Because of its independence vis-à-vis the judicial power and its constitutional prerogatives, the Constitutional Court cannot (unlike the U.S. Supreme Court as the last appellate court of the judicial pyramid, and also unlike the *Bundesverfassungsgericht*, at least concerning constitutional questions) directly decide the case and can only provide an interpretation of the statute (Article 134 of the Italian constitution). However, the statute is not considered abstractly, but in terms of its real effects in actual circumstances; what is abstract is the language and the rhetoric of the Constitutional Court opinion.

We said at the beginning that the diffused/centralized dichotomy is part of the canonical opposition between the American judicial review and the European constitutional adjudication. Now it should be apparent that this opposition works only in a very limited perspective. It is true that Italian (ordinary) judges cannot nullify and even refuse to enforce statutes, but having a kind of quasi-monopoly of the referral, they effectively have in their hands the key that opens the door of the Constitutional Court and even more so in enforcing its decision, so it seems evident that they play a crucial role both *before* and *after* the opinion of the Constitutional Court. *They put it in motion and enforce its decision*. Without the cooperation of ordinary judges, the Constitutional Court would be a *vox clamans in deserto*. Moreover, this quasi monopoly extends beyond their constitutional role: ordinary Italian (like other European) judges can directly refer questions to the Court of Justice of the European Union and also enforce the CJEU's rulings within Italy.

This shows also how myopic were the leftist members of the Constituent Assembly opposing the Constitutional Court. The judicial body in Italy is the only branch of the central government able, with the cooperation of the Constitutional Court, to exercise an active counterpower vis-à-vis the political branches: the Parliament and the government. In a parliamentary *Parteienstaat*, like Italy, Germany, and France (notably since the introduction of the *quinquennat* that makes very unlikely the *cohabitation*, the French version of the American "divided government"), an elective counterpower is impossible (even though conflicts inside the governing majority are not impossible and may limit the power abuses by the elected branches). Moreover, the control *per via incidentale*, coming from the concrete questions that judges have to adjudicate, seems to be the best mechanism to protect individual rights. By that we do not mean only the rights of individuals in general (like voting or freedom of speech and religion) or those of groups that can organize themselves and act on the political system by lobbying or election. We mean the rights of individuals who have no access to the political process because they are too weak to coalesce or not rich or numerous enough to lobby (especially in countries that have almost no equivalent of the American Civil Liberties Union [ACLU]). A referral to the Constitutional Court costs, in principle, nothing.[20] Furthermore, its members are not up for reelection so that they can care a bit more about justice than about consent.

In a more important sense, constitutional adjudication of the Italian type puts an end to the myth of the negative legislator as it allows us to redefine the old and obsolete doctrine of the governmental functions. It is not any more believable to claim that the legislators enact statutes and the judges apply them. But legislative and judicial organs each have normative power, in the Kelsenian language, the power of *Rechtserzeugung* – each can produce legal norms. The Parliament enacts general and abstract norms, so to speak, under a veil of ignorance. Even Portalis, the father of the French postrevolutionary codification, recognized that the legislator cannot foresee everything[21] and even less, we would add, the effects of the general and abstract enacted statutes. The Constitutional Court with the help of the ordinary courts of justice rewrites, partially, statutes on the basis of the often unforeseeable consequences of them. And if needed, it can exercise the function of *eipieikeia*,[22] which abstract laws cannot really recognize.

[20] The plaintiff does not need to hire a counsel; hearings are not necessary for the Italian Court's decision, and the referral comes from the judge *a quo*, not from a lawyer.

[21] "Nous nous sommes également préservés de la dangereuse ambition de vouloir tout régler et tout prévoir. Qui pourrait penser que ce sont ceux mêmes auxquels un code paraît toujours trop volumineux, qui osent prescrire impérieusement au législateur, la terrible tâche de ne rien abandonner à la décision du juge?

Quoi que l'on fasse, les lois positives ne sauraient jamais entièrement remplacer l'usage de la raison naturelle dans les affaires de la vie. Les besoins de la société sont si variés, la communication des hommes est si active, leurs intérêts sont si multipliés, et leurs rapports si étendus, qu'il est impossible au législateur de pourvoir à tout." Jean-Étienne-Marie Portalis, Discours préliminaire du premier projet de Code civil (1801), p. 16. Online at http://classiques.uqac.ca/

[22] Suspending the law in a specific case if its enforcement would produce injustice.

The control *incidentale* starting from concrete cases has also another important function as constitutional counterpower, notably versus the possible exorbitant power of the elected majority controlling both the parliament and the executive in parliamentary democracies. An example can explain what we have in mind. The Berlusconi government in 2008 passed a statute (124/2008, known as *Lodo Alfano* from the name of the attorney general who introduced the bill) making impossible to put on trial the prime minister for whatever crime he is supposing to have committed in his life during the exercise of his political functions (no crime was excluded, from stealing an apple to murder). Evidently because the same majority controls the two houses of the Italian Parliament and because the executive is the expression of this majority, the opposition cannot do anything except hoping to win the next elections and then change the law. But ordinary *judges* could send the statute immediately to the Constitutional Court, asking if they have to apply it (meaning, in this case, cancelling the trial), in effect asking the Constitutional Court to check the constitutional character of the statute. In this case, this happened immediately, because the prime minister was under trial in different courts in Italy. And in October 2009, the Constitutional Court nullified the statute arguing that it violated the constitutional principle of citizens' equality in front of the law (Judgment No. 262, year 2009).

The model introduced in Italy in 1948 and that exists also in Germany, Spain, and a variety of other countries has now been introduced in France after a so-called *organic law* specifying the Article 61–1 of the constitution has been approved (Pasquino 2009). And, as we are finishing writing this chapter, the French *Conseil Constitutionnel* has, for the first time in France's history, nullified a statute, based on a referral of a constitutional question from a court.[23]

LATIN AMERICAN CIRCUMSTANCES

Julio Rios-Figueroa has written a very useful survey of constitutional practices in Latin America that he presented at the 2009 meetings of the American Political Science Association (APSA).[24] He was able to demonstrate, among other things, a striking increase in the independence of constitutional judges in recent years. He also showed an increase in the number of constitutional organs situated outside the judiciary (six such entities have been created since 1950 and only one was abolished). Most interestingly, he also argued that the powers of the constitutional

[23] The new French constitutional law permitting referrals to the *Conseil Constitutionnel* does not permit ordinary judges to make referrals but restricts that right to the supreme courts (the *Cassation* and the *Conseil d'Etat*).

[24] JulioRios-Figueroa, "Institutions for Constitutional Justice in Latin America," *op cit.*

adjudicator have increased steadily since 1950 as well. His paper also provides an illuminating breakdown that allows the reader to see precisely how changes have occurred year by year. He demonstrated that the biggest change has been in the availability of abstract, centralized and a posteriori review. Such review was available in less than half of the eighteen nations he studied in 1945, whereas more than three-quarters of them have such a possibility now. There has been relatively little change in the (already high) levels of concrete a posteriori review (mostly the various forms of *amparo*, but it also would include the Columbian *tutela* – roughly 80 percent of the countries have both centralized and decentralized forms of such review – and would also include one aspect of the Italian model). At the same time, there has been a substantial rise in *erga omnes* effects of constitutional review (from about 25 percent to nearly 50 percent).

While Rios-Figueroa's classification is quite abstract, it shows that the biggest change is roughly in the direction of one aspect of the Italian model (which exhibits both concrete and abstract, centralized a priori review) with, perhaps, a smaller move in the direction of the German model (via increasing the availability of centralized *amparo* rulings with *erga omnes effect*), although it is difficult to be sure of this because he does not give comparative detail about the time point at which constitutional review is available. His classification says little about two other issues that we believe are important features of the Italian case: the development of a specialized constitutional tribunal that has a monopoly over specifically constitutional issues (we noted earlier that there have been six new constitutional courts created since 1950); and the allocation of the power to refer questions to this tribunal to ordinary judges (a priori review can occur in many different ways – either through referral from an ordinary court, from a high court, or from direct petition as with the various forms of *amparo*). As we have said, however, Rios-Figueroa's classification is too abstract to capture these important aspects of the Italian model, so we cannot really make any stronger claim for developments in this direction over the whole region.

It may be useful, however, to examine one particular case to see concretely how some of these transformations may have occurred. For that purpose we draw on another paper that was presented at the same 2009 APSA panel, where Rios-Figueroa first presented his results and which describes recent developments in Chile. Couso and Hilbink (2011), in their extraordinarily rich and detailed paper, describe traditional Chilean courts as deferential to political authorities and not at all inclined to intervene to provide constitutional guarantees against the sitting government. They argue that courts in Chile have traditionally isolated themselves from political developments in various ways as a means to protect their institutional prerogatives and have functioned mostly as appliers of legislated codes. But they note that this traditional pattern appears to be changing as courts are showing more willingness, for example, to examine the conduct of the earlier military regime, and specifically to look into institutional protections for its members and to embrace international human rights standards. From our point of view, the most interesting institutional development is the reinvigoration (or maybe the invigoration) of the Constitutional Tribunal (which was itself established under the Pinochet regime, but was until very recently reluctant to use its powers of constitutional adjudication[25]), which has become an important actor in these changes.

Couso and Hilbink's work surveys the main changes in the administrative structure of the judiciary after 1990 and almost reads (to us) like a textbook for transforming a conservative and apprehensive judiciary into an institution capable and willing to assert and defend constitutional claims, and specifically human rights claims, against the government. "[T]his change is most dramatic at the level of the Constitutional Court and in pockets of the lower ranks of the regular judiciary, but it is almost imperceptible at the high echelons of the of the judiciary, such as the Courts of Appeals and the Supreme Court" (Couso and Hilbink 2011: 35) Traditionally, the judicial career in Chile did not attract high-quality talent and was itself carefully regulated by a Supreme Court, anxious to defer to executive authority, to read statutory texts literally and to avoid political entanglements. After the Pinochet period, however, successive presidents attempted a number of judicial reforms including some of a technical nature that were aimed at improving the quality and training of new judges and restricting the control over their careers by the high court. Others were more substantive and had the effect of making ordinary judges more interested in taking on human rights cases. These transformations have been very important, but the authors suggest that they would not have effected a substantial change in Chilean jurisprudence without some positive change at the top. The key changes concerned the membership and jurisdiction of the Constitutional Court (in 2005), specifically "the elimination of the members of the Supreme Court from the Constitutional Court and their replacement with legal academics and former politicians" and the "transfer of the *recurso de inaplicabilidad* to the Constitutional Court" (Couso and Hilbink 2011: 37). The results of these changes have been dramatic in producing two interlinked transformations: first a rise in judicial activism by ordinary judges, and second the rise in a powerful and independent constitutional court.

We refer the reader to the Couso-Hilbink paper for a description of the changes in the judicial career and the makeup and dispositions of the lower judiciary (i.e., the rise of judicial activism): They link this to the removal of control of the judicial career by the Supreme Court, the development of judicial schools, and the

[25] The Constitutional Tribunal initially was restricted to a priori abstract review, to be conducted prior to the promulgation of a legislative statute, as was the case of the French *Conseil Constitutionnel* until this year.

introduction of new (adversarial and oral) criminal trial procedures, all of which increased the independence and prestige of ordinary judges. Here, we are more interested in the rise of the Constitutional Court.

Couso and Hilbink point to two key changes. First, the Constitutional Tribunal was no longer to have Supreme Court members sitting on it (three of the seven justices were from the Supreme Court before 2005). Second, the *recurso de inaplicabilidad* was transferred from the Supreme Court to the Constitutional Tribunal, which "gave lower-court judges and average citizens access to the latter for the first time" (Couso and Hilbink 2011: 18). This permitted the Constitutional Tribunal for the first time "the power to decide actual cases" (Couso and Hilbink 2011: 18). The transfer "provoked a dramatic increase in the caseload of the Constitutional Court" (Couso and Hilbink 2011: 19). Decided cases "increased ten-fold," making membership on the Constitutional Court a full-time job. Overall the effect has been to make the Court more active and visible to ordinary citizens because it "can directly address their concerns via the *recurso*, often in a highly visible fashion without directly confronting the government." At the same time, this newly active Court has been "more likely to directly confront the government in its abstract a priori jurisdiction" (Couso and Hilbink 2011: 19).

From our viewpoint, a key aspect of the reform is that "transfer of the *recurso de inapplicabilidad* from the Supreme Court to Constitutional Court also opened a new opportunity for ordinary judges at any level to challenge the constitutionality of a law that affects a case before them" (Couso and Hilbink 2011: 19). By *empowering ordinary judges to send questions directly*, after 2005, Chile's justice system has been transformed decisively in the direction of the Italian model. Our reading of the Couso-Hilbink paper suggests that, in effect, the 2005 transformation leveraged the ongoing changes in the lower judiciary accomplished in the reforms, which the authors describe in detail, in a way that effectively created a new alliance, the one between the ordinary judge and the Constitutional Tribunal. The ordinary judge, who is now more highly educated and less dependent on judicial superiors, is now invited to play an active role in defending constitutional rights just as Italian judges can.

We do not mean to say that all of the important changes that Rios-Figueroa describes can be seen as a move to the Italian model. The region has seen a great number of innovations at the constitutional level, many of them drawing on local traditions. But the Italian model opens a new avenue for constitutional adjudication, which works partly by developing the competence and powers of the judiciary itself and partly by enlisting its members in the project of constitutionalism that can be pursued outside the channels of the judiciary. The interesting politics of this transformation has the capacity to break down older political alliances and replace them with new alignments that seem likely to enhance the legal protections for fundamental rights and liberties.

CONCLUSION

In conclusion, we offer a tentative assessment of the properties of the three models of constitutional adjudication that we introduced at the beginning of this chapter – an assessment based both on the dimension of temporality and the mechanism of access to Constitutional Courts.

In the (old) *French model*, control is immediate (*if asked*)[26] but unable to take into account the effects of the enforcement of the statute, which is scrutinized by the Constitutional Council "under a veil of ignorance," meaning without knowing the concrete forms and effects of its enforcement in real cases and controversies. As Guy Canivet (the ex-president of the French Supreme Court – the *Cour de cassation*) claims, the French Constitutional Council has to anticipate possible effects of the statute enforcement, which is not really possible. Moreover, the French constitutional adjudication is so far (before the reform of Article 61–1) exclusively internal to the "representative circuit": Citizens are excluded from the control likewise the judicial power.[27]

The *German* system presents opposite features. The access is very large and open virtually to every human being – one does not even need to be a German citizen to

[26] Guy Carcassonne has drawn attention to the so-called *non-saisines*, meaning the statutes that for different reasons are not referred to the *Constitutional Council* ("Les non saisines," in "*Trente ans de saisine parlementaire du Conseil Constitutionnel*," Economica [2006], p. 45–48).

[27] *En premier lieu, que l'acte à contrôler soit un traité, une loi organique ou une loi ordinaire, le Conseil constitutionnel ne peut être saisi que par des acteurs de la vie politique: l'exercice du droit de saisine ne dépend donc pas de l'intensité de l'atteinte portée aux droits des individus, mais de la simple appréciation de l'opportunité politique faite par les détenteurs du droit de saisine. De fait, des lois portant gravement atteinte aux droits de l'homme peuvent ne pas être contestés par des hommes politiques peu soucieux de défendre, par exemple, les droits des membres d'une minorité peu populaire dans l'opinion publique ou des droits traditionnellement mal défendus. C'est une première faiblesse du système français.*

En effet, ce qui est demandé au Conseil constitutionnel, ce n'est pas d'apprécier à la lumière de la Constitution les effets produits par l'application d'une règle de droit à l'individu. Ce qui est demandé au juge constitutionnel français, c'est tout autre chose: il doit soit constater qu'il y a une sorte de contradiction flagrante entre les règles du droit constitutionnel et les dispositions contenues dans le texte examiné, soit de pronostiquer que le texte examiné produira à l'avenir des effets juridiques qui seront en contradiction avec les règles constitutionnelles. La première hypothèse est nécessairement exceptionnelle: elle correspond en réalité à la notion de violation directe de la règle de droit dans le contentieux administratif. C'est donc la seconde hypothèse qui est la plus importante. Or, dans cette seconde hypothèse, il est demandé au Conseil constitutionnel d'imaginer tous les cas dans lesquels le texte examiné est susceptible de produire des effets incompatibles avec la Constitution, ce qui est une tâche impossible à faire, surtout lorsqu'on se souvient qu'il doit rendre sa décision dans un délai très bref. [...] le contrôle ne peut pas être déclenché au moment de l'application de la loi, c'est-à-dire au moment où la loi est susceptible de manifester sa malfaisance; enfin le contrôle repose sur de simples suppositions. Le contrôle se ramène à un exercice de pronostic.

Michel Fromont, "La justice constitutionnelle en France : l'exception française," *Le nouveau constitutionnalisme. Mélanges en l'honneur de Gérard Conac*, sous la direction de Jean-Claude Colliard et Yves Jegouzo, Paris: Economica, 2001, p. 177.

send a constitutional complaint to *Karlsruhe* (Lübbe-Wolff 2006). But the waiting period is normally very long because the GCC is an appellate court for constitutional complaints (*Verfassungsbeschwerden*), in a way similar to the U.S. Supreme Court. The difference with U.S. judicial review is that German inferior courts cannot hear constitutional complaints so they can be heard only after exhaustion of the regular litigation process (there are exceptions, but we are describing the rule).

As a result, Germany has produced a kind of "popular" constitutionalism. Citizens as such are involved in a dialogue with the GCC about the meaning of their Constitution. They do not need any political (France) or institutional (Italy) mediation to access the organ that guarantees their rights. A negative side-effect could be considered the huge caseload. With more than 5,000 complaints each year, the GCC has barely the time to be a deliberative body (most of the decisions concerning constitutional complaints are taken by single justices in panels of three of them, and only exceptionally do they reach the plenum of one of the two "Senates" – the groups of eight justices who make up the GCC).

The Italian model (*ricorso incidentale*)[28] allows rather quick control, because any statute can be sent to the Constitutional Court even the first time of its possible enforcement (like in the case of the *Lodo Alfano*), and the enforcement of the law is suspended until the judgment/decision by the Constitutional Court. Citizens (*litigants*) are involved through the ordinary courts where the judges are nowadays normally willing – when they do not take the initiative themselves – to send the questions to the Constitutional Court. The Constitutional Court is, moreover, a very deliberative organ because all the decisions are taken by the Court sitting in its *plenum*. A limit of the model is nonetheless that administrative and judicial decisions are not object of constitutional scrutiny which is restricted to parliamentary statutes. Why does the "Italian system" seem attractive? In a country that takes rights seriously, it is a way to give rapid access to rights protections to citizens, avoiding at the same time the flood of individual complaints. Moreover, the concrete review has an effect *erga omnes* and not just on the specific case like for the *amparo*.

In France, there was an additional reason at the origin of Article 61–1, which introduces a variation of the Italian model: The European Courts were increasingly creating a way for judges or ordinary people to circumvent French courts on some issues. The Court of Justice of the European Union permits direct (Italian-

[28] To avoid misconceptions or useless objections, let us remind in a footnote that we are speaking here of *Idealtypen*. The Italian Court has four major constitutional competences: (1) the control of constitutional legitimacy of statutes sent to it by ordinary judges – historically the essential bulk of its activity; (2) the resolution of conflicts concerning the respective legislative powers of the regions and the national parliament; (3) the resolution of constitutional conflicts among the branches of the national government; and (4) last but not least, the *ex ante* control of the constitutional admissibility of popular referendums cancelling statutes passed by the Parliament.

style) referrals by ordinary judges. Additionally, the European Court of Human Rights permits litigants to appeal (German-style) when their rights are violated after exhausting all legal remedies. As a result, a number of disputes about French legislation were bypassing internal legal controls, so that the government and President Sarkozy suggested to bring some element of that type of litigation under the control of French institutions, meaning the *Conseil Constitutionnel*.[29]

We argued in the beginning of the chapter for two kinds of implications: one for the litigants and protections of rights, and the other for ordinary judges. Here we mostly have been addressing the first, but we have to come back to the second too, especially because one of the things that seem to have been happening in Latin America (and maybe in Eastern Europe) is that Italian-style adjudication empowers ordinary judges and makes them more likely to play more active, and even aggressive, judicial roles than they have done previously. We think the Italian model has begun to play an important role in fostering this transformation of the judiciary and in its capacity to protect human rights. It also may well lead to a strengthening of constitutional controls on the political branches overall, in a region that has long resisted such limitations.

REFERENCES

Carcassonne, Guy, **Les « non saisines » in** *Trente ans de saisine parlementaire du Conseil Constitutionnel*, ed. by D. Mauss and A. Roux, Paris: Economica, (2006), 45–48.

Couso, Javier and Lisa Hilbink, "From Quietism to Incipient Activism: The Institutional and Ideological Roots of Rights Adjudication in Chile," in *Courts in Latin America*, ed. by G. Helmke and J. Rios-Figueroa (New York: Cambridge University Press, 2011), 99–127.

Favoreu, L., "American and European Models of Constitutional Justice," in D. Clark (ed.), *Comparative and Private International Law. Essays in Honor of John Merryman* (Berlin: Duncker & Humblot, 1990).

Ferejohn, John and Pasquale Pasquino, "Constitutional Courts as Deliberative Institutions: Toward an Institutional Theory of Constitutional Justice," in Wojciech Sadurski (ed.), *Constitutional Justice, East and West: Democratic Legitimacy and Constitutional Courts in Post-Communist Europe in a Comparative Perspective* (The Hague: Kluwer Law International, 2002).

"Constitutional Adjudication: Lessons From Europe," *University of Texas Law Review*, 82 (2004), 1671–704.

Fromont, Michel, "La justice constitutionnelle en France: l'exception française," *Le nouveau constitutionnalisme. Mélanges en l'honneur de Gérard Conac*, sous la direction de Jean-Claude Colliard et Yves Jegouzo Paris : Economica, (2001), 177.

[29] See the article on the 61–1 by P. Pasquino and the exhaustive research by Alyssa King on the French Conseil Constitutionnel: "Un récit à propos d'un projet de loi: la réforme de l'article 61–1 de la Constitution et le justiciable en droit constitutionnel français," Mémoire soutenu à l'EHESS, July 2009.

Ginsburg, Tom, *Judicial Review in New Democracies* (Cambridge: Cambridge University Press, 2003).

Habermas, Jürgen, *A Berlin Republic. Writings on Germany* (Cambridge: Polity Press, 1998).

Helmke, Gretchen and Julio Ríos-Figueroa, "Institutions for Constitutional Justice in Latin America," in G. Helmke and J. Rios-Figueroa (eds.), *Courts in Latin America* (New York: Cambridge University Press, (2011), 27–54.

Lübbe-Wolff, Gertrude, "The German Federal Constitutional Court from the Point of View of Complainants in Search of Their Constitutional Rights," in P. Pasquino (ed.), *La giustizia costituzionale ed i suoi utenti* (Milano: Giuffrè, 2006,).

Pasquino, Pasquale, "L'origine du contrôle de constitutionnalité en Italie: Les débats de l'Assemblée constituante (1946–47)," *Rivista trimestrale di diritto pubblico*, 1 (2006), 1–11.

"New Constitutional Adjudication in France: The Reform of the Referral to the French Constitutional Council in Light of the Italian Model," *Indian Journal of Constitutional Law*, 3 (2009), 105–17.

Portalis, Jean-Étienne-Marie, "Discours préliminaire du premier projet de Code civil (1801)," p. 16. Online at http://classiques.uqac.ca/

Rios-Figueroa, Julio, "The Institutional Setting for Constitutional Justice in Latin America (2009). APSA 2009 Toronto Meeting Paper. Online at http://ssrn.com/abstract=1450840

Sadurski, Wojciech, "Judicial Review in Central and Eastern Europe: Rationales or Rationalizations?" Paper presented to the conference "Judicial Review: Why, Where, and For Whom?" Hebrew University of Jerusalem, May 31–June 1, 2009

"Twenty Years after the Transition: Constitutional Review in Central and Eastern Europe," presented to a conference on Constitutional Courts, Human Rights, Democracy and Development at the Konrad Adenauer Stiftung and Max Planck Institute, Heidelberg, Germany, November 12–13, 2009.

Sternberger, Dolf, *Verfassungspatriotismus* (1979, in *Schriften*, Frankfurt am Main: Insel Verlag, 10 [1992], 13–16, translation by Allison Brown). Online at http://germanhistory-docs.ghi-dc.org/pdf/eng/Chapter14Doc6Intro.pdf

12

Tyrannophobia

Eric A. Posner and Adrian Vermeule

Tyranny looms large in the American political imagination. For the framers of the Constitution, Caesar, Cromwell, James II, and George III were anti-models; for the current generation, Hitler takes pride of place, followed by Stalin, Mao, and a horde of tyrants both historical and literary. Students read *1984* and *Animal Farm* and relax by watching Chancellor Palpatine seize imperial power. Unsurprisingly, comparisons between sitting presidents and the tyrants of history and fiction are a trope of political discourse. Liberals and libertarians routinely compared George W. Bush to Hitler, George III, and Caesar. Today, Barack Obama receives the same treatment, albeit in less respectable media of opinion. All major presidents are called a "dictator" or said to have "dictatorial powers" from time to time.[1]

Yet the United States has never had a Caesar or a Cromwell, or even come close to having one, and rational actors should update their risk estimates in the light of experience, reducing them if the risk repeatedly fails to materialize. By now, 233 years after independence, these risk estimates should be close to zero. Why then does the fear of dictatorship – tyrannophobia – persist so strongly in American political culture? Is the fear justified or irrational? Does tyrannophobia itself affect the risk of dictatorship? If so, does it reduce the risk or increase it?

The plan of this chapter is as follows. The first section offers some definitions and conceptual distinctions, principally to identify the varieties of tyrannophobia that we consider. The second section examines fears of dictatorship in American history. The third section examines comparative evidence on the causes of dictatorship and

[1] *For example*, Stuart Taylor Jr., "The Man Who Would Be King," *Atlantic Monthly* (Apr. 2006) 25–26, quoted in Sanford Levinson, *Our Undemocratic Constitution: Where the Constitution Goes Wrong (And How We the People Can Correct It)* (New York: Oxford University Press, 2006) p. 81. For another prominent example of tyrannophobia, see Arthur Schlesinger, Jr., *The Imperial Presidency*, 1st Mariner Books ed. (New York: Houghton Mifflin, 2004) p. 377 (arguing that Jefferson's prophecy of "the tyranny of executive power . . . appeared on the verge of fulfillment" [writing in 1973]); and see his apocalyptic introduction to the 2004 edition, Schlesinger (2004): ix–xxiv.

introduces new evidence on the relationship across countries between dictatorship and tyrannophobia. We find no evidence that tyrannophobia prevents dictatorship.

The fourth section evaluates the relationship between tyrannophobia and dictatorship in American history. As to the original constitutional design, we suggest that the framers' choice of an independently elected executive may have created a risk of dictatorship in an earlier day, but that in the present day, elections and independent demographic factors – notably the wealth of its population – now ensure that the United States is unlikely to lapse into dictatorship. The very economic and political conditions that have created powerful executive government, in the modern administrative state, have also strengthened informal political checks on presidential action. The result is a president who enjoys sweeping de jure authority, but who is constrained de facto by the reaction of a highly educated and politically involved elite, as well as by mass opinion.

Overall, our argument is in the alternative. One possibility is that tyrannophobia has no effect on the risk of dictatorship; we provide some evidence for that hypothesis. Alternatively, tyrannophobia might both reduce the risk of dictatorship (a benefit) and also block desirable grants of authority to the executive (a cost). If so, we suggest that the benefit is minimal, because demographic factors and the basic framework of elections provide an independent and sufficient safeguard against dictatorship; hence the cost of tyrannophobia exceeds the benefit.

CONCEPTS AND DISTINCTIONS

Tyrannophobia is the fear of dictatorship, but what is dictatorship? The term is slippery in a family-resemblance sort of way, with many competing definitions and a great deal of vague usage. One recent treatment distinguishes "tinpot" dictators, who maximize personal consumption, from "totalitarian" dictators, who maximize power (Wintrobe 1998: 43, 47). In general usage, "dictatorship" takes many forms. In one version, dictatorship is the endpoint of a continuum that runs from fully autocratic rule by one person alone, through oligarchy, to democracy. In this version, talk of democratic dictatorship, or perhaps even constitutional dictatorship, would be oxymoronic. In another version, dictatorship refers to the nature of the policies that government institutes; a "democratic" or populist government that violated civil liberties and arbitrarily confiscated property could coherently be called dictatorial. A third theme, especially pronounced in Anglo-American discourse, focuses on the executive and equates dictatorship with unchecked executive power, in which case legislative dictatorship would be the oxymoron.

Rather than attempting to identify a natural kind of dictatorship, which probably does not exist anyway, we will combine the first and third accounts by stipulating that dictatorship is a political system of legally unchecked rule by one person or an identified small group of persons. Legal checks can be divided into two categories: the requirement that the leader obtain the consent of other government officials (for example, legislators) before acting; and the requirement that the leader submit to periodic popular elections. Dictatorships tend to exist when both types of checks are weak or nonexistent. On this account, dictatorship lies on a continuum and is thus a matter of degree, so usage implicitly varies: The fewer the checks, the more plausible the "dictator" label becomes, but some people use the label to refer narrowly to unelected leaders, some to elected leaders who need no consent from others, and some use "dictatorship" hyperbolically, to refer to abuses even by an (elected) executive who is subject to some legal checks. On our definition, this last usage is erroneous, yet there is an important substantive issue here about the risk of abuses-short-of-dictatorship; we address the issue later in the chapter.

As intensional definitions of "dictatorship" are so slippery, extensional definition may help indicate our interests. The paradigm cases we have in mind include absolute monarchies (but not constitutional monarchies), fascist dictatorship based on leader worship, military dictatorships and juntas, and most of the stock tyrannies mentioned earlier. We mean to exclude various large-scale oligarchies and systems of collective rule, such as the Chinese communist party. Dictatorship is fully consistent with the existence of de facto political checks on the ruler; there will almost always be political forces the dictator(s) must be careful to reward or appease, such as the military or security services, mass public opinion, or an elite "selectorate" (Bueno de Mesquita et al. 1999) that influences the choice of dictators.

Indeed, it is common in the political economy literature on dictatorships to assume that a dictator stays in power by satisfying the preferences of some group – a subgroup such as the elites but potentially the entire population (Acemoglu and Robinson 2006; Boix and Svolik 2009). If the dictator fails to satisfy this group, it will overthrow him. A democratic government is assumed to satisfy the preference of the median voter;[2] if it does not, the median voter will select a different government. Accordingly, the dictator and the democratic government may act identically when the dictator needs the support of a majority of the entire population. The only difference is that the democratic government is constrained by the de jure power of the median voter, whereas the dictator is constrained by the de facto power of the median citizen.

Given this definition of dictatorship, one of our major aims is to identify several varieties of tyrannophobia, and to do this, several distinctions are necessary. The tyrannophobe may fear dictatorship in the extreme sense we have identified – the end-point of the continuum, where the leader faces no legal checks at all, either

[2] In these models; the median voter theorem is controversial and authors make other assumptions as well.

elections or the consent of others for lawmaking – or else the tyrannophobe may fear dictatorship in a weaker sense, such as abuses by an elected executive. In general, our claims will be stronger if the tyrannophobe's fears are more extreme, weaker if the tyrannophobe is more moderate; the problems have a sliding-scale quality.

Another key distinction involves the nature of the fear that occurs in tyrannophobia. Some fears are rationally warranted by the evidence and can be described as justified fear. Alternatively, fear may be an emotional response that short-circuits rational consideration of the evidence, and thus constitutes an unjustified fear. Tyrannophobia is intrinsically ambiguous and can refer to either variety of fear, so we discuss both. We should note, however, that if tyrannophobia is rational – if it refers to a belief about the probability of dictatorship that reflects Bayesian updating – then the label has no explanatory value. In understanding (for example) why constitutional framers put constraints on the executive, we would refer to their justified beliefs rather than the emotion of fear. Tyrannophobia is interesting to the extent that it reflects irrational beliefs, in which case one wants to understand why people have these irrational beliefs and what effect these beliefs have on constitutions and other political outcomes. Although we will discuss both versions of tyrannophobia, our focus will be on the irrational version.[3]

Furthermore, risks are a product of both the probability that an event will materialize – here, that a dictator will take power – and the harms that will occur if the risk does materialize. On the margin of probability, the unjustified variety of tyrannophobia takes the form of exaggerated perception of the risk that a dictatorship will occur, through the creeping expansion of executive power, through a sudden seizure of executive power in a crisis, or through some other sequence. We consider versions of these claims in the third and fourth sections.

On the margin of harm, the question is whether the tyrannophobe rationally considers the evidence about the costs and benefits of dictatorship.[4] Liberal legalists sometimes imply that dictatorship has catastrophic effects on welfare, but this is a caricature, not supported by the evidence. It is not even clear whether authoritarian governments systematically offer different public policies than democracies do. A comparison of democracies and noncommunist non-democracies between

3 This paper can thus be thought of as a step in the direction of thinking about constitutional design from a behavioral law and economics perspective. That literature so far has largely focused on private law and some nonconstitutional public-law issues. *See, e.g.*, Cass R. Sunstein (ed.), *Behavioral Law and Economics* (Cambridge: Cambridge University Press, 2000).

4 Mark Tushnet helpfully noted to us that in principle, one should distinguish the long-run costs and benefits of consolidated dictatorship from the short-run costs of a *transition* to dictatorship. If transition costs are very high, the switch to a dictatorship might be bad even if, in a steady state, dictatorship is no worse than democracy. (Of course, the same point might apply in reverse, to a switch from dictatorship to democracy). However, we are unaware of large-number evidence on the transition question; the discussion in text refers to evidence on the long-run effect of dictatorship.

1960 and 1990 finds that the two regime types offer very similar substantive public policies; they differ principally in terms of policies related to winning or maintaining public office, in that non-democracies are more likely to select leaders through violence (Mulligan et al. 2004). More generally, "[a]lthough some studies have established a significant positive link between measures of political freedom and [income] growth . . . others have found that authoritarian regimes have better growth records" (Mueller 2003: 423). Likewise, a recent survey finds that "there is no evidence that constraints on the executive predict growth" (Glaeser et al. 2004: 282). Yet the most recent study finds that dictatorships do produce fewer public goods than democracies do (Deacon 2009: 243). Some of these findings can be reconciled by the hypothesis that dictatorial regimes exhibit higher variance than democratic regimes and a higher dispersion of growth rates (Glaeser et al. 2004: 285); perhaps democracy has both a lower downside and a lower upside.[5] Whether that trade-off is desirable depends on the nature of the status quo ante, the risk aversion of the population, and on the absolute level of performance under the democratic alternative.[6]

It is not our contention that dictatorship is superior to democracy. Among other problems, political freedom and equality are themselves components of welfare. Certainly, in the developed world, where democracies function well, dictatorship has little to recommend it. The cross-country evidence we have cited suggests more ambiguity about the developing world. It may be that a dictatorship that keeps order and delivers a few other public goods is superior to a democracy that quickly degenerates into anarchy. Our more modest point is just that institutional design of democratic institutions should not assume that the loss of well-being caused by a transition from democracy to dictatorship is higher than it in fact is.

Another distinction involves different types of safeguards against dictatorship. Even if dictatorship is a real risk, and even if it would be harmful if it occurred, the requisite precautions might be either institutional or else political and cultural. The former typically arise through deliberate constitutional design, involving familiar institutions such as legislative oversight, judicial review for statutory authorization or constitutionality, and (in some systems) the separation of powers. Political and cultural precautions arise, if at all, through decentralized action by many individuals. They can be arranged on a continuum from relatively formal modes of political organization, such as political parties capable of resisting dictatorship, to unwritten

5 Mueller (2003): 424 (citing Jody Overland, Kenneth L. Simons, and Michael Spagat, "Political Instability and Growth in Dictatorships" (2000) (unpublished working paper, later published in *Public Choice* 125 [2005], 445).

6 Philippe Aghion, Alberto Alesina, and Francesco Trebbi, "Endogenous Political Institutions," *Quarterly Journal of Economics* 119 (2004) 575, present a model in which a leader with relatively low insulation – meaning a leader who must gain the approval of (many) others before acting – is relatively more desirable as the risk aversion of the population increases.

constitutional norms and conventions (Elster 2009) – such as the long-standing convention that no president should stand for a third term (until Roosevelt did so) – to a loosely defined ethos of libertarianism. We will examine the relationship between institutional and noninstitutional constraints in later sections.

A last type of tyrannophobia has a temporal dimension. There is a long history of *time-limited dictatorships* (Rossiter 2002: 8). In the ancient Roman republic, for example, the senate could appoint a dictator to address an emergency for a term that typically expired after six months. Some renaissance Italian republics had a similar position. And many modern constitutions grant executives special (although usually not absolute) powers during emergencies. By our definition, time-limited dictatorships are not true dictatorships because the dictator derives his authority from the people or from elected officials.[7] But time-limited dictatorships loom large in the imagination of the tyrannophobe because many time-limited dictators have refused to step down.

TYRANNOPHOBIA IN AMERICAN HISTORY

The Founding

The Declaration of Independence is the urtext of tyrannophobia in the United States. Britain at the time had a constitutional monarchy, and the king was by no means the sole or even leading figure in determining colonial policy, but shared power with Parliament. Yet the Declaration focuses not on Parliament, or the British people, but on the king, and his supposedly tyrannical methods: "The history of the present King of Great Britain is a history of repeated injuries and usurpations, all having in direct object the establishment of an absolute Tyranny over these States. To prove this, let Facts be submitted to a candid world."[8] A long list of the king's outrages end in this climax: "In every stage of these Oppressions We have Petitioned for Redress in the most humble terms: Our repeated Petitions have been answered only by repeated injury. A Prince, whose character is thus marked by every act which may define a Tyrant, is unfit to be the ruler of a free people."[9]

7 We thus by stipulation exclude certain types of "constitutional dictatorships" in the United States – the arguable cases being wartime presidential power. See Rossiter (2002). For a critical discussion of constitutional dictatorships, *see* Sanford Levinson and Jack M. Balkin, "Constitutional Dictatorship: Its Dangers and Design" 94 *Minnesota Law Review* 1789 (2010). Levinson and Balkin believe that the U.S. executive currently has excessive power, which lends itself to abuse; and although they believe that to some extent constitutional dictatorship is unavoidable, they advocate increased checks on executive power to curb abuses and prevent unlimited dictatorship.

8 *The Declaration of Independence* (U.S. 1776): para. 2.

9 *The Declaration of Independence* (1776): para. 30.

Parliament receives only a passing reference in the next paragraph. British policy toward the American colonies, although very much a joint product of king and Parliament, is personified in the king, a tyrant.

Why did Jefferson employ this rhetorical strategy? Parliament, whatever its defects, was a quasi-representative body. If Parliament was to be blamed for the injuries suffered by the American colonies, then so have to be the British people. Yet Americans had deep ties with the British – not just by consanguinity, as noted by the Declaration, but also commercial, religious, and ideological. Given Britain's mastery of the seas, it would have been difficult to imagine that the colonies, after independence, could flourish without some sort of accommodation with the British. Indeed, the Declaration's references to the British people are notably gentle:

> Nor have We been wanting in attentions to our British brethren. We have warned them from time to time of attempts by their legislature to extend an unwarrantable jurisdiction over us. We have reminded them of the circumstances of our emigration and settlement here. We have appealed to their native justice and magnanimity, and we have conjured them by the ties of our common kindred to disavow these usurpations, which, would inevitably interrupt our connections and correspondence. They too have been deaf to the voice of justice and of consanguinity. We must, therefore, acquiesce in the necessity, which denounces our Separation, and hold them, as we hold the rest of mankind, Enemies in War, in Peace Friends.[10]

The effort to separate out the king for special obloquy, and to distinguish him from the British people and their parliament, exploited British historical memory and political currents in Britain at that time. British hostility to its own monarchy extended back to the seventeenth century, culminating in the regicide of Charles I. By the eighteenth century, there was an uneasy compromise between the Crown and the people, but George III was not a popular figure. He was the target of a powerful political movement that accused him and the parliamentary leadership of corruption. "Country" critics of the king and Parliament argued that the Crown used offices and revenues at its disposal to bribe members of Parliament who would therefore no longer serve as a counterweight to executive power (see, e.g., Edling 2003: 66). Many Americans shared these views (Id.: 67–68). Although Americans greatly respected, even idealized, the king earlier in the eighteenth century, while having only a vague notion of what Parliament was, by the revolutionary period he had attracted intense hostility on the ground that he had violated the social contract (McConville 2007: 8–9, 311). The exaggerated beliefs about the king's power, and the correspondingly vague sense of Parliamentary power, may explain why the king was blamed for British colonial policy. It was thus an obvious strategy to blame the king for the injuries that made the American revolution necessary, and absolve the

[10] *The Declaration of Independence* (1776): para. 31.

British people as much as possible, in this way exploiting divisions in the British political class and laying the foundations for a return to friendly relations in the future.

The words were not just rhetoric. American political institutions during and after the revolution were notable for the weakness of the executive office. State legislatures inherited the executive powers of royal governors; state governorships were mostly weak, ministerial offices (Wood 1969: 135–36). The Articles of Confederation failed to establish an executive office for the national government. Suspicion of the executive ran deep. Yet as state legislatures used their newfound powers to cancel debts, redistribute wealth, and persecute dissenters, it soon became clear that "legislative tyranny" – a term that came into use at that time – was just as dangerous as executive tyranny (Wood 1969: 404–12). Meanwhile, at the national level, the absence of a powerful executive hampered the war effort, limited the ability of the national government to respond to internal rebellions, and put the American people at a disadvantage in commercial disputes with foreign nations.

Hence one of the chief motivations for holding a constitutional convention was to strengthen the national executive (Wood 1969: 466–67; 550–51). The Federalists were pragmatists who were willing to abandon their earlier opposition to a strong executive because intervening experience had taught them that a weak executive spelled ruin (Schlesinger 2004: 2). But they ran into a strong tide of opposition. Indeed, the anti-federalists could simply cite the Revolution-era criticisms of George III. Again, the names of Caesar, Cromwell, and other historical tyrants were invoked.[11] Republics are often weak and internally divided, hence vulnerable to a charismatic leader who can promise unity and who controls the military. Once powerful figures obtained the office of the executive, institutional barriers against abuse would fall away. Anti-federalists adopted the Country party's rhetorical "logic of escalation," "by which it tended to see in every limited act of government a larger plan aiming to subvert popular liberty" (Edling 2003: 67). For the Country critics, Britain was constantly in danger of sliding back into the royal absolutism from which the Glorious Revolution had only temporarily and imperfectly saved the nation. For the anti-federalists, a powerful executive office in the United States would pose similar dangers. They imitated the tyrannophobic rhetoric of the Country party even after the United States was no longer threatened by Britain's monarchical institutions and even though circumstances in the United States differed from those in Britain. Thus did tyrannophobic tropes enter American political discourse at an early stage, transplanted from a country that had experienced real tyrants in its recent past, but

[11] *See, e.g.*, Morton Borden (ed.), *The Antifederalist Papers* (East Lansing: Michigan State University Press, 1965) No. 3, p. 8; No. 25, p. 66; No. 70, p. 204. The papers are replete with references to "tyranny," "despotism," etc.

taking root in the soil of a country for which royal absolutism had no party. The rhetoric persisted after its foundation had vanished.

The debate about executive abuse was not resolved in the Constitution. The founders created a presidency and vested it with undefined executive powers. A handful of more specific powers that would turn out to be consequential did not have a clear meaning at the time of negotiations. The veto power might be understood just to mean the right to veto unconstitutional legislation, not legislation that the president rejected on policy grounds. The commander-in-chief power could refer only to tactical control, not military strategy and foreign policy in general. The power to receive ambassadors could refer to a ceremonial role, not (as it was later interpreted) the power to recognize states and governments. It was possible to conceive of the presidency as a ministerial position, similar to that of any number of weak governorships that existed in the American states, or as a much more important figure.[12] Ambiguous language papered over these disputes, and the debate continued into the Washington administration.[13]

Post-Founding American History

The trend of presidential power over two centuries resembles a graph of GDP or the stock market – a gradual trend upward but with cyclical peaks and valleys along the way. The canonical list of powerful presidents includes Washington, Jackson, Polk, Lincoln, Theodore Roosevelt, Wilson, Franklin Delano Roosevelt, and Nixon.[14] Each powerful president was followed by one or more weak presidents, at least if we include among the weak Truman, who cemented American dominance of world institutions and ran an essentially unilateral war in Korea, but who also became highly unpopular and (thus) lost a major showdown with the Supreme Court.[15] Each powerful president was accused, at one time or another, of Caesarism (as were many weak presidents). Discomfort with the concentration of power in the hands of one man may well have led to a political backlash in each case, hampering the ability of the successors to exercise power. Many of these presidencies were also followed by formal constitutional and legislative changes designed to limit the power of future

12 Indeed, in Hamilton's comparison of the president to the British king and to American governors, he repeatedly emphasizes the more limited interpretations of the president's constitutional powers. *See* Alexander Hamilton, *The Federalist* No. 69.

13 Of particular interest are the founders' disagreements about the executive prerogative to violate laws in order to protect the nation, and the intellectual history of this view. For reasons of space, we cannot recount this story. For a brief, lucid account, *see* Balkin & Levinson (2010); for a recent book-length treatment, *see* Benjamin Kleinerman, *The Discretionary President: The Promise and Peril of Executive Power* (Lawrence: University Press of Kansas, 2009).

14 For a standard account, *see* Schlesinger (2004).

15 Youngstown Sheet & Tube Co. v. Sawyer, 343 U.S. 579 (1952).

presidents.[16] In other cases, the weakness of succeeding presidents may have owed more to the hostile political climate toward executive power that the powerful president left in his wake.

FDR's administration was the watershed (Schlesinger 2004: 122–23, 409). Many of the presidencies that followed it were powerful – Truman's for a time, Eisenhower's, Johnson's, Nixon's, Reagan's. Of these, only Nixon's abuses created a backlash, leading to the weak presidencies of Ford and Carter and to a series of framework statutes intended to check executive power. Historians usually invoke the Cold War and the rise of the administrative state as the explanatory factors giving rise to the imperial presidency. The United States was, for the first time in its history, continuously engaged in a life-or-death struggle with a foreign power, over decades rather than years. A powerful executive was always thought necessary for planning and conducting military operations; accordingly, the powerful executive was institutionalized (Schlesinger 2004: 127–28, 163–70). Meanwhile, the United States had developed a true national market that required regulation at a national level. Technological problems in the modern era seemed to require continuous monitoring and adjustment, tasks that only an executive bureaucracy can handle (Schlesinger 2004: 210–12).

But if American presidents have gained more legal and political power over time, they remain vastly more constrained, at least politically, than the Caesars and the Cromwells that the founders feared. Indeed, the United States – unlike many other countries, including Germany, of course – has never had a dictator in the sense of unchecked rule by one person for an indefinite period.[17] Every president has humbly submitted to quadrennial elections and respected their results. George Washington, in many respects a model of the constrained executive, devoted much of his Farewell Address to warning his fellow citizens about the risks and evils of tyranny.[18] Lincoln violated the law at the start of the Civil War but felt that he needed to obtain congressional ratification of his actions after the fact, and stood for election at the end of his first term. Wilson and Roosevelt also had tremendous power to

16 *For example*, Administrative Procedure Act, Pub. L. No. 79–404, 60 Stat. 237 (1946) (codified in various sections of 5 U.S.C.); term limit amendment after FDR, U.S. CONST. amend. XXII; various framework statutes after Nixon (War Powers Resolution, Pub. L. No. 93–148, 87 Stat. 555 (1973) (codified at 50 U.S.C. §§ 1541–1548 (2000)); National Emergencies Act, Pub. L. No. 94–412, 90 Stat. 1255 (1976) (codified as amended at 50 U.S.C. §§ 1601–1651 (2000 & Supp. III 2003)); International Emergency Economic Powers Act, Pub. L. No. 95–223, 91 Stat. 1626 (1977) (codified as amended at 50 U.S.C. §§ 1701–1706 (2000 & Supp. III 2003)); Ethics in Government Act, Pub. L. No. 95–521, 92 Stat. 1824 (1978) (codified as amended at 28 U.S.C. §§ 591–598 (2000)); and Foreign Intelligence Surveillance Act, Pub. L. No. 95–511, 92 Stat. 1783 (1978) (codified as amended at 50 U.S.C. §§ 1801–1863 (2000 & Supp. III 2003))).

17 As noted earlier, we exclude from our definition of dictator the time-limited dictator; arguably, certain wartime presidents such as Lincoln and FDR had time-limited dictatorial powers.

18 George Washington, *Farewell Address*, September 17, 1796.

conduct war, but presidential power has always contracted with the return to peace. Peacetime dictatorships have never taken place.

The peculiar danger reflected by Caesar and Cromwell, and later Napoleon, was that a charismatic military leader would become a dictator by popular acclamation. This never happened in the United States. The closest example is Andrew Jackson, and although he used his powers aggressively – notably, by ignoring a Supreme Court ruling and by refusing to comply with a statute that required the Treasury to deposit funds with the Bank of the United States – no historian considers him a dictator. Although Jackson's impact on the presidency was large in the long term – he was the first charismatic, populist president, and helped establish the modern party system – like so many other strong presidents, he provoked a backlash (Yoo 2008: 521) and was followed by a string of mediocrities (aside from Polk, who, however, served only one term). A few historians think that Douglas MacArthur could have staged a coup d'état after being fired by Truman. This judgment is questionable; MacArthur quickly became a figure of ridicule (Manchester 1978: 679–83). Eisenhower, while arguably a strong president, used his powers moderately. Americans admire the military, but the culture is not militaristic; aside from Washington, Eisenhower, and Jackson, no great military leader has had any success as a politician.[19]

The worst decade for democracy was the 1930s, when global economic upheaval produced dictatorships around the world. Conditions were worse in the United States than in many of these countries. For a very brief period, some Americans admired Mussolini, who seemed to be able to get things done. In 1927, Studebaker even named one of its cars the "Dictator."[20] But the rise of dictatorship in Europe and elsewhere, especially when it took an ugly turn in the 1930s, spurred a backlash in the United States. The only serious American politician who could even remotely seem to fit the fascist mold was Huey Long, the governor of Louisiana from 1928 to 1932 and senator from 1932 to 1935. As governor and leader of a political party, Long advanced a populist platform of redistribution and public works. He was a charismatic leader who some believe sought to create a cult of personality and to obtain dictatorial powers (Swing 1970). Whether or not he had this goal, he never came close to achieving it at the national level. He was assassinated before he had any serious prospect of obtaining national power.

Stepping back from the details, two points stand out. The most powerful, quasi-dictatorial presidents are often the very presidents who have obtained the approval

[19] A few other distinguished military leaders became minor presidents, including William Henry Harrison, Zachary Taylor, and Ulysses Grant. Theodore Roosevelt, a great president, could not be considered a great military leader on the basis of his minor exploits in the Spanish-American War.

[20] Benjamin L. Alpers, *Dictators, Democracy, and American Public Culture: Envisioning the Totalitarian Enemy, 1920s–1950s* (Chapel Hill: University of North Carolina Press, 2003), p. 15. The name would be dropped in 1937.

of history; Lincoln and Roosevelt are exemplars. Such presidents overcame the gridlock of ordinary politics and supplied new policies that made them enduringly beloved. If there is consensus about anything in American history, it is that Lincoln and Roosevelt were great presidents. Moreover, even the quasi-dictatorial presidents have obeyed basic constraints, such as the need to stand for election and respect the results. These two features plausibly flow from the same source: presidential sensitivity to public opinion and the judgment of fellow citizens.

Hypotheses

This quick historical sketch suggests several hypotheses about the role of tyrannophobia in American history. The first is that the inheritance of tyrannophobia, as reflected in the Declaration of Independence and founding debates, has served Americans well by providing a bulwark against abuse of executive power – either by motivating de jure constraints on the executive or by popular skepticism toward demagogues who sought executive office. Such people could not gain traction at a national level or for any amount of time because they awoke historical memories of Caesar and Cromwell. Popular presidents like FDR faced similar tyrannophobic resistance (Alpers 2003: 105–07, 205–06). Tyrannophobia damaged FDR's standing when he tried to pack the Supreme Court, and tyrannophobia would lead to the enactment of institutional constraints on the executive after FDR's administration ended, such as the Twenty-Second Amendment, which limited the president to two terms, and the Administrative Procedure Act, which imposed procedural constraints on executive administration.[21] On this view, a central feature of American political psychology – fear of executive power – serves as a constraint on the executive every bit as important as the separation of powers and other institutional constraints.

The second hypothesis is that American tyrannophobia has been a fundamentally irrational phenomenon that has interfered with needed institutional development. Caesar took control of a highly militarized and hierarchical society. The seventeenth-century England of Cromwell and the Stuarts was also profoundly different from that of the United States – agrarian, poorly educated, riven by violent religious conflicts, aristocratic, and centered on a hereditary monarchy. What relevance could these examples have for the United States – relatively educated, egalitarian, and religiously peaceful from the founding, and then industrialized, highly educated, and secular over time? We might think of tyrannophobia as similar to other prejudices that perhaps had some social function under radically different circumstances in the distant past, but that have no place in modern times, and only

[21] Pub. L. No. 79–404, 60 Stat. 237 (1946) (codified in various sections of 5 U.S.C.).

retard institutional change that is needed to address modern challenges.[22] Indeed, if the aim is to minimize the risk of dictatorship, or just to take optimal precautions against it, tyrannophobia might be counterproductive, for reasons we will discuss.

The first two hypotheses treat tyrannophobia as a causal factor; another possibility is that it is epiphenomenal. Americans fear the executive, but this fear does not make the risk of dictatorship greater or less. Tyrannophobia is an effect, not a cause. We take up these hypotheses in the sections that follow, from a comparative perspective (the third section) and as applied to the United States (the fourth section).

COMPARATIVE TYRANNOPHOBIA

One way to evaluate the hypotheses mentioned earlier is by doing cross-country comparisons. In this part, we attempt to test the hypothesis that tyrannophobia helps prevent dictatorship. We find no evidence to that effect. Across polities, tyrannophobia is no safeguard of democracy. The literature attributes dictatorship to general demographic variables; our own look at the evidence leaves this conclusion undisturbed.

Does Tyrannophobia Prevent Dictatorship?

The hypothesis is that public fear of dictatorship – tyrannophobia – explains why some states never become dictatorships while others do. To test this hypothesis, one needs a measure of tyrannophobia. In our discussion of American history, we appealed to documentary sources. We do not have the expertise to conduct a similar analysis for other countries, nor is it obvious how one could convert documentary evidence into a quantifiable variable.

Indeed, tyrannophobia might be a culturally specific phenomenon, unique to the United States. It is difficult to think of another country where fear of the executive is such an important part of political discourse (although, as we will see, American tyrannophobia appears to be an elite phenomenon, not shared by the general population). Many countries are, of course, authoritarian, and people in authoritarian countries rarely criticize the government openly. Consider China and Russia. Among democracies, some have an authoritarian streak, such as France with its Gaullist tradition. In Germany, the touchstone for political discourse is not dictatorship but nationalism. Britain, not threatened by dictatorship since the seventeenth

[22] Alpers, for example, argues that what we call tyrannophobia – an excessive fear of tyranny – led to persecution of dissenters and others who opposed American foreign policy during World War II and the Cold War, which was presented by the government as a conflict with dictatorship. Alpers (2003): 301–02.

century, is comfortable with its ceremonial monarchy, powerful parliament, and (hence) exceptionally powerful prime minister. One might think that tyrannophobia would flourish in countries that have recently moved from dictatorship to democracy, such as Brazil, Argentina, Chile, and Indonesia, but one must recall that in many of those countries, partisans of the defunct authoritarian regime remain and wield substantial influence. By contrast, the United States kicked out its Tories after the revolution.

We have searched for quantitative proxies for tyrannophobia and the best we have found are results from the World Values Survey.[23] We focus on two questions. The first question asks whether having a "strong leader" is very good, fairly good, bad, or very bad.[24] The second question asks whether "democracies are indecisive and have too much squabbling" and gave respondents the choice of answering: agree strongly, agree, disagree, and strongly disagree.[25] We assume that tyrannophobes are more likely to answer the first question with "very bad" and the second question with "strongly disagree."

We put together a data set that includes the survey results (in both cases, the variable equals the sum of the percentages of the two positive responses), along with the Polity IV democracy score for 2000 (from 0 to 10, reflecting increasing democratization), per capita GDP for 2000, and information regarding whether the country was governed by a dictatorship at any time after 1950 (Lijphardt 1999: 132–33). Table 12.1 provides the information for twenty-two countries.

Our data set is cross-sectional, so we cannot directly test whether a democracy with a tyrannophobic population is less likely to become a dictatorship. Instead, we simply looked for correlations. We do not find statistically significant correlations that support the psychocultural hypothesis.[26] A tyrannophobic public (as measured by answers to the survey questions) is just as likely to live in a non-democracy as in a democracy. There is thus no evidence that tyrannophobia prevents the rise of dictatorships.

Alternative Explanations for the Absence of Dictatorship

If tyrannophobia does not prevent dictatorship, what does?

[23] *World Values Survey*, http://www.worldvaluessurvey.org (last visited July 15, 2009). The surveys we use were conducted over a ten-year period from 1999 to 2008; different countries were surveyed in different years.

[24] *World Values Survey*: question E114.

[25] *World Values Survey*: question E121.

[26] The two survey variables are highly correlated. Our data set consists of 191 countries, but we have survey results for only 84 countries (in the case of Strong Leader) and 65 countries (in the case of Democracies Squabble). For Strong Leader, the mean was 35%, ranging from 3% to 78%. For Democracies Squabble, the mean was 49%, ranging from 13% to 80%.

TABLE 12.1. *Survey results for selected nations*[27]

Country	"Strong Leader"	"Democracies Indecisive"	Polity IV Democracy (2000)	Per Capita GDP (2000)	Period of Dictatorship (1950–2007)
Australia	24%	–	10	$23,200	–
Belgium	33%	61%	10	$25,300	–
Brazil	64%	–	8	$6,500	1964–1984
Canada	22%	50%	10	$24,800	–
China	36%	35%	0	$3,600	1950–2007
Columbia	31%	–	7	$6,200	1950–1956
Egypt	16%	29%	0	$3,600	1952–2007
France	33%	74%	9	$24,400	–
Germany	17%	35%	10	$23,400	–
India	64%	66%	9	$2,200	–
Indonesia	24%	25%	7	$2,900	1957–1998
Iran	74%	28%	4	$6,300	1950–1996 2004–2007
Japan	24%	43%	10	$24,900	–
Mexico	58%	62%	8	$9,100	1950–1987
Nicaragua	19%	–	8	$2,700	1950–1983
Russia	57%	72%	7	$7,700	1950–1991
South Africa	44%	52%	9	$8,500	–
Spain	33%	36%	10	$18,000	1950–1975
Sweden	18%	48%	10	$22,200	–
United Kingdom	28%	45%	10	$22,800	–
United States	33%	39%	10	$36,200	–
Vietnam	9%	–	0	$1,950	1954–2007

[27] *World Values Survey*, http://www.worldvaluessurvey.org (last visited July 15, 2009); Polity IV Annual Time-Series 1800–2007: Excel time-series data, http://www.systemicpeace.org/inscr/p4v2007.xls (last visited July 30, 2009); Central Intelligence Agency World Factbook, http://cia.gov/library/publications/download/download-2001/factbook_2001.zip (last visited July 30, 2009) (All values in 2000 dollars.). Data were obtained through the Online Data Analysis feature using both the fourth wave (1999–2004) and the fifth wave (2005–2008) of the World Values Survey. The primary survey data used were from the responses to "Political system: Having a strong leader (E114)," and "Future changes: Greater respect for authority (E018)" from the fifth wave. These data were supplemented with fourth-wave data from those two questions and "Democracies are indecisive and have too much squabbling (E121)." Where there were data from both waves, only the most recent survey results were used. When the survey results had two options for positive responses, the response rates were aggregated. The Polity IV Democracy score "is an additive eleven-point scale (0–10). The operational indicator of democracy is derived from codings of the competitiveness of political participation (variable 2.6), the openness and competitiveness of executive recruitment (variables 2.3 and 2.2), and constraints on the chief executive (variable 2.4)." Monty G. Marshall and Keith Jaggers, "Polity IV Project: Political Regime Characteristics and Transitions, 1800–2007 Dataset Users' Manual" 13, http://www.systemicpeace.org/

Demographics

Probably the most robust result of cross-country empirical work on dictatorship is that the best safeguard for democracy is wealth. No democracy has fallen in a nation whose average per capita income was greater than a little more than $6,000 in 1995 dollars.[28] (In Weimar Germany in 1933, average per capita income was $3,556, down from $4,090 in 1928) (Maddison 2003: 62). Stated in 2008 dollars, average per capita income in the United States is no less than $39,751.[29] If this pattern reflects causal forces, the United States is unlikely to become a dictatorship in the foreseeable future simply because of its enormous wealth.

What causes the association between wealth and the stability of democracy? The causes are uncertain, even if the pattern itself is robust. One account is that "the intensity of distributional conflicts is lower at higher income levels." (Przeworski et al. 1996). On this model, as income rises, the marginal utility of further increases in income declines, so the relatively poor will have less to gain (in utility terms) from subverting the democratic order to redistribute wealth to themselves, whereas the relatively rich will have less to lose from majoritarian redistribution under democracy. The poor will accept less redistribution, the rich will accept more, the set of policies that are politically acceptable to both sides expands, and no social group thinks it is worthwhile to gamble on a bid for dictatorship.

A different but compatible model focuses on inequality between elites and masses (Acemoglu and Robinson 2006; Boix 2003: 21–23, 37–38). Democracy, in the sense of the electoral franchise, arises when masses can credibly threaten to revolt and to expropriate the wealth of rich elites. The elites want to buy off the masses with a measure of redistribution, but a promise to make direct transfers is not credible; the masses realize that once the revolutionary crowd has dispersed, elites will have no incentive to redistribute. Understanding this, elites offer the masses voting power so as to credibly commit to share the wealth.[30] In a majoritarian democracy with a skewed distribution of wealth, the median voter will vote for transfers from rich

inscr/p4manualv2007.pdf (last viewed July 30, 2007). The period of dictatorship was determined by looking at both the Democracy score and the actual Polity IV score, which is the composite of the Democracy score and the Autocracy score (Marshall and Jaggers 2007: 15).

[28] *See* Adam Przeworski et al., "What Makes Democracies Endure?" *Journal of Democracy* 7 (1996), 41 (citing Seymour Martin Lipset, *Political Man: The Social Bases of Politics*, Johns Hopkins Paperbacks ed., [Baltimore: Johns Hopkins University Press, 1981], p. 51); Angus Maddison, *The World Economy: Historical Statistics* (Paris: Organisation for Economic Co-Operation and Development, 2003), pp. 58–69, 87–89, 100–01, 105, 110, 142–48, 180–87, 218–24.

[29] Per Capita Personal Income by State, http://bber.unm.edu/econ/us-pci.htm (last visited July 24, 2009).

[30] A problem with this model is that it is unclear why the promise of the franchise is any more credible than would be a promise of direct redistribution; if the revolutionary masses cannot reassemble, elites can revoke the franchise they previously promised or else engage in vote rigging, as in Iran in 2009. The model must add an epicycle, to the effect that revoking elections is a more clear betrayal of the promise to redistribute and will thus create a focal point that allows the masses to coordinate

to poor. The model implies that democracy will come into existence only when inequality is neither too high nor too low; if inequality is very high, the elites will have too much to lose from redistribution and will choose to fight it out, whereas if inequality is very low, the masses will have too little incentive to organize for revolution in the first place.

So both wealth in the absolute sense and the distribution of wealth are relevant to both the emergence of democracy and its stability over time. Empirically, factors besides wealth and moderate redistribution can also help create or sustain democracy, although these factors appear less important (Benhabib and Przeworski 2006: 275). A higher average level of education lowers the costs to citizens of mobilizing en masse to create a credible threat against elites, lowers the costs of obtaining and processing information about government action, and socializes citizens in the putative virtues of the democratic order in which they live. Ethnic and linguistic homogeneity are positively correlated with the stability of democracy,[31] perhaps because homogeneity lowers the costs of mass organization. Finally, where there is heterogeneity, the existence of overlapping cleavages – cross-cutting social structures rather than unified and hostile subgroups – helps democracy as well (Benhabib and Przeworski 2006: 274).

The upshot is that most factors favor democracy in the United States, including wealth, education, and overlapping cleavages. Although the United States is a heterogeneous country, it has been uniquely effective at assimilating immigrants with different backgrounds. The most worrisome factor is inequality: The United States in recent years has achieved levels of inequality higher than that of most countries (for which there are calculations), placing it in an uncomfortable group consisting mostly of developing countries with weak political institutions.[32]

Institutional Design

The institutional design hypothesis is that constitutional structure and rights prevent dictatorship. A central controversy in the literature involves a possible connection between presidentialism and the failure of democracy. A number of scholars

on an uprising. *Cf.* Barry R. Weingast, "The Political Foundations of Democracy and the Rule of Law," *American Political Science Review* 91 (1997) 246. If this is common knowledge among elites and masses, then the initial promise of the franchise will be credible.

[31] There is a vigorous debate in comparative politics about whether the facts show that homogeneity – of ethnicity, language, religion, or wealth – is conducive to or even necessary for democracy. Yet the weight of the findings holds that homogeneity on these dimensions is at least appreciably correlated with democracy. (For a recent overview of the literature and an argument against the conventional view, see M. Steven Fish and Robin Brooks, "Does Diversity Hurt Democracy?" *Journal of Democracy* 15 [2004] 154).

[32] *See* List of Countries by Income Equality, Wikipedia, http://en.wikipedia.org/wiki/List_of_countries_by_income_Equality

have argued that presidential systems are more brittle than parliamentary ones, in the sense that presidential systems are more likely to collapse into authoritarian rule (Przeworski et al. 1996: 44–47). A key mechanism behind this result is that presidential systems "are highly vulnerable to legislative-executive deadlocks" (Przeworski et al. 1996: 47; see also Linz 1994: 3, 6–8). In times of economic or political crisis especially, such deadlocks create public demand for the strong hand of a dictator, and an elected president can more easily stage an autogolpe than can any other official.

On this view, presidentialism is especially risky in the presence of a fragmented party system (Mainwaring 1990; Wintrobe 1998). Where parties multiply, gridlock follows, and an independently elected executive can appear to stand above party, offering decisive action while facing little in the way of organized countervailing power. The framers failed to anticipate the development of the modern political party (Ackerman 2005: 27–35), and in America's early history, parties were fluid, fragmentary, and ill-defined, so this path to dictatorship was a live possibility – at least if the theory is correct. However, an alternative view is that the empirical pattern is an artifact of selection effects: Presidential systems collapse into dictatorships because presidential systems are selected in unstable countries (Cheibub 2007). At present, there is no scholarly consensus on the issue.

Where does this leave us? The demographic hypothesis looks stronger than ever in light of the weak or ambiguous results for the competitors. To be sure, our data analysis has been extremely tentative and crude. We think there is enough here, however, to justify skepticism toward the psychological hypothesis that tyrannophobia preserves democracy against the threat of dictatorship.

DICTATORSHIP AND TYRANNOPHOBIA IN AMERICA

Against this historical and comparative background, we turn to the relationship between tyrannophobia and dictatorship in the United States. If tyrannophobia were a crucial safeguard against dictatorship, it would have benefits. However, we believe that tyrannophobia is either not a safeguard against dictatorship (as the evidence presented in the third section suggests), or is at best an unnecessary and costly one, akin to placing one's house underground to guard against the trivial risk of a meteor strike. In the administrative state that flowered in the twentieth century, demographic factors and the basic constraint of elections jointly provide an independent and sufficient buffer against dictatorship. The United States of 2009 is too wealthy, with a population that is too highly educated, to slide into authoritarianism. An implication is that even if tyrannophobia reduces the risk of dictatorship, it must also constrain grants of power to the executive that are otherwise desirable. The former effect is a benefit, the latter a cost; but the benefit is minimal, because demography and elections, taken together, independently prevent dictatorship. Accordingly, either tyrannophobia has no effect on the risk of dictatorship, or else it produces social costs for little in the way of offsetting benefits.

Causes of Tyrannophobia

As we saw in the second section, tyrannophobic rhetoric, possibly rational, played an important role in the American founding. The puzzle is that, even if it was justified in that period as a prophylactic against dictatorship (and it may well not have been), why has it persisted across two hundred years of political stability?

Bounded Rationality

Psychologists have offered a number of hypotheses for why people have incorrect beliefs about the risk of an event. These hypotheses center around bounded rationality, particularly cognitive biases and reliance on mental shortcuts called heuristics (Plous 1993). People exaggerate risks of events that inspire them with dread (cancer deaths rather than ordinary illnesses); over which they have no control (nuclear accidents rather than car accidents); and that have unusual salience. The first tendency is related to loss aversion, the attribution of greater weight to losses than to identical gains against an arbitrary reference point. People are also imperfect Bayesians: They update probability estimates in light of new information as they should, but they do not do this very well or very quickly. Instead they give too much weight to their initial estimates and discount new information that conflicts with it. Past probability estimates are stickier, over time, than would be the case with unbounded rationality.

Let us compare a relatively unconstrained executive and an executive who takes orders from a legislature. There is a straightforward trade-off: the first executive can adopt policies very easily; the second must obtain the consent of a majority of the legislature. Accordingly, the first executive can more easily act to advance and undermine the public good; the second executive will have to choose from a narrower range of policy outcomes, with a limited upside and downside for the public.

We can immediately see that the executive's ability to inflict worse as well as better outcomes will engage the public's loss aversion. People will irrationally overweight the bad outcome, and hence they will exaggerate the downside of the strong executive relative to the upside. The limited executive, with its limited downside, will therefore be more appealing. More speculatively, it is possible that people feel that they have less control over the executive – a remote figure with a national constituency – than over the legislature, by virtue of their representation by an individual with whom they are more likely to have contact (or to know someone who knows him or her, etc.). Further, the president is a salient figure, the personification of government and the focus of the national media. It follows that the risks and consequences of executive power are also more salient than the risks of legislative and judicial power. Finally, and even more speculatively, imperfect Bayesian updating implies that possibly justified fears of executive overreaching that existed in earlier periods, including the founding, could outlast changes in circumstances.[33] Bayesian updating is an attribute of individual decision making, of course, but perhaps such a phenomenon could take place at a collective level. Successive generations inherit attitudes toward the executive held by previous generations; attitudes that might be justified at an earlier time are not adjusted by later generations in light of changed circumstances, such as the improved education of the citizenry.

One might even suggest that in a country such as the United States, with strong traditions of equality and individualism, the president will frequently be the target of strong feelings of resentment and envy. The pomp of the office sits uneasily with republican sensibilities. The suspicion that any president will secretly attempt to obtain dictatorial powers might help resolve cognitive dissonance between these feelings and the evident inability of presidents to do much more than respond to crises and implement a tiny portion of their political agenda.[34] Tyrannophobia is an element of the broader paranoid style in American politics, which attributes vast, wrenching social changes to the machinations of individuals or small groups thought to have extraordinary power.[35]

Overall, then, the suggestion is that ongoing tyrannophobia in the United States can be explained by cognitive biases and other psychological phenomena. Just as a single nuclear accident can cause people to overestimate the risks of nuclear energy and hence demand that government shut down that industry, with the result that no further accident can ever occur, the pre-founding brush with executive tyranny – followed by the dictatorships of such figures as Mussolini, Hitler, Stalin, and Mao – has caused Americans to overestimate the risk of executive power and hence recoil against even reasonable moves toward greater executive authority. Even though

33 See our discussion in the third section regarding the greater likelihood that tyranny takes place in poorer societies (as the United States was before modern times) than in richer societies.

34 *See generally* Alexis de Tocqueville, *Democracy in America*, Harvey C. Mansfield & Delba Winthrop (trans.) (Chicago: University of Chicago Press, 2000) (1835), especially Part II, chapter 9 and Part IV, chapters 1 and 6. Tocqueville believes that American mores, ideological commitments, and institutions pose a number of dangers, but despotism in the usual sense is not one of them.

35 *See* Richard Hofstadter, "The Paranoid Style in American Politics," in *The Paranoid Style in American Politics and Other Essays* (Cambridge, MA: Harvard University Press, 1967), pp. 3, 29–40; Richard Hofstadter, "The Pseudo-Conservative Revolt – 1954," in *The Paranoid Style in American Politics and Other Essays*, pp. 41, 46.

dictatorship has never existed in the United States, Americans fear dictators and refuse to support anyone who seems to have dictatorial ambitions, and are reluctant to support legislative and constitutional changes that could increase executive power; this reluctance persists even though circumstances have changed, and the actual risks of dictatorship are far lower than in the past.

Rational Updating

There is a second and related possibility, which resonates with American political culture; we state it only briefly. On this account, the relaxation, over time, of de jure checks on the presidency has fed tyrannophobia, because the growth of de facto checks on the presidency is ignored. Tocqueville (1835: 257–58) observed that Americans are legalistic, and it is still a striking fact of American political discourse that even elites tend to equate the absence of *legal* checks on the executive with the absence of *any* checks on the executive. Political checks on the executive are more amorphous and vague than legal checks; they do not often produce the sort of highly salient constitutional showdowns that occur when presidential power is tested and constrained by a decision of the Supreme Court. The epistemic costs of acquiring and processing information about political checks are higher than for legal checks, so even rational citizens might underestimate the extent and strength of the former relative to the latter. The consequence is that as legal checks erode, the populace will increase its estimate of the risks of dictatorship, even though the actual risk may remain constant or even decline, depending on the actual strength of the political checks.

On this account, tyrannophobia does not need to rest on bounded rationality in the sense of psychological quirks. It is merely an overestimate of the risks of dictatorship arising from positive information costs – more precisely, differences in the cost of acquiring information about different types of constraint on the executive. An implication is that if the costs of political information fall, owing to the Internet and other technological advances, the public will know more about political checks on the executive, and tyrannophobia will abate.[36]

The Effects of Tyrannophobia

Tyrannophobia and the Risk of Dictatorship

Tyrannophobia might itself affect the risk of dictatorship. This effect, if it exists, might run in either of two directions: widespread tyrannophobia among the public or elites

[36] This implication is, however, in tension with the data suggesting that in richer (and presumably technologically more advanced) societies, people are more likely to disapprove of a strong executive. See the third section of this chapter for a discussion.

might either reduce the risk of dictatorship or actually increase it. A third possibility, suggested by the survey results discussed in the third section, is that tyrannophobia has no independent causal force at all. We will consider these possibilities in turn.

On the first possibility, tyrannophobia is a fear that provides its own remedy. Perhaps the United States has never come close to dictatorship in part because tyrannophobia is widespread, causing political actors to take stringent precautions against executive abuses, including hyperbolic assertions that any increase in executive power is the harbinger of dictatorship. In the most optimistic version of this account, the framers premised central institutions of American constitutional law on the fear of dictatorship and geared them to minimize the risk, but this is desirable because the risk is high; eternal vigilance is the price of liberty. If the risk has never materialized, that is because our vigilance has never lapsed. Moreover, the longer the period with no dictatorship – a risk that has occasionally materialized in other nations, even seemingly liberal and democratic ones – the more the framers' fears of dictatorship seem justified, in a cycle of self-confirming expectations.

Unfortunately, that optimistic possibility is observationally equivalent to two other possibilities: (1) dictatorship is not observed in the United States because it was never a real risk in the first place, even without the institutions erected to guard against it; (2) the precautionary institutions actually had the perverse effect of increasing the risk of dictatorship, but fortuitously that risk never materialized. In either case, the elaborate safeguards against dictatorship built into the constitutional structure are costs that create no expected benefit or that even create expected harm. A firm that hires expensive security guards and then experiences no robberies should realize that several different inferences are possible: (1) the guards' presence prevents the robberies (the optimistic scenario); (2) the risk was lower than initially feared and the guards are an unnecessary expense; (3) the guards' presence actually exacerbates the risk of robberies by signaling that the firm has valuables it needs to protect. The available information does not discriminate among these possibilities. A symptom of unjustified tyrannophobia is the assumption that the optimistic story simply must be correct.

In the worst possible case, tyrannophobia might actually increase the risk of dictatorship and thus prove self-defeating. Two mechanisms might bring this about. In the first, tyrannophobic constitutional designers set up elaborate vetogates such as bicameralism and a committee system; legislative and judicial oversight of executive action; and other checks and balances, all with an eye to minimizing the risks of executive dictatorship. However, these checks and balances create gridlock and make it difficult to pass necessary reforms. Where the status quo becomes increasingly unacceptable to many, as in times of economic or political crisis, the public demands or at least accepts a dictator who can sweep away the institutional obstacles to reform (Hartlyn 1994: 295–96). Here the very elaborateness of the designers' precautions against dictatorship creates pent-up public demand that itself leads to dictatorship. Comparative politics provides (contested) evidence for this story (Hartlyn 1994; Linz 1994; Przeworski et al. 1996: 44–46), and if Lincoln or Roosevelt had become a genuine dictator, a similar account would be natural. On this view, the United States was lucky not to have experienced dictatorship during earlier periods of its history; we return to this point shortly.

In another mechanism, tyrannophobic constitutional designers create oversight bodies to check the executive, yet these oversight bodies themselves become tyrannical. In this way, tyranny sneaks up behind the back of the tyrannophobe, who is gazing vigilantly in the wrong direction. In Honduras in 2009, a democratically elected president proposed a constitutional amendment to abolish presidential term limits. Citing the risk of executive dictatorship, legislators and soldiers dragged him from his bed and hustled him into exile – a classically dictatorial move. There are no such lurid cases in the United States, but mechanisms of legislative oversight have sometimes produced a kind of legislative tyranny writ small, as in the case of Joe McCarthy, many of whose abuses were effected through committee oversight of executive branch personnel and decision making. The fear of "Government by Judiciary" (Berger 1977) is best understood as a fear that judicial checks, intended to prevent legislative or executive tyranny, will themselves produce either judicial tyranny or, more plausibly, judicial gerontocracy.

Both these mechanisms suggest that precautions against tyranny can create the risks they aim to avert.[37] Institutional design must then trade off two competing risks of tyranny, which can arise either because there are no institutional checks in place, or because of and through the very institutions set up to guard against it. Checks against tyranny embody a kind of precautionary principle. Here as elsewhere, however, precautionary principles can be self-defeating if precautions exacerbate the risk itself, so precautions must be entered on both sides of the cost-benefit ledger (Sunstein 2005: 27–32).

So in the abstract, it is plausible that tyrannophobia prevents dictatorship, but it is also plausible that it exacerbates the risks. Finally, tyrannophobia might simply have no effect on the risk of dictatorship at all. The comparative evidence surveyed in the third section clearly suggests this, although it does not conclusively demonstrate it. Across a large set of democracies and non-democracies, levels of tyrannophobia, defined as the inverse of support for a strong executive, are not significantly

[37] As another possible example of self-defeating precautions against tyranny, term limits on the executive might induce coups or other constitutional crises. Anticipating that they will be barred from standing for reelection, powerful executives might decide to subvert the constitutional order altogether. See THE FEDERALIST NO. 72 (Hamilton) (an executive facing term limits "would be much more violently tempted to embrace a favorable conjuncture for attempting the prolongation of his power, at every personal hazard"). There is some evidence to this effect. See Ginsburg et al. (2011)

correlated with the type of political regime. Tyrannophobic publics are as likely to live in non-democracies as in democracies. Tyrannophobia probably does not constitute a safeguard against dictatorship, in the United States or elsewhere.

Alternative Explanations

If tyrannophobia has not protected America from dictatorship, what has? We will examine two competing hypotheses: that America has avoided tyranny through the excellence of its constitutional design, and that America has avoided tyranny in virtue of its demographics. The second hypothesis has much more support.

Institutions: On Presidentialism and Luck. One theory is that America has never experienced dictatorship because of the foresight of the framers. Fearing Caesarism, Cromwellism, and monarchical prerogative, the framers on this account set up an elaborate system of separated powers accompanied by checks and balances. The premise of the system was that the union of executive, legislative, and judicial powers in the same hands "may justly be pronounced the very definition of tyranny."[38] The framers also limited the executive's emergency powers, in part by providing safeguards against suspension of the writ of habeas corpus, whose central function is to ensure judicial review of executive detention.[39]

Perhaps these institutional devices have succeeded in some broad sense, even considering the rise of the so-called imperial presidency in the twentieth century. Roosevelt failed to pack the Court, in part because of widespread fear of executive dictatorship (Leuchtenburg 1995: 137, 146); the Administrative Procedure Act, forced through despite a reluctant executive, creates procedural and judicial checks on executive power; Nixon was forced from office by the threat of impeachment; and Congress set up the framework statutes of the 1970s, such as the War Powers Resolution[40] and the National Emergencies Act,[41] to constrain future abuses. In each of the cases, the basic separation of powers – implying a powerful and independent legislature – hampered executive aggrandizement because the legislature resisted it. Although the separation of powers in the legal sense has undoubtedly been weakened in the twentieth century, in part by the death of the nondelegation doctrine and the grant of massive rulemaking powers to the executive, its functions have been taken up, in part, by competition between political parties (Levinson and Pildes 2006).

[38] Clinton Rossiter (ed.), THE FEDERALIST NO. 47, at 301 (James Madison) (New York: New American Library, 1961).

[39] Amanda L. Tyler, "Suspension as an Emergency Power," *Yale Law Journal* 118 (2009) 627–30; Boumediene v. Bush, 128 S. Ct. 2229, 2247 (2008).

[40] Pub. L. No. 93–148, 87 Stat. 555 (1973) (codified at 50 U.S.C. §§ 1541–1548 (2000)).

[41] Pub. L. No. 94–412, 90 Stat. 1255 (1976) (codified as amended at 50 U.S.C. §§ 1601–1651 (2000 & Supp. III 2003)).

Viewed in terms of comparative constitutional design, however, the framers' choices seem in hindsight to have been poor ones, at least from the standpoint of minimizing the risk of dictatorship. The central decision to create an independently elected executive – although rationalized in the Federalist Papers as a tyranny-prevention measure – was in fact adopted *faute de mieux*, after a protracted stalemate at the convention that came very close to adopting a parliamentary model in which the executive would be selected by the majority party in Congress (McDonald 1985: 250). In comparative perspective, the choice of a presidential system turns out to have been risky, although to be fair, the framers lacked the information needed to understand this.

As we saw in the third section, some scholars believe that presidential systems are more likely to collapse into authoritarian rule than parliamentary systems are, at least at low levels of wealth and especially in the presence of fragmented parties. If these scholars are correct, the separation of powers in the American sense of a separately elected executive is a risk factor for dictatorship rather than a precaution against it; to the extent that this is true, and if tyranny prevention was the framers' major aim, the framers blundered (Ackerman 2005: 643–46). By a happy accident of history, however, America inherited the first-past-the-post electoral system from Britain, and that system has a well-documented tendency to create, over time, two dominant parties,[42] in turn reducing the risks of presidentialism. Thus the risks that a fragmented party system may create, under presidentialism, were avoided.[43] Here again the framers acted from ignorance, but their choices were fortuitous. In addition, the decision to give emergency powers to Congress (in the suspension clause), rather than the president, probably did not help forestall a dictatorship. Lincoln violated the clause, and Congress acquiesced.

This is not to say that institutional choice did not matter at all. After all, the founders could have, but did not, establish a dictatorship. One could plausibly argue that the federalist structure of the constitution helped deter the formation of a *national* dictatorship. Anyone who aspired to absolute power would have to contend with independent power centers in the states even after subjugating Congress and the federal judiciary. Federalism also weakens incentives to form a dictatorship in a state: ease of exit would deprive the dictator of rents. An independent judiciary, as

[42] Duverger's law. Maurice Duverger, *Political Parties: Their Organization and Activity in the Modern State*, Barbara North and Robert North, trans., Wiley Second English ed., revised (London: Routledge Kegan & Paul, 1963), p. 217.

[43] There are significant scholarly controversies here. For a finding that fragmented parties do not create risks to democracy, and indeed that fragmentation and proportional representation (usually thought to produce fragmentation) are *negatively* correlated with democratic collapse, see Abraham Diskin et al., "Why Democracies Collapse: The Reasons for Democratic Failure and Success," *International Political Science Review* 26 (2005) 299–300.

opposed to one maintained and funded by the executive, also would be a nuisance to an aspiring dictator. All that said, however, it is at least plausible that the United States has avoided tyranny largely despite its constitutional design, not because of that design.

Demography and the Administrative State. The best explanation for the lack of dictatorship in America – at least in America today, as opposed to the nineteenth century – is neither psychological nor institutional, but demographic. The third section examined the strong comparative evidence that wealth is the best safeguard for democracy. Equality, homogeneity, and education matter as well. How does the United States, circa 2009, fare on these dimensions? Ethnic, religious, and linguistic homogeneity have declined, and inequality has risen, but because of its high performance on other margins, there is little cause for concern about American democracy. The United States has an enormously rich, relatively well-educated population and multiple overlapping cleavages of class, race, religion, and geography. Simply by virtue of its high per capita income, the likelihood of dictatorship in the United States is very low, at least if the historical pattern reflects causation. The high-water mark of the modern presidency's approach to domestic dictatorship – Nixon's "third-rate burglary" of the offices of his political opponents – was pathetic stuff in historical and comparative perspective, and immediately put Nixon on a slippery slope to disgrace. Likewise, comparisons between Weimar Germany and the United States of the George W. Bush administration[44] were, to say the least, exaggerated.

We add a less obvious point. Legal scholars, especially those of a libertarian or civil-libertarian bent, often express concern that the formal separation of powers has atrophied over the course of the twentieth century. On this account, economic and security crises, the rise of the administrative state, the death of the nondelegation doctrine, the imperial presidency, the ineffectual character of the War Powers Resolution and the other framework statutes of the 1970s, all mean that in many domains presidents operate without substantial legal checks, although they have political incentives to cooperate with Congress and to seek statutory authorization for their actions. Among the framer's miscalculations was their failure to understand the "presidential power of unilateral action" (Moe and Howell 1999) – the president's power to take action in the real world, with debatable legal authority or none at all, creating a new status quo that then constrains the response of other institutions. In the most overheated version of this view, such developments are taken to pose a real risk of executive tyranny in the United States (Schlesinger 2004: 377).

We suggest, however, that the same large-scale economic and political developments that have caused a relaxation of the legal checks on the executive have

[44] Entering the terms "Bush" and "Hitler" into Google yields 6,820,000 hits; "Obama" and "Hitler" yield twice that.

simultaneously strengthened the nonlegal checks. Legal checks on the presidency have been relaxed largely because of the need for centralized, relatively efficient government under the complex conditions of a modern dynamic economy and a highly interrelated international order. Yet those economic and political conditions have themselves helped create de facto constraints on presidential power that make democracy in the United States extremely stable.

The modern economy, whose complexity creates the demand for administrative governance, also creates wealth, leisure, education, and broad political information, all of which strengthen democracy and make a collapse into authoritarian rule nearly impossible. Modern presidents are substantially constrained, not by old statutes or even by Congress and the courts, but by the tyranny of public and (especially) elite opinion. Every action is scrutinized, leaks from executive officials come in a torrent, journalists are professionally hostile, and potential abuses are quickly brought to light. The modern presidency is a fishbowl, in large part because the costs of acquiring political information have fallen steadily in the modern economy, and because a wealthy, educated, and leisured population has the time to monitor presidential action and takes an interest in doing so. This picture implies that modern presidents are both more accountable than their predecessors and more responsive to gusts of elite sentiment and mass opinion, but they are not dictators in any conventional sense.

More tentatively, we also suggest that the relaxation of legal checks may *itself* have contributed to the growth of the political checks, rather than both factors simply being the common result of a complex modern economy. On this hypothesis, the administrative and presidential state of the New Deal and later has, despite all its inefficiencies, plausibly supplied efficiency-enhancing regulation, political stability, and a measure of redistribution, and these policies have both added to national economic and cultural capital and dampened political conflict. The administrative state has thus helped create a wealthy, educated population and a supereducated elite whose members have the leisure and affluence to care about matters such as civil liberties, who are politically engaged to a fault, and who help check executive abuses. Whereas the direct effects of wealth, education, and other factors on the stability of democracy are clear in comparative perspective, there is more dispute about the overall economic effects of regulation and the administrative state (Jalilian 2007: 87–88), so we offer this as a hypothesis for further research.

The Costs and Benefits of Tyrannophobia

We have suggested that the framers' tyrannophobia, combined with the lack of dictatorship in later periods, plausibly fuels contemporary tyrannophobia, insofar as contemporary actors infer that the framer's design choices are what has allowed democracy to endure. However, the inference is invalid, for the key choice of presidentialism may itself have been a risk factor for dictatorship; if it was, then the framers inadvertently put self-government at risk, but were favored by fortune. Likewise, whereas it is possible that tyrannophobia has an endogenous tyranny-preventing effect, it is equally possible that it perversely increases the risk, and the most plausible conclusion of all is that it has no effect in either direction; to ignore the latter two possibilities is itself a major symptom of tyrannophobia. Tyrannophobia in the United States is real, and it may well be the result of the psychological and informational factors discussed earlier, but there is no evidence that it contributes to the absence of dictatorship in the United States, and there is some affirmative evidence that it does not do so.

Even if tyrannophobia has a weak effect of that sort, it seems clear that wealth and other demographic factors in all likelihood prevent dictatorship in the United States, quite apart from its tyrannophobic political culture. So even if tyrannophobia once checked dictatorship, that check is unnecessary today, in light of the exceptional stability of advanced democratic polities like the United States. The main possible benefit of tyrannophobia is therefore illusory. On the other hand, if tyrannophobia hampers useful grants of power to the executive, it creates social costs, namely an entrenched reluctance to transfer necessary powers to the executive. Elsewhere, we have described a range of institutions and policy initiatives that would increase welfare by increasing executive power, especially in the domain of counterterrorism, but that are blocked by "libertarian panics" and tyrannophobia.[45] Overall, then, the cost-benefit ledger of tyrannophobia shows real costs and illusory benefits.

To be sure, even if tyrannophobia is not needed to prevent dictatorship, it might usefully prevent executive abuse that falls short of dictatorship. Consider the possibility, for example, that executives are naturally inclined to use their powers to spy on and otherwise harass political opponents – not to establish dictatorship, but just to obtain a marginal advantage in the next election.[46] This is harmful behavior that should be deterred. If institutions can deter this behavior only with difficulty because executive officials all answer to the president, perhaps tyrannophobia can deter it. The executive, expecting overreaction by the public if word leaks out, does not engage in the abusive behavior in the first place.

This is certainly possible, and if the choice is between tyrannophobia and a completely inert and indifferent public, tyrannophobia might seem preferable. Better still, however, would be a rational and informed public that would express

[45] For examples of "tangible security harms" resulting from civil-libertarian rules that constrain executive power, see Eric A. Posner and Adrian Vermeule, *Terror in the Balance: Security, Liberty, and the Courts* (New York: Oxford University Press, 2007), pp. 24–26. See also Adrian Vermeule, "Libertarian Panics," *Rutgers Law Journal* 36 (2005).

[46] Nixon and many of his predecessors engaged in such behavior.

the appropriate amount of outrage when the executive engages in abuse, and that could distinguish gradations of abuse rather than treat all such actions as steps on the road to dictatorship. Modern economies, which feature falling information costs and a leisured elite, tend to create such publics, although for the reasons we have discussed tyrannophobia persists as well.

This version of the case for tyrannophobia – as a deterrent to low-level executive abuses – is more plausible than the more ambitious argument that tyrannophobia is justified because it deters dictatorship. Low-level executive abuse has taken place in the United States in living memory, and so one might want to nourish tyrannophobia so that executives fear that even minor abuses will lead to a harsh public reaction, and are thus deterred. However, this weaker argument is vulnerable to the same kinds of objection as the stronger argument. There is no evidence that tyrannophobia deters low-level executive abuse; it is equally plausible that overheated rhetoric about dictatorship discredits critics of the executive in the eyes of the uncertain majority, and that it limits beneficial grants of power to the executive. As before, the benefit side of this trade-off is likely to be illusory at least in part, for an educated and leisured population, combined with the regular cycle of elections, will themselves check executive abuses – as evidenced by the 2006 and 2008 elections in the United States. The problems here have the same structure as the problem whether tyrannophobia deters dictatorship proper, only with all the costs and benefits diluted to an uncertain degree.

There is one last case for tyrannophobia. Suppose that rational members of the public would free-ride on each other, with the result that actual public scrutiny of the presidency falls short of the optimal. Instilling people with tyrannophobia might give them the emotional impetus to overcome the collective-action problem. But the presidency already has intrinsic interest for the public. "As the parties wasted away, the Presidency stood out in solitary majesty as the central focus of political emotion, the ever more potent symbol of national community" (Schlesinger 2004: 210). On this account, presidents already receive close public scrutiny; judiciaphobia and legislatophobia would be healthier political emotions.

CONCLUSION

Tyrannophobia is a central element of American political culture, and has been since the founding. We have offered several claims and hypotheses to illuminate its origins and importance. We suggest that tyrannophobia arises from the interaction between history and the quirks of political psychology, or from the differential costs of information about legal and political checks on the executive; that dictatorship in the strong sense is not a real possibility in the United States today because of demographic factors and the electoral constraint; that dictatorship in the weak sense of executive abuse is not a problem that overheated rhetoric about tyranny can successfully address;[47] and that tyrannophobia, therefore, has little social utility in modern circumstances. Either tyrannophobia produces no benefits (as the evidence suggests), or it produces minimal benefits and substantial costs.

Whatever its possible utility in the past, a question on which we are agnostic, tyrannophobia today is just another misperception of risk, akin to a fear of genetically modified foods. Indeed, in light of the current evidence on the determinants of democratic stability, tyranny should be at the very bottom of the scale of public concern. The modern entrepreneurs of tyrannophobia – from George Orwell to George Lucas – ought not be lionized as defenders of the liberal state, but instead shunned as purveyors of political misinformation.

ACKNOWLEDGMENTS

Thanks to John Carey, Adam Cox, Jacob Gersen, Tom Ginsburg, Jack Goldsmith, Alison LaCroix, Sandy Levinson, Jonathan Masur, Mark Tushnet, participants in the 2009 University of Chicago Conference on Comparative Constitutional Design, and participants in a workshop at the University of Kansas Law School for helpful comments, and to Charles Woodworth and Sergei Zaslavsky for excellent research assistance.

REFERENCES

Acemoglu, Daron & James A. Robinson, *Economic Origins of Dictatorship and Democracy* (New York: Cambridge University Press, 2006).

Ackerman, Bruce, "The New Separation of Powers," *Harvard Law Review* 113 (2000) 633–729.

The Failure of the Founding Fathers: Jefferson, Marshall, and the Rise of Presidential Democracy (Cambridge, MA: Harvard University Press, 2005).

Administrative Procedure Act, Pub. L. No. 79–404, 60 Stat. 237 (1946) (codified in various sections of 5 U.S.C.)

Aghion, Philippe, Alberto Alesina, and Francesco Trebbi, "Endogenous Political Institutions," *Quarterly Journal of Economics* 119 (2004) 565–611.

[47] We do not claim, however, that we live in the best of all possible worlds. When the executive engages in abuses, legal or constitutional reform may be justified. *See, e.g.*, Levinson and Balkin (2010), who propose a number of creative reforms. However, we believe they go astray by starting with the premise that the United States already has a kind of constitutional dictatorship or nearly so, and then arguing that (therefore?) additional checks are justified. Indeed, this last argument is in tension with their recognition that some type of discretionary executive action is necessary in cases of emergency (Levinson and Balkin 2010: 5). The paper is motivated by the historical fear that republican governments are in danger of collapsing into dictatorships (Levinson and Balkin 2010: 4–5). Our argument is that this historical fear is (by now) exaggerated.

Alpers, Benjamin L., *Dictators, Democracy, and American Public Culture: Envisioning the Totalitarian Enemy, 1920s–1950s* (Chapel Hill: University of North Carolina Press, 2003).

Benhabib, Jess and Adam Przeworski, "The Political Economy of Redistribution under Democracy," *Economic Theory* 29 (2006) 271–90.

Berger, Raoul, *Government by Judiciary: The Transformation of the Fourteenth Amendment* (Cambridge, MA: Harvard University Press, 1977).

Boix, Carles and Milan Svolik, "The Foundations of Limited Authoritarian Government: Institutions and Power-Sharing in Dictatorships," Unnumbered working paper, March 2, 2009. Available at http://ssrn.com.ezp-prod1.hul.harvard.edu/abstract=1352065

Boix, Carles, *Democracy and Redistribution* (Cambridge: Cambridge University Press, 2003).

Borden, Morton (ed.), *The Antifederalist Papers* (East Lansing: Michigan State University Press, 1965).

Boumediene v. Bush, 128 S. Ct. 2229 (2008).

Bueno de Mesquita, Bruce et al., "Policy Failure and Political Survival: The Contribution of Political Institutions," *Journal of Conflict Resolution* 43 (1999) 148.

Central Intelligence Agency World Factbook, http://cia.gov/library/publications/download/download-2001/factbook_2001.zip (last visited July 30, 2009).

Cheibub, José Antonio, *Presidentialism, Parliamentarism, and Democracy* (Cambridge: Cambridge University Press, 2007).

Deacon, Robert T., "Public Good Provision under Dictatorship and Democracy," *Public Choice* 139 (2009) 241–62.

Diskin, Abraham et al., "Why Democracies Collapse: The Reasons for Democratic Failure and Success," *International Political Science Review* 26 (2005) 291–309.

Duverger, Maurice, *Political Parties: Their Organization and Activity in the Modern State*, Barbara North and Robert North, trans., Wiley Second English ed., revised (London: Routledge Kegan & Paul, 1963).

Edling, Max M., *A Revolution in Favor of Government: Origins of the U.S. Constitution and the Makings of the American State* (New York: Oxford University Press, 2003).

Elster, Jon, "Unwritten Constitutional Norms," unpublished manuscript, Columbia University (2009).

Ethics in Government Act, Pub. L. No. 95–521, 92 Stat. 1824 (1978) (codified as amended at 28 U.S.C. §§ 591–598 [2000]).

Fish, M. Steven and Robin Brooks, "Does Diversity Hurt Democracy?" *Journal of Democracy* 15 (2004) 154–66.

Foreign Intelligence Surveillance Act, Pub. L. No. 95–511, 92 Stat. 1783 (1978) (codified as amended at 50 U.S.C. §§ 1801–1863 (2000 & Supp. III 2003)).

Ginsburg, Tom, James Melton, and Zachary Elkins. "On the Evasion of Executive Term Limits," *William & Mary Law Review* 52 (2011) 1807–72.

Glaeser, Edward L., Rafael LaPorta, Florencio Lopez-de-Silanes, and Andrei Shleifer, "Do Institutions Cause Growth?" *Journal of Economic Growth* 9 (2004) 271–303.

Hartlyn, Jonathan, "Presidentialism and Colombian Politics," in *The Failure of Presidential Democracy: The Case of Latin America* (Baltimore: Johns Hopkins University Press, 1994).

Hofstadter, Richard, "The Paranoid Style in American Politics," in *The Paranoid Style in American Politics and Other Essays* (Cambridge, MA: Harvard University Press, 1967).

"The Pseudo-Conservative Revolt – 1954," in *The Paranoid Style in American Politics and Other Essays* (Cambridge, MA: Harvard University Press, 1967).

International Emergency Economic Powers Act, Pub. L. No. 95–223, 91 Stat. 1626 (1977) (codified as amended at 50 U.S.C. §§ 1701–1706 (2000 & Supp. III 2003)).

Jalilian, Hossein, Colin Kirkpatrick, and David Parker, "The Impact of Regulation on Economic Growth in Developing Countries: A Cross-Country Analysis," *World Development* 35 (2007) 87–103.
Kleinerman, Benjamin, *The Discretionary President: The Promise and Peril of Executive Power* (Lawrence: University Press of Kansas, 2009).
Leuchtenburg, William E., *The Supreme Court Reborn: The Constitutional Revolution in the Age of Roosevelt* (New York: Oxford University Press, 1995).
Levinson, Daryl J. and Richard H. Pildes, "Separation of Parties, Not Powers," *Harvard Law Review* 119 (2006) 2311–86.
Levinson, Sanford, *Our Undemocratic Constitution: Where the Constitution Goes Wrong (And How We the People Can Correct It)* (New York: Oxford University Press, 2006).
Levinson, Sanford and Jack M. Balkin, "Constitutional Dictatorship: Its Dangers and Design," 94 *Minnesota Law Review* 1789 (2010).
Lijphart, Arend, *Patterns of Democracy: Government Forms and Performance in Thirty-Six Countries* (New Haven, CT: Yale University Press, 1999).
Linz, Juan J., "Presidential or Parliamentary Democracy: Does It Make a Difference?" in Juan J. Linz and Arturo Valenzuela (eds.), *The Failure of Presidential Democracy: The Case of Latin America* (Baltimore: Johns Hopkins University Press, 1994).
Lipset, Seymour Martin, *Political Man: The Social Bases of Politics* (Baltimore: Johns Hopkins University Press, 1981).
List of Countries by Income Equality, Wikipedia, http://en.wikipedia.org/wiki/List_of_countries_by_income_equality
Maddison, Angus, *The World Economy: Historical Statistics* (Paris: Organisation for Economic Co-Operation and Development, 2003).
Mainwaring, Scott, "Presidentialism in Latin America," *Latin American Research Review* 25 (1990) 157–79.
Manchester, William, *American Caesar: Douglas MacArthur, 1880–1964* (New York: Little, Brown and Company, 1978).
Marshall, Monty G. and Keith Jaggers, "Polity IV Project: Political Regime Characteristics and Transitions, 1800–2007 Dataset Users' Manual" 13, http://www.systemicpeace.org/inscr/p4manualv2007.pdf (last viewed July 30, 2007).
McConville, Brendan, *The King's Three Faces: The Rise and Fall of Royal America, 1688–1776* (Chapel Hill: University of North Carolina Press, 2007).
McDonald, Forrest, *Novus Ordo Seclorum: The Intellectual Origins of the Constitution* (Lawrence: University Press of Kansas, 1985).
de Mesquita, Bruce Bueno et al., "Policy Failure and Political Survival: The Contribution of Political Institutions," *Journal of Conflict Resolution* 43 (1999) 147–61.
Moe, Terry M. and William G. Howell, "The Presidential Power of Unilateral Action," *Journal of Law, Economics, and Organization* 15 (1999) 132–79.
Mueller, Dennis C., *Public Choice III* (Cambridge: Cambridge University Press, 2003).
Mulligan, Casey B., Ricard Gil, and Xavier Sala-i-Martin, "Do Democracies Have Different Public Policies than Nondemocracies?" *Journal of Economic Perspectives* 18 (2004) 51–74.
National Emergencies Act, Pub. L. No. 94–412, 90 Stat. 1255 (1976) (codified as amended at 50 U.S.C. §§ 1601–1651 (2000 & Supp. III 2003)).
Overland, Jody, Kenneth L. Simons, and Michael Spagat, "Political Instability and Growth in Dictatorships" (2000) unpublished working paper, later published in *Public Choice* 125 (2005) 445–70.

Per Capita Personal Income by State, http://bber.unm.edu/econ/us-pci.htm (last visited July 24, 2009).
Plous, Scott, *The Psychology of Judgment and Decision Making* (New York: McGraw-Hill, 1993).
Polity IV Annual Time-Series 1800–2007: Excel time-series data, http://www.systemicpeace.org/inscr/p4v2007.xls (last visited July 30, 2009).
Posner, Eric A. and Adrian Vermeule, *Terror in the Balance: Security, Liberty, and the Courts* (New York: Oxford University Press, 2007).
Przeworski, Adam et al., "What Makes Democracies Endure?" *Journal of Democracy* 7 (1996) 39–55.
Pub. L. No. 79–404, 60 Stat. 237 (1946) (codified in various sections of 5 U.S.C.).
Pub. L. No. 93–148, 87 Stat. 555 (1973) (codified at 50 U.S.C. §§ 1541–1548 (2000)).
Pub. L. No. 94–412, 90 Stat. 1255 (1976) (codified as amended at 50 U.S.C. §§ 1601–1651 (2000 & Supp. III 2003)).
Rossiter, Clinton (ed.), *The Federalist Papers* (New York: New American Library, 1961).
Rossiter, Clinton, *Constitutional Dictatorship: Crisis Government in the Modern Democracies*, new edition (Rutgers, NJ: Transaction Publishers, 2002).
Schlesinger, Arthur, Jr., *The Imperial Presidency*, 1st Mariner Books ed. (New York: Houghton Mifflin Company, 2004).
Sunstein, Cass R. (ed.), *Behavioral Law and Economics* (Cambridge: Cambridge University Press, 2000).
Sunstein, Cass R., *Laws of Fear: Beyond the Precautionary Principle* (Cambridge: Cambridge University Press, 2005).
Swing, Raymond Gram, "Forerunner of American Fascism," in Hugh Davis Graham (ed.), *Huey Long* (New York: Prentice Hall, 1970).
Taylor, Stuart , Jr., "The Man Who Would Be King," *Atlantic Monthly* (April 2006) 24–25.
The Declaration of Independence (U.S. 1776).
Tocqueville, Alexis de, *Democracy in America*, Harvey C. Mansfield & Delba Winthrop (trans.) (Chicago: University of Chicago Press, 2000) (1835).
Tyler, Amanda L., "Suspension as an Emergency Power," *Yale Law Journal* 118 (2009) 600–94.
U.S. Constitution amendment XXII.
Vermeule, Adrian, "Libertarian Panics," *Rutgers Law Journal* 36 (2005) 871–88.
War Powers Resolution, Pub. L. No. 93–148, 87 Stat. 555 (1973) (codified at 50 U.S.C. §§ 1541–1548 (2000)).
Washington, George, *Farewell Address*, September 17, 1796.
Weingast, Barry R., "The Political Foundations of Democracy and the Rule of Law," *American Political Science Review* 91 (1997) 245–63.
Wintrobe, Ronald, *The Political Economy of Dictatorship* (Cambridge: Cambridge University Press, 1998).
Wood, Gordon S., *The Creation of American Republic, 1776–1787* (Chapel Hill: University of North Carolina Press, 1969).
World Values Survey, http://www.worldvaluessurvey.org (last visited July 15, 2009).
Yoo, John C., "Andrew Jackson and Presidential Power," *Charleston Law Review* 2 (2008) 521–84.
Youngstown Sheet & Tube Co. v. Sawyer, 343 U.S. 579 (1952).

13

Do Executive Term Limits Cause Constitutional Crises?

Tom Ginsburg, Zachary Elkins, and James Melton

In February 2010, Niger President Mamou Tandja was deposed in a coup, some six months after pushing through a constitutional referendum to allow himself to remain in office beyond his final five-year term. That same month, President Alvaro Uribe of Colombia found himself stymied by the Constitutional Court in his attempt to serve a third term. These leaders are hardly alone in attempting to remain in office beyond their initial allocated term: In recent years, term limits extensions have been an issue in many countries in Latin America (Carey 2009), Africa (Posner and Young 2007) and elsewhere. In many instances, such as the prominent case of Manuel Zelaya in Honduras in 2009, term limits seem to have been at the center of constitutional crises.

This latest wave of term limit evasions invites a number of questions that we seek to address in this article. First, are term limit violations increasing in frequency? Second, what are the determinants of term limit violations? And third, what are the consequences of term limit violations, particularly with regard to crisis? Surprisingly, we have little evidence on any of these questions to date, notwithstanding normative claims that term limits ought to be part of the universal architecture of presidential democracy (Maltz 2007).

We begin by describing the prevalence and type of limits on executive tenure across time and space. We then ask whether term limits "work," in the sense of actually and effectively constraining executives from remaining in office (Breslin 2009). This section takes advantage of a unique set of data on the content of historical constitutions (the Comparative Constitutions Project).[1] This data set includes information on a host of constitutional provisions, including any restrictions on executive tenure. To these de jure data, we can compare the de facto record of executive tenure compiled by Goemans, Gleditsch, and Chiozza (2009). Together these sources

[1] *See* Comparative Constitutions Project, http://www.comparativeconstitutionsproject.org.

can provide a sense of the manner and timing of executives leaving office. They also answer some basic empirical questions that have long gone unexplored.

Next, we examine the determinants of term limit violations, examining an array of characteristics associated with the context, the leaders in question, and the nature of the term limitation. Finally we examine the historical association of term limits with constitutional crises. We conclude that term limits are surprisingly effective in constraining executives from extending their terms, at least in democracies. There is no evidence that term limits are associated with the death or disability of democracy, even if in some circumstances they may induce early constitutional replacement.

EXECUTIVE TERM LIMITS: ORIGINS AND RATIONALE

We define an executive term limit as a constitutional restriction on the number of fixed terms (consecutive or otherwise) the head of state can serve. The origins of executive term limits go back as far as the ancient republics, but the modern practice gained currency with the creation of the presidency at the American founding. The founding fathers debated the length of the presidential term, including the question of whether reelection ought to be allowed. Many of the framers were concerned that the prospect of reelection would force the president to curry favor with Congress – an undesirable outcome that they associated with failing to take into account the national interest (Stein 1943: 6). Others, such as Alexander Hamilton, argued that artificially jettisoning leaders would deprive the country of needed experience during times of crisis. In the end, of course, the U.S. Constitution initially omitted term limits, much to the chagrin of Thomas Jefferson, who declared the omission to be one of the defects of the document.[2]

Those in favor of term limits focus on the potential for tyranny by an executive. As Simon Bolivar put it (before reversing his position once he assumed executive office himself), "Nothing is more perilous than to permit one citizen to retain power for an extended period. The people become accustomed to obeying him, and he forms the habit of commanding them; herein lie the origins of usurpation and tyranny. ... Our citizens must with good reason learn to fear lest the magistrate who has governed them long will govern them forever" (Carey 2009: 80). Bolivar identifies the perverse advantages of incumbency: the current office holder can, either intentionally or not, come to seem like the only alternative. Incumbency may have indirect effects on political competition, serving as a barrier to entry, so that other

[2] Thomas Jefferson, Letter to James Madison, December 20, 1787 (expressing concern over incumbency advantage and stating that "the power of removing him every fourth year by the vote of the people is a power which will not be exercised.")

good candidates might refrain from entering a contest against an established incumbent (Elhauge 1997: 154–65).

Opponents of term limits, on the other hand, argue that they are antidemocratic. Term limits, in this view, serve as an artificial and illiberal constraint on the choice of the polity from retaining an executive who it may otherwise wish to keep. In theory, the polity can always vote the incumbent out of office it so chooses, and so there is no need to categorically limit candidates from continued participation in elections. This argument has been adopted by both scholars and courts.[3] Opponents of term limits also argue that governance, like other activity, requires experience, and that practitioners of government may get better over time (Polsby 1991; see also Hume 1752).

Opponents and proponents of term limits tend to differ in their prediction of likely executive behavior in the final term. Whereas proponents argue that term limits will free up the executive to act in the public interest, opponents note that the lack of electoral check can also give way to corruption and pursuit of policies for personal gain. Hamilton was particularly concerned with the potential for manipulation by a term-limited leader to remain in office. As he put it, "(A)s the object of his ambition would be to prolong his power, it is probable that in case of a war, he would avail himself of the emergency to evade or refuse a degradation from his place." For this reason Hamilton favored a life term during good behavior, a kind of elective monarchy for the United States that in any event would not have a large quantum of power. Another founding father, Gouverneur Morris, argued that the final period would induce unconstitutional behavior by a leader. Should the possibility of reelection be foreclosed, he argued, a leader may seek to retain it by the sword. The implication is that it makes sense to incentivize leaders with the possibility of continued office to avoid last-period problems.

There is little empirical evidence to sort out the claims of proponents and opponents of term limits. One helpful theoretical perspective, however, is to view term limits from the perspective of default rules (Ayres and Gertner 1989). Like other provisions of the constitution, term limits can be overcome by constitutional amendment and so will not constrain a sufficiently popular executive, although they raise the costs of remaining in office. Franklin Roosevelt, for example, initially denied wishing to run again in 1940 after his second term, in keeping with the unwritten constitutional norm of the time (Stein 1943; Doron and Harris 2001). But with the New Deal in full swing, his popularity was such that his party insisted that he run again. Term limits did form some constraint, in that Roosevelt's popularity had to be high enough to overcome the default norm of the unwritten constitution: No doubt some (unspecified) number of voters who might otherwise have been

3 U.S. Term Limits v. Thornton, 512 U.S. 1286 (1994).

inclined to vote for him declined to do so because of the unwritten limitation. But the threshold could be overcome. Once the Twenty-Second Amendment was adopted, the degree of political support necessary shifted again: A future president would require enough support to sustain a constitutional amendment reversing the Twenty-Second Amendment – a much higher threshold (Lutz 1994).

Term limits can be thus said to raise the degree of political support required for an executive to maintain office from the ordinary electoral majority to the amendment threshold. It is not clear *ex ante* that the amendment threshold is always optimal, however, in terms of offsetting the incumbency advantage. It may be that the amendment threshold is too low, so that it does not constrain the executive in any real way. Alternatively, the amendment threshold may be so high as to exceed the incumbency advantage. In such instances, a popular president whom the polity would otherwise prefer to retain will be forced to leave office because of term limits.

To illustrate, suppose that the net advantage of being an incumbent in presidential elections is 10 percent – the average incumbency advantage for members of the U.S. Congress since 1975 (Gelman and King 1990). This means that a candidate will obtain the additional votes of 10 percent of the electorate relative to the support she would receive were she not an incumbent. Suppose further that the incumbent candidate is forbidden by the constitution from running for a second term, but the constitution can be amended by referendum with the support of two-thirds of the population. In this example, the amendment supermajority exceeds a majority plus the incumbency advantage. An incumbent who has the support of 62 percent of the population would have been elected by a majority (even without the incumbency advantage) but will be prevented from running by term limits. An incumbent who has the support of 70 percent of the public, on the other hand, will be able to secure an amendment and remain in office. Arguably the term limit rule in this example is excessively restrictive: It does more than simply offset the incumbency advantage.

If the default rule is not sufficiently sensitive to real-world conditions, it is likely to provoke pressures for change, which can lead to constitutional crises. By constitutional crises, we mean a situation in which constitutional politics become so heated that they suspend the operation of normal politics. Constitutional politics are those that involve struggles over the meaning and enforcement of the constitution; ordinary politics involve issues to be decided within the governance structure established by the constitution (Buchanan and Tullock 1961). When an executive suspends the operation of term limits in order to remain in power, there is likely to be a severe reaction from other parts of the political system and this can suspend ordinary political processes.

These crises do not always rise to the level of midnight abductions of the President a la the Honduran case. However, street protests, name calling, and lamentations about the country's standing as a "democracy" are not infrequent. It seems very clear that an executive who reaches the end of his allowed tenure, remains highly popular, and wishes to stay presents his citizens with an unhappy dilemma. The resulting conflict is one between a majority (or plurality) that yearns for "four [or five or six] more years" and a minority that demands the implementation of constitutional rules. Either side can make a compelling argument for their position from the perspective of democratic theory, but a satisfactory reconciliation of the two sides is unlikely. Even if the crisis does not result in violence, the personalization of the conflict – over whether a particular individual can retain office – distinguishes a term limits crisis from other types of constitutional crisis, which might arguably have beneficial effects down the road (Posner and Vermuele 2008).

Four resolutions to the crisis are possible, with varying welfare consequences. The possible resolutions are: (1) the executive departs; (2) the executive remains and *amends* the constitution; (3) the executive remains and *replaces* the constitution; and (4) the executive remains and *ignores* the constitution. The first outcome – the only one in which term limits work as designed – is seemingly unproblematic, except for those who argue (reasonably) that the executive's departure denies the majority's will.[4] The second and third outcomes represent two methods of constitutional adaptation, with one preserving the constitution and the other eviscerating it. Although we remain agnostic about the effects of amendment to abolish term limits, replacement seems to be of greater concern. In part this is because the welfare effects of constitutional replacement can be negative (Elkins, Ginsburg, and Melton 2009). Replacing a constitution entails costly renegotiation along many dimensions and can perpetuate broader instability. The fourth solution, in which an executive remains without any legal basis, may undermine the very idea of a constitutional order more broadly. In short, replacing and ignoring the constitution will have systemic consequences, whereas the departure of the executive will also leave the polity devoid of an effective or popular leader.

Even the second solution (amendment) may be problematic, even though it adheres nominally to constitutional guidelines. Democracy is ultimately about processes, not personalities, and there is something unseemly about rulers who reengineer higher law to facilitate personal ambition. Of course, one might adopt a qualified approach to amendments designed to evade term limits by focusing on the *process* of evasion. Carey (2009) distinguishes extensions of executive term brought about by negotiations between the president and opposition from those brought about by plebiscite. In the former case (which he associates with strategies chosen by Latin American leaders Carlos Menem, Fernando Cardoso, and Alberto Uribe),

4 The manner of the executive's departure may make a difference as well. For example, removal of the president through military intervention might be deemed more damaging to the constitutional order than allowing the executive to remain in place.

the extension of term is accompanied by limits on power, and so the risk of tyranny is mitigated. With referenda, subsequent constraints on the executive may be less effective. Another alternative is informal amendment through supreme or constitutional court interpretation, as in Nicaragua, Ukraine, and Kyrgyzstan.

In short, the normative debate over term limits turns on various empirical and theoretical claims. Proponents fear executive tyranny, and more generally the effects of incumbency on political competition. They also believe there to be positive benefits from encouraging leaders to develop successors and political organizations that can extend their policies into the future. Opponents argue that term limits are anti-democratic and form an artificial restriction on choice. One way to help inform this debate is to examine the consequences of term limits, and the propensity of their violation, which in turn requires understanding the population of potential cases.

EXECUTIVE TERM LIMITS: THEIR TYPES AND INCIDENCE

We can get a better sense of the prevalence of term limits by consulting the data on constitutions in the Comparative Constitutions Project.[5] In that project, we have collected the written constitutions for all independent countries since 1789 and recorded their characteristics across a wide number of dimensions. Our sample for this article includes 428 constitutional systems from the universe of 960 systems that we have identified as existing in independent states (including microstates) from 1789 to 2006. The sample is restricted to those constitutions that provide the head of state with a fixed term in office (i.e., presidential and semi-presidential systems). Of these, more than 60 percent (n = 269) place some limit on the number of terms the head of state is eligible to serve.[6] Another 10 percent of fixed-term constitutions explicitly state that there are no term limits, leaving roughly 30 percent that are silent on the subject. For most of the last group we infer that there is no limit, although certainly some such limits may be imposed by ordinary law or unwritten custom (e.g., as many assert existed in the United States until the passage of the Twenty-Second Amendment).[7]

Executive term limits come in several varieties. Historically, the most common species (27 percent of all fixed-term constitutions) allows multiple terms, but not in succession – an approach that institutionalizes some alternation in power.[8] The U.S. model, in which only two terms are permitted (as of 1951), is also found with

5 *See* Comparative Constitutions Project for further details on data and coding.

6 We exclude parliamentary systems with figurehead heads of state, such as India. Seventy-five percent of in-force presidential and semi-presidential constitutions have term limits for the head of state.

7 In this sense, our data may understate the true extent of actual term limits in operation.

8 Some of these constitutions extend the succession limitation to the vice-president, to avoid the president and vice-president from alternately succeeding each other. *See, e.g.*, Constitution of Argentina (1994).

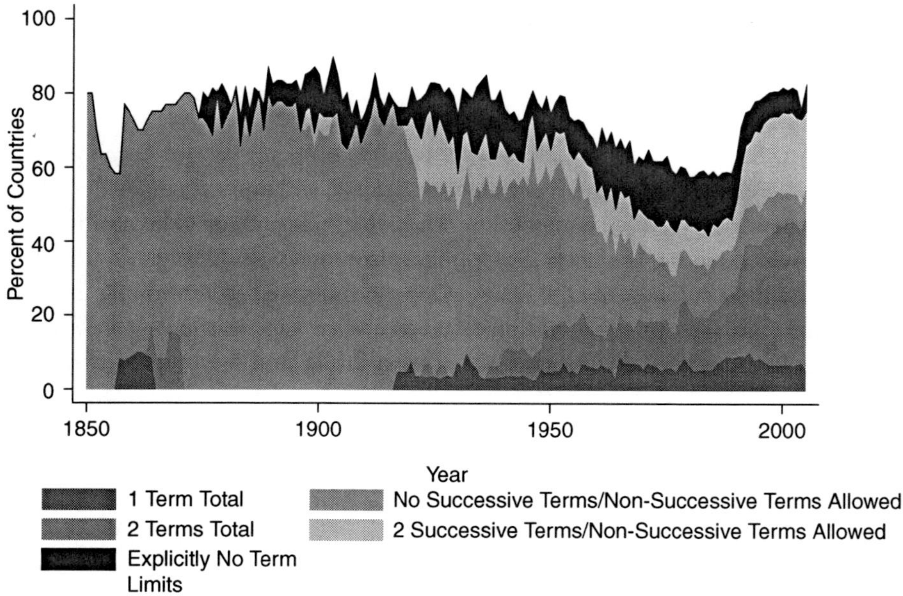

FIGURE 13.1. Percent of countries with executive term limits, by type of limits
Note: Universe: constitutional systems with fixed-term heads of state, since 1850.

some frequency (20 percent).[9] In addition, some eight percent of constitutions combine these two models, so that two successive terms are permitted, after which the candidate must sit out at least one term before returning. Some Latin American constitutions have a prohibition on consecutive terms combined with a specification of the number of terms the executive must remain out of office. For example, the constitutions of Ecuador 1830 and 1897, Panama 1956 and 1994, Uruguay 1918, and Venezuela 1961 require two terms to elapse before the executive can be reelected. Limitations of the executive to a single term, such as the provision at issue in Honduras's constitutional crisis this summer or Mexico's *sexenio*, are relatively rare. Historically, only eighteen constitutions (or 3 percent of fixed-term constitutions) have included such a provision.

Figure 13.1 provides a historical sense of the distribution of executive term limits. The majority of fixed-term constitutions have always had term limits. In the post–World War II era, however, we observe a drop in their popularity, mostly because of the influx of non–Latin American constitutions to the population. Since the third

[9] A small number of constitutions allow three terms those of Kiribati (1995), Rwanda (1973), the Seychelles (1979 and 1993), and the Republic of Vietnam (1962). The largest number of terms is found in the Rwanda Constitution of 1962, which allows four successive terms. Some of these allow a subsequent term after a term out of power.

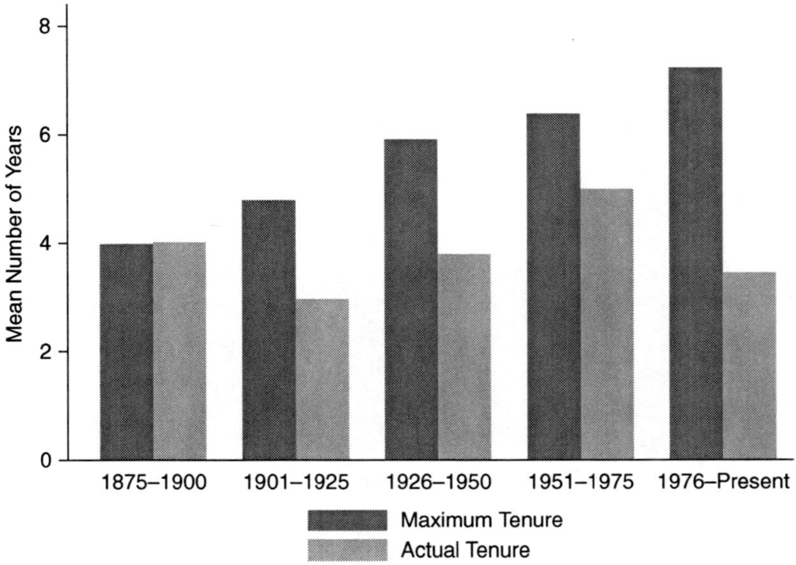

FIGURE 13.2. Mean tenure and mean permitted tenure[10] over time.
Note: Universe: fixed-term executives who served their maximum tenure, since 1875.

wave of democratization, executive term limits have come back into fashion and are now as popular as ever. Although term limits retain great popularity, constitutions now provide executives with a more generous period to govern than did early constitutions. Prior to World War II, few countries with limits allowed their heads of state to serve more than one consecutive term. Since World War II, most countries with term limits have settled on two terms as the appropriate threshold, with roughly half of those allowing a return to office following a sitting-out period and the other half not allowing any return.

Not only is the *number* of permitted terms on the rise, but so too is the *length* of terms. The most common term lengths for heads of state are four, five, and six years – 84 percent of constitutions specify one of these term lengths. The prevalence of four-year terms has been on the decline since early 1900s. In 1900, 60 percent of constitutions that had a specified term length for the head of state provided for a four-year term. By 2000, however, that number had decreased to 18 percent. This drop may be yet another indicator of the decline of popularity of the U.S. constitutional model (Elkins, Ginsburg, and Melton 2009: 194). The share of constitutions granting a five-year term, on the other hand, has increased dramatically since the 1930s, from almost none to about 60 percent of those constitutions with a specified term.

[10] By "permitted tenure" we mean the product of term length and the number of terms allowed.

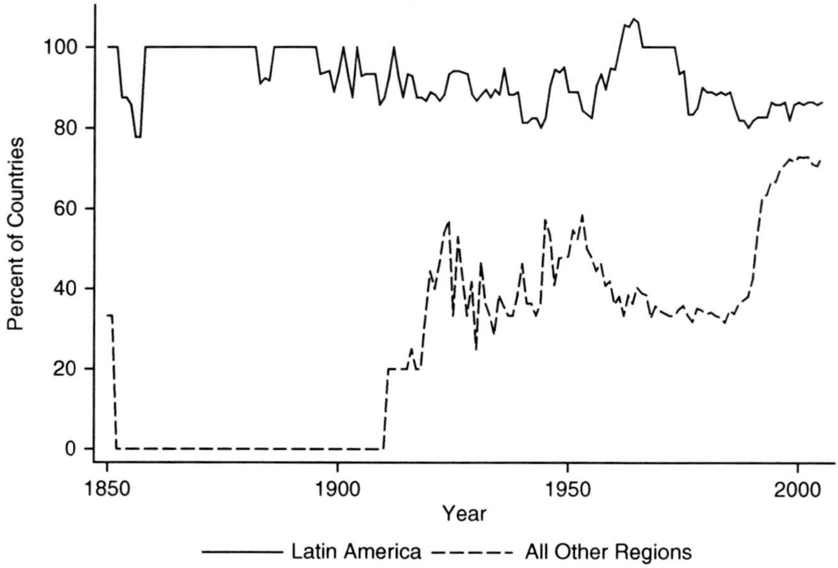

FIGURE 13.3. Percent of countries with executive term limits, by region.
Note: Universe: constitutional systems with fixed-term heads of state, since 1850.

The combination of longer terms and an increase in the number of permitted terms has stretched considerably the maximum time heads of state are constitutionally allowed to hold office; indeed, the average permitted tenure has *doubled* since 1875. As Figure 13.2 shows, the average maximum tenure for executives has increased from slightly more than four years in 1875 to nearly eight years in 2006. For much of this time period, the observed tenure of executives has also increased. Recent years, however, have witnessed a drop in actual time served.

There is an interesting regional pattern to these data (Figure 13.3). In Latin America, a region that has been universally presidentialist since state formation, nearly all constitutions through the turn of the twentieth century and well more than 90 percent of constitutions through World War II contained executive term limits. In the postwar era, however, the proportion of cases in Latin America with limits has dropped. Among constitutions currently in force in Latin America, only 85 percent contain executive term limits, down from 95 percent immediately after World War II. On the other hand, constitutions in the rest of the world have gone in the other direction. Whereas only 47 percent of constitutions outside of Latin America provided for term limits in 1950, 73 percent now do. With respect to term limits at least, Latin America is starting to look more like the rest of the world at the same time that the rest of the world becomes more like Latin America.

Upon closer inspection, the data also suggest distinctive regional and temporal styles with respect to the type of limits. One-term limits are relatively rare in the modern era, and they are nearly all found in Latin America (with most such cases allowing non-successive terms). In the post-Soviet and sub-Saharan African countries, on the other hand, two-term limits are more popular, and whereas the post-Soviet countries are split on non-successive terms, the sub-Saharan African countries tend to explicitly prohibit such a return by the executive.

Overall, the data suggest that term limits are an almost universal and enduring part of presidential democracy. They are prominent not only in Latin America – a region where their usage has eroded in recent years – but also in other regions where presidentialism and (especially) semi-presidentialism have become fashionable. It does appear, however, that restrictions on executives have softened over the years. Leaders are permitted to stay twice as long as they used to be. Still, the apparent wave of evasions cited at the outset of this article suggested that even these longer limits may not be enough to contain executive ambition. We turn now to an analysis of these sorts of evasions.

HOW OFTEN ARE TERM LIMITS HONORED?

Understay, Punctual Exit, and Overstay

Conceptually, executives subject to a fixed term can (1) leave office early (*understay*), (2) serve through their maximum tenure and leave punctually, or (3) *overstay*, defined as staying longer than the maximum term as it stood when one originally came to office. The focus here is on the latter two categories. We can classify leaders into one of the three categories by comparing de jure constitutional information on term limits with the period of time that leaders actually served. The former can be assessed with data from written constitutions, combining information on both the *number* and the *length* of terms that leaders are permitted. These two elements combine to produce a measure of the maximum allowed tenure. Figure 13.4 describes the distribution of this measure, whose mean of roughly eight for this sample corresponds to the U.S. model of two terms of four years and out. The modal value of ten, likewise, corresponds to the increasingly popular formula of two terms of five years.

This measure is fairly easy to compare with the career of leaders who served consecutive terms. Of course, any such comparison depends on good information on the tenure of world leaders, and for that we employ a very useful set of data from the Archigos Project (Goemans, Gleditsch, and Chiozza 2009), which records the dates leaders took and left office and by what means they left, for leaders across the world since 1875. The analysis of the two sets of data thus begins in 1875, even though we have data on constitutional provisions dating to 1789. The sample includes 644

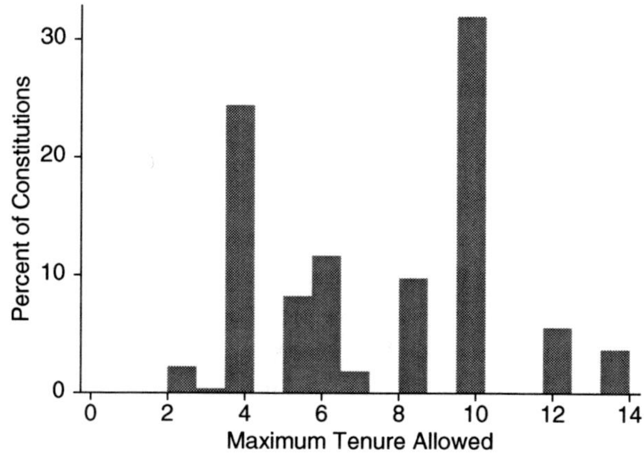

FIGURE 13.4. Maximum tenure for heads of state (combines term length and term limits).
Note: Universe: constitutional systems with fixed-term heads of state, since 1789.

heads of state subject to limits, of whom 45 percent (292) understayed, 44 percent (281) served their maximum tenure and then stepped down, and 11 percent (71) overstayed.

For the purposes of this article, we are primarily interested in the last two groups of executives, but given that the plurality of leaders understay, a brief look at this group seems warranted. Leaders might leave early for a number of reasons. Table 13.1, which draws on the reasons for exit as coded by Goemans and colleagues, sheds some light here. Most understayers (51 percent) are removed from office through "regular means," which for the executives in this set means regularly scheduled elections (although these elections may not be "free and fair"). Another 12 percent either died of natural causes or retired citing health reasons. Thus, more than 60 percent of executives who did not serve their maximum tenure left through "regular" means, leaving the formal constitution intact.[11] On the other hand, a nontrivial number of understaying executives (32.3 percent) were forced from office by some extra-constitutional leadership change, such as a military coup. The third row of Table 13.1 concerns those who serve their maximum time in office and then leave punctually. Roughly 90 percent of these executives leave office through "regular" means. Thus, it appears that those who leave office early are less likely to leave through constitutionally prescribed procedures than are those who leave "on time."

[11] Some 4% of understaying executives are still in office. The fate of these executives is undecided. They may turn out to be understayers. They may also serve their maximum tenure or beyond.

TABLE 13.1. *Punctuality and mode of exit*

Punctuality of exit	Mode of exit					
	Still in office	Regular means	Died in office	Retired	Irregular means	N
Not Subject to Term Limits	6 (2.9%)	153 (74.3%)	10 (4.9%)	2 (1.0%)	35 (17.0%)	206
Understay	11 (3.8%)	150 (51.4%)	26 (8.9%)	11 (3.8%)	94 (32.3%)	292
Exit at Maximum Permitted Tenure	22 (7.8%)	228 (81.1%)	4 (1.4%)	6 (2.1%)	21 (7.5%)	281
Overstay	18 (25.4%)	26 (36.6%)	7 (9.9%)	0 (0.0%)	20 (29.0%)	71
Means of Overstay						
Amendment	14 (48.3%)	8 (27.6%)	2 (6.9%)	0 (0.0%)	5 (17.2%)	29
Replacement	2 (7.4%)	13 (48.2%)	2 (7.4%)	0 (0.0%)	10 (37.0%)	27
Coup/Emergency/ Suspension	1 (20.0%)	1 (20.0%)	1 (20.0%)	0 (0.0%)	2 (40.0%)	5
Disregarded/Not Specified	2 (22.2%)	4 (33.3%)	1 (11.1%)	0 (0.0%)	3 (33.3%)	9
All	57 (6.7%)	557 (65.5%)	47 (5.5%)	19 (2.2%)	170 (20.0%)	850

Note: Universe: fixed-term executives, since 1875.

Some subset of those leaders that understay or leave on time would likely have preferred to remain in office. Another subset probably tried to remain in office, despite limits, but without success. (Indeed, Honduran President Zelaya "understayed" only because he failed in his attempt to overstay.) At this stage, we cannot estimate the population in these groups precisely. Unrealized attempts to extend power do not reveal themselves easily, at least in the large sample we consider here. We can, however, say something about the degree and kind of overstays.

Overall, overstayers do not constitute a significant segment of the population of leaders (11 percent). Yet, if we restrict the analysis to those executives who actually had the opportunity to overstay (i.e., omitting understayers), the overstayers are a significant group. This sort of restriction makes sense because an executive's age, popularity, and other factors restrict opportunities for overstaying. So, of those leaders who served at least their maximum tenure, *more than 20 percent stayed longer than allowed*. Overstayers managed this through various means. Sometimes the executive may engineer a constitutional amendment or judicial interpretation to ensure continued tenure in office, either by extending the current term or by removing prohibitions on reelection. If an amendment is unavailable, the executive may formally suspend the constitution's operation, perhaps through the use of emergency powers, or simply ignore the constitution. In some cases, the executive may commission the writing of a new constitution more amenable to longer terms. Such rewriting can extend the term of the executive, remove the limit on the number of terms the executive is able to serve, or simply reset the clock, so to speak, by reducing the number of full terms the executive served under the constitution currently in force. Thus, both overstay and understay can come in both constitutional and extra-constitutional varieties. Some recent work suggests that extra-constitutional modes of term limit transgression are becoming less common (Posner and Young 2007).

To examine the propensity of overstay in more detail, we analyze every instance of potential executive overstay, meaning all leaders who stayed until at least the expiration of their term. This more careful examination resulted in a smaller number of overstays than observed in the Archigos data. Out of 352 potential overstayers, 89 (25.3 percent) attempted stay beyond their term.[12] Of these, 79.8 percent (n = 71) were successful. This means that in 20.2 percent of cases (71 of 352), term limits were not effective predictors of actual term served. The cases of unsuccessful attempts to overstay might also be considered constitutional failures from an ideal of self-enforcement, but from another perspective they reflect the effective (albeit active) enforcement of the constitution.[13]

Of the seventy-one cases in which executives successfully overstayed, twenty-nine involved constitutional amendment and hence are relatively unproblematic from a normative point of view.[14] In another twenty-seven cases, the constitution was replaced, and in five cases, the constitution was suspended or set aside. The

[12] The most common method of *seeking* an overstay was a constitutional amendment (n = 40) followed by constitutional replacement (n = 29). Constitutional suspension or coup occurred in five cases, and in fifteen cases the constitution was simply disregarded or the mechanism of overstay was unclear.

[13] Our data suggests that many of these are failed amendments. Attempts to overstay through amendment succeed in 72.5% of attempts, whereas attempts through replacement and suspension were successful in more than 95% of cases.

[14] From an empirical standpoint, overstay through amendment also seems relatively unproblematic. Executives who extend their maximum tenure through the amendment process typically only stay in office for an extra four years – about one term. However, executives that extend their maximum tenure through replacement or suspension of the constitution typically stay in office for six or ten extra years, respectively. These numbers would likely be even higher if such a large number of executives who overstay via replacement or suspension were not removed through irregular means (see Table 13.1). Of course, there are exceptions to this general rule, like Zine El Abidine Ben Ali of Tunisia, who served as president since 1987 to 2011 via an amendment in 2002 that abolished term limits in the country; in general, however, those who extend their term limits through constitutional amendment overstay fewer years than those who use other means. Moreover, as discussed later in the chapter, the consequences of overstay tend to be less severe when overstay is achieved through amendment.

remaining ten cases indicate the constitution simply being disregarded or are cases for which the mechanism of overstay is unclear, at least according to the historical sources we consulted. Setting aside those who overstayed through constitutional amendment, we can say that roughly forty-two cases of overstay (11.9 percent of all potential overstayers) resulted in a severe break to the constitutional order (and another eighteen attempts to overstay were unsuccessful). Whether this is considered a large or small number depends on a view of the proverbial glass being half-full or half-empty, but it is at least arguable that a figure of one in eight represents a serious level of risk for the constitutional order, even if we can celebrate the fact that the constitution "works" in the other seven cases.

Even these numbers may overstate the incidence of punctual exit. Sometimes an executive can leave on time yet violate the spirit of term limits. Vladimir Putin's amendments that created a more powerful prime ministerial office, and thus provided a "golden parachute" for the ex-president, is one example. Dominican dictator Rafael Trujillo cited American practice of limiting the presidency to two terms when in 1938 he stated that he refused to run, despite what he interpreted to be the wishes of his people (Hartlyn 1998). Trujillo proceeded to step down in favor of his vice-president. But, after President Roosevelt ran for a third term in 1942, Trujillo followed suit and reassumed the presidency for two more terms, stepping down again in favor of his brother Hector in 1952.[15] The analysis of evasions of term limits in this article does not fully capture these "false negative" instances of overstay.[16]

Figures 13.5 and 13.6 illustrate patterns of term limit evasion both over time and across space. Both figures report the number of evasions among potential overstayers (that is, the number of leaders who were supposed to leave in a given year) as well as a smoothed (lowess) line that indicates the probability of overstay. These figures provide a sense of the incidence of term limit evasion over time. Figure 13.5, which plots the incidence for all potential overstayers, reminds us that overstaying term limits is a time-honored practice. The incidence of term limit evasion has

[15] Perhaps anticipating such manipulation, some Latin American constitutions forbid relatives from succeeding the president. *See* Constitución Política de la República de Nicaragua art. 171 (1948).

[16] Another type of term evasion involves those who violate the limit on the number of nonconsecutive terms. As noted in Figure 13.1, constitutions increasingly eliminate executives' ability to serve nonconsecutive terms. With these new limits on executive tenure comes the possibility that an executive may run after an intermediary term when they are constitutionally barred from office. The only such evasion we were able to identify was by Rafael Nunez of Colombia. Nunez was president from August 11, 1884 to April 1, 1886, and despite a restriction in the 1863 constitution that a full two-year term must elapse before a president is eligible to serve again, he took office again on June 4, 1887. However, it is unclear whether this is an overstay, because Nunez's two terms were served under two different constitutions. For the sake of inclusiveness, we count it as one.

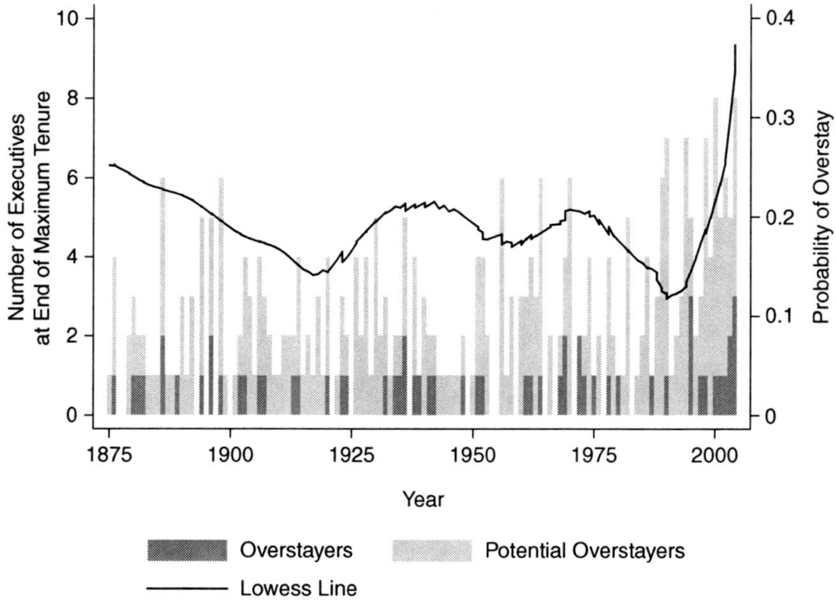

FIGURE 13.5. Probability of maximum tenure evasions by executives by year.
Note: Universe: fixed-term executives who served their maximum tenure, since 1875.

remained fairly stable since 1875, albeit with an apparent increase in the last ten years. Although term limit evasion is not a modern problem, it appears to be growing more acute.

Figure 13.6 describes the offenders by region and over time. Latin America clearly has the longest history of evasion, as it does the longest history of presidential democracy. We count forty-two instances of tenure evasion in Latin America since 1875. But the overall rate of overstay is lower in Latin America than in other regions: Only 15.6 percent of potential overstayers actually overstay. If anything, term limit evasion is on the decline in Latin America relative to the historical pattern.[17]

Our primary concern in this section has been to estimate the overall risk of term limit evasion. Tolerance for term limit evasion will no doubt vary, but an overall risk of 11.9 percent of constitutional rupture (overstay without following amendment procedures) seems somewhat high and worthy of further analysis. The upward trend in term limit evasion also invites a more thorough evaluation of the causes and consequences of evasion. The next two sections take on these tasks.

[17] It should be noted, however, that this analysis does not incorporate the most recent round of evasions in Latin America that have occurred since 2006.

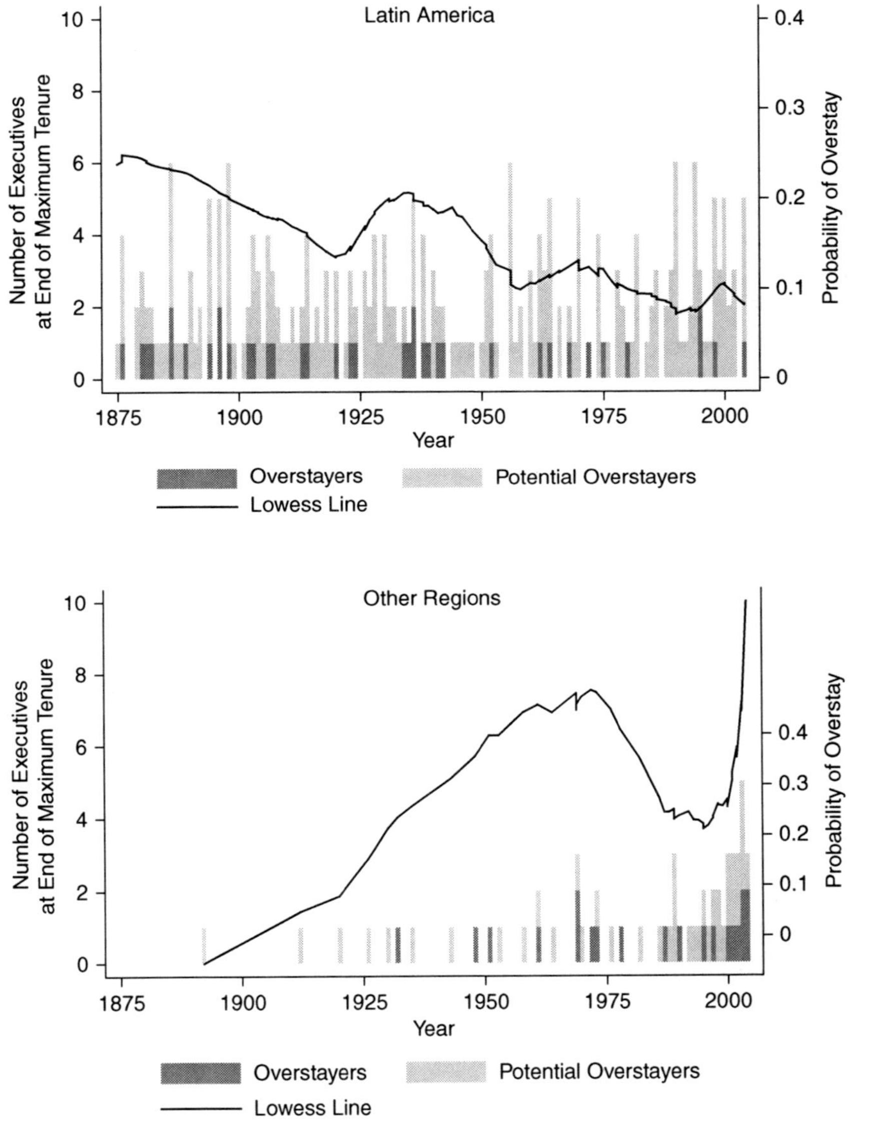

FIGURE 13.6. Probability of maximum tenure evasions by executives by year and region. *Note*: Universe: fixed-term executives who served their maximum tenure, since 1875.

Determinants of Overstay

This section explores the determinants of overstay more rigorously in a multivariate analysis. The dependent variable in this analysis is the odds of overstay, and the sample is all potential overstayers. The analysis includes several variables that might be thought to predict overstay. We ask whether *age of the leader* matters, with the hypothesis being that older leaders will be more likely to overstay under the assumption that they are less likely to assume another powerful position in their working life. (We also include a squared term to test whether this effect is nonlinear due to the debilitating effects of aging.) We examine the *leader's profession*, categorized as lawyer, military, or other. The former two categories were most frequent, and the expectation is that military leaders would be more likely to violate on the grounds that they have more opportunity because of military support. Lawyers might be less likely to overstay, at least if they have a professional habit of law-abidingness. Other leader characteristics in the analysis include the *number of terms* the leader has previously served and whether the leader himself came into power through *irregular means* such as a coup.

Beside characteristics of the leader, we examine the type of term limit at issue to see whether single or multiple terms increase the propensity of violation. We also look at country characteristics such as the number of previous overstays in the country's history, the democratic health of the country at the time the leader took office (using the widely used Polity database),[18] the age of both the regime (i.e., democratic or authoritarian) and that of the constitution,[19] and the number of executives to account for differences in executive-legislative relations. The hypothesis is that older constitutions are more likely to be enforced and thus discourage violators of term limits. Finally, the model includes dummy variables for different regions of the world and the decade in which the potential overstay occurs. To estimate the model, we employ logistic regression, which is appropriate for binary dependent variables.

Figure 13.7 provides the results, which are largely consistent with the hypotheses. Older leaders are indeed more likely to violate term limits (although the negative sign on the squared term indicates that this is not true of very old leaders). Leaders around ages thirty and fifty-four exhibit the baseline predicted probability of overstay (model baseline = 0.10),[20] with leaders in their mid-forties having the highest probability.[21] The probability that military leaders will overstay is 0.13 higher than that

[18] Polity IV Database: Political Regime Characteristics and Transitions 1800–2008, available at http://www.systemicpeace.org/polity/polity4.htm (last accessed February 22, 2010).

[19] One might suspect that the age of the constitution will be highly correlated with the age of the regime. In the sample we analyze, the correlation is moderately high (R = 0.54) but not sufficiently high to suggest that multicollinearity will be a problem.

[20] This baseline is calculated while holding the values of all independent variables (except age) at their means. All of the marginal effects discussed in this paragraph and the next are in reference to this baseline and are also calculated while holding all other independent variables at their means. For example, when we state that leaders in their mid-forties have a 0.07 higher probability of overstay than leaders aged thirty or fifty-four, this means that leaders in their mid-forties have a 0.17 probability versus a 0.10 probability for leaders aged thirty or fifty-four.

[21] 0.07 higher than the baseline.

of nonmilitary leaders, but we find no apparent "law-abidingness" effect for lawyers. Leaders who themselves took office through irregular means have a probability of overstaying that is 0.26 higher than those who took office through regular means. Leaders who previously served nonconsecutive terms are just as likely as leaders who served no previous terms to violate.

The results show that executives who are initially allowed to serve two or more terms have a probability of overstaying 0.33 higher than executives who initially face either a single-term limit or no term limit at all – an interesting finding we discuss later in the chapter. The presence of both democracy and older constitutions tends to decrease the propensity to overstay. The coefficient for the number of executives is close to statistically significant, indicating that the probability that executives in presidential systems will overstay is 0.09 lower than that for executives in semi-presidential systems. On the other hand, a number of country-level variables have no significant effect on overstay, including the prohibition of nonconsecutive terms, a history of previous overstays, and the age of the regime. We also find no regional or temporal effects (except for an apparent dearth of overstays in the 1890s). These null findings suggest a certain universality of term limit evasion in that the attributes of violators do not correspond to a particular political, geographic, or historical profile.

One might suspect that the mechanisms affecting leaders' desires and ability to overstay might vary by regime type. To test this possibility, we reran the logistic regression models in Figure 13.7 on samples restricted to autocracies or democracies, measured at the first year of the leader's term.[23] Interestingly, the variables that predict overstay in democracies are different from those that do so in autocracies. In democracies, only the military background of the leader and the age of the constitution remain statistically significant. In autocracies, many of the same variables that were statistically significant in the full sample remain so, including age, military background, form of entry, number of terms allowed, and Polity score.[24]

To summarize, several interesting findings emerge from the analysis of the determinants of term limit violation. The results demonstrate that former military leaders are significantly more likely to overstay, regardless of the kind of regime in place when they take office. In autocratic regimes, the term limit faced by the executive influences their decision to overstay, as leaders are much more likely to overstay if

[23] These models are on file with the authors. For this analysis, we classify country-years as democratic if their Polity score is 3 or greater and as autocratic if their score is less than 3. This is a relatively low threshold compared to the one traditionally used in the literature, because we wanted to be sure to include new and marginal democracies in the sample.

[24] The only differences between the autocracy-only model and the full-sample model are that in the autocracy-only model, the confidence intervals of the number of executives variable shrink and the age of the constitution is no longer statistically significant. Thus, the only variable that predicts overstay regardless of regime type is military background.

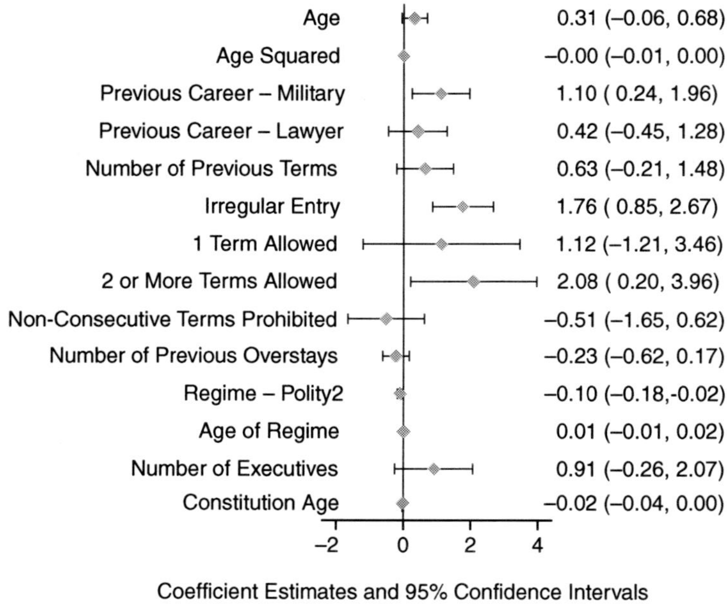

FIGURE 13.7. Logistic regression model predicting successful term limit violations.[25]
Note: Universe: fixed-term executives who served their maximum tenure, since 1875 (n = 350).

they are initially allowed two or more terms than if they face no term limit or are only allowed one term. Perhaps leaders develop a taste for power in their second term, or have accumulated sufficient power to be able to manipulate the tools of government to allow an overstay. The results also show that executives elected in democracies are less likely to violate constitutions. This is consistent with the intuitive idea that constitutions "matter" more in democracies than in autocracies.

Consequences of Overstay

Even if overstay through constitutional rupture occurs with some frequency (one in eight cases), it does not follow that these actions result in constitutional crisis, as opposed to something closer to a consensual shift in constitutional norms. A more

[25] The figure contains results from a logistic regression model with coefficient estimates indicated by the markers and 95% confidence interval indicated by the bars. Positive coefficients indicate that the variable is associated with higher levels of term limit evasion, whereas negative coefficients indicate a lower likelihood of evasion. Variables whose 95% confidence interval does not overlap 0 – as indicated by the vertical reference line – are considered statistically significant. Regional and decade dummies are omitted from the figure. The full results of this model as well as results from several additional models are available from the author.

TABLE 13.2. *Average number of years with a conflict by overstay status*[26]

	All years of term	Last 2 years of actual tenure	Last 2 years of permitted tenure	N
No Term Limits	2.4 (54.2%)	0.8	–	97
Understay	1.7 (75.4%)	1.1	–	209
Exit at Maximum Permitted Tenure	3.3 (60.0%)	1.1	1.1	202
Overstayer	6.5 (46.5%)	0.6	0.7	54
By Means of				
Amendment	4.7 (44.0%)	0.4	0.4	35
Replacement	7.6 (58.4%)	1.1	0.9	21
Coup/Emergency/ Suspension	5.3 (20.1%)	0.5	0.5	4
Disregarded/Not Specified	9 (58.9%)	0.8	0.4	9
All	2.9 (63.4%)	1.0	1.0	562

Note: Universe: fixed-term executives, since 1875.

thorough investigation of the consequences of term limit violations is required. The remainder of this section offers some suggestive evidence.

To evaluate the effect of term limits on crisis propensity, we need some sense of the baseline incidence of crisis. Unfortunately, there is no generally accepted indicator of constitutional crisis of the type we are considering. One way to get at the question is to examine the percentage of constitutional deaths (instances in which a constitution is suspended or replaced, as opposed to merely amended) that results from the quest for overstay (Elkins, Ginsburg, and Melton 2009: 55). By this metric, term limits pose a moderate threat to constitutions. Thirty-two constitutions (less than 5 percent of all constitutions) have met their demise as a result of term limit violations. When compared to some important environmental threats to constitutions (e.g., war, coups, regime change), term limit violations are not associated with a large number of deaths.

Examining formal constitutional changes alone, however, does not fully capture the extent that the conflict over term limit violations interrupts normal politics. Perhaps a better measure of constitutional crisis is the occurrence of political conflict. To operationalize political conflict, we use Bank's data on assassinations, strikes, guerilla warfare, government crises, purges, riots, and revolutions.[27] Table 13.2 captures the average number of years of political conflict for all years of rule by category

[26] The cells contain the mean level of democracy with the standard deviation in parentheses.

[27] Cross National Time Series Data Archive, http://www.databanks.sitehosting.net/Default.htm (last accessed February 20, 2010).

of leader (with respect to the punctuality of their exit). One observes that overstayers experience fewer years of conflict than do non-overstayers. This is somewhat understandable, in that an overstayer will either be sufficiently popular to minimize political conflict or sufficiently strong to repress it. A similar trend is apparent even if we account for crisis during the last two years of an executive's term, that during the two years prior to a term limit violation, and even for the means of overstay. Furthermore, the level of political conflict is relatively low in systems in which there are no term limits at all. It is hard to sort out the story here because of selection effects, but the overall conclusion seems inconsistent with the conjecture that term limits induce higher levels of political conflict through overstays. Alexander Hamilton, it seems, was wrong about this point.

Despite little evidence that term limit violations induce constitutional crisis, term limit violations may have other negative effects. One potential consequence is an increased likelihood of future overstays. However, perhaps surprisingly, a national history of overstay does not seem to predict future occurrences. Executives in a country with no history of overstay are *more* likely to violate than are those in a country with at least one previous occurrence (24.9 percent vs. 15.1 percent). And the probability generally declines with the number of previous overstays in the country (Table 13.3).[28] Thus, it appears that overstay does not breed future overstay.

Another potential consequence of term limit violations is that they might degrade democracy. Table 13.4 assesses this possibility. Democracy in these figures is measured by the widely used Polity index.[29] The results demonstrate that levels of democracy do not tend to change much across leaders' tenures, regardless of whether the leader is an overstayer or not, and this trend is the same regardless of initial regime type or the means of overstay. In fact, if there is any trend, it is that in initially democratic regimes, democracy increases slightly during the tenure of overstayers. This is especially surprising given that the removal of term limits might itself penalize a country's score on democracy, based on the conceptualization employed by Polity.

Another way to get at the consequences of term limit evasion is to trace particular case histories. The Appendix to this chapter lists every violator of term limits, sorted by whether the country was a democracy or autocracy at the time the leader took

[28] Leaders who take office in a country with a history of overstay through means other than amendment show a higher propensity for future violation (greater than 20%), but this higher propensity is still less than that of leaders who take office in a country with no history of overstay.

[29] The raw scores from Polity should be interpreted with some caution, as the rating methodology is likely to include the fact of overstay as part of its explicit criteria through the executive constraint subcomponent. If this was driving our results, then we would expect overstay to lead to large changes in democracy, which is exactly the opposite of what we find. Nonetheless, to ensure that our results are not influenced by our choice of democracy measure, we checked them with the Unified Democracy Scores (UDS), which deliver substantively similar results.

TABLE 13.3. *Analysis of overstay recurrence*

Previous Overstays	Number of executives	Number of overstays	Percentage of overstays
None	165	41	24.9%
At Least 1	185	28	15.1%
Number of Previous Overstays			
1	57	16	28.1%
2	75	8	10.7%
3	42	2	4.8%
4	1	1	100%
5	10	1	10.0%
Means of Previous Overstay			
Amendment	75	7	9.3%
Replacement	64	14	21.9%
Coup/Emergency/Suspension	5	1	20.0%
Disregarded/Not Specified	41	6	24.0%
All	350	69	19.7%

Note: Universe: fixed-term executives who served their maximum tenure, since 1875.

office. Of the democratically elected leaders who overstayed in recent years, several did so through amendment and thus may fit the model of the popular leader who works around the default rule to remain in office. Carlos Menem in Argentina and Fernando Cardoso in Brazil revised their constitutions to allow a second term, and both turned over the office to opposition parties after their second terms were over (although Menem tried to stay on before his attempt was ruled unconstitutional). Alexander Lukashenko in Belarus, on the other hand, used amendment to consolidate power and moved his country from the ranks of democracies to a "competitive authoritarian" regime. Others who pursued this strategy either replaced the constitution wholesale (Alberto Fujimori, Ferdinand Marcos) or simply suspended it after failing to secure amendment (Tandja Mamadou in Niger).

The nineteenth-century cases are also mixed. For example, Costa Rica enacted a single four-year term limit with its 1871 constitution. President Tomás Miguel Guardia Gutiérrez, who had been part of a coup ousting the previous president, overstayed several months, then ceded power to a puppet leader briefly before being reelected to continue his overstay until his own death. Term limits were then observed for some time. In 1889, President Ramón Bernardo Soto Alfaro attempted to overstay after holding the "first honest election" in the country – but mass protests prevented him from succeeding (Busey 1961: 58). The regime of his successor Jose Joaquin Rodriguez marked a turning point for democracy. Thereafter, only one leader has overstayed (Castro in 1898) and has done so through constitutional

TABLE 13.4. *Mean level of democracy (as measured by polity) by initial regime type and overstay status*[30]

	N	Autocracies (Polity < 3)			Democracies (Polity ≥ 3)		
		Start year	Violation year	End year	Start year	Violation year	End year
No Term Limits	225	−4.8 (2.80)	–	−4.5 (2.80)	8.7 (1.85)	–	8.7 (1.77)
Understay	304	−3.0 (3.02)	–	−3.0 (2.98)	6.9 (2.05)	–	7.0 (2.00)
Exit at Maximum Permitted Tenure	279	−2.5 (3.16)	–	−2.3 (3.19)	7.3 (2.28)	–	7.3 (2.31)
Overstay	69	−4.4 (3.37)	−4.6 (3.44)	−4.4 (3.49)	6.6 (1.76)	7.1 (1.36)	7 (1.34)
By Means of							
Amendment	38	−5.0 (3.38)	−4.7 (3.68)	−4.4 (4.05)	7.2 (1.57)	7.75 (1.71)	7.8 (1.72)
Replacement	29	−4.2 (2.95)	−5.1 (3.33)	−4.6 (3.34)	6.0 (2.00)	6 (–)	8 (–)
Coup/Emergency/ Suspension	5	−5.0 (4.24)	−5 (4.24)	−4.8 (3.95)	5.0 (–)	–	–
Disregarded/Not Specified	15	−2.3 (3.80)	−4.2 (4.21)	−3.1 (3.98)	6.0 (1.41)	6.5 (0.71)	6 (1.00)
All	877	−3.3 (3.18)	–	−3.2 (3.18)	7.7 (2.19)	–	7.8 (2.15)

Note: Universe: fixed-term executives, since 1875.

amendment.[31] The Costa Rican story appears to be one in which attempted evasion leads to mass enforcement, ultimately leading to stable democracy.

Contrast Venezuela, the country in the sample with the largest number of overstays (six). Five of these occurred in the forty years prior to 1913 (see Appendix), a period of successive military strongmen who sometimes overstayed while other times governed through puppet leaders that would leave office on time. There was no effective enforcement of term limits, and their application seemed to depend on

30 Castro attempted another constitutional amendment in 1902 to allow himself to remain in power, but was defeated. *See* Wikipedia Rafael Yglesias Castro, http://en.wikipedia.org/wiki/Rafael_Yglesias_Castro (last accessed February 20, 2010).

31 The percent of country-years leaders experienced conflict during their terms is the variable analyzed in the table. A country-year is coded as experiencing a conflict if there were any of the following events in that year: assassinations, strikes, guerrilla warfare, government crises, purges, riots, or revolutions. The data for this variable are from Banks (2001) and spans from 1919 to 2003. We prefer this measure to Bank's conflict index because we are interested in instances of conflict rather than the severity of conflict.

the whim of the ruler. After democracy was reestablished in 1959, term limits were regularly observed. Hugo Chavez, however, initiated constitutional reform after his initial election in 1999, and then in 2007 attempted to amend the new constitution to remove term limits. His first referendum attempt failed narrowly, but Chavez was able to hold another referendum in 2009, which succeeded. Chavez seems to represent a return to an earlier, less democratic tradition in Venezuela.

Ferdinand Marcos of the Philippines exemplifies an executive who suspended democracy to remain in office. The Philippines was considered a democracy at the time of his initial election in 1965. The presidential term was four years, with a limit of eight consecutive years in office. In 1969, Marcos won an unprecedented second term, but thereafter became increasingly dictatorial and developed a cult of personality. With rising insecurity and a communist uprising, Marcos declared martial law in 1972, suspending Congress. He then wrote a new constitution that allowed him to remain in power, and his dictatorship continued until the "People Power" revolution of 1986. Since the reestablishment of democracy, however, the Philippine political system has weathered many attempts to engineer overstay, and has rebuffed them all. Like Costa Rica, an incident of successful enforcement seems to have facilitated a pattern of observance of term limits thereafter.

To summarize the main results of the empirical analysis: Some form of constitutional rupture occurs in roughly 12 percent of cases in which a leader has the potential to overstay, and in eighteen additional cases an executive attempted to overstay. However, overstayers are not associated with higher levels of violent political conflict. Overstay does not breed future overstay, nor does it lead to regular decline in levels of democracy. Furthermore, many overstayers seem to leave office after one additional term, particularly those who achieve their extended term through constitutional amendment. Democracy, on the other hand, seems to reduce the prospect of overstay. In sum, these results suggest that executive overstay is not as problematic as recent events suggest.

CONCLUSION

Term limits are designed to discourage tyranny and to address real problems of incumbency in democratic governance, but have been subject to competing claims by proponents and opponents. Some, such as Bolivar, have argued that term limits are necessary to curb executive ambition. Others, including Hamilton and other American founders, argued that term limits would induce executives to seek to remain in office, and perhaps even generate crises to allow themselves to do so. The theoretical debate has proceeded without the benefit of much empirical analysis. One of the objectives of this article has been to inform the normative debate with data on the frequency of overstay.

Our evidence is not definitive, but on balance suggests that, for democracies at least, constitutional crisis induced through term limit violations is relatively rare. Constitutional enforcement of term limits appears to operate routinely in democracies, and even in many autocracies (such as Mexico before 1994). Term limits seem to work in the vast majority of cases, in that those who have the possibility of overstaying do not frequently seek to do so. Of those who do seek to overstay, 20 percent fail in the attempt, which can also be considered constitutional enforcement of sorts, even if it sometimes coincides with a crisis as defined here.

Even when term limits are violated, the consequences are not always negative. Our large-n evidence suggests that overstay does not lead to the denigration of democracy, on average. Of the recent overstayers in democracies, some (Menem and Cardoso, for example) fit the profile of popular leaders who were able to amend the default rule so as to serve a single extra term. Only a small number of leaders in recent years – Fujimori in Peru, Marcos in the Philippines, and Chavez in Venezuela – have completely replaced the constitution to allow themselves extra time. Some such leaders, such as Niger's Mamadou Tandja, have subsequently found themselves replaced through military coup.

The finding that term limits operate as default rules whose amendment does not always lead to future disruption has implications for the study of executive-legislative relations. Linz (1990) famously criticized presidential democracy and focused in part on fixed terms. In his view, he saw the fixed term as a factor in institutionalizing conflict between branches, leading to deadlock and higher incentives to take extra-constitutional action. As Mainwaring and Scully (1995: 33) put it: "[B]ecause of fixed terms of office, if a president is unable to implement her/his program, there is no alternative but deadlock." Although the current state of the literature is more agnostic (Cheibub 2007), the assumptions of the Linzian position are still widely held. Yet if executives in presidential systems frequently overstay (or understay) their term, we might think of presidential systems as de jure rigid but in practice flexible in the number of years an executive serves.

The very simplicity of term limits – easily comprehensible by the average citizen – may have something to do with their effectiveness. Simple and clear rules, it seems, can facilitate effective constitutional enforcement (Weingast 1997). Constitutional text provides a focal point for enforcement behavior, and such enforcement is likely to be easier when everyone understands the rules. Drawing a line of four or eight years as a maximum term in office has elements of arbitrariness, but the very clarity of a bright-line rule ensures that the line will, more often than not, be observed. In contrast with Alexander Hamilton's conjecture, term limits restrain rather than promote conflict. In the matter of constraining executive ambition, then, most constitutions seem to work most of the time.

ACKNOWLEDGMENTS

We thank Jose Cheibub, Henry Dietz, Rosalind Dixon, Lee Ann Fennell, David Fontana, Jennifer Gandhi, Guadalupe Gonzalez, Donald Horowitz, Wendy Hunter, Aziz Huq, Brian Kalt, Brian Leiter, Raul Madrid, Anup Malani, Eric Posner, Adam Przeworski, Julio Rios-Figueroa, Adam Samaha, Alexei Trochev, Adrian Vermeule, and Kurt Weyland for their comments and suggestions. Kristen McKeown and Carolyn Tan provided helpful research assistance.

APPENDIX

TABLE A1. *List of democratic overstayers (Democracy = Polity> = 3)*

Country	Year	Leader	Means of overstay	Overstay year	Level of democracy	Age of democracy
Argentina	1988	Menem	Amendment	1995	8	5
Belarus (Byelorussia)	1994	Lukashenko	Amendment	2006	7	3
Brazil	1995	Cardoso	Amendment	1998	8	10
Colombia	1884	Nunez	Replacement	1886	8	17
Colombia	2002	Alvaro Uribe Velez	Amendment	2006	7	45
Costa Rica	1870	Guardia	Disregarded/ Not Specified	1876	5	29
Costa Rica	1885	Bernardo Soto Alfaro	Disregarded/Not Specified	1886	7	44
Costa Rica	1894	Rafael Yglesias Castro	Amendment	1898	10	4
Honduras	1933	Carias Andino	Replacement	1936	5	7
Namibia	1990	Nujoma	Amendment	2000	6	0
Niger	1999	Mamadou	Coup/ Emergency/ Suspension	2009	5	0
Peru	1990	Fujimori	Replacement	1995	8	10
Philippines	1965	Marcos	Replacement	1973	5	15
Uruguay	1931	Terra	Replacement	1935	3	27
Venezuela	1999	Hugo Chavez	Replacement	2004	7	30

TABLE A2. *List of autocratic overstayers (Autocracy = Polity<3)*

Country	Year	Leader	Means of overstay	Overstay year	Level of democracy	Age of democracy
Algeria	1999	Bouteflika	Amendment	2009	−3	4
Angola	1979	Dos Santos	Disregarded/Not Specified	2007	−7	4
Argentina	1946	Peron	Amendment	1952	−8	0
Bolivia	1920	Saavedra	De Facto Control	1924	2	40
Bolivia	1971	Banzer Suarez	Disregarded/Not Specified	1975	−7	0
Brazil	1930	Vargas	Replacement	1938	−4	0
Chad	1990	Deby	Amendment	2006	−7	4
Chile	1973	Pinochet	Replacement	1980	−7	0
Colombia	1904	Reyes Prieto	Amendment	1907	−5	0
Congo, Democratic Republic Of	1965	Mobutu	Replacement	1969	−9	0
Ecuador	1895	Aloy Alfaro Delgado	Replacement	1896	−1	65
Ecuador	1906	Aloy Alfaro Delgado	Coup/ Emergency/ Suspension	1906	−3	76
El Salvador	1871	Gonzalez	Replacement	1873	−1	12
El Salvador	1876	Zaldivar	Replacement	1880	−1	17
El Salvador	1935	Hernandez Martinez	Replacement	1939	−9	4
Eritrea	1993	Afeworki	Disregarded/Not Specified	2007	−6	0
Gabon	1967	Bongo	Amendment	2003	−7	7
Guatemala	1885	Barillas	Amendment	1889	2	6
Guatemala	1898	Estrada-Cabrera	Disregarded/Not Specified	1903	2	0
Guatemala	1931	Ubico Castaneda	Amendment	1934	−9	0
Guinea	1984	Conte	Amendment	2001	−7	26
Haiti	1957	Duvalier, Francois	Replacement	1962	−5	7
Honduras	1963	Lopez Arellano	Replacement	1968	−1	27
Kazakhstan	1991	Nazarbaev	Amendment	2005	−3	0
Lebanon	1943	EL Khoury	Amendment	1948	2	0
Lebanon	1989	Elias Hrawi	Amendment	1995	0	0
Lebanon	1998	Emile Lahoud	Amendment	2004		0
Liberia	1944	Tubman	Amendment	1951	−6	60
Lithuania	1926	Smetona	Replacement	1932	0	0
Mali	1968	Traore	Amendment	1987	−7	8
Nicaragua	1893	Zelaya	Amendment	1896	−5	55
Nicaragua	1911	Adolfo Diaz	Disregarded/Not Specified	1914	−3	73
Nicaragua	1937	Anastasio Somoza Garcia	Replacement	1942	−8	1

Country	Year	Leader	Means of overstay	Overstay year	Level of democracy	Age of democracy
Nicaragua	1967	Anastasio Somoza Debayle	Replacement	1972	–8	31
Panama	1920	Belisario Porras Barahona	Amendment	1920	–3	17
Paraguay	1880	Caballero	Disregarded/Not Specified	1882	–4	10
Paraguay	1954	Stroessner	Coup/ Emergency/ Suspension	1964	–9	0
Peru	1919	Leguia	Replacement	1923	–4	0
Peru	1933	Benavidez	Disregarded/Not Specified	1936	2	0
Rwanda	1973	Habyarimana	Replacement	1990	–7	12
Sierra Leone	1968	Stevens	Replacement	1978	1	0
Sudan	1989	Al-Bashir	Replacement	2008	–7	0
Taiwan	1950	Chiang Kai-shek	Coup/ Emergency/ Suspension	1961	–8	1
Tajikistan	1992	Rakhmonov	Amendment	2003	–6	0
Togo	1967	Eyadema	Amendment	2002	–7	7
Tunisia	1957	Ben Ali Bourguiba	Amendment	1969		
Tunisia	1987	Zine Al-Abidine Ben Ali	Amendment	2004	–5	0
Uganda	1986	Museveni	Amendment	2005	–7	0
Uruguay	1938	Baldomir	Coup/ Emergency/ Suspension	1941	0	4
Uzbekistan	1991	Karimov	Amendment	1997	-9	0
Venezuela	1870	Guzman Blanco	Replacement	1873	-5	40
Venezuela	1879	Guzman Blanco	Replacement	1881	-5	49
Venezuela	1894	Joaquin Crespo	Replacement	1894	-3	64
Venezuela	1899	Cipriano Castro	Replacement	1902	-3	69
Venezuela	1908	Gomez	Replacement	1913	-3	78
Yugoslavia (Serbia)	1945	Tito	Amendment	1972	-7	0

REFERENCES

Albert, Richard. 2009. The Fusion of Presidentialism and Parliamentarism. *American Journal of Comparative Law* 57: 531–78.

Ayres, Ian and Robert Gertner. 1989. Filling Gaps in Incomplete Contracts: An Economic Theory of Default Rules. *Yale Law Journal* 99: 87–130.

Breslin, Beau. 2009. *From Words to Worlds: Exploring Constitutional Functionality*. Baltimore: Johns Hopkins University Press.

Buchanan, James and Gordon Tullock. 1961. *The Calculus of Consent*. Ann Arbor: University of Michigan Press.

Busey, James L. 1961. The Presidents of Costa Rica. *The Americas* 18: 55, 58.

Carey, John. 1998. *Term Limits and Legislative Representation*. Cambridge: Cambridge University Press.

2009. The Re-Election Debate in Latin America, in *New Perspectives on Democracy in Latin America: Actors, Institutions and Practices*, edited by William C. Smith. Malden, MA: Blackwell Publishing, pp. 79–89.

Cheibub, Jose. 2007. *Presidentialism, Parliamentarism, and Democracy*. New York: Cambridge University Press.

Cheibub, Jose, Zachary Elkins, and Tom Ginsburg. 2009. Beyond Presidentialism and Parliamentarism: On the Hybridization of Form. Unpublished manuscript.

Doron, Gideon and Michael Harris. 2001. *Term Limits*. Lanham, MD: Lexington Books.

Elhauge, Einer. 1997. Are Term Limits Undemocratic? *University of Chicago Law Review* 64: 83–201.

Elkins, Zachary, Tom Ginsburg, and James Melton. 2009. *The Endurance of National Constitutions*. New York: Cambridge University Press.

Horwill, Herbert W. 1925. *The Usages of the American Constitution*. London: Oxford University Press.

Hume, David. 1752. "Idea of a Perfect Commonwealth" in *Hume: Political Essays*, edited by Knud Haakonssen. New York: Cambridge University Press.

Gelman, Andrew and Gary King. 1990. Estimating Incumbency Advantage without Bias. *American Journal of Political Science* 34: 1242–64.

Gersen, Jacob. 2009. Unbundled Powers. *Virginia Law Review* 96: 301–58.

Gersen, Jacob and Christopher Berry. 2007. The Unbundled Executive. *University of Chicago Law Review* 75: 1385–434.

Goemans, H. E., Kristin Gleditsch, and Giacomo Chiozza. 2009. Introducing Archigos: A Dataset of Political Leaders. *Journal of Peace Research* 46(2): 269–83.

Grofman, Bernard, ed. 1996. *Legislative Term Limits: Public Choice Perspectives*. Boston: Kluwer.

Hartlyn, Jonathan. 1998. *The Struggle for Democratic Politics in the Dominican Republic*. Chapel Hill: University of North Carolina Press.

Linz, Juan. 1990. The Perils of Presidentialism. *Journal of Democracy* 1: 51–69.

Lutz, Donald. 1994. Toward a Theory of Constitutional Amendment. *American Political Science Review* 88: 355–70.

Mainwaring, Scott and Timonthy R. Scully, eds. 1995. *Building Democratic Institutions: Party Systems in Latin America*. Stanford: Stanford University Press.

Maltz, Gideon. 2007. The Case for Term Limits. *Journal of Democracy* 18(1): 128–41.

Polsby, Nelson W. 1991. Constitutional Mischief: What's Wrong with Term Limitations. *American Prospect* 6: 40–43

Posner, Daniel N. and Daniel J. Young. 2007. The Institutionalization of Political Power in Africa. *Journal of Democracy* 18(3): 126–40.

Posner, Eric and Adrian Vermuele. 2008. Constitutional Showdowns. *Pennsylvania Law Review* 156: 991–1048.

Stein, Charles W. 1943. *The Third Term Tradition*. New York: Columbia University Press.

Sunstein, Cass. 2001. *Designing Democracy: What Constitutions Do*. New York: Oxford University Press.
Sutter, Daniel. 2003. Durable Constitutional Rules and Rent Seeking. *Public Finance Review* 31(4): 413–28.
Weingast, Barry. 1997. The Political Foundations of Democracy and the Rule of Law. *American Political Science Review* 91: 245–63.

Index

CPSIA information can be obtained at www.ICGtesting.com
Printed in the USA
LVOW100033080213

319002LV00002B/3/P

9 781107 020566